# CULTIVATING COACHING MINDSETS

# Also Available

Best Practices of Literacy Leaders, Second Edition:
Keys to School Improvement
*Edited by Allison Swan Dagen and Rita M. Bean*

The Literacy Specialist, Fourth Edition:
Leadership and Coaching for the Classroom, School,
and Community
*Rita M. Bean and Virginia J. Goatley*

The Power of Instructional Coaching in Context:
A Systems View for Aligning Content and Coaching
*Jacy Ippolito and Rita M. Bean*

# Cultivating Coaching Mindsets

**SECOND EDITION**

## An Action Guide for Instructional Leaders

**Rita M. Bean**
**Jacy Ippolito**

*Foreword by Allison Swan Dagen*

THE GUILFORD PRESS
New York   London

Copyright © 2025 The Guilford Press
A Division of Guilford Publications, Inc.
www.guilford.com

All rights reserved

Except as noted, no part of this book may be reproduced, translated, stored in a retrieval system, or transmitted, in any form or by any means, electronic, mechanical, photocopying, microfilming, recording, or otherwise, without written permission from the publisher.

Printed in the United States of America

This book is printed on acid-free paper.

Last digit is print number:  9  8  7  6  5  4  3  2  1

---

LIMITED DUPLICATION LICENSE

These materials are intended for use only by qualified professionals.

The publisher grants to individual purchasers of this book nonassignable permission to reproduce all materials for which permission is specifically granted in a footnote. This license is limited to you, the individual purchaser, for personal use or use with students. This license does not grant the right to reproduce these materials for resale, redistribution, electronic display, or any other purposes (including but not limited to books, pamphlets, articles, video or audio recordings, blogs, file-sharing sites, internet or intranet sites, and handouts or slides for lectures, workshops, or webinars, whether or not a fee is charged). Permission to reproduce these materials for these and any other purposes must be obtained in writing from the Permissions Department of Guilford Publications.

---

**Library of Congress Cataloging-in-Publication Data**

Names: Bean, Rita M., author. | Ippolito, Jacy, author.
Title: Cultivating coaching mindsets : an action guide for instructional leaders / Rita M. Bean, Jacy Ippolito ; Foreword by Allison Swan Dagen.
Description: Second edition. | New York : The Guilford Press, 2025. | Includes bibliographical references and index. |
Identifiers: LCCN 2024035340 | ISBN 9781462556434 (paperback) | ISBN 9781462556441 (cloth)
Subjects: LCSH: Literacy—Study and teaching. | Language arts teachers. | Language arts.
Classification: LCC LC149 .B42 2025 | DDC 372.6—dc23/eng/20240809
LC record available at *https://lccn.loc.gov/2024035340*

# About the Authors

**Rita M. Bean, PhD,** is Professor Emerita in the School of Education at the University of Pittsburgh. Prior to joining the university, she taught at the elementary school level and served as a reading supervisor for grades K–12. Dr. Bean has published numerous articles, book chapters, and books on topics including professional learning and the role of reading specialists and literacy coaches. She is a member of the Reading Hall of Fame and a former board member of the International Literacy Association. Dr. Bean is a recipient of the University of Pittsburgh's Chancellor's Distinguished Teaching Award and Distinguished Service Award, among other honors.

**Jacy Ippolito, EdD,** is Professor in the McKeown School of Education at Salem State University in Massachusetts, where he teaches courses in literacy and leadership, co-directs graduate programs in educational leadership, and is the co-founder and co-leader of the Center for Educational Leadership. Prior to joining Salem State, Dr. Ippolito was a middle school reading specialist, drama teacher, and literacy coach. His research, teaching, and consulting focus on the intersection of coaching, leadership, adolescent/disciplinary literacy, and school reform. He is the author of numerous journal articles and books.

# Foreword

The field of education has significantly shifted since the first edition of *Cultivating Coaching Mindsets* was published in 2016, creating an even greater need for knowledgeable instructional coaches to provide ongoing support for all teachers through job-embedded, high-quality coaching. The COVID-19 pandemic has reshaped the educational landscape, given its effects on student learning, and leading to $190 billion in funding for Elementary and Secondary School Emergency Relief. Schools and districts have been encouraged to make changes in curricula and instruction to address student needs, including in both literacy and mathematics. Social and emotional learning has garnered increased attention. Equity, diversity, and inclusion efforts have been both celebrated and challenged. Schools have also been investigating the possibilities of virtual instruction and coaching as potential solutions to these instructional dilemmas. *Cultivating Coaching Mindsets, Second Edition: An Action Guide for Instructional Leaders* addresses these issues and suggests possible strategies and practices for those responsible for supporting teacher professional learning through coaching.

As a faculty member and program leader at West Virginia University, I have had the privilege of teaching from *Cultivating Coaching Mindsets* (*CCM*) since its initial publication. I have introduced the book and its coaching-mindsets framework to hundreds of graduate students in the literacy education/reading specialist program in the introductory course. Other faculty members also use the mindsets framework, which enables both faculty and students to share a common framework across courses throughout the graduate program. When our reading specialist candidates, who are all classroom teachers, graduate, they leave with a keen understanding of the work of a school-based coach, a four-part mindset framework, and knowledge of the influence of instructional coaching. Their new learning provides them with the confidence and candid desire to work in schools alongside their colleagues to address new and long-standing issues in their schools, all to achieve meaningful school improvement through instructional coaching. Given that I advocate for and teach from this book, it is a great honor to reintroduce the main themes and summarize the significant changes to this second edition.

In this updated edition, the authors' objectives are to (1) offer insights into the unique mindsets required for coaching adult learners and (2) propose many approaches, accompanied by practical strategies and protocols, for working effectively with educators. In this edition, Bean and Ippolito reaffirm coaching as not simply a role, but a set of activities and responsibilities that many individuals in a school can assume. The book's foundational principles remain steadfast: leadership, relationships, equity, mission/vision, and systems thinking. These principles serve as the guiding forces behind effective coaching practices, empowering educators to elevate learning experiences and foster inclusive environments.

At the heart of this second edition of *CCM* is an updated conceptual framework, a product of the groundwork laid in Bean and Ippolito's previous work and tightly connected to the newly published *The Power of Instructional Coaching in Context* (2024). The revised framework underscores the essential alignment among content, coaching processes, and the contextual nuances of school systems. Moreover, in this second edition, Bean and Ippolito delve deeper into the content and mindsets of coaching while emphasizing the pivotal role of organizational systems and school culture in helping coaching programs thrive—both with individual teachers and to create systemwide change.

One of the most notable changes in the second edition is the shift from a singular focus on literacy coaching to a broader lens encompassing instructional coaching across all disciplines. This transition reflects Bean and Ippolito's understanding of how coaching, as a reform initiative, can be broadened to effectively address all grades and subjects to support the needs of all educators and learners.

While the core mindset framework—change agent, facilitator, designer, and advocate—remains foundational, it has been refined. The foundational framework serves those interested in working with adult learners in schools quite well. The phrase "thinking like a [mindset]" is a structure reinforcing the promise of habits of mind. These four mindsets reflect the enduring pillars of leadership, adult learning, relationships, and collaboration within a school's overarching vision, mission, and systems thinking.

Also new to the second edition, Bean and Ippolito emphasize the importance of coaching for equity, diversity, and belonging, including how coaches and educators might continue to navigate the challenges and opportunities presented by virtual instruction and coaching. This emphasis underscores the adaptability and agility required of coaches in an ever-evolving educational landscape. In this edition, Bean and Ippolito include five phenomenally detailed coaching cases in the final chapter to illustrate many of the ideas introduced across the book. Two cases have been updated, while three are new, with two focusing on secondary-level coaching and disciplinary literacy. These cases support the shift from literacy coaching to instructional coaching across various content areas, stretching from elementary to high school. The cases are ideal for class discussions or as part of a professional learning community group's exploration of coaching.

Readers will find familiar features in this edition, such as Guiding Questions, Voices from the Field, Stop and Reflect, and Put into Practice. These features and engaging activities across chapters are designed to support active participation in navigating the possibilities, complexities, and dilemmas of coaching. Further Readings and Resources are provided at the end of the chapters, and the Web Resources have also been assembled as a supplement on the book's website (see p. xx for details), allowing readers to link to these online materials directly. Bean and Ippolito have skillfully used all these features to provide practical insights. They have also updated the appendices with multiple protocols for active engagement with the book's content.

With the publication of the second edition of *Cultivating Coaching Mindsets*, Guilford's selection of books now comprises a captivating quartet tailored to school leaders, graduate programs, educators, reading/literacy specialists, and all those focused on instructional coaching and literacy leadership. In addition to the present book, these texts include *The Power of Instructional Coaching in Context*; *Best Practices of Literacy Leaders, Second Edition*; and *The Literacy Specialist, Fourth Edition*. What unites all four texts is Rita Bean's remarkable vision and lifelong dedication to advancing literacy/instructional leadership and the role of specialists, coaches, and coordinators in school improvement. Having used all four texts in my graduate program, I encourage readers of this second edition of *CCM* to consider it in the context of its three sister books!

In summary, the second edition of *Cultivating Coaching Mindsets* is a timely resource that addresses evolving needs and provides practical strategies for effective coaching. As readers—whether familiar with the text or new to it—embark on their journey with the second edition, I am confident they will find inspiration, practical wisdom, and renewed purpose as they continue to champion excellence in education through their coaching collaborations.

ALLISON SWAN DAGEN, PhD
*West Virginia University*

# Preface

*Cultivating Coaching Mindsets* (2016) was the first major writing project that we (Rita and Jacy) undertook together, and it was the beginning of an exciting and productive professional relationship and friendship. Since then, we have worked on several research projects, written multiple articles and books, and consulted with school districts across the country to support them in their efforts to implement effective coaching programs. Working together has provided us with stimulating learning opportunities, where we continue to debate, challenge, and *coach* each other in thinking about how to share research and best practices about coaching as a means of improving teaching and learning in schools across the United States and beyond.

Our goal for this second edition of *Cultivating Coaching Mindsets* was to write a book that built on our recent research and experiences in schools. We identified several important objectives. First, given the many and varied coaching processes and school contexts that affect coaching across all disciplines and levels, we expanded our focus to that of *instructional coaching* (as compared to focusing solely on literacy coaching in the first edition) and updated the book's subtitle accordingly. We have seen a recent and understandable shift across contexts to instructional coaching, and we have therefore shifted the content in this second edition to address the work of all who coach across all disciplines and grade levels in schools. Our second objective was to highlight and extend the knowledge and theory that we proposed in our previous book, *The Power of Instructional Coaching in Context* (PICIC)—specifically, acknowledgment of the importance of and need for contextual support at the district and school levels to develop and implement effective coaching programs. We thought it critical to marry the systems focus of *PICIC* with the coaching mindsets presented in this text.

As a result, this second edition provides readers with opportunities for learning, reflecting, and raising questions about the connections between their habits of mind, ways of coaching, the systems in which they coach, and our ideas for how to improve both individual coaching work and coaching as a system of professional learning. As coaches ourselves, and as researchers and consultants working with coaches for decades, we have always valued the ways in which coaches are the first to model lifelong professional learning in service of leading schoolwide efforts to improve teaching and learning. We believe this second edition is a useful guide for all who wish to take on such work. Finally, we hope this book will serve as a call to action for all readers, a reference that is turned to again and again over time, to support individual and systemic improvement processes. While readers may start with Chapter 1 and move through the book sequentially at first, we imagine that, over time, readers may dip in and out of the book to reference specific coaching moves and processes.

Whatever your coaching context, we hope the book provides the just-in-time guidance you need to best support colleagues and continue your own journey of continual learning!

# Acknowledgments

*From Rita:* I dedicate this book to my husband, Tony Eichelberger, who died in January 2024. Tony was my partner and best friend, and served as my North Star. I thank him for his love and all he did to encourage and support me in life and in my professional work. Many thanks also to my family: Erin Eichelberger, Derek and Barbie Eichelberger, and their children, Ethan, Ava, and Dylan—they make life joyful and meaningful. My appreciation also to my professional colleagues and literacy students who have served as inspiration and a source of learning throughout the years.

*From Jacy:* I dedicate this book to all the coaches I have collaborated with and learned from over the past 20 years. Being able to support the personal and professional learning of others—through coaching—has been one of my greatest honors, and I'm deeply indebted to all the coaches who have shown me the way. I also want to thank my wife, Victoria, for her unwavering support and thought partnership. Projects like this book would never be possible without her. Finally, I want to thank my two kiddos, Milo and Emily, and my parents, Jim and Elaine, for collectively coaching me on my ever-evolving journey as a father.

*From us both:* Together, we want to acknowledge and thank the coaches and leaders who contributed their voices and ideas to this book, including:

- Adam Brieske-Ulenski, Associate Professor of Reading Education, Bridgewater State University, Massachusetts
- Linda DiMartino, Literacy Supervisor, Agawam Public Schools, Massachusetts

- Ellen B. Eisenberg (Executive Director) and Bruce P. Eisenberg (Associate Director), The Professional Institute for Instructional Coaching, Pennsylvania
- Michael P. Henry, Teacher and Instructional Coach, Reavis High School, Burbank, Illinois
- Shauna Magee, Literacy Specialist and Coach, Triton Public Schools, Massachusetts
- Kristi Sacha, Teaching and Learning Consultant, Educational Service Center of Northeast Ohio
- Christina Steinbacher-Reed, Executive Director, BLaST Intermediate Unit 17, Williamsport, Pennsylvania
- Marsha Turner-Hall, Teacher and Instructional Coach, Lincoln County Schools, North Carolina
- Emily Veader, Elementary Math Instructional Coach, Arlington Public Schools, Massachusetts

Our thinking, and this book, are immeasurably enriched by your contributions—thank you for staying in conversation with us.

Additionally, we would like to thank our partners at Instructional Empowerment (and Learning Sciences International), especially Meg Bowen and Michael Toth, for making the first edition of this book possible. We want to thank all the amazing editors and staff at The Guilford Press for bringing the second edition of this book to life, especially Craig Thomas and Jeannie Tang, for their unwavering support and constructive feedback. And lastly, we wish to thank our respective universities, the University of Pittsburgh and Salem State University, for their ongoing support of our research and writing efforts. We are incredibly grateful.

# Contents

**CHAPTER 1**   Cultivating Coaching Mindsets    1
to Support Systemwide Improvement

    Meeting Melinda    1
    Why Is Coaching Still a Critical Part of School Improvement?    2
    Core Beliefs and Major Assumptions about Coaching    3
        *Coaching Is Best Viewed as a Set of Activities, Not Just a Role*    4
        *Coaching Is Helpful for All Educators, All Grades, All Disciplines*    5
        *Coaching Is Fundamentally Nonevaluative*    5
        *Coaching Should Continually Develop Teacher Capacity*    6
        *Coaching Is Most Effective When Focused on Both Individuals and Systems*    7
        *Differences between Elementary and Secondary Coaching Are a Matter of Degree*    8
        *Content Matters*    8
        *Context Also Makes a Difference*    9
        *Coaching Can Have an Impact*    10
    A Conceptual Framework to Support Coaching and School Improvement    11
        *Why Mindsets Matter*    14
        *Why Leadership, Relationships, Mission/Vision, and Systems Thinking Matter*    15
    Summary    17
    Reflections    17
    Activities    18
    Further Readings and Resources    18

**CHAPTER 2**   Exploring the Coaching Mindsets    20

    A Shift for Melinda    20
    Four Essential Mindsets    20
        *Mindset 1: Thinking Like a Change Agent*    21
        *Mindset 2: Thinking Like a Facilitator*    25
        *Mindset 3: Thinking Like a Designer*    32
        *Mindset 4: Thinking Like an Advocate*    35
    Summary    39
    Reflections    39
    Activities    39
    Further Readings and Resources    40

## CHAPTER 3 Understanding and Shaping School Culture through Systems Thinking     42

Melinda Begins to Consider School Culture   42
What Do We Mean by Culture?   43
   *Shared Leadership Is Key to Building a Collaborative Culture*   44
School Culture: How Important Is It?   45
Leading Organizational Change to Improve Instruction   47
   *1. Focus on Mission, Vision, and Commitment*   48
   *2. Focus on Distributing Leadership*   49
   *3. Focus on Collaboration and Relationships*   50
   *4. Focus on Using Data for Decision Making*   51
Diversity, Equity, and Belonging: The Core of a School's Mission/Vision   51
   *Diversity, Equity, and Belonging: Focusing on Human Capital*   52
   *Developing Awareness of and Appreciation for Cultural Differences*   52
   *Transforming Curriculum and Instruction*   53
   *Engaging the School Community*   53
Partnering with Principals to See and Shape Culture   54
   *The Principal's Role in Supporting Coaching*   55
   *How Coaches Can Support Principals*   57
Partnering with Allied Professionals to Support a Culture of Collaboration   59
Example of a School Change Initiative: The Importance of Systemwide Change   60
Summary   61
Reflections   61
Activities   62
Further Readings and Resources   62

## CHAPTER 4 Introduction to Ways of Working with Teachers     64

Melinda Begins Thinking Like a Facilitator   64
Avoiding the Expertise Trap by Thinking and Working Like a Facilitator   65
   *1. Focus on Facilitating Teacher Learning (Not Sharing Your Own Expertise)*   65
   *2. Focus on Inquiry, Dialogue, and Thought Partnership (Not Pontificating)*   66
   *3. Focus on Lifelong Learning (for the Coach Most of All)*   67
The Power of Language: Talking with Individuals and Groups of Teachers   67
   *First and Foremost, Be an Active Listener*   67
   *Be Aware of Your Nonverbal Communication*   68
   *Use Effective Questioning Techniques*   68
Discussion-Based Protocols as Critical Coaching Tools   72
Coaching Activities for Developing Relationships with Individuals and Groups of Teachers   74
High-Leverage Facilitative Coaching Moves   79
   *Using an Agenda for Individual and Group Coaching Sessions*   79
   *Facilitating Initial Problem Solving*   80
   *Co-Planning*   81
   *Facilitating Assessment and Data-Based Conversations*   81
   *On-the-Fly Coaching*   82
   *Making the Rounds (Informally)*   82
   *Facilitating or Participating in Group Meetings*   83
Summary   84
Reflections   84
Activities   85
Further Readings and Resources   85

| CHAPTER 5 | **Working with Individual Teachers to Analyze and Transform Practice** | 87 |
|---|---|---|

    Melinda Begins to Work with Teachers One-on-One   87
    Powerful Ways of Coaching Individual Teachers   88
    Modeling   90
        *Establish Goals*   90
        *Involve Teachers as You Model*   91
        *Talk and Reflect with the Teacher Soon after the Lesson*   91
        *Follow Up*   91
        *A Few Cautions*   91
    Co-Teaching   92
        *Teaching and Assisting/Monitoring*   93
        *Parallel Teaching*   93
        *Station Teaching*   94
        *Turn Taking or Team Teaching*   94
        *Final Thoughts on Co-Teaching*   94
    Observing   95
        *Observations Should Assist in Improving Instruction*   96
        *A One-Time Observation Is Just a Snapshot*   96
    Unpacking the Observation Cycle   97
        *Pre-Observation/Planning Conversation*   98
        *Observation*   99
        *Analysis of the Observation*   102
        *Post-Observation/Debriefing Conversation*   104
    Summary   110
    Reflections   110
    Activities   111
    Further Readings and Resources   111

| CHAPTER 6 | **Working with Groups to Build a Culture of Adult Learning** | 113 |
|---|---|---|

    Melinda Begins to Consider Group Coaching and Facilitation Skills   113
    Why Coaches Work with Groups   115
        *Working with Groups Can Spur Change*   116
        *Group Coaching Is Connected to Targeted Coaching with Individuals*   116
        *Working with Groups Increases Efficiency*   116
    General Guidelines for Working with Groups of All Sizes   117
        *Craft Community Agreements for Participation and Review Them Periodically*   117
        *Be the "Guide on the Side"*   119
        *Remember That Engagement Is Important*   120
        *Balance Routine and Repertoire*   121
    Strategies for Working with Small Groups   121
    Strategies for Working with Large Groups   128
        *Making a Virtual Presentation*   130
        *Suggestions for Follow-Up*   130
    Group Activities That Support the Development of Professional Learning Communities   131
        *Book Clubs or Study Groups*   132
        *Lesson Study*   133
        *Data Meetings*   133
        *Grade-Level Meetings*   133
        *Classroom Learning Walks*   133
        *Collaborative Cycles of Inquiry*   134
    Summary   135

Reflections   135
Activities   136
Further Readings and Resources   136

**CHAPTER 7  Using Assessment to Guide Student Learning     138
and School Improvement**

Melinda Wades into Assessment Work   138
How This Chapter Can Help Melinda and All Coaches to Think
    about Assessment   140
Assessment of Student Learning: The What and Why   140
   *Summative Assessments*   142
   *Formative Assessments*   145
Ideas for Coaches: Using Data to Improve Classroom Instruction   146
   *Recommendation #1: Make Data an Essential Aspect of the Instructional
       Improvement Cycle*   146
   *Recommendation #2: Teach Students to Self-Assess and Set Their Own Goals*   150
   *Recommendation #3: Use Data to Establish a Vision for School
       and District Improvement*   151
   *Recommendation #4: Develop a Culture That Uses Data for Instructional
       Decision Making*   154
Summary   154
Reflections   155
Activities   155
Further Readings and Resources   156

**CHAPTER 8  Developing, Implementing, and Sustaining     157
Schoolwide Instructional Programs**

Melinda Tackles School-Level Work with the Instructional
    Leadership Team   157
The Role of Coaches in Improving Schoolwide Learning   158
How Coaches Can Support Instructional Leadership Teams   160
The Needs-Assessment Process   163
   *What Is a Needs Assessment?*   163
   *Stages of the Needs-Assessment Process*   164
Moving from Needs Assessment to Action Planning   168
   *Crafting the Action Plan*   168
   *Disseminating the Action Plan*   169
   *Implementing the Action Plan: Managing Change*   169
   *Shifting from Initial Implementation to Sustainability*   171
Guidelines for Developing or Selecting Curriculum and Materials   172
   *Technology as a Tool to Support Student Learning*   173
   *Considering Uses of Technology across Classrooms*   174
   *Coaches' Role in Developing Teachers' Ability to Use Technology Effectively*   176
Advocating for Programs or Materials   177
   *Maintaining a Dual Focus on Individuals and Systems*   177
Summary   178
Reflections   179
Activities   179
Further Readings and Resources   180

**CHAPTER 9  Working with Families and Communities     181**

Melinda Begins to Look Beyond the School Walls   181
The Importance of Engaging Families and Communities   182

Ideas for Developing a School Culture That Understands, Values,
    and Celebrates the Diversity of Its Communities  183
Build Two-Way Communication Channels to Enhance Family Understanding
    and Involvement  185
  *Find Ways to Communicate with Families*  186
  *Provide Activities and Programs That Support Families in Their Efforts to Guide
    Their Children's Learning*  186
  *Involve Families in Decision Making and Encourage Their Participation as Partners
    in Efforts to Educate Their Children*  188
  *Help Develop Teachers' Understanding of How to Talk
    with and Support Families*  188
Capitalizing on Community Resources by Establishing Relationships  189
  *Working with Local Preschool Providers*  190
  *Working with Local Libraries*  191
  *Working with Local Universities*  191
Grant Writing: Accessing Resources from External Sources  192
Summary  194
Reflections  194
Activities  194
Further Readings and Resources  195

**CHAPTER 10  Coaches as Lifelong Learners**  196

Melinda Considers Her Own Ongoing Professional Learning  196
A Reminder about Adopting an "Expert" Stance  197
Knowledge That Supports Coaching Work  199
  *Keep Apprised of National and State Standards*  200
  *Find or Form a Professional Network*  200
  *Keep a Journal*  201
  *Join a Professional Learning Organization*  201
  *Strive for a Balanced Professional Reading Diet*  201
  *Keep an Eye on State and National Education News and Policy*  202
  *Take "Lifelong" Seriously*  202
Self-Assessment and Reflective Tools to Encourage Lifelong Learning  202
  *Self-Assessment*  203
  *Seeking Feedback*  205
Self-Reflection Related to Our Coaching Mindsets  206
Summary  206
Reflections  207
Activities  207
Further Readings and Resources  208

**CHAPTER 11  Coaching Cases: Stories of Coaches and Coaching**  209

Case 1: The Evolution of a Coach  209
  *School-Based Coach (2003–2005)*  210
  *A Change in Direction*  211
  *Supervisor of Coaches (2006–2010)*  212
  *External Coach (2010–2015)*  213
  *Executive Director (2017–Present)*  214
Case 2: School-Based Elementary Math Coach  216
Case 3: A Coaching Mindset in the Classroom  219
  *Coaching as a Part-Time Responsibility*  220
  *Importance of the Relationship with Administrators*  221
  *Mindset Is Key*  221
  *Frameworks*  221

   *Protocols* 222
   *How This Has Changed Me as a Classroom Teacher* 223
  Case 4: Mentoring Instructional Coaches: An Eight-Year Journey 224
   *Working at the District Level: Leading and Guiding Coaches* 225
   *Five Lessons Learned* 225
  Case 5: Changing the Community of Teaching, Learning, and Practice:
   A State Coaching Initiative 229
   *Coaching Framework* 229
   *The BDA Cycle of Consultation* 230
   *Mentoring* 230
   *Content Framework* 231
   *Updates about This Statewide Initiative* 231
  Final Thoughts about the PIIC 233

| | | |
|---|---|---|
| **APPENDIX A** | Thinking and Working Like a Coach: Note-Taking Organizer | 235 |
| **APPENDIX B** | Note-Taking Organizer When Coach Is Modeling Instruction | 240 |
| **APPENDIX C** | Observation Protocol for Discipline-Specific Instruction | 241 |
| **APPENDIX D** | Lesson Analysis Guide for Post-Observation Coaching Conversations | 244 |
| **APPENDIX E** | Analysis of State and District Assessments | 246 |
| **APPENDIX F** | A Sample Process for Guiding Assessment-Focused Self-Study and Professional Learning | 247 |
| **APPENDIX G** | Assessing Teacher Perceptions of Professional Learning Experiences | 249 |
| **APPENDIX H** | Template for a Professional Learning Action Plan | 251 |
| **APPENDIX I** | Coach Skills, Knowledge, and Dispositions Self-Assessment Tool | 254 |
| **APPENDIX J** | Sample Disciplinary Literacy Protocols Shared by Michael P. Henry | 258 |
| | References | 261 |
| | Index | 277 |

---

Purchasers of this book can download and print larger versions
of select materials at *www.guilford.com/bean3-materials*
for personal use or use with students (see copyright page for details).

# CHAPTER 1

# Cultivating Coaching Mindsets to Support Systemwide Improvement

> **GUIDING QUESTIONS**
>
> 1. Why might coaching in schools matter more now than ever before?
> 2. What are our own major assumptions and core beliefs about coaching?
> 3. What are the four mindsets that guide coach thinking and work?
> 4. In what ways does our framework for thinking and working like a coach depend on strong leadership, collaborative relationships, a clear mission/vision, and systems thinking?

## Meeting Melinda

When her principal asked Melinda, an experienced classroom teacher, to take on an instructional coaching role to support teaching and learning in her K–5 school, Melinda began to search for resources that would help her better understand her new responsibilities. While Melinda was excited to take on coaching work, she was also quite nervous about shifting from working solely with students to working predominantly with adults. Her principal told Melinda that she would have a great deal of input in defining her coaching work. While this seemed like an amazing professional opportunity, Melinda worried that so much of her role was undefined. How might Melinda begin to think about her new role? How might she focus her thinking and work? How might she know if she is making a difference in classroom instruction and student learning?

In many ways, this book presents both the research and resources that we think can support Melinda in accomplishing her goals. While fictional, Melinda represents a compilation of the many instructional coaches and teacher leaders with whom we have worked over the years. Having both personally walked in Melinda's shoes and mentored many teachers and coaches like Melinda, we have chosen to begin each of our chapters with a brief snapshot of the tasks that Melinda might take on and the questions that she might ask along the way. Each chapter then serves as a resource for helping all who coach to answer questions like Melinda's.

Therefore, the two main purposes of this book are to (1) provide those who coach with an understanding of how coaching requires particular *ways of thinking* about coaching adult learners in schools and (2) suggest numerous related *ways of working* with adult learners, including dozens of practical strategies and tools. In this introductory chapter, we begin by presenting several major reasons that instructional coaching in schools is now as important as ever before, if not more so, and some core beliefs and fundamental assumptions about coaching that guide our work. We end by presenting the framework at the heart of this book, which supports coaching across a wide variety of school contexts.

## Why Is Coaching Still a Critical Part of School Improvement?

Coaching, although still a relatively new phenomenon in the history of public schooling, has gained momentum during the past several decades. In business, there are executive coaches; in medicine, health coaches and life coaches; and in education, instructional coaches. Educational coaches come with a variety of titles (e.g., instructional, academic, change, literacy, social-emotional, peer), and a dizzying and diverse number of roles and responsibilities. However, all those who coach, whether in business, medicine, or education, share a fundamental similarity, a desire to support the work of colleagues while continually improving their own practice.

Atul Gawande, an internationally known surgeon and writer, realizing that he had reached a plateau in his learning, worked with a coach to further develop his technical skills and his ability to work with other members of his team. Gawande (2011) makes several key points about coaching; specifically, he notes that "the allegiance of the coach is to the people they work with; their success depends on it. And the existence of a coach depends on the acknowledgement that even expert practitioners have significant room for improvement" (para. 95). Gawande continues, in his 2017 TED Talk on the same subject, by asking the fundamental questions: "How do professionals get better at what they do? How do they get great?" A big part of his answer is: "Everybody needs a coach. Everyone. The greatest in the world needs a coach" (Gawande, 2017). In other words, all of us can always improve as professionals, and coaches can play an important part in helping us get there. It is from this simple idea, the notion that everybody needs a coach to improve professionally, that we begin this book exploring the coaching mindsets that support the continual improvement work that educators and schools need to create equitable opportunities and outcomes for all students.

For teachers working in the post-COVID-19 era of education, professional learning has perhaps never been more important nor more complex. We find ourselves in the middle of a historical inflection point, in which educators must rapidly and continually adapt to think differently about how they teach. Student populations are diversifying along every continuum (race, gender, language, neurodiversity, and so on). Delivering high-quality instruction in an age where artificial intelligence, online and hybrid learning, and digital devices are pervasive requires educators to constantly question which fundamental skills students of all ages must acquire. As a result, educators must regularly update their research-based disciplinary and pedagogical knowledge in literacy, math, science, social studies, the arts, and more. Moreover, we are witnessing a revolution in terms of teachers needing to attend more than ever to students' social-emotional learning (SEL). Students in the 2020s are wrestling with global issues of climate change, poverty, food scarcity, and social unrest in ways that make school, college, and workplace demands far more complicated.

All of this points to a need for today's educators to be ready and willing to adapt their instructional practices to meet ever-shifting student and schooling needs. Traditional teacher preparation and professional learning methods simply will not be enough to meet the myriad existing and emerging demands. While we still believe that there is no silver bullet, no one idea or tool that will solve all dilemmas (Ippolito & Bean, 2024), we also know from research and experience that coaching can and should be a big part of the solution. At its best, instructional coaching is a powerful job-embedded, educator-responsive form of professional learning that can adapt to emerging student, teacher, and school needs. Coaching can be the very solution that many school leaders are seeking as they try to support teachers in this era of rapid societal change. While we fully acknowledge the many ways in which coaching may not live up to its potential in specific school contexts—in part because of the ways that school systems and structures may not fully support coaching efforts (for more on supporting larger coaching systems, see Ippolito & Bean, 2024; Woulfin et al., 2023)—in this book, we zoom in on the habits of mind and ways of working that all those who work with adult learners in schools can adopt. By thinking and working like a coach, all educators can make a difference in one another's practice.

Before sharing the framework at the heart of this book, we first wish to share some of our own core beliefs and assumptions about coaching. These beliefs have shaped our work in schools, our research, and most certainly this book; therefore, we think it important to show our cards at the outset of this book.

## Core Beliefs and Major Assumptions about Coaching

In this section, we introduce a handful of core beliefs and major assumptions that we hold as central to successful coaching. We then continue to refer to these assumptions throughout the book.

### *Coaching Is Best Viewed as a Set of Activities, Not Just a Role*

Not all who coach in schools have followed similar journeys into their roles and responsibilities. Some educators become coaches through formal graduate coursework, certification programs, or degree programs. Others take on coaching work via school and district mentoring and preparation pathways. Many others begin to coach via informal routes, much like our own experiences as coaches in which our respective school leaders tapped us and asked us to begin working with colleagues (very similar to Melinda's experience at the outset of this chapter). This diversity of coach preparation and professional support pathways has certainly shaped our own thinking about how best to make sense of coaching over time.

Therefore, one of our core beliefs mentioned throughout this book is that many educators in schools take on coaching responsibilities, from those with the formal title of "coach" to others such as specialists/interventionists, teacher leaders, cooperating and mentor teachers, team leaders and facilitators, consultant teachers, department heads, assistant principals, and even at times principals. In other words, we have come to view coaching fundamentally as an *activity* rather than only as a *role*. Many individuals, regardless of title, may assume coaching responsibilities, which run the gamut from serving as a resource or mentor to others, to co-planning and co-teaching, to observing and providing feedback, and so on. Interventionists and specialists often take on coaching responsibilities (see Shauna Magee's Voices from the Field). Teacher leaders and grade-level or content-area teachers often are tasked with coaching colleagues with a similar disciplinary focus. The notion that many educators hold coaching responsibilities in schools is consistent with current research evidence that schools with a culture of shared leadership and collaboration are well positioned to increase student learning (Bryk et al., 2015; Bryk et al., 2010; Donohoo & Katz, 2017; Donohoo et al., 2018; Louis et al., 2010). Ultimately, if we limit coaching responsibilities to only those who hold the formal title of "coach," then we risk losing or undermining the wealth of experience, knowledge, and savvy of many capable teachers and leaders. Consequently, this book is written for *all who coach adults in schools*, regardless of formal title.

> **VOICES FROM THE FIELD**
>
> In 2013–2014, the district made the decision to transition the specialists into coaches. Up until that time, the reading specialist's main role was intervention and direct service of students. When the transition was made, administration suggested a 60% coaching and 40% intervention balance; however, the coaching model has looked different at each school, and even from year to year based on budget/staffing cuts, administrative changes, etc. Currently, I spend about 50% of my day working with students and 50% coaching.
>
> —Shauna Magee, Literacy Coach

## Coaching Is Helpful for All Educators, All Grades, All Disciplines

This brings us to our second foundational belief: Coaching can be critically important to improving teaching and learning in schools, across *all* educators, grade levels, and disciplines. Certainly, coaching can be beneficial for those responsible for teaching in elementary schools—for teachers working with the youngest learners who are just beginning to learn the basics of decoding sound–symbol connections, mastering their first sight words, learning early math facts, and developing a sense of wonder about the world and how to explore it via disciplinary lenses in the humanities, sciences, and arts. However, while coaching of teachers in the earliest grades makes great sense, we must not forget how beneficial coaching can be for those educators working in upper grades, as the instructional focus shifts to more complex vocabulary and comprehension instruction, sophisticated and abstract mathematical concepts, and extremely detailed and discipline-specific learning in history, science, and arts classes. A greater emphasis on teaching disciplinary literacy strategies to students as they move into middle school, high school, and university settings only increases the need for coaching teachers within and across disciplines across all grades as a means of improving students' content learning (Burke & Kennedy, 2024; Gabriel, 2023; Ippolito et al., 2024; Moje, 2015; C. Shanahan & Shanahan, 2014; T. Shanahan & Shanahan, 2008, 2012). In other words, coaching is key to helping teachers across all grades and subjects take on the challenge of merging content goals with discipline-specific literacy teaching and learning (Botel & Paparo, 2016).

## Coaching Is Fundamentally Nonevaluative

Most educators who write about coaching do not view it as an evaluative process, one in which coaches participate in the formal evaluation of teacher practices or performance. Yet, in some districts, coaches are indeed asked to assume such an evaluative role, especially with the current emphasis on teacher performance evaluation. For example, in one district, teachers identified as "exemplary" were assigned as consulting teachers or coaches to work with and then monitor the work of beginning teachers and veterans who were experiencing teaching difficulties (Goldstein, 2009). Galey-Horn and Woulfin (2021), in a study of 41 instructional coaches across five educational systems, found that coaches often served as mediators of evaluation policy. These coaches collaborated with teachers to help them develop an understanding of evaluation and to support them in thinking about how to reach the goals the teachers had set for themselves. In other words, important questions have been raised recently about how coaches might be formally included in teacher evaluation practices as part of more coherent improvement and evaluation systems in schools (Woulfin & Rigby, 2017). However, in practice, coaches can struggle when asked to assume both supportive coaching roles and evaluation roles. As stated by Toll (2006), evaluation responsibilities may make it difficult for coaches to develop trusting relationships with teachers.

In our experience, coaches are best positioned as colleagues who work with their peers as thought partners—tackling problems of practice, collaboratively inquiring, reflecting, and partnering to make decisions about how best to improve instructional practices. Although coaches can support teachers who have been identified as needing to improve by formal school leaders, in our experience, we believe that coaches should not formally evaluate teachers. As we have written about before (Ippolito & Bean, 2024), we have found it best for principals and coaches to clarify for all educators the "evaluation role of the principal and the supportive role of the coach" (p. 198). This joint message, that coaches are supportive peers and not evaluating supervisors, truly does need to come from both principals and coaches simultaneously.

Whether informally or formally, when educators such as coaches are asked to assume any evaluative role, they can learn much from the coaching literature and from this book about how to work with teachers in positive ways, provide constructive feedback, and encourage teachers to become more reflective about their teaching and learning. We suggest, however, that individuals who hold formal evaluative positions be given titles other than "coach."

> **VOICES FROM THE FIELD**
>
> Business flows because coaching comes with a "no judgment" guarantee.
> —LINDA DIMARTINO, Literacy Supervisor

### *Coaching Should Continually Develop Teacher Capacity*

Many coaches with whom we have worked have indicated surprise that teachers in their schools continued to seek the same sorts of support from them, even though these teachers have participated in various coaching activities over several years. There may be many reasons for this, including that the coaching perhaps focused almost entirely on early relationship-building activities, rather than slowly nudging teachers to internalize the work and take more ownership over their own professional learning. How often have we reverted to practices with which we are familiar or comfortable when we didn't have the support (and pressure) to keep using new practices (e.g., learning a new way to grip a tennis racket or a golf club)?

Therefore, coaching initiatives must offer both support and pressure, over time, in service of continually developing teacher capacity. In other words, coaching is not meant to—nor can it—*inoculate* individuals so that eventually there is no need for coaching. Remember Atul Gawande's (2017) powerful statement: "Everybody needs a coach. Everyone. The greatest in the world needs a coach." The implications of this notion are far-ranging. There are always new students, new frameworks, and new dilemmas for coaches and teachers to discuss. At all stages of their careers, all teachers and coaches can learn from one another. At the same time, the focus of coaching should be on helping teachers grow professionally. As stated in the Learning Policy Institute Report (Darling-Hammond et al., 2017) on effective teacher professional learning, educators must be prepared to teach in ways that enable students to achieve the competencies needed to handle the complex demands required for success in the 21st century. In this review, coaching is identified as one of the important features of any professional learning effort. Coaches can provide the guidance and support that builds teachers' capacity to "use new curricula, tools, and approaches" (p. 13); they can facilitate teacher reflection about their instructional practices and how to use student data to improve instructional decision making.

## *Coaching Is Most Effective When Focused on Both Individuals and Systems*

We always encourage those who take on coaching work to simultaneously focus on both the needs of individuals and larger systems. All too often smart, talented coaches and leaders exhaust themselves by exclusively attending to the needs of teachers one-on-one. Similarly, others fail to make inroads with teachers because they tilt exclusively toward systems-level thinking, constantly planning for larger-group and whole-school initiatives, without attending to the individual differences and needs that arise among faculty. Others get caught up in management tasks—such as organizing assessment results, ordering and arranging materials, and so forth—that reduce the time and energy for coaching.

Mangin and Dunsmore (2015) highlight what many in the field have guessed for some time: that while coaches are often asked to support systemwide instructional change, coach preparation and support more often prepares them to work with individuals, "respond[ing] to teachers' individualized needs" (p. 187). Maintaining this dual focus on individuals and systems simultaneously requires clear communication with school and district leadership about the vision and theory of action for systems-level change. Questions that coaches can ask themselves as they endeavor to adopt a dual focus on individuals and systems include:

- To what extent are the principal, coach, and district-level leaders all on the same page about the goals of instructional change efforts?
- How clearly can each of these stakeholders articulate shared goals and action steps?
- How clearly have systemwide change efforts been communicated to (and solicited from or generated by) teachers across grades and schools?
- To what degree must work with individual teachers fit within a larger framework for change versus simple support of individual teachers' interests and needs?

As Mangin and Dunsmore (2015) suggest, without clearer alignment of focus at both the system and individual levels, coaches may default to thinking that "the sum of individual changes across teachers [might be] equivalent to systemic reform" (p. 203), which we would argue is rarely the case, particularly in large schools and districts. By maintaining a dual focus on individuals and the larger system, coaches act as organizational glue, building the collective capacity of teachers and leaders to move toward common, effective instructional practices.

### *Differences between Elementary and Secondary Coaching Are a Matter of Degree*

As we have written elsewhere (Ippolito & Lieberman, 2012, 2020), we believe that there are real differences between coaching at elementary and secondary levels, but we see those differences more as differences of *degree* rather than of fundamental distinctions. Those who coach in the early grades and in the later grades must think about both the content of instruction as well as the coaching processes they might use. They need background knowledge and preparation about disciplinary standards, curriculum, and instruction, and they need to know how to work with individuals, groups, and systems. Further, scheduling is a challenge for all coaches, with both elementary and secondary coaches struggling to find time to work with teachers (as opposed to getting bogged down in administrative work).

While both elementary and secondary coaches have more in common than not, there are some differences in degree that seem to matter. For instance, secondary coaches are often expected to work with much larger groups of teachers, both within and across disciplines. Secondary coaches often need deeper background knowledge and preparation in content-area curriculum to best support content-area teachers in history, math, science, and so on. Finally, we often see the biggest differences when we look at elementary versus secondary coaches' pathways into coaching: More elementary coaches come to the role as experienced general classroom teachers or specialists, while more secondary coaches come to the role with a deeper content-area instructional background (e.g., former high school English, history, math, or science teachers). We believe that differences between elementary and secondary coaching are important to consider in both initiating and sustaining coaching programs; however, we also caution readers to not overemphasize the differences, and instead to look for commonalities across all roles that include coaching responsibilities.

### *Content Matters*

Those who coach, and the school leaders who support them, must also pay careful attention to the ways in which coaching is shaped by the focus or "content" of that coaching work. As we have argued before (Ippolito & Bean, 2024), the instructional core of students, teachers, curriculum, and the classroom tasks that connect all three

(City et al., 2009) can have a direct and dramatic effect on coaching work. Fundamentally, school leaders and coaches must be sensitive to the ways in which the target of coaching work, the "content" that coaches and teachers discuss, shapes the overall coaching initiative; otherwise, coaching work may be too generic or diffuse to make much of a difference in teaching and learning.

In general, instructional coaches who are experts in the foundational disciplinary and pedagogical knowledge associated with their coaching work (e.g., literacy, math, SEL, and so on) are better able to facilitate teacher learning and to assist in the design and implementation of teaching and learning experiences. For example, literacy coaches unfamiliar with the research about effective phonics instruction will be less able to identify specific trouble spots, or areas where a teacher might provide a series of classroom experiences more closely connected to the research on how young students' brains learn to read. Likewise, at the secondary level, a math instructional coach without an awareness of the very real differences in student outcomes when memorizing equations versus describing and understanding deep connections between mathematical operations and real-world applications will be limited in what they can share with their teacher partners.

All of this points to the need to hire and support instructional coaches who are ready and willing to continually grow their disciplinary and pedagogical content knowledge. This speaks directly to the need for collaborative, ongoing professional learning for teachers and coaches together (Woulfin et al., 2023). For example, although more and more schools acknowledge the value of collaboration among teachers, too often neither the structure (i.e., scheduling) nor the support (e.g., availability and capacity of teachers to collaborate) are available (Bryk et al., 2015; National Center for Literacy Education, 2014). According to the report *Remodeling Literacy Learning Together: Paths to Standards Implementation* (National Center for Literacy Education, 2014), American schools do many things right, but at the same time, there is a need for *remodeling* to build an even better system. This is especially true if we are to create schools in which all students have equal access to educational opportunity. Coaches with deep content knowledge and expertise are poised to lead the way.

### Context Also Makes a Difference

While content undoubtedly matters in shaping coaching efforts, more attention has been given recently to the notion that context also greatly influences coaching work. Coaching programs will look different depending on the context in which they are implemented (Hannan & Russell, 2020; Ippolito & Bean, 2024; Woulfin et al., 2023). School size, leadership structures, student demographics, experiences and backgrounds of teachers, experiences and backgrounds of coaches, and the existing culture of the school all have an impact on coaching initiatives. Other factors, such as union issues or written job descriptions, also influence the ways in which coaching initiatives function. Such factors can affect the type of coaching model implemented (e.g., more directive, responsive, or balanced), the responsibilities of the coach (e.g., working with all teachers or only those who request support), and even the workload of the coach (e.g., full-time or part-time hours). These variables, across contexts, account for some of the difficulty in evaluating the effectiveness of coaching. As we have argued before (Ippolito & Bean, 2024), we can no longer conceptualize or enact coaching work without taking seriously the context-specific needs of each school and district. Successful coaching in one school or district cannot simply be transposed, without adaptation, to another context.

### *Coaching Can Have an Impact*

Over the past several decades, researchers have been studying various aspects of coaching, including the roles and responsibilities of coaches and the effects of coaching on teacher practices. As mentioned, given the complexities of coaching, obtaining unequivocal evidence about its impact, especially on student learning, has been difficult. However, there appears to be growing evidence that coaching, if implemented effectively, can in fact influence and change teacher practices and student learning (Bean et al., 2010; Biancarosa et al., 2010; Elish-Piper & L'Allier, 2011; Kraft & Blazar, 2017; Kraft et al., 2018; Matsumura et al., 2013; Piper & Zuilkowski, 2015).

Coaching can also influence teachers' beliefs and attitudes (Gibbons & Cobb, 2017; Kinnucan-Welsch et al., 2006; Vandeburg & Stephens, 2010). However, there continues to be a need for ongoing, rigorous studies that investigate coaching's multifaceted dimensions (e.g., coach preparation and qualifications, coaching activities, and the context in which coaching appears) (Swan Dagen & Bean, 2014). There is also a need for studies in which content, coaching processes, and context are all considered simultaneously; that is, in what ways might each affect the others?

> **STOP AND REFLECT**
>
> With a small group of professional colleagues, reread this section on core beliefs about coaching work. Use the Four A's protocol from the Center for Leadership & Educational Equity and the School Reform Initiative (see Web Resources at the end of this chapter) to discuss the beliefs. What **a**ssumptions are being made? What do you **a**gree with? What do you want to **a**rgue with? What, if anything, do you want to **a**spire to or **a**ct upon? Compare notes with colleagues and use this opportunity to clarify your own initial beliefs and assumptions about coaching. It may be worth keeping notes or recording these for yourself, to see if any of your beliefs shift or sharpen as you continue to read this book.

Having shared some of our core beliefs related to coaching, we now share the conceptual framework that will shape the rest of the book. We have come to use this framework with both coaches and school leaders to describe the larger enterprise of coaching work (including the effects of content and context on coaching) and to articulate and explore the habits of mind and ways of working that lead to effective coaching.

## A Conceptual Framework to Support Coaching and School Improvement

We view coaching as a process of *facilitated* inquiry that enables teachers to make decisions, solve problems, and set or achieve both individual goals as well as the goals of the organization, specifically to improve classroom instructional practices and student learning. Further, such *collaborative* inquiry contributes to cultural and organizational changes necessary for improving the learning of all students.

We see effective coaching as being guided by an underlying set of coaching mindsets, that is, an established set of attitudes, beliefs/values, and feelings that influence coach behavior and support the ways in which coaches lead adult learning and collaboration, all in service of the continual improvement of teaching and learning. Such coaching mindsets ultimately guide the wide array of coaching activities that take place weekly in schools (e.g., holding conversations with teachers designed to increase awareness and reflection about instructional issues, modeling various interventions or strategies, observing, facilitating meetings about instruction or data, and so on) and can focus on individuals or groups. Although the stance of the coach, or how the coach approaches interactions with teachers, may differ depending upon teacher knowledge, experience, and receptivity to professional learning, coaching must always be built upon a foundation of respect for the goals and beliefs of individual teachers about teaching, learning, and content. Beyond the mindsets that influence the work of individual coaches, and to help coaches and the schools they serve to achieve their improvement goals, our framework also includes ideas related to the context in which coaches work, the subject-area content they're addressing, and the coaching processes they might choose to use. We believe this framework helps explain the ways in which coaching can become a powerful lever for supporting school improvement.

Over the years, given our own work as instructional coaches and subsequent research into the roles, responsibilities, and effects of coaching, we now often think about coaching from a systems perspective. In our most recent book, *The Power of Instructional Coaching in Context* (Ippolito & Bean, 2024), we introduced the Content and Coaching in Context (CCIC) Framework (see Figure 1.1). The CCIC Framework suggests that successful coaching is not just the result of expert coaches with good intentions and quality coaching processes, working with individual teachers.

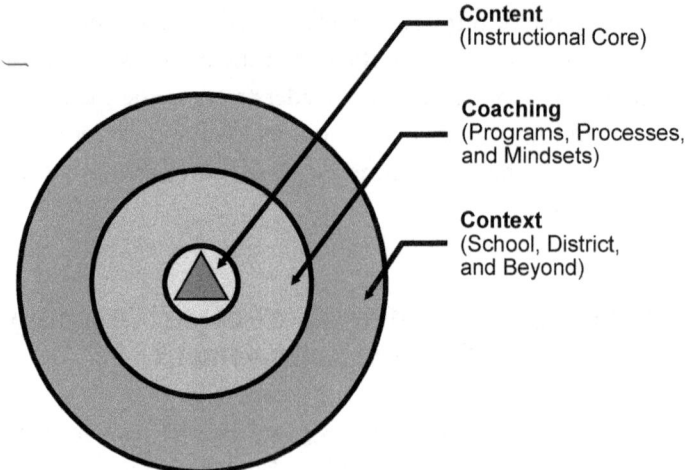

**FIGURE 1.1.** The Content and Coaching in Context (CCIC) Framework. Adapted from Ippolito and Bean (2024, p. 13). Copyright © 2024 The Guilford Press.

Instead, successful coaching also requires and may be more accurately described as the *alignment* of content (a clearly articulated instructional core or target for coaching work) with coaching programs and processes, all embedded within a supportive school and district context. Alignment of these domains (content, coaching, and context) can ultimately produce improved teaching and learning, as well as equitable opportunities and outcomes for all students.

In this current second edition of *Cultivating Coaching Mindsets*, we update and expand upon our previous work (Bean & Ippolito, 2016; Ippolito & Bean, 2018, 2024) by adding a layer of detail and complexity to our CCIC Framework, now detailing the mindsets that drive coaching work within the middle ring of our framework. We view these mindsets as those that instructional coaches must adopt to successfully influence the instructional core *and* the larger school or district context that shapes all coaching, teaching, and learning work. Therefore, we have embedded the mindsets within the coaching ring of our CCIC bullseye heuristic. While the four broad coaching mindsets we present in this second edition are not an exhaustive list of the ways in which coaches think and work, they do form a foundation for excellent job-embedded professional learning within and across disciplines, grade levels, and schools.

Our four revised and updated mindsets include thinking and working like a change agent, facilitator, designer, and advocate (see Figure 1.2). As change agents, coaches continually work to refine and improve teaching and learning processes in schools. As facilitators, coaches guide adult learning for individuals and groups. As designers, coaches work with teachers and leaders to reframe instructional dilemmas as design challenges to be solved. Finally, as advocates, coaches regularly lobby for the needs of students, teachers, parents, and the community. We see these four mindsets as interwoven throughout all work within an effective coaching program, guiding the work of all those who coach and interacting with the content and context of schooling.

Inspired by the work of Jim Collins (2001, 2005) in his descriptions of "good to great" companies and schools, we also see our coaching mindsets as deeply connected to larger notions of leadership, adult relationships, mission/vision, and systems thinking within schools. We have seen these four interrelated notions act as drivers of coaching and school improvement, or what Collins (n.d., 2019) refers to as the "flywheel effect" for organizations. The term *flywheel* "comes from mechanics, where it refers to a very heavy wheel that is used to generate and transfer energy to other parts of a machine" (Adisa, 2020). The flywheel effect in education refers to many individual and early efforts that serve to build momentum and generate a cycle of ongoing improvement. In other words, coaching is incredibly difficult to enact successfully without the presence of strong leadership, collaborative relationships, a clear mission/vision, and a focus on systems thinking in a school. Over time, these four elements can support both coaching and rich learning for educators and students alike. Therefore, in addition to highlighting the four primary coaching mindsets across this book, you will also see many references to and connections with issues of leadership, relationships, mission/vision, and systems thinking.

Thus, our four coaching mindsets influence and are influenced by the beliefs and actions of coaches, teachers, leaders, and systems within schools. Coaches who adopt and model these mindsets—change agent, facilitator, designer, and advocate—are

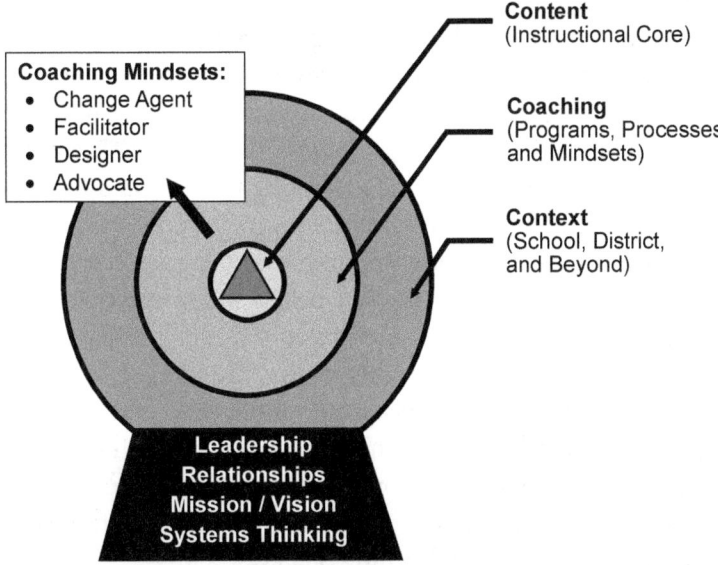

**FIGURE 1.2.** Framework for thinking and working like a coach.

well positioned to make a significant impact in their schools. Furthermore, as you may have surmised by now, we view these mindsets as adoptable by more than just formal instructional coaches. Teacher leaders, specialists/interventionists, special educators, librarians, principals, assistant principals, directors/coordinators, and more can adopt these mindsets as they go about their own work as leaders of adult and professional learning in schools.

Across this second edition, we zoom in on the various ways in which these four coaching mindsets can guide and shape the work of all who coach within schools. While each chapter may focus more on one or two mindsets, we have endeavored to make a connection to each mindset to some extent in each chapter.

## *Why Mindsets Matter*

How you *think* about the process of improving teaching and learning matters a great deal as you strive to make changes in individual classrooms as well as in entire schools and districts. As scholars of organizational learning have written about extensively (see McDonald & Cities and Schools Research Group, 2024; Schein, 2010; Schön & Rein, 1994), the *mental models* or *frames* that we hold, and through which we view the world, matter enormously. Our mental models and frames shape how we think about our work and how we think about change processes. This is why we have chosen to highlight four critical coaching mindsets, or frames, and related actions across this book. To briefly illustrate, let's discuss the simple but powerful mental shift from thinking about change as a technical process versus an adaptive one. This is perhaps the first step in thinking like a change agent (discussed in greater depth in Chapter 2).

Much of coaching work is about helping colleagues to become more reflective practitioners and shift their instruction slowly to improve outcomes for students. However, if the work of coaching is viewed through a purely technical lens (Heifetz et al., 2009) or as single-loop learning (Argyris & Schön, 1974, 1996)—in other words, learning that simply requires detection of a problem and implementation of a known solution—then this frame for coaching will likely not produce the deep, systemic changes that most leadership work is meant to provoke. Instead, if coaching work is to result in deep changes in teachers' beliefs and instructional practices, then coaches must push toward adaptive (Heifetz et al., 2009) or double-loop learning (Argyris & Schön, 1974, 1996)—in other words, the kind of learning that results in a fundamental questioning of beliefs, assumptions, and practices as steps toward transforming teaching and learning (rather than simply tinkering around the edges). Adaptive learning processes involve not just the analysis of current dilemmas but the analysis and shifting of an organization's fundamental beliefs, assumptions, and ways of operating as a result of the learning process.

Consider this example of the difference between a technical and adaptive change agent focus when coaching a fifth-grade math team. After identifying fifth graders' poor math homework performance, the fifth-grade team of teachers assign a modified homework packet, simply reducing the number of problems and increasing the number of points assigned. In other words, they adopt a technical change mindset. The team is then surprised two weeks later that student performance has not shifted. At this point, the elementary math instructional coach begins to work with the team to take a more adaptive approach to the dilemma. The coach facilitates two separate "looking at student work" protocol-based discussions, encouraging the team to delve more deeply into the types of problems students are completing and those that are causing frustration. A number of insights emerge, about both the types of problems being assigned for homework and the relationship between direct instruction, students' independent practice in class, and success on the homework. The group of teachers begins to question the purpose of the homework assignments, and they quickly reconsider and reinvent the homework tasks, with the coach's assistance, to present students with menus of homework options to better practice the conceptual, computational, and communication skills and knowledge each student needs.

This shift, from a technical approach to a more adaptive and collaborative approach to change, may not occur without direct support from an instructional coach who has adopted the "change agent" mindset. Such adaptive learning requires educators (both teachers and coaches) to analyze their own assumptions about teaching and learning as part of the problem-solving process. While instructional coaches may be eager to help teachers solve current teaching and learning dilemmas quickly, the work of Argyris and Schön (1974, 1996), and Heifetz et al. (2009) reminds us that to effectively solve both current and future dilemmas, coaches need to think about their own adult learning and work habits.

In Chapter 2, we further review the four mindsets, or mental models, that we have found effective instructional coaches to hold over time. These mindsets, when applied consistently by dedicated coaches and informal leaders, produce the longest-lasting and biggest changes in teaching and learning. Most importantly, these frames are most successful when they align with the content, coaching practices, and context of each specific school. The alignment between espoused theory (i.e., what we *say* we do) and theories-in-use (i.e., what we *actually* do) (Argyris & Schön, 1974) is of utmost importance as instructional coaches talk the talk *and* walk the walk of organizational learning.

## *Why Leadership, Relationships, Mission/Vision, and Systems Thinking Matter*

We end this chapter with a brief discussion of leadership, relationships, mission/vision, and systems thinking as key drivers and supports of instructional coaching. As research continues to investigate the ways in which school culture and context shape instructional coaching work (Woulfin et al., 2023), our own thinking about the deeply contextualized nature of coaching has evolved (Ippolito & Bean, 2024).

Over time, and as systems-focused research on school change has emerged (e.g., Bryk et al., 2015), we have found that the most effective coaching programs are those that pay great attention to the interdependent nature of these four factors and how they relate to the work of instructional coaches.

- **Leadership** is the foundation upon which all successful instructional coaching work rests. Principals, assistant principals, curriculum directors/coordinators, and other formal school and district-based leaders who deeply understand and support coaching efforts can make all the difference in fostering a schoolwide culture of collaborative inquiry and ongoing adult professional learning. Leaders can promote the work of coaches, encourage teachers to connect with coaches frequently, and release leadership responsibilities to both coaches and teachers (those closest to students). By promoting an environment in which teachers and coaches have real authority to make critical decisions about teaching and learning, school leaders pave the way for coaching success.
- **Relationships** are the well-researched, strong conduits for professional growth in schools. We are hard-pressed to find any successful coaching initiative that does not have strong relationships at its very core. Research on social networks in schools (Daly & Little, 2010), collective efficacy (Donohoo & Katz, 2017; Donohoo et al., 2018), and collaborative school improvement processes (Bryk et al., 2015) provide us with a rich understanding of the ways that strong interpersonal relationships in schools can support positive shifts in teaching and learning. Moreover, coaching is an inherently relational activity, with a growing body of evidence suggesting that coaches are successful not just because of *what* they share with teachers but because of *how* they collaborate (Ippolito, 2010; Robertson et al., 2020b). Without a fundamental focus on building and sustaining strong relationships among adults in schools, coaching may never realize its true potential.
- **Mission and vision** guide the work of not just coaches but also the entire school community. We like to think of *mission* as the essential reasons for any organization to exist, tied closely to a school's core beliefs and values. In the case of many schools, the mission is to provide equitable and rich learning opportunities to all students, in service of promoting lifelong learning and robust opportunities for all. Mission-driven work includes all the nuts and bolts and the day-to-day work that helps a school achieve its goals. Meanwhile, we think of *vision* as the ability of an organization to paint a clear picture of the future, and to steer adult professional work carefully (adhering to mission) to eventually realize the goals of the organization. Schools with clearly articulated mission/vision statements, and lots of adult and student work to demonstrate how the mission and vision are being enacted every day, are fertile environments in which coaching initiatives can thrive. Schools in which mission/vision is muddy or constantly shifting struggle to support healthy coaching work.

- **Systems thinking** refers to the notion that coaches, as well as teachers and leaders, must not only deeply consider the efficacy of their own roles and work, but they must also consider how their work fits into the larger systems in operation in a school and district. As we discuss in the following chapters, shared goals and collective efforts across roles are what ultimately make coaching effective. As we have written about before (Ippolito & Bean, 2024), alignment across content, coaching, and context—or, alignment across systems of teaching, learning, coaching, and leading—is where success lies.

Increasingly, as we work not just with instructional coaches and coaching programs but also the teachers, leaders, and systems impacted by coaching, we find ourselves returning again and again to these domains of leadership, relationships, mission/vision, and systems thinking as important foundations for all effective coaching initiatives. We return to these ideas, interwoven with our coaching mindsets and related coaching practices, across the remainder of this book.

## Summary

In this chapter we began by introducing Melinda as a focal figure who will be learning and thinking about coaching alongside us across this book. We then summarized some of the reasons why coaching matters more today than ever before. We shared nine core beliefs and major assumptions about coaching that we have developed over the years. Ultimately, we ended the chapter by introducing the framework that guides the remainder of this book, followed by brief discussions of why coaching mindsets matter and how leadership, relationships, mission/vision, and systems thinking undergird all good coaching work in schools. We now turn to Chapter 2, in which we further explore and articulate the four coaching mindsets at the heart of this book.

## Reflections

- Which of the core beliefs and assumptions about coaching from this chapter do you most agree with? Disagree with? Which additional beliefs and assumptions do you bring to coaching work, given your own professional experiences?
- Look again at Figure 1.2 and consider the ways in which our four coaching mindsets—change agent, facilitator, designer, and advocate—connect to your work. Which mindset(s) do you already adopt in your own work? Which mindset(s) may be an area of growth for you? Which elements of the framework prompt questions or even confusion? Talk with colleagues about your thinking. Record questions that arise, in service of finding and composing answers as you read further in the book.

## Activities

1. Read the *Kappan* article "How Coaches Get In" (see Web Resources at the end of this chapter). This article details a variety of ways that instructional coaches across content areas "gained access to teachers' classrooms" to best support teaching and learning work. Consider the ways in which the coaches highlighted in this article may have employed the coaching mindsets outlined in this chapter. Note the ways in which leadership, relationships, mission/vision, and systems thinking may have been drivers to support this coaching work.

2. Talk with two different individuals with coaching responsibilities. Use the following questions to guide the discussion (note: the questions could also easily be turned into a short questionnaire or an interview protocol, depending on your context and purposes). Be prepared to discuss the similarities and differences in how individuals respond to your questions and how their responses connect to the content of this chapter.

   a. How do you and your school district define coaching? Are your definitions similar? Different? In what ways?

   b. What do you see as the major focus or foci of your role(s): working with students, teachers, leaders, systems (e.g., school, district)?

   c. What are your major coaching activities? (That is, how do you spend your days?) Do you spend more time with individuals or groups of teachers?

   d. Which coaching mindsets do you think guide your work? How might the larger leadership, relationships, mission/vision, and systems thinking present in your school influence how you think about and carry out your work?

   e. To what extent do teachers understand your coaching role? (That is, how would other teachers define your role?)

   f. What are the stated goals that you are trying to achieve as a result of your coaching work (e.g., increased student achievement, changes in literacy practices)? To what extent are these goals related to the learning goals in your school? What supports your coaching work? What supports would you like to see put into place?

## FURTHER READINGS AND RESOURCES

**Print Resources**

Aguilar, E. (2024). *Arise: The art of transformational coaching.* Jossey-Bass.

Costa, A., & Garmston, R. (2015). *Cognitive coaching: Developing self-directed leaders and learners* (3rd ed.). Rowman & Littlefield.

Gibbons, L. K., & Cobb, P. (2016). Content-focused coaching: Five key practices. *The Elementary School Journal, 117*(2), 237–260.

Gibbons, L. K., & Cobb, P. (2017). Focusing on teacher learning opportunities to identify potentially productive coaching activities. *Journal of Teacher Education, 68*(4), 411–425.

Ippolito, J., & Bean, R. M. (2024). *The power of instructional coaching in context: A systems view for aligning content and coaching.* Guilford Press.

Woulfin, S. L., & Rigby, J. G. (2017). Coaching for coherence: How instructional coaches lead change in the evaluation era. *Educational Researcher, 46*(6), 323–328.

Woulfin, S. L., Stevenson, I., & Lord, K. (2023). *Making coaching matter: Leading continuous improvement in schools.* Teachers College Press.

## Web Resources (see www.guilford.com/bean3-materials for live links)

Center for Leadership & Educational Equity and the School Reform Initiative. (2024). Four "A's" text protocol. *www.clee.org/resources/four-as-text-protocol*

Knight, J. (Host). (2024). Art Costa & Bob Garmston. *Coaching conversations with Jim Knight* [Audio podcast]. Apple Podcasts. *http://podcasts.apple.com/au/podcast/art-costa-bob-garmston/id1649791348?i=1000638305772*

Munson, J., & Saclarides, S. (2023). How coaches get in. *Kappan. http://kappanonline.org/how-academic-coaches-get-access-munson*

# CHAPTER 2

# Exploring the Coaching Mindsets

> **GUIDING QUESTIONS**
>
> 1. What are some of the habits of mind and ways of working adopted by those who coach adult learners?
> 2. Which theories and research support these coaching mindsets?
> 3. How might these ways of thinking and working guide coaches as they support teachers, leaders, students, and schools as organizations?

## A Shift for Melinda

Melinda was a confident teacher. She knew how to engage her second-grade students in active learning and felt knowledgeable about all aspects of her curriculum. She also felt that she had good relationships with her fellow teachers. Still, Melinda was a bit surprised when her principal tapped her to take on coaching responsibilities. The idea of moving from a peer relationship with her colleagues to a coaching relationship made her somewhat nervous and uncomfortable. In fact, she wasn't quite sure where to begin or even how to think about her new roles and responsibilities. What shifts in thinking and working might Melinda adopt to help her step into her new coaching role? How might her new ways of thinking connect with new ways of working?

## Four Essential Mindsets

In this chapter, we expand upon the big ideas and habits of mind introduced in Chapter 1 that guide coaching work, shape how coaches think about their work, and greatly impact both the processes and results of coaching. Here, in Chapter 2, we further outline the four mindsets that successful coaches employ as they think about and enact their roles. The subsequent chapters in this book then focus on the ways that effective instructional coaches translate these habits of mind into ways of working. These are the four mindsets that we see as essential:

1. Thinking like a change agent
2. Thinking like a facilitator
3. Thinking like a designer
4. Thinking like an advocate

## Mindset 1: Thinking Like a Change Agent

Over the past 20 years, we have conducted research and talked with numerous instructional coaches across the United States and beyond. We have spent a great deal of time considering the ways that coaches think and work to improve teaching and learning in schools. Through our work with coaches, we have found the mindset of *change agent* to be one of the most important mental frames to adopt. By its very nature, the role of the instructional coach serves as a force for persistent and steady improvement in schools. By hiring and supporting instructional coaches in schools, leaders signal clearly to all educators that a core value of the organization is the continual refinement of teaching and learning processes. Thus, in many ways, coaches become both a figurative and a literal lever for change in schools.

### Managing Change Requires Particular Mental Frames and Skills

Inherent in the term *change agent* is the suggestion that effective instructional coaches must understand, make visible, and manage change processes intentionally. Too often, as teachers like Melinda are tapped to step into informal and formal instructional coaching roles, not enough attention is paid to how coaches must adopt a larger view of schools and the change processes within them. Yet, how are coaches to begin this work? Thinking and operating like a change agent in a school is no easy feat. It requires cutting against the grain of the status quo in schools, and "coaching for transformation" (International Literacy Association, 2018a, p. 4).

To begin, we have always appreciated the work of Michael Fullan in articulating both the challenges and the successes of change efforts in schools. In talking about educators as change agents, Fullan (1993) neatly captures the cognitive dissonance of focusing on change in schools:

> But we are facing a huge dilemma. On the one hand, schools are expected to engage in continuous renewal, and change expectations are constantly swirling around them. On the other hand, the way teachers are trained, the way schools are organized, the way educational hierarchy operates, and the way political decision

makers treat educators results in a system that is more likely to retain the status quo. (p. 12)

This tension is as much true today, in our post–COVID-19 pandemic schools and educational systems, as it was over 30 years ago when Fullan first wrote these words. In some ways, as schools continue to recover from multiple years of COVID-19 pandemic teaching and learning, Fullan's statements seem remarkably prescient. Schools have stampeded back to the status quo despite participation in the global natural experiment of shifting to virtual and hybrid teaching and learning. So, what is the way forward? How do we make sense of the perennial tension between expectations of continuous renewal and the de facto return to the status quo in schools?

Fullan's (and our) answer to this question is to "make explicit the goals and skills of change agentry" (1993, p. 12). In other words, one of the ways that schools systematically break free from the status quo and intentionally bring to life their espoused values of continual improvement is to invest in coaches, teachers, and leaders as change agents. Fullan (1993) names four qualities that compose the change agent mindset: personal vision-building, inquiry, mastery, and collaboration (pp. 13–14). We summarize these four ways of thinking and working briefly here.

1. **Personal vision-building.** With this notion, Fullan reminds us that larger organizational changes, including specific changes in teaching and learning, emerge in part from the intentional visioning that coaches, teachers, and leaders undertake individually and together. When coaches adopt the mindset of a change agent, they take on the responsibility of helping both teachers and leaders craft intentional, realistic, and optimistic visions of the future for teaching and learning. If they don't paint a clear picture of the future for the entire school community, then school improvement processes may feel directionless.

2. **Inquiry.** By focusing on inquiry, Fullan reminds us that change processes in schools are not linear, simple, or finite. Contrariwise, instructional coaches who operate as change agents would do well to keep the notion of inquiry front and center for themselves and the teachers and leaders with whom they work. The continual improvement of teaching and learning is a "perennial quest," and an inquiry stance is required for "forming and reforming personal purpose" (Fullan, 1993, p. 13). We remind ourselves and the coaches with whom we work that it is far better to adopt an inquiry stance rather than an expert stance. Coaches who engage others in inquiry are better equipped to build a collective vision for the what and why of improvement processes.

3. **Mastery.** While vision and inquiry are necessary aspects of thinking and working like a change agent, Fullan also reminds us that mastery is equally important. As Fullan (1993) states, "People *behave* their way into new visions and ideas, [they don't] just think their way into them" (p. 13). This notion reminds us that

coaches who think and work as change agents must focus on iterative experiments both in adult collaborations and in classroom teaching and learning work. This part of the mindset helps us to roll up our sleeves to try new processes and practices. A mastery focus bolsters coaches when supporting teachers and schools in piloting new work, repeating and tinkering with promising practices, and refining those practices that result in equitable and excellent student outcomes.

**4. Collaboration.** Finally, the notion of collaboration highlights that change agent work is not isolated work. The best change agent coaches are not those who sit alone in offices dreaming of grand future visions. Effective change agents are always in conversation with colleagues, collaborating around the thorniest teaching and learning dilemmas. Coaching and collaboration push against the invisible and perennial norms of autonomy, egalitarianism, and seniority in schools (Donaldson et al., 2008; Lortie, 1975). These long-standing norms can sometimes undermine coaching, which is built upon a foundation of collaboration, shared goals, and efforts to make teaching practice public. Therefore, change agent coaches would be wise to always keep collaboration in mind as both a goal and an expected (though often challenging) part of coaching processes.

Thus, by focusing on vision, inquiry, mastery, and collaboration, coaches can begin to adopt the mindset of a change agent. However, several other ingredients are important to name as part of effective change agent thinking and action: seeing the systems at work in schools, attending to school culture, and focusing on collective efficacy.

### Seeing and Managing Systems, Culture, and Collective Efficacy

Much has been written about schools as organizations that are both changing all the time and perennially change-resistant (Bryk et al., 2015; Elmore, 2004; Fahey et al., 2019; Fullan, 2015). Change processes in schools are a topic to be studied carefully by coaches tasked with shifting teaching and learning practices across multiple classrooms and entire schools (see Further Readings and Resources at the end of this chapter for more on this topic). Savvy instructional coaches must not only continue their professional learning within the discipline(s) that they are coaching (e.g., literacy, math, science, social studies, SEL, technology, and so on) but must also become students of schools as organizations.

As we have written about extensively (Ippolito & Bean, 2024), one of the first steps in understanding and managing change processes in schools requires us to "see the systems" at work in schools (pp. 23–44). To do this, coaches must climb to the proverbial balcony (Heifetz et al., 2009) and observe the larger patterns of communication and collaboration among teachers and leaders in the school. This may involve thinking about the social networks in operation at the school (Daly &

Little, 2010)—how teachers, leaders, coaches, and other specialists are connecting (or not) with one another over time. Or it may entail considering the ways in which forces from outside of the school (e.g., state and national standardized tests, shifting curricular standards, updated teacher licensing policies and practices, and so on) interact with unique characteristics and forces within the school (e.g., the specific school personnel, shifting student demographics and needs, the particular layout and quality of the school's facilities, and so on). The interaction of outside and internal forces on school change processes must be a focus of a coach thinking and working as a change agent (Elmore, 2004; Galey-Horn, 2020).

As coaches begin to uncover and see the systems at work in schools, they are also exposing and disturbing school culture (Fahey et al., 2019; Ippolito & Bean, 2024; Woulfin et al., 2023). Given the perennial and often invisible norms of autonomy, egalitarianism, and seniority at work in schools, coaches who are simply going about their daily work will find themselves naturally violating deeply held cultural norms. Consider the novice coach, perhaps like Melinda at the outset of this chapter, who is seeking collaboration, access to teachers' classrooms, and permission to provide collegial feedback (to both novice teachers and teachers who may have worked at the school longer than the coach themself). These all represent instances of disruptions to school culture, especially in schools steeped in traditional ways of working, where each teacher operates quite independently. Coaches operate as cultural change agents when they see and begin to shape both the wider school culture and the microcultures that exist within grade-level and content-area teams.

Finally, much of thinking and working like a change agent connects directly to the notion of supporting collective efficacy in schools. Collective efficacy refers to the simple but powerful idea that educators can make a greater impact on students' learning and lives when they collectively believe that they are more effective together. As stated by Donohoo et al. (2018): "When a team of individuals share the belief that through their unified efforts they can overcome challenges and produce intended results, groups *are* more effective" (p. 41). This does not mean that all educators agree on every single aspect of teaching and learning—quite the opposite, as we have come to learn (Preston & Donohoo, 2021). Collective efficacy must be slowly built and intentionally facilitated (as we argue in the next section), and coaches must not shy away from navigating disagreements or differences of opinion. In fact, coaches who are able to help teachers both agree and disagree productively will find themselves well along the road to creating strong school cultures with high degrees of collective efficacy—as opposed to groups who "work to maintain a *culture of nice* and in doing so, avoid critical conversations about ineffective instruction and assessment practices" (Preston & Donohoo, 2021, p. 29).

While we have shared some initial thoughts as to what it might mean to think and work like a change agent here, we delve more deeply into this mindset and how coaches can surface and shift school culture in Chapter 3 as well as across the book.

> **STOP AND REFLECT**
>
> Think about your own coaching and leadership experiences. What do you see as your strengths related to change agent work? What might be your growing edges? Which aspects of thinking and working like a change agent might feel most comfortable? Least comfortable?

## *Mindset 2: Thinking Like a Facilitator*

Our second coaching mindset is a frame that many teacher leaders and coaches can easily name and yet still may struggle to adopt effectively: thinking like a *facilitator*. Much debate in both the field and research literature has centered on the particular roles of instructional coaches in schools (Bean et al., 2015; Deussen et al., 2007; International Literacy Association [ILA], 2015; Killion & Harrison, 2017; Knight, 2017). However, a great deal of this debate centers on how coaches intentionally facilitate different types of conversations and professional learning experiences with adult colleagues. Here we share just a few of the ways coaches might begin to think and operate more like facilitators as they support ongoing adult professional learning.

### *Considering Coaching Stance and Positionality*

First, coaches must consider their facilitative stance when working with colleagues. How should they approach colleagues and position themselves in relation to adult peers in schools? While this may be a simple question to ask, it is a complex one to answer and enact. In fact, determining how to position oneself as a coach in relationship to adult colleagues is often one of the early challenges that any coach like Melinda might face. This is especially true for those who take on coaching work in a school where they previously taught. Making the shift from peer teacher to coaching colleague can be exciting, but also initially uncomfortable because of the uncertainty of positionality, a tension that Melinda exemplified at the outset of this chapter. Thus, how coaches position themselves in relationship to teachers and leaders matters a great deal.

Much of the debate about the roles of coaches and their positionality revolves around the tension of coaches operating fundamentally in responsive, directive, or balanced ways (Ippolito, 2010), or what McKenna and Walpole (2008) describe as "soft" versus "hard" coaching (pp. 14–15). (Others have termed this "light" versus "heavy" coaching; for more related to this way of thinking about coaching, see Killion, 2008, 2010; Wilder, 2013.) Coaches who operate from a fundamentally *responsive* stance see their role as responding to teachers' needs, following teachers' interests, and encouraging teachers' self-reflection as they analyze and improve their practice in ways that teachers themselves articulate. This stance is built on a history of cognitive coaching (Costa & Garmston, 2002, 2015). On the other hand, coaches who operate from a fundamentally *directive* stance see their role as guiding teachers toward particular practices, sharing their own expertise, and holding teachers accountable. This stance is more closely aligned with the kinds of coaching associated with specific curricular programs or frameworks, where the implementation of set practices is key. Recent evidence suggests that some balance of these stances is important, as coaches and teacher leaders shift back and forth between more responsive and directive ways of interacting with colleagues to achieve particular professional learning goals (Ippolito, 2010; Mangin & Dunsmore, 2015; Robertson et al., 2020b).

While the notion of balancing responsive and directive stances makes a great deal of sense to coaches, it is challenging to navigate in schools where there is not a tight alignment of purposes and practices across the instructional core, the coaching program, and the larger school and district context (see Ippolito & Bean, 2024). For example, in some schools, the coaching stance is determined by a specific change initiative mandated by the district, as was evident in many schools that participated in the large-scale federal Reading First initiative. Such a school or district might adopt a more directive coaching approach overall, requiring coaches and teachers to implement specific curricular programs or models. However, even in such instances, oftentimes coaches and teacher leaders can still find ways to balance responsive and directive stances in their daily interactions with teachers.

For example, Coburn and Woulfin (2012), in a study of coaches in a Reading First school, discuss ways in which those coaches were able to support teachers in their efforts to implement the literacy framework adopted by the school and, at the same time, address the needs of individual teachers. In another, more recent study of how instructional coaches across content areas gained entry into teachers' classrooms (Munson & Saclarides, 2023), the 28 coaches in the same district were found to deploy a wide variety of relational and structural strategies (e.g., from more responsive relationship-building techniques to more directive approaches including targeting particular teachers for offers of modeling, co-teaching, and so on) in order to make a difference in classroom instruction. Ultimately, paying close attention to coaching stance, and shifting as needed in the moment and over time, is one of the primary ways that coaches can think and work as facilitators of adult learning.

In sum, coaches should consider how clearly, quickly, and effectively they can provide the support and feedback teachers need to initiate appropriate instructional changes for students that address schoolwide goals and values. In some instances, teachers are ready and eager for direct support and appreciative of receiving specific ideas for moving ahead. They may not have the knowledge to reflect on the reasons for their instructional dilemmas at this time, and the coach has the responsibility to ensure that classroom instruction will improve. Moreover, effective relationships can often be established when coaches are able to provide credible, simple strategies that might help the teacher solve some immediate difficulties. The following section on differentiating coaching provides additional thinking about this issue.

## Differentiating Coaching to Meet Adult Learners' Needs

A second way that instructional coaches can think and work as facilitators is to carefully consider the adult learning needs of professional colleagues. While most instructional coaches are experts in child and adolescent development and take into consideration students' developmental needs when designing and supporting instruction, it is the truly savvy coach who remembers that adults also range in their developmental and professional learning needs over time (Berger, 2019; Breidenstein et al., 2012; Drago-Severson, 2009; Drago-Severson & Blum-DeStefano, 2017; Fahey et al., 2019). While many resources that coaches consult suggest that an understanding of adult learning is imperative (see, e.g., Aguilar, 2016; Knowles et al., 2020), few resources offer guidance on how to make sense of and lead adult learning *and development*.

Breidenstein et al. (2012) argue that "the work of school reform—or improving student learning—is inextricably connected to the learning of the adults who work in schools" (p. 12). In other words, without a clear vision for how to lead adult learning and development, and without a culture of adult learning in place, there is little hope for significant student growth over time. Breidenstein et al. (2012) go on to argue that we need to "support the learning not only of individual educators but also of the teams, groups, departments, schools, and districts in which they work" (p. 8). But how might a coach productively think about organizing this adult learning?

In response, Breidenstein et al. (2012) build on the adult development work of Robert Kegan (1998) by proposing adult learning structures and routines that map onto the diverse ways in which adults in schools make sense of their work. Kegan's original constructive-developmental theory suggests that "(1) adults continually work to make sense of their experiences [constructive] and (2) the ways that adults make sense of their world can change and grow more complex over time [developmental]" (Breidenstein et al., 2012, p. 5). While Kegan (1998) proposes different stages of adult development focused on how adults' meaning-making systems grow more complex over time (see Ippolito & Bean, 2024, Chapters 2 and 7, for a more extensive review), Breidenstein et al. (2012) map Kegan's theory onto the professional learning experiences of groups of educators in schools.

Therefore, Breidenstein et al.'s (2012) big contribution is not distinguishing among instrumental, socializing, and self-authoring individuals (Kegan's original "stages" of adult development, describing how adults might see the world in qualitatively different ways). Instead, Breidenstein et al. suggest that leaders, such as coaches, spend more of their energy thinking about the *types of learning* that groups of adults in a school might need at any given time. They propose that, fundamentally, adults might engage in three different types of learning activities that support adults' current ways of thinking and working, and that also nudge them toward more complex thinking and action.

- **Instrumental learning.** Instrumental professional learning activities support adults by providing explicit information, concrete learning about specific curricula or instructional practices, and guidance that suggests a right/wrong way of moving forward. All educators, across their careers, appreciate and need instrumental learning occasionally, especially when learning something new (e.g., learning how to teach over Zoom or Google Meet during the height of the COVID-19 pandemic provided many coaches with opportunities to offer explicit instrumental learning opportunities to teachers). Examples of instrumental learning activities might include coach-facilitated presentations on new curricula or instructional practices, learning directly from a professional text and trying text-based suggestions, or following stepwise directions provided in a video on how to lead an effective classroom discussion.

- **Socializing learning.** Socializing professional learning activities support adults by providing opportunities for educators to meet with one another, align thinking and practices, and come to shared understandings of both instructional dilemmas and potential solutions. We argue that this type of professional learning opportunity is how coaches might make the biggest difference in teaching and learning at the team level, within content-area departments, and even across entire schools. By working with groups of educators and helping them to share and align thinking and practices, coaches can encourage larger-scale changes in teaching and learning. Examples of socializing learning activities include professional learning communities, grade-level team planning sessions, data-analysis sessions, or even instructional leadership teams (ILTs), all of which can involve, or be led by, coaches.

- **Self-authoring learning.** Finally, self-authoring professional learning activities support adults by providing opportunities for individuals and groups to reflect on and articulate their own criteria for success. So often in schools (and in the wider world!) we turn to leaders, standards, or each other as we try to measure our own success. In self-authoring professional learning activities, individuals and groups are instead encouraged to consider outside criteria but then truly articulate their own professional benchmarks, growing edges, and goals. Self-authoring learning invites educators to ask inquiry questions that arise from their own instructional dilemmas, to research those dilemmas (independently and/or with colleagues), and then to pilot new practices with attention to their own self-defined criteria for achievement. Examples of self-authoring learning activities include individual and group inquiry cycles, independent instructional design and teaching projects, coach-led individual or group coaching cycles focused on teachers' own dilemmas and criteria, or even supporting educators as they apply for National Board Certification.

Coaches who wish to create professional learning "holding environments" (Drago-Severson & Blum-DeStefano, 2017, pp. 52–54), in which they can both fully support adult learners and also nudge them toward more complex ways of thinking and teaching, would do well to differentiate their coaching work to include a variety of instrumental, socializing, and self-authoring opportunities over time. See Further Readings and Resources at the end of this chapter for additional resources to help build a richer understanding of coaching with attention to adult development and learning.

## Putting It All Together as Coaches Increase Intensity across Facilitative Work

Finally, another way that we talk with coaches about thinking and acting like a facilitator is to continually consider how they might increase the intensity of their work with teachers over time. We often introduce a version of our Levels of Intensity graphic (see Table 2.1) as a way to illustrate the ways that a coach might slowly move from less-intense (Level 1) coaching activities to more-intense activities (Level 2 and Level 3) across a school year, or even across multiple years.

If we consider one of the goals of coaching to be supporting individuals and groups as they engage in a variety of instrumental, socializing, and self-authoring learning experiences (Breidenstein et al., 2012; Drago-Severson, 2009; Fahey et al., 2019), then we might look for opportunities at different levels of intensity to support adult learners in each of these ways. Moreover, coaches might consider when and how to vary intensity across the school year, use the Levels of Intensity as a reflective tool with teachers and leaders about the nature and direction of professional learning work, and ultimately create familiar sequences of professional learning activities that provide teachers support over time. For example, a coach might first assist with assessment of students to gauge instructional needs (Level 1), then use a discussion-based protocol to help a grade-level team analyze students' work (Level 2), then engage in some co-planning, co-teaching, and inquiry-focused coaching cycles to pilot new instructional practices to better support students (Levels 2 and 3). Thus, the Levels of Intensity model can be used in a variety of ways to help differentiate professional learning experiences for educators. (For more suggestions of how to use the Levels of Intensity, see Ippolito & Bean, 2024).

Having worked as instructional coaches ourselves, and mentored hundreds of instructional coaches over the past several decades, we now believe that thinking like a facilitator (working with awareness of stance, positionality, adult learning/development needs, and intensity of work) can truly promote deep and long-lasting changes in teaching and learning. When a coach thinks and behaves like a facilitator, they naturally move toward the balanced ways of working that seem

**TABLE 2.1. Levels of Intensity in Coaching**

| Level 1: Building Relationships (informal/less intense) | Level 2: Analyzing Practice (semiformal/slightly more intense) | Level 3: Transforming Practice and Making Teaching Public (more formal/intense) |
|---|---|---|
| • Having conversations with colleagues (getting to know one another, identifying issues or needs, setting goals, problem solving)<br>• Establishing schedules for meeting with groups of teachers and individuals<br>• Establishing agreements for collaboration and conversation<br>• Developing and providing materials for or with colleagues<br>• Developing curriculum with colleagues<br>• Participating in professional learning (PL) opportunities with colleagues (conferences, workshops)<br>• Leading or participating in study groups<br>• Assisting with assessment of students<br>• Instructing students to learn about their strengths and needs<br>• Coaching on the fly (having unscheduled, brief meetings with teachers that provide opportunities for additional coaching) | • Having conversations with individual colleagues about teaching, learning, and literacy (analyzing data, lessons)<br>• Co-planning lessons<br>• Modeling and discussing lessons<br>• Revisiting agreements for collaboration and making certain they facilitate group work<br>• Visiting classrooms and providing feedback to teachers as part of a planning/observation/debrief coaching or inquiry cycle<br>• Introducing discussion-based protocols to assist in the analysis of student work, holding group conversations about student–teacher work, and so on<br>• Analyzing student work to assist teachers in planning instruction<br>• Analyzing and interpreting assessment data (using results for instructional decision making)<br>• Leading team meetings (grade level, data, department)<br>• Making presentations at PL meetings<br>• Providing online PL | • Having conversations focusing on co-planning, co-teaching, and teaching dilemmas<br>• Co-teaching lessons<br>• Expanding the range of discussion-based protocols used, including those that require higher degrees of risk/trust and surface assumptions related to issues of equity and social justice<br>• Helping individuals and groups design their own discussion-based protocols and collaboration routines<br>• Facilitating learning walks with small groups of teachers (or with teachers and leaders together) as a means of learning more about classroom instruction across grades or subject areas<br>• Conducting individual and group analysis of video-recorded lessons of teachers<br>• Engaging in lesson study with teachers<br>• Participating in and leading professional learning communities<br>• Participating in and leading individual and collaborative inquiry work with teachers<br>• Providing support to teachers as a result of teacher performance evaluation outcomes<br>• Involvement in efforts to improve school programs<br>• Facilitating school–community partnership work |

*Note.* Adapted from Ippolito and Bean (2024, p. 127). Copyright © 2024 The Guilford Press. From *Cultivating Coaching Mindsets, Second Edition: An Action Guide for Instructional Leaders* by Rita M. Bean and Jacy Ippolito. Copyright © 2025 The Guilford Press. Permission to photocopy this material, or to download and print enlarged versions (www.guilford.com/bean3-materials), is granted to purchasers of this book for personal use or use with students; see copyright page for details.

to produce the best coaching relationships. Ultimately, coaches who operate as facilitators:

- Recognize and respect the individual and varying needs of the teachers being coached and their attitudes and beliefs about coaching and learning.
- Provide safe learning opportunities for individuals and groups, with the goal of increasing collective capacity to reflect on student learning and instructional practice.
- Focus on creating opportunities for genuine, deep learning (and understand that this can sometimes produce short-term confusion, frustration, and the questioning of deeply held assumptions).
- Create opportunities for inquiry, for colleagues to draw their own conclusions and craft their own responses, rather than always attempting to provide quick, right answers.
- Focus on encouraging "participation, ensuring equity, and building trust" (McDonald et al., 2013, p. 11).
- "[Ask] difficult questions of the group, [take] responsibility for the arc of the group's learning, and persistently [push] towards deeper learning" (Fahey & Ippolito, 2015, p. 4).
- Use clear agendas and discussion-based protocols (an "agreed upon set of rules that guide coach/teacher/student work, discussion, observation, and interactions") (Ippolito & Lieberman, 2020, p. 79).
- Respect and value the contributions of teachers, encouraging them to participate as colleagues in conversations and decision making.
- Observe and listen as a means of deciding how to respond, what clarifying questions to ask, what feedback to give, and how to solicit responses from all members of the group.

As can be seen from this list of the role of a facilitator, coaches and teacher leaders who operate as facilitators are always seeking to build shared ownership and understanding of instructional practices and student learning among teachers. Facilitators are neither entirely directive (introducing and prescribing specific instructional moves) nor entirely responsive (catering to individual and group requests). In fact, operating as a facilitator can free coaches from feeling as if they must always have all the right answers at their fingertips. Instead, they can focus on how to help teachers find *better* answers through individual and group processes that promote ownership and build confidence. One of our coaching colleagues calls this "finding the right tool for the job," signaling that, ultimately, facilitation is about matching purpose with participants and learning processes. Facilitative work is the day-to-day work of a coach. Those who do not focus specifically on improving their facilitative skills are limiting their ability to positively influence colleagues. We further explore the ways in which coaches think and act as facilitators across Chapters 4, 5, and 6.

> **STOP AND REFLECT**
>
> - Think about your own past experiences participating in professional learning. Which experiences helped you to grow the most? What did the coach/facilitator do to support you before, during, and after the professional learning experience? How did the experiences connect with our notions of thinking and working like a facilitator?
> - Now consider a professional learning experience you may have designed and led. What made the experience successful for participants? What would you revise? What (if any) connections do you see between your role as a facilitator and the successes and challenges you experienced?

### *Mindset 3: Thinking Like a Designer*

Another powerful mindset that a coach can adopt is that of thinking like a *designer*. Design thinking focuses on collaborative problem solving, addressing both technical and adaptive challenges (Heifetz et al., 2009) by collaboratively surfacing hidden assumptions, sources of confusion, structural and logistical obstacles, and procedural inefficiencies and then engaging individuals and teams in a process of designing effective responses. Coaches who approach student learning and instructional challenges with a design mindset can engage colleagues in a process that builds reflective and problem-solving capacity—it helps coaches position themselves as facilitators, harnessing the power and knowledge of the group, instead of being narrowly defined as the sole expert in the room.

There are roughly three areas that we have seen effective coaches address when they adopt the mindset of a designer: curriculum and instruction, collaborative learning structures, and assessment. We discuss each briefly here, and then elaborate in later chapters.

**1. Curriculum and instruction.** Although many schools adopt specific curricular programs and practices for use in various subject areas, coaches must often provide guidance in how to adapt or modify these materials to meet the needs of students in their schools. This guidance can be provided to individual teachers, but quite often design issues arise at grade-level or subject-area meetings (e.g., "Even after teaching the lessons on phonemic awareness, many of our kindergarten students don't seem to get it? What are some other ideas we can use?"). Sometimes, coaches must use their knowledge to identify more intensive ways of teaching, or it may be a matter of helping teachers learn how to better teach the strategies identified in the school's adopted program. It may also be a matter of encouraging additional practice exercises, with students needing additional learning opportunities. All of these are design issues that can be addressed by the coach in collaboration with teachers. When supporting teachers in their own design work of crafting instructional units and lessons, coaches often consult state and professional standards, consider students' needs in their particular context, and take into account the skills, knowledge, and practices of their teaching colleagues. In other words, when coaches recommend or co-develop new strategies, materials, or routines with teachers, all the aforementioned factors are in the back of their minds, and they are serving as designers thinking strategically about end results and efficient routes to those results. We elaborate on these ideas in Chapters 7 and 8.

**2. Collaborative learning structures.** When coaches are choosing and creating collaborative learning structures for teachers, they are best served by thinking as a designer and then as a facilitator. Choosing whether to offer a content-based workshop, a study group, or a series of co-teaching opportunities requires coaches to adopt a design mindset and consider which dilemmas are most pressing and which collaborative learning structures might most efficiently address the dilemmas at hand. Sometimes a particular protocol or collaborative learning routine may not work without a bit of adaptation, and the act of adapting a traditional routine to fit the needs of a particular group can benefit from design thinking. We explore this kind of thinking further in Chapter 6, where we zoom in on group coaching.

**3. Assessment.** When coaches consider assessment issues, they are best served by thinking as designers. Most coaches know that excellent teaching and learning begins with sound assessment practices. When thinking like a designer, coaches might strategically use Google Forms or other tools to design targeted needs-assessment surveys to determine which areas of teaching and learning faculty feel are most in need of improvement. Assessment work is also focused on the analysis of student data, including both formative and summative assessment results. All these data become part of the initial stages of design work, wherein a coach can lead teams of teachers through analysis, design, and implementation phases. We dive into the coach's role in assessment work in-depth later in Chapter 7.

These ways of thinking and working map onto what has recently been called *design thinking*, and we highlight one of our favorite resources that helps educators and coaches adopt this frame. We have used and pointed many coaches to the overview of design thinking and related resources offered by IDEO, and specifically their resource Design Thinking for Educators, which includes the downloadable guide *Design Thinking for Educators Toolkit* (IDEO, n.d.; see also the Web Resources at the end of this chapter). These materials encourage teachers and instructional coaches to engage in a five-step process (discovery, interpretation, ideation, experimentation, and evolution) that helps individuals and groups move from identifying and understanding a challenge to designing possible solutions. Along with a description of the five-step process for participating in and engaging others in design work, the *Design Thinking for Educators Toolkit* (IDEO, n.d.) suggests particular ways of thinking about design work that are most productive, including the following:

- Thinking of yourself as a designer by being intentional in your creative problem-solving work
- "Embrac[ing] your beginner's mind" (p. 16) by adopting a learning stance, allowing for mistakes along the way, and not expecting the "right" answer to emerge immediately
- "Stepping out of your comfort zone" (p. 16) by leaving your classroom, routine, and established patterns of thinking and collaborating to try something entirely new
- Understanding that "problems are just opportunities for design in disguise," focusing you optimistically on a better future and helping you to ask, "What if?" instead of "What's wrong?" (p. 16)

Notably, by adopting a design mindset, coaches can shift the way they work with both individuals and larger groups to focus on productive problem solving instead of getting stuck in less productive cycles of blame and avoidance. At the systems level, adopting a design mindset might mean the collaborative design of group cycles of collaborative inquiry, action research, and coaching across grades and content areas. It means moving from the strategic large-group parsing of standards and deliberation about a set of core instructional practices that might meet those standards to individual instructional design work that pushes beyond standards to meet particular students' needs, such as meeting the needs of multilingual learners or students with learning differences.

Adopting a design mindset as an organization suggests that the answers to both technical and adaptive challenges lie within the expertise and skills of the teachers and leaders in schools (perhaps with some assistance from outside resources as well); however, it positions coaches and teacher leaders as agents of change and designers, as protagonists in their own stories instead of extras on a movie set.

Above all else, thinking like a designer allows coaches to try new approaches with an eye toward tinkering and refining, without expecting excellence or success immediately upon implementation. The related notion of "prototyping" is powerful (Scharmer, 2009). Coaches and teachers can try new ways of working, with some impunity to say, "Well, that didn't quite work the way we expected; let's figure out what didn't work and try something slightly different tomorrow!" It is this kind of design thinking that fosters a positive, collaborative, inventive culture where teachers and leaders turn to each other to discuss and collaboratively solve instructional dilemmas (Nash, 2019).

> **STOP AND REFLECT**
>
> When have you been invited into design thinking as part of your teaching, coaching, and leadership work in schools? What supported you in engaging in design thinking? Thinking back, what might have supported your work even more when engaging in design thinking? How might you keep this mindset front and center in your work moving forward?

## *Mindset 4: Thinking Like an Advocate*

As any fan of the musical *Hamilton* will be able to tell you: If you don't stand for something, then you may fall for anything. This adage has never been truer than for coaches who, by nature, find themselves toggling between the different viewpoints of students, teachers, and leaders. Often, coaches have little formal authority, yet they are perhaps in the best position to influence teachers and leaders alike. This is why it is critically important to "stand for something" as a coach—in other words, to know what is most important to you and then to advocate for it.

> **VOICES FROM THE FIELD**
>
> I see my role as providing the support teachers need as they work to guarantee the academic success of their students. Teachers have so much responsibility, and they need the support [and advocacy] of others to make that a reality. "Consistent Student Achievement through Sustained Educator Growth" is my professional philosophy that drives my work. When I find myself conflicted with additional responsibilities or outside demands, this statement reminds me that it's educator growth that will lead to student achievement. This helps me to prioritize my time and efforts.
> —Marsha Turner-Hall, Teacher and Instructional Coach

Some scholars have suggested that advocacy work is a vital part of teaching and leading in schools (Ferman, 2017), and this is perhaps most true for instructional coaches. When coaches are able to adopt the frame of thinking like an advocate, they are in a powerful position to leverage research, personal experience, and relationships not only to *improve* but also to *transform* teaching and learning. When thinking like an advocate, coaches engage in the following: advocating for students, advocating for teachers, advocating for community partnerships, and advocating for particular practices, models, and programs. We discuss each next.

> • • • • • • • • • **Put into Practice** • • • • • • • • • •
>
> In what ways do you serve as an advocate in your school or district? Talk with colleagues about the sorts of specific advocacy efforts that would improve teaching and learning in your school or district.

### Advocating for Students

At the heart of all professional learning and improvement work is a laser-like focus on student access, opportunity, and success. Regardless of their formal titles, coaches can serve a vital role in schools by advocating for rights for students, including early identification of students' needs, multiple tiers of instruction and intervention (typically as part of a multi-tiered system of supports), and authentic reading, writing, and communication tasks and associated resources. For more about advocacy for students' rights, we suggest a short article from Medium on "Four Ways to Advocate for Your Students" (see Web Resources at the end of this chapter).

One of the most frequent queries we receive from pre-service and currently practicing coaches is this: "Should I raise concerns when I believe that current materials, instruction, schedules, or systems aren't truly meeting students' needs?" While the devil is in the details, our answer is almost always *yes*! Students' needs are the highest priority, and often, specialists, special educators, and coaches have extensive, specialized knowledge and experience to identify dilemmas and support colleagues as they begin to address gaps. Of course, every school has limitations regarding its budget, space, staffing, and materials; however, if current conditions are not meeting students' needs (as evidenced by both quantitative and qualitative data), then coaches can confidently and respectfully advocate for change with teachers and leaders. In fact, advocating for change based on clear documentation of students' needs (and gaps between needs and current practices) is perhaps the strongest advocacy position to adopt.

### Advocating for Teachers

While many coaches report feeling like "neither fish nor fowl" (Ippolito, 2010, p. 169), operating neither as formal classroom teachers nor as formal school leaders, this middle-road position can be a powerful place from which to advocate for the betterment of conditions so that teachers can deliver the best instruction possible. This kind of advocacy work is delicate and must always be grounded in evidence related to students' needs; however, there are times when coaches are completely justified in arguing for lengthier instructional blocks of time, common planning time for teams of teachers to meet and review student data and related teaching practices, specific professional learning experiences to support new instructional practices, or even more coaching opportunities for teachers.

When advocating for teachers' needs, we have found it best to do the following:

- Draw clear connections between students' needs and teachers' needs. If teachers' needs are not related to students' needs, then little change can be expected.
- Build a coalition before approaching administrators. Do the informal relationship-building work of talking with both allies and possible naysayers before going public or making a case with administration. Not all teachers necessarily need to completely agree with a recommended change, but without broad support, coaches will find themselves fighting a battle on multiple fronts.
- Look for implementation examples in the literature and in schools and districts nearby to paint a clear picture of the future after a proposed change has been adopted. If arguing for longer instructional blocks, more flexible small-group instructional opportunities, or classroom libraries, for example, be prepared to demonstrate how these elements have proven successful elsewhere.
- Develop a rough plan before approaching administration, including possible benefits and rationales for drawbacks related to proposed changes. Going to an administrator with a problem without also brainstorming some possible solutions will likely lead to frustration and wasted time. Remember the importance of adopting the mindset of a designer.

### Advocating for Community Partnerships

Beyond advocating for students and teachers, coaches are also often able to advocate for stronger school–community partnerships. While we expand on the coach's work with the community in Chapter 9, we note here that coaches are well positioned to advocate for better school–community connections.

Some have argued that strong school–community relationships are the key to school reform, particularly in our neediest urban schools (Hong, 2020; Warren, 2005). We completely agree. The more invested parents, politicians, and business leaders are in a community's local schools, the stronger a school's position to seek and receive support in the form of funding, volunteers, and wraparound services that provide students with the targeted assistance they need beyond school hours. The more that coaches know about community-based services, and the more that community members are invited into schools, the better equipped both the school and the community will be to meet students' needs. However, coaches advocating for stronger school–community partnerships must do so with the knowledge, consent, and support of school- and district-based leadership, as well as a broad coalition of teachers. We have seen coaches design and advocate for creative, ongoing curriculum-focused programs; implement volunteer tutoring programs that invite retired community members to partner with elementary school students; and sponsor multilingual-family education support services that invite parents to join their children at different times of day to learn a language together. Coaches have also invited community members to offer elective mini-courses for students, freeing teachers for short periods to engage in professional learning experiences. More frameworks and examples for school–community advocacy work can be found in Chapter 9.

### *Advocating for Particular Practices, Models, and Programs*

Finally, we have witnessed coaches judiciously advocating for particular practices, models, and programs. We believe that both homegrown and prepackaged curricula must be created, chosen, and adapted based on a synthesis of research-based best practices and a deep understanding of each school's context and its students' needs. Given this, there are times when coaches are well positioned to advocate for or question the selection of particular programs.

Many schools and districts seek to purchase and implement prepackaged curricular programs. We certainly see the value in terms of providing teachers with guidance, aligning practices, and offering students (particularly in schools and districts with high degrees of student mobility) similar experiences across grades and schools. However, not all curricular programs and models are created equal. Coaches are perhaps best positioned to help teachers and school leaders evaluate existing (and homegrown) curricular programs and models to ensure that authentic materials, rigorous cognitive tasks, and research-based best practices are forefront.

While not all schools or coaches will have complete freedom in choosing curricular programs or models, it is perfectly reasonable for coaches (as part of routine self-assessment practices) to collaboratively assess whether a specific program is in fact meeting students' needs. If not, then advocating for change makes sense. We end this section with a short list of tenets for coaches engaged in advocacy work:

- Spend time working with faculty to help them understand and believe in the importance of advocacy work. Marshal research, policy, and site-based data and evidence to support your position—don't simply assume that colleagues will adopt your stance without well-supported documentation.
- Adopt an evidence-based stance—encourage experimentation and the testing of hypotheses, with a willingness to move in a different direction when classroom-level evidence is suggesting that something isn't working.
- Passion is important, but reason will win the day. Try to avoid battles of will, petty disputes, or personality conflicts.
- Always remain open to the possibility that you're wrong—nothing works 100% of the time across all contexts, and something you think is right might work differently in different contexts.
- When a final decision is made, by a formal leader or group of colleagues, accept the decision and show your support through words and actions. It is

always better to advocate for the next change than to spend time mourning the loss of a current debate.

Now that we have reviewed our four coaching mindsets, we want to introduce a quick tool to use as you reflect on your own coaching work and continue reading this book. Appendix A provides a simple template that allows you to take notes as you read, keeping track of which habits of mind are dominant in each area of coaching work and which habits of mind you have already adopted (or might consider adopting). We will refer to Appendix A throughout the book, but you may want to download and print a copy of it or create your own version now before reading on.

## Summary

In this chapter, we have described why savvy coaches adopt the mindsets of change agent, facilitator, designer, and advocate to best support students, teachers, and schools as learning organizations. These mindsets not only help when adopting a coaching stance but also suggest productive ways of working to support the improvement of teaching and learning in individual classrooms as well as across entire schools and districts. As Melinda thought about these mindsets, she realized that she had some real strengths (e.g., as a facilitator and advocate), but that there was much she could learn about the other two mindsets. The notion of being a change agent seems exciting and challenging at the same time! In the following chapters, we elaborate on and illustrate these mindsets in action.

## Reflections

- Which of the four coaching mindsets explored in this chapter most closely match your own understanding of the role of a coach in your school, district, or current setting? Which of the mindsets pushes your thinking the most? Which would be easy for you to adopt? Which might be a stretch?
- If you were to make your own list of "coaching mindsets," what would you include in addition to the four introduced in this chapter? How might you look for and keep track of those additional mindsets as you continue to read this book?

## Activities

1. Look at, print, or create your own version of the chart in Appendix A. Before reading further in the book, conduct a quick self-assessment. As you look across

the columns of the template, which mindsets come most naturally to you? From which mindset do you typically engage in coaching work? Which frame of mind is your biggest blind spot at the moment? What actions are you already taking to build that set of skills?

2. Now, as you look down the rows of the chart in Appendix A, consider the topics of the upcoming chapters. Which domains are areas of strength? Any blind spots?

3. Finally, look for overlaps by viewing the intersections between ways of thinking (column headings) and ways of working (row headings) addressed in the book. Look for strengths. Similarly, note possible blind spots, where your ways of thinking and ways of working may need bolstering (e.g., thinking like a change agent when leading school-change initiatives). How might doing this quick self-assessment shape your reading of the book and your subsequent work as a coach?

## FURTHER READINGS AND RESOURCES

### Print Resources

*For more on thinking and acting like a change agent (see also Chapter 3):*

Bryk, A. S., Gomez, L. M., Grunow, A., & LeMahieu, P. G. (2015). *Learning to improve: How America's schools can get better at getting better.* Harvard Education Press.

Wagner, T., Kegan, R., Lahey, L. L., Lemons, R. W., Garnier, J., Helsing, D., et al. (2012). *Change leadership: A practical guide to transforming our schools.* John Wiley & Sons.

*For more on thinking and acting like a facilitator (see also Chapters 4–6):*

Berger, J. G. (2019). *Unlocking leadership mindtraps: How to thrive in complexity.* Stanford University Press.

Breidenstein, A., Fahey, K., Glickman, C., & Hensley, F. (2012). *Leading for powerful learning: A guide for instructional leaders.* Teachers College Press.

McDonald, J. P., Mohr, N., Dichter, A., & McDonald, E. C. (2013). *The power of protocols: An educator's guide to better practice* (3rd ed.). Teachers College Press.

### Web Resources (see www.guilford.com/bean3-materials for live links)

*For more on thinking and acting like a designer (see also Chapters 7–8):*

Booker, L., & Russell, J. L. (2022). *Design principles for improving practice with instructional coaching.* EdResearch for Action. https://edresearchforaction.com/research-briefs/design-principles-for-improving-practice-with-instructional-coaching/

Dimitriadis, M. (2024). *What is design thinking? A handy guide for teachers.* Makers Empire. www.makersempire.com/what-is-design-thinking-a-handy-guide-for-classroom-teachers/

IDEO. (n.d.-a). *Design thinking.* www.ideou.com/pages/design-thinking

IDEO. (n.d.-b). *Design thinking for educators* [with toolkit]. http://page.ideo.com/design-thinking-edu-toolkit

Stanford D.School. (2024). *Getting started with design thinking for K12.* https://dschool.stanford.edu/resources-collections/getting-started-with-design-thinking

*For more on thinking and acting like an advocate (see also Chapter 9):*

Bolden, F. (2023). *How instructional coaches can support the mental health of educators.* The Learning Counsel. *https://thelearningcounsel.com/articles/how-instructional-coaches-can-support-the-mental-health-of-educators/*

Jewett, L. (2022). Teachers as advocates and leaders of the profession. *Homeroom: The Official Blog of the U.S. Department of Education. https://blog.ed.gov/2022/09/teachers-as-advocates-and-leaders-of-the-profession/*

McGraw Hill. (2019). *Four ways to advocate for your students.* Medium. *https://medium.com/inspired-ideas-prek-12/four-ways-to-advocate-for-your-students-31bc2c367b51*

National Youth Rights Association. (n.d.). *Student bill of rights. www.youthrights.org/issues/student-rights/student-bill-of-rights*

# CHAPTER 3

# Understanding and Shaping School Culture through Systems Thinking

### GUIDING QUESTIONS

1. In what ways can systems thinking influence school culture, leadership, and organizational change?
2. What does research suggest for coaches working to improve organizational culture? How does this work lead to improvements in teaching and learning?
3. In what ways can coaches work with teachers to develop a culture of understanding and appreciation for the diversity that exists in schools? In what ways can coaches work with teachers to create equitable instructional opportunities that meet the needs of all students?
4. In what ways can coaches and principals work together to build a culture of coaching and collaboration?

## Melinda Begins to Consider School Culture

Melinda understood that in her new role as a coach, she was being asked to support teachers in addressing the newly established district mission and vision. She valued the perspective of her principal, who consistently asked teachers, "What do you expect your students to learn? How will you know when they have learned it, and how will you respond when they don't learn it? How will you respond when they already know it?" (adapted from DuFour et al., 2016). The principal reminded teachers that they were in this together and wanted to know what resources and professional learning would help them to improve student learning. In Melinda's school, teachers were encouraged to work collaboratively to identify and solve problems. The culture seemed conducive to coaching, a place of learning for all students and adults. But, as a coach, how might Melinda work as a change agent in continuing to encourage and expand her school's culture of coaching, collaboration, and continual improvement? Which aspects of culture should Melinda attend to most closely? Who might be her allies in continuing to shape the larger culture to positively affect student learning? And an even larger question, what leadership role does Melinda play in addressing issues related to how the various parts of the system can be aligned to generate a culture of communication, collaboration, and collective efficacy?

As mentioned in Chapter 1, a culture conducive to coaching is one of the key tenets of our Framework for Thinking and Working Like a Coach (see Figure 1.2). In this chapter, given the impact of culture on coaching, as well as the impact of coaching on culture, we address several topics related to school, and to some extent district, culture. First, we define *culture*—what it is, and its influence on life in a given school or district. We then provide some background on its importance and describe organizational features of schools found to be critical when initiating any instructional changes. Specific notions for improving the culture of schools are discussed. We also address diversity and equity as important dimensions of culture and provide ideas for coaches to consider when working with teachers in developing an awareness and understanding of diversity and equity as essential components of effective curricular and instructional programs. We then detail how principals can specifically support coaching, highlighting the ways that coaches and principals can work together to engage in culture-building and culture-refinement work. Finally, we conclude with a specific example of a whole-school organizational change initiative to improve student learning.

## What Do We Mean by Culture?

> Culture is both a dynamic phenomenon that surrounds us at all times, being constantly enacted and created by our interactions with others and shaped by leadership behavior, and a set of structures, routines, rules, and norms that guide and constrain behavior.
> —Schein (2010, p. 1)

Professionals in schools, like those in other organizations, have specific views or beliefs about the culture in which they work. They may indicate that "teachers in this school really enjoy working with the students," or at the other extreme, that "teachers don't believe their students can learn." Likewise, they behave in ways that reflect their attitudes toward students and colleagues. They may interact with peers, seeking advice or resources about how to improve instruction. Or perhaps they close their classroom doors, ignoring schoolwide efforts to change curriculum or instruction. In some schools, the cultural norms are such that teachers readily participate in community events or are willing to stay after school to attend a special professional learning activity, even if it occurs beyond required hours. But, before delving into the many ways that coaching is impacted by and shapes culture, we first must define what we mean when we say "culture." To begin, we borrow heavily from the organizational researcher and theorist Edgar Schein.

Schein (2010), as quoted earlier, views culture as a "dynamic phenomenon," and elaborates on three distinct levels of culture. The first level is that of *artifacts*, or observable aspects of culture. For example, artifacts might include the banners or signs on display when one enters the school (e.g., "We are better together," "Focus on student learning"), the ways in which the classrooms are organized (e.g., small-group settings for discussions, tables and chairs set in rows), or even the ways in which teachers interact with their students or their colleagues. The second level, that of *espoused values*, focuses on the goals or ideals identified by the organization (e.g., mission or vision statements, widely articulated values such as "actively engage students in every lesson every day"). The third level, and the most difficult to discern, is that of the *underlying assumptions* of the organization (e.g., what do we believe about the students we teach? Their parents? How supportive are we of the direction of the school, the efforts of administration, and so on?).

Notice, given Schein's definitions, that much of what we think of as culture is invisible, like an iceberg where only a small portion is visible above the waterline. For example, although teachers in a specific school where the student population has changed over the years might not verbalize any negative views about the students they now teach, there may be an implicit, unstated set of beliefs that current students don't come to school with the background, motivation, or ability to learn. And teachers may behave in ways that reflect these beliefs.

### *Shared Leadership Is Key to Building a Collaborative Culture*

Those who write about culture often discuss the importance of leadership and its influence on the culture and climate of an organization. We agree with Schein that leadership is critical to creating and managing the culture in an organization, and therefore is not just a single role assigned to a specific individual. As such, all personnel in an organization have leadership responsibilities that include developing trusting relationships among colleagues. As we mention in Figure 1.2, leadership and relationships are building blocks essential to designing a culture conducive to coaching. Certainly, the principal plays a major leadership and relationship-building role in schools, especially by facilitating and supporting others as leaders. While there is general acceptance of the principal as the primary leader in schools, given the authority of the position, those who have coaching responsibilities also have leadership responsibilities. For coaches, their leadership roles are informal, and therefore they tend to lead from the middle by encouraging, nudging, and convincing others to support organizational goals and visions.

Further, those who coach are leaders who must think and act like change agents; that is, they need to understand the ever-shifting culture in a school and the meaningful role of their leadership as critical to creating organizational or systemic change. Effective coaches/leaders know how to manage and change the culture, rather than having the culture manage them. We have always appreciated John F. Kennedy's words on this topic, delivered at an address in the Assembly Hall in Frankfurt, Germany, on June 25, 1963: "Change is the law of life. And those who look only to the past or present are certain to miss the future" (Kennedy, 1963). We see evidence of change in schools all the time. For example, look at the influence of the global pandemic, which generated new paradigms that contribute to what we know about virtual teaching and engagement for deep learning. Change is indeed inevitable in schools, as well as in society (Fahey et al., 2019; Fullan & Langworthy, 2014).

## School Culture: How Important Is It?

Although there are many attempts in today's schools to improve the quality of teaching in individual classrooms—for example, measuring teacher performance and then rewarding or penalizing individual teachers for their work—there is research evidence that such efforts alone are not sufficient. More emphasis needs to be placed on improving the organization to ensure that all parts of the system interrelate and work together seamlessly (Bryk et al., 2015; Bryk et al., 2021; Leana & Pil, 2006; Reeves, 2023; Taylor, 2011; Woulfin et al., 2023).

Leana and Pil (2006), based on their large-scale research, identified and discussed two important constructs that influence organizational culture: *human capital* and *social capital*. These two notions are, in our experience, critical ideas for coaches to hold onto as they begin to understand and shape school culture. The first construct, human capital, relates to the human resources in the school—the staff (e.g., teachers, administrators, specialized personnel) and their experiences, backgrounds, education, and dispositions. The second construct, that of social capital, can be subdivided into internal and external social capital. *Internal social capital* refers to the patterns of interactions and relationships between and among all individuals in the school (e.g., how committed are they to the goal of improving student learning? Do they have high expectations and a shared vision for student outcomes? To what degree have all been involved with establishing a common mission and vision?). Meanwhile, *external social capital* refers to the relationships of the school with its families and other community agencies or organizations (e.g., libraries, businesses) that have an impact on a school's success.

Several key notions related to social capital are essential to the work of coaches. First, building social capital relies on building trusting and low-risk relationships in which teachers feel comfortable discussing problems or needs. Leana and Pil (2006) found, for example, that teachers, when faced with a problem, tended to seek out their peers for advice more than they did a coach or principal, perhaps because they trusted these colleagues and felt comfortable talking with them. Second, building social capital relies on providing opportunities for interaction so that such collaboration can occur; teachers need time to work together. These two aspects of social capital can provide coaches with a way to understand, assess, and shape cultural elements within a school.

Accordingly, to answer the question in the heading of this section, culture is *extremely* important! Meaningful, long-term, and sustained change will not happen when efforts are focused at the individual level only (Ippolito & Bean, 2024; Mangin & Dunsmore, 2015; Woulfin et al., 2023). As described by Leana (2011), one can use the analogy of "tinker toys" when thinking about school culture. The circles or nodes represent human capital, but one must also use the rods to make connections between the circles—in other words, building social capital. It is here that real and sustained change occurs. In Figure 3.1, we illustrate the importance of both human and social capital, highlighting the need for both. If a school has high human capital but low social capital, it falls in the box in the upper left-hand quadrant (e.g., there are effective teachers in the school, but little collaboration nor a sense of collective effort to achieve a common goal). These are schools where quality teaching is occurring in isolated classrooms. Often, parents will request a specific teacher or teachers for their children! Teachers who are experiencing difficulties with instruction may feel as though they have little guidance or direction and aren't sure exactly where they can seek help.

If the school has high social capital but low human capital, it falls in the lower right-hand quadrant. Teachers in these schools collaborate, but only a few have much experience or knowledge about the content or pedagogy for which they are responsible. Teachers may be involved in professional learning communities, but the leaders lack facilitation and leadership skills to guide thinking and learning; thus, the meetings tend to be unproductive. Conversations aren't focused on teaching and learning, and there may be a lack of support and follow-through with implementation ideas.

If both high social and human capital are evident in the school, it falls in the upper right-hand quadrant—the place to be! Teachers in these schools participate in meaningful dialogue in which they raise questions about their own work and that of others, with a focus on providing effective instruction for all students. Experienced, knowledgeable teachers and novices learn from each other in a risk-free environment, and coaches provide necessary resources, guidance, and support. The principal provides leadership that encourages and supports this work by establishing the structure and facilitating the collaborative work of teachers and coaches.

The least desirable situation is one in which there is both low social and low human capital (the lower left-hand quadrant). Much must be done to improve or remodel these schools. Moreover, coaches who work in such environments will have a difficult task; they will need to work with administrators, perhaps at the district level, or even bring in external consultants to assist in developing strategies to create

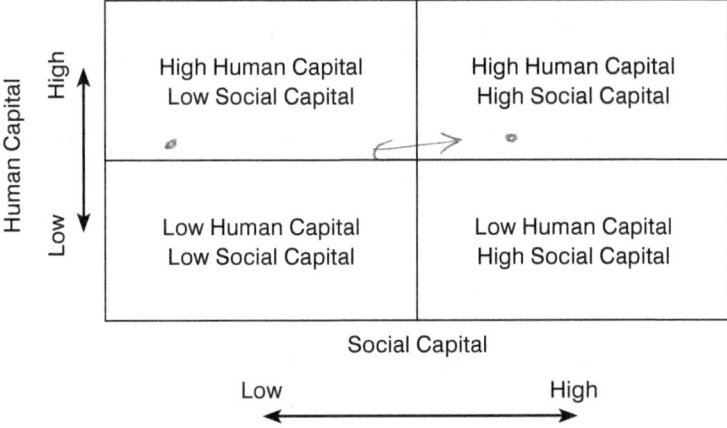

**FIGURE 3.1.** Human and social capital relationships. From Ippolito and Bean (2024, p. 27). Copyright © 2024 The Guilford Press. Reprinted with permission.

better working conditions. They will also need to collaborate with the principals and district leaders in supporting teachers. This means not only providing the professional learning that teachers need to develop key pedagogical knowledge and skills but also facilitating experiences that help teachers develop a sense of self- and collective efficacy and a commitment to achieving the overall goals of the school and district.

> • • • • • • • • • • **Put into Practice** • • • • • • • • • • • •
>
> Introduce Figure 3.1 to your colleagues. Ask them to think individually about where they would place your school in terms of human and social capital. Then ask group members to discuss their individual responses and the rationale for them. How similar or different were the responses? Discuss whether there is a need to make changes in the school and how.

## Leading Organizational Change to Improve Instruction

Building on the work of Tony Bryk and colleagues (Bryk, 2021; Bryk et al., 2015), in which they provide a comprehensive view and a number of essential elements about how to improve education in America's schools, in this chapter we focus on the importance of seeing the system. We focus on how coaches might become aware of the "interactions among the people engaged with it, the tools and materials they have at their disposal, and the processes through which these people and resources come together to do work" (Bryk et al., 2015, p. 58). They make the point that education is a complex system, and making all the parts of the system work together productively isn't an easy task. Too often, schools have looked for a silver bullet, the current fad or the quick solution (e.g., a new literacy program, a streamlined performance evaluation, and so forth). However, unless all parts of the system are aligned and "problems of coordination, communication, and system sensing" (Bryk et al., 2015, p. 60) are addressed, then there is little chance of meaningful change taking place. Bryk et al. (2015), in fact, describe coaching as one of those reforms that, because of its complexity, requires adaptive integration if it is to be productive at the system level. In other words, coaching must be adapted to meet specific contextual system features and challenges if in the long run it is going to influence not only school culture but also teaching and learning.

In the following sections, we identify what we consider to be critical guidelines for those involved in systems-level coaching work. These guidelines are supported by a number of research syntheses (Bryk et al., 2015; Bryk, 2021) and connect directly to our framework in Figure 1.2.

## *1. Focus on Mission, Vision, and Commitment*

In Chapter 1, we include mission and vision as important factors in our Framework for Thinking and Working Like a Coach (See Figure 1.2). Both short- and long-term goals must be identified, recognizing that change occurs over time and that it may take between two and five years for schools to accomplish their overall goals (Fullan, 2020; Taylor, 2011; Zigmond et al., 2011). (For more on this, see the Further Readings and Resources at the end of the chapter.)

Achieving a vision requires more than "buy-in" from teachers. When teachers are involved in decision making and work collaboratively to craft the vision, there is much more potential for successful and sustainable change (Bryk, 2021). Further, there will be greater awareness of the need for additional adult learning and related changes in teaching. Here are four ideas for coaches who are helping teachers and leaders establish a common instructional vision:

- **Support the establishment of an instructional leadership team.** An ILT that includes principals, coaches, and teachers can lead the change process by facilitating discussions and work activities related to school needs and goals, relative to student learning within and across disciplines. We elaborate on this suggestion in Chapter 8.
- **Provide opportunities for teachers to reflect together.** Coaches and school leaders can help teachers reflect on what they do well and what they think needs to change if they are to improve student learning in the school. Reflective dialogue is one of the keys to sparking transformation (Fahey et al., 2019; Mezirow, 2000). Start by working in small groups, such as grade-level or departmental teams, and then

share information in large groups so that there are opportunities to look both vertically and horizontally at the curriculum and instruction in the school.

- **Focus!** There seems to be strong evidence (Bryk et al., 2015; Collins, 2001; Schmoker, 2011) of the importance of having a laser-like focus (building on current school strengths) that addresses both the *what* and the *how* of achieving change goals. For example, middle school educators, to achieve the goal of improving writing across the curriculum, must recognize the importance of the goal, receive support from a coach with deep knowledge and understanding of writing instruction, and work collaboratively to achieve the goal. One of our oft-repeated adages to coaches and school leaders is that if you are going to put a new initiative or project *onto* teachers' plates, then consider what you are taking *off* their plates! Effective change does not occur simply by adding more and more initiatives or moving blindly from one to another and falling victim to "solutionitis" (Bryk, 2015).

- **Provide top-down as well as bottom-up support.** Closely related to focus, when a school is implementing a specific initiative, they need support from the district, that is, top-down support. If a district is moving in a different direction from that identified by the school, there will be little chance of success. School personnel such as coaches, principals, and teachers need to know that their vision and goals are recognized as important and that they will receive the necessary support to work toward their goals. And as stated above, any initiative at the school level will be more successful when there is teacher involvement and decision making when change efforts are being considered.

## 2. Focus on Distributing Leadership

Again, leadership is identified in our graphic in Chapter 1 (Figure 1.2) as an important driver of school improvement. Leadership can be defined in many ways: as a position (e.g., superintendent, principal); as someone who possesses specific characteristics (e.g., communicates well, is knowledgeable); as a style (e.g., charismatic, democratic, laissez-faire, authoritative, adaptive); or even as one who can influence or persuade others to behave in specific ways (e.g., how a coach can encourage followership [Evans, 2007]). Leadership style or approach may vary, depending on where a school is in terms of its change process. During the initial stages of a change process, someone who can motivate and ignite action may be needed, whereas at later stages, the school may benefit from leadership that is more calming and focused on implementation and sustainability issues (e.g., what needs to be done to provide essential organizational supports and pressures).

Taking all these views of leadership into account, in this text we define leadership as "any activity or set of activities associated with working with others to reach or accomplish a common goal" (Bean & Goatley, 2021, p. 100). We define leadership this way because we see great power in distributing leadership across roles in schools, encouraging coaches and teacher leaders to take lead roles in school improvement efforts. Coaches especially play important leadership roles by supporting teachers directly: listening to them, helping them solve problems, and keeping them focused on the identified goals and action steps necessary to achieve those goals. An important assumption in this book is that there are many leaders in schools, from the principal who plays a key leadership role in developing a collaborative environment in which teachers feel empowered to make decisions, to teachers whose role as leaders is too often understated. Leaders must be able to see the big picture—that is, to be "thought leaders"—and, at the same time, manage the day-to-day occurrences that can facilitate or hinder progress toward a specific goal. Ultimately, to be successful, any change initiative in a school must focus on (and likely distribute) leadership across multiple individuals, roles, and groups.

### *3. Focus on Collaboration and Relationships*

There is strong evidence of the importance of collaboration as a means of developing collective efficacy in schools. What is exciting is that researchers (e.g., Donohoo et al., 2018; Hattie, 2012, 2016) indicate that a focus on collective efficacy can "make a difference in student learning, even greater than the impact of communities and homes" (Ippolito & Bean, 2024, p. 69). Teachers need opportunities to work together to address real, meaningful problems. Such collaboration requires administrative leaders to develop schedules that enable groups of teachers—grade level, departmental—to meet on a regular basis. Such meetings need to be facilitated by those who understand how to develop a clear set of norms for group work, protocols for guiding discussion, and approaches for managing conflicts and arriving at decisions. Collaborative work requires thinking like a designer, with coaches engaging colleagues in problem-solving conversations about students, curriculum, instruction, and so on. Effective design work also requires careful observation of those doing the work (teachers and students) and consideration of how context and available tools influence the work being done.

Before undertaking systemic change efforts, coaches, leaders, and teachers might consider crafting a shared understanding of their own school culture or climate, creating a starting point for establishing a common vision for both teaching and learning, and for developing curricula that are evidence-based and meet the needs of students. Such a visioning activity requires all educators in a school to participate in dialogue that builds the capacity of individuals and teams. Both the process and the end results can position a school to better support teacher learning and instructional efforts. The National Center for Literacy Education (NCLE) Framework for Capacity Building identifies six conditions and practices that support effective collaboration and have an impact on student learning: deprivatizing practice, enacting shared agreements, creating a collaborative culture, maintaining an inquiry stance, using evidence effectively, and supporting collaboration systematically (NCLE, 2014,

p. 33). We suggest that leaders consider using the inventory to facilitate discussion about collaborative work and how it can be improved. A useful resource that can aid schools in thinking about collaborative work and how it can be improved is the Professional Learning Communities Survey tool provided by the Center for Leadership & Educational Equity (CLEE) and the School Reform Initiative (SRI) (see Web Resources at the end of this chapter).

### 4. Focus on Using Data for Decision Making

Data can be a school's greatest friend, if used appropriately. Taylor (2011), for example, use the term "principled" use of data, which identifies data use as a tool, not a goal. She indicated the need to use a broad array of data sources, from student work samples to standardized test scores, highlighting the importance of using student, teacher, and school data as three important sources of information to guide decision making. We also often point coaches who are thinking like designers to consult the *Data Wise* series (Boudett et al., 2020) and Safir and Dugan's (2021) *Street Data* book as powerful sources to read and discuss with teachers, ILTs, and school leaders. (See more about data and its use in Chapter 7.)

> **STOP AND REFLECT**
>
> Think carefully about the four focus areas for coaches involved in systems-level work. Which of these would you identify as strengths in your school, and why? Which of these might appear to be challenges, and why? What might be your next steps in terms of addressing any noted challenges (and with whom might you collaborate)?

## Diversity, Equity, and Belonging: The Core of a School's Mission/Vision

In thinking about a school's culture, systems, and all that they encompass, a discussion of diversity, equity, and belonging in schools, communities, and our society overall is essential. Our society is becoming increasingly diverse, and regardless of the locale of the school, students must be engaged in activities and curriculum that help them understand diversity as a source of strength and potential. Coaches have the responsibility of supporting teachers in implementing instructional practices that promote equity and social justice, and of advocating for change if inequities exist. Learning about and addressing equity in schools is a lifelong professional endeavor; therefore, in the next two sections we offer some important thoughts and resources for coaches.

### *Diversity, Equity, and Belonging: Focusing on Human Capital*

As defined by Coleman et al. (2011), diversity is a "multidimensional, broadly inclusive concept that acknowledges and embraces the richness of human differences . . . the term 'diversity' is not code for race, ethnicity, or gender by themselves" (p. 20). Rather, it is more encompassing of many different attributes, including academic achievement, gender, age, religion, sexual orientation, and marital status, as well as race and ethnicity. Diversity of students, teachers, and staff in schools and in the surrounding community contributes in positive ways to the culture of the school, providing opportunities for learning. To establish a culture that builds on diversity, coaches can work with teachers to support them in working effectively with a wide range of learners and their families to create an atmosphere that respects the value that each individual brings to the overall group. Given the challenge that teachers face in addressing the multiple ways that the students in their classrooms differ, coaches play an important role in developing teacher knowledge about equity and diversity, and in supporting teachers as they implement differentiated instruction in classrooms.

We view diversity, equity, and belonging as topics central to any discussion about developing the school culture as an effective place for learning, so we encourage all coaches and leaders to go beyond the brief ideas presented here for a more in-depth study of diversity and equity, their influence, and their impact on your work (see Further Readings and Resources at the end of this chapter). Here we simply note three key ideas to consider in your work with educators.

### *Developing Awareness of and Appreciation for Cultural Differences*

Although raising and addressing issues of diversity and equity can be challenging, it is critical that coaches build their skills in bringing issues of diversity and equity to the surface in their work with teachers. A large majority of the teachers in U.S. schools tend to be white, middle class, and English-speaking, and often they have not had the experiences that prepare them to work with the increasingly diverse student body in their schools. Too often, they aren't given the opportunity to talk about race and culture, their own and their students', in meaningful, open ways. Asking educators to share their own stories, their cultural traditions, biases, and perceptions, can be helpful in raising issues and discussing the diversity that exists in the school. Talking about our own cultural experiences can often open the door to even more meaningful conversations about how to develop learning experiences that build on students' experiences. In some schools, external consultants are brought in to lead discussions about the topics of diversity and culture. In other schools, teachers may be given opportunities to read articles about culture and diversity and then hold discussions about them. We often point coaches to the CLEE/SRI protocols (see

Web Resources at the end of this chapter): discussion-based protocols designed to support adult educators committed to meaningful work around diversity issues (e.g., Diversity Rounds, Equity Stances), which can be used to initiate discussions about diversity and equity in schools. In sum, by developing an awareness of and appreciation for cultural differences (in our view, just a first step), coaches and leaders can lay the foundation for teachers to develop curriculum and instruction that builds on students' strengths, a focus of the next section.

## *Transforming Curriculum and Instruction*

Coaches are well positioned to assist teachers in developing curriculum and instruction that build on student assets. Together, coaches and teachers can discuss exactly where there are gaps in the curriculum and which activities, or instructional strategies, might address those gaps. For example, is there a need to improve instruction for multilingual learners? Is there a need to help students understand and value diversity (in its broadest sense)? Is there a need for more culturally responsive curriculum that addresses issues related to racial and cultural diversity in schools, especially as it relates to discipline-specific learning?

## *Engaging the School Community*

There is strong evidence of the effects of a positive relationship between family and community involvement in schools and student achievement (Lazar et al., 2012; Paratore et al., 2020). Results of the Programme for International Student Assessment (PISA) in 2022 indicated that parents play a key role in many different ways, from influencing attitudes toward learning and schools to providing direct support that reinforces the value and importance of learning (Organisation for Economic Co-operation and Development [OECD], 2023). The results also indicate the importance of developing positive school and family relationships. However, too often, school–parent relationships have been built on a deficit model that assumes the "school knows best" and positions the school as the expert, ignoring the strengths that parents bring to the conversation. Boutte and Johnson (2014) call for strength-based involvement programs that place schools in the position of learners willing to acknowledge and value the funds of knowledge (Moll, 2000) that families bring to schools, to learn from and with them. As stated by Boutte and Johnson (2014), "Instead of viewing families as 'struggling,' perhaps it is useful for educators to think of the struggles that they are facing . . . and how to circumvent and transcend these" (p. 179). For a more in-depth discussion of family and community involvement, see Chapter 9.

There is a great deal more to consider regarding coaching, leadership, and diversity issues, beyond the scope of this book. However, now we turn our attention to the critical role of the principal in supporting coaching work. Without strong building-based leadership, issues of diversity, equity, and culture writ large cannot be adequately addressed.

## Partnering with Principals to See and Shape Culture

Substantial evidence exists that principals play key roles as instructional leaders and have a powerful effect on teaching and learning in schools (Bean & Lillenstein, 2012; Bean et al., 2015; Bean et al., 2018; Berebitsky et al., 2014; Bryk et al., 2015; Schwanke, 2024; Supovitz et al., 2010). One of the important leadership tasks of principals is that of developing and distributing leadership in schools, that is, identifying and supporting teacher leaders, creating schedules that allow for collaboration, supporting teachers in their change efforts, and providing support for those changes. Effective principals understand, facilitate, and support both formal and informal coaching efforts. In a study of the implementation of Response to Intervention (RtI) systems in five schools (Bean & Lillenstein, 2012), the principal was found to be the "central person for promoting a risk-free environment, leading the effort in establishing norms for collaboration, and facilitating shared responsibility and accountability" (p. 497). Matsumura et al. (2009) found positive and significant relationships between specific behaviors of principals and effective implementation of coaching in schools. When principals were actively involved in the change initiative, identified and supported coaches as sources of expertise, and trusted coaches to manage their own schedules, teachers were more frequently involved in coaching activities. Increasingly, researchers are finding that principals directly influence coaches' access to classrooms and efficacy when collaborating with teachers (Munson & Saclarides, 2022; Saclarides & Munson, 2024). Therefore, in the following section, we discuss first how principals can support the work of coaches and then ways that coaches can most effectively work with principals.

> **VOICES FROM THE FIELD**
>
> As new principals were hired, they would attend state-sponsored coaching trainings that typically focused on a purely directive approach. The principal began seeing the coaching role as that of compliance monitor, data manager, or assessment coordinator. Once a principal developed this mindset, it was incredibly difficult to change that perception. During my second year, I focused more attention on building the principals' understandings of effective coaching practices. Slowly this helped to build a shared model of coaching, and I learned the importance of including principals in building our system of coaching.
> —Christina Steinbacher-Reed,
> Executive Director, BLaST Intermediate Unit 17

### *The Principal's Role in Supporting Coaching*

Principals play an important role in shaping and influencing the culture in the school, including the culture of coaching. In all coaching efforts with which we have been involved, coaches have identified, first and foremost, the key role of principals in assuring that the coaching initiative will be successful (Bean et al., 2015; Bean & Lillenstein, 2012; Ippolito & Bean, 2019, 2024). Below we identify and describe ways that principals can facilitate the work of coaches.

- **Understand the role of coaches and the importance of coaching.** This includes understanding not only what coaching is and what it can do, but what it is not and what it cannot do. For example, principals must understand that effective coaching relationships cannot be forged if the coach is asked to serve as an evaluator of teacher performance. Furthermore, principals should not ask coaches to identify the weaknesses of specific teachers. At the same time, effective principals recognize they can learn much from the coach relative to instruction if they take the time to listen to the coach describe instructional needs in the school broadly (e.g., student work samples indicate the need for more in-depth student work with fractions at the fourth-grade level; the eighth-grade team wants to learn more about how to actively engage their students in discussions across content areas). In other words, coach–principal interactions might most productively focus on the needs of groups of students and teachers, rather than focusing on the specific dilemmas of individual teachers.

- **Identify coaches as an important source of expertise.** Principals can do this in many ways. They can speak positively in school meetings or with individual teachers about coaching and its value for improving student learning; they can suggest ways that teachers may choose to work with the coach or identify topics for discussion. A caution: Such suggestions should not just be made to a teacher who has been identified by the principal as having some weaknesses, given that such recommendations may cause teachers to think that coaching is only for teachers who are struggling. Rather, the principal can suggest to all teachers that they may want to meet with the coach to share what they are doing and to gain some additional ideas and resources for their work. An excellent teacher at one school mentioned that the coach in their building never approached her, indicating that she, the teacher, had no need of coaching. Yet this teacher believed that an opportunity for interaction with the coach would have given her a chance to raise some questions about specific students and discuss new instructional ideas.

- **Protect and prioritize coaches' time by co-developing schedules.** In collaboration with the school's ILT, principals can support coaches by co-developing coaching calendars and schedules. By directly co-developing coaching schedules, principals can identify and protect specific chunks of time for coaches to work with grade-level or content-area teams of teachers. Principals can also show direct support by occasionally acting as a substitute in a classroom when the coach needs to hold a debriefing conference with a teacher. Additionally, it is always important to "expect the unexpected," and to acknowledge that coaches might need to step in and support teachers and leaders on a regular basis, sometimes taking them away from their primary coaching duties. As instructional coach Marsha Turner-Hall suggests in the following Voices from the Field, it is critical to manage and reduce the number and types of interruptions to coaching that can occur. Principals play a large role in ensuring disruptions are minimized.

> **VOICES FROM THE FIELD**
>
> Coaching teachers on classroom management or academic rigor is the easy part. What is difficult is coaching teachers within the context of external forces: adhering to the demands of building administration, having to cover classes due to teacher absences, or handling student discipline. Coaching doesn't occur in a vacuum, and effective coaches must prepare for and create a process flexible enough to handle those interruptions.
> —MARSHA TURNER-HALL, Teacher and Instructional Coach

- **Communicate regularly with the coach.** The type and timing of conversations may differ, depending on principal and coach preferences, but regular communication is essential. Some principals may prefer a weekly summary of activities and a set of suggestions or recommendations. Other principals may suggest that the coach set a regular time to meet every week or two. In addition to conversations that include only the principal and the coach, regularly scheduled meetings of the principal and the ILT can be especially useful for sharing perceptions, clarifying and elaborating upon any recent decisions, and deciding which members of the team are responsible for specific tasks. Principals can be especially supportive if they make it clear that, if circumstances warrant it (i.e., there is a specific problem or concern), the coach is welcome to stop by for an impromptu meeting at any time.
- **Provide feedback to the coach.** Coaching can be a lonely job, and although we recommend that coaches form networks where they can interact informally with others in a similar role, getting feedback (warm and cool) from the principal can be helpful. The principal can share with the coach the fact that several teachers were very excited about their work with the coach, or can make suggestions about how the coach might reach out to teachers or about how to use time more productively. Taking the time as a principal to ask the coach how they can be helpful—rearranging schedules, putting the coach on a meeting agenda for a brief mini-lesson—can be part of this interaction.
- **Involve the coach in leadership activities.** Ask the coach to serve on various leadership teams or to conduct professional learning workshops for teachers in

the school (or even in the district), and to participate in walk-throughs with various leaders and teachers as a learning exercise. Work collaboratively, seeking input from the coach when designing schedules and assigning students or teachers to specific instructional groups.

## *How Coaches Can Support Principals*

Leadership in a school can be distributed in different ways, depending on the experience and knowledge base of the principal. As mentioned above, and as we have heard from many principals, coaches who are experts in their discipline(s) can be a powerful source of learning for principals themselves. Moreover, principals see that coaches play important leadership roles, not only in coaching individual teachers but in helping teachers understand data and how to use them, and in leading small groups of teachers in making instructional decisions (Bean et al., 2018). While principals may have deep disciplinary knowledge in one or more domains (e.g., literacy, math, science), it is the rare principal who feels completely confident in all disciplines and across all grade ranges. Therefore, coaches can be incredible sources of both content and pedagogical knowledge in the school. In such instances, the principal may ask the coach to take on more responsibilities for leading instructional efforts in the school in collaboration with the principal. Both can discuss data results and their implications for instruction. Together, they can take informal walk-throughs through the school, gaining a deeper sense of the students in the classrooms and teaching and learning practices. In schools where the principal has a strong instructional background, the coach and principal can work together with teachers to make short- and long-term decisions about instruction at the classroom and school levels. Specific ideas for those who coach and how they can support the principal follow.

- **Ensure that coaching feedback is consistent with that offered by the principal.** Principals routinely provide feedback to teachers about their practice, both formally as part of evaluation systems and informally as part of instructional rounds or classroom walk-throughs. Where coaches can be most supportive is by coordinating with principals and ensuring that both principal and coach feedback to teachers is coherent and consistent. Otherwise, principal and coach feedback might conflict and leave teachers confused about next steps for improving teaching and learning. Coaches can share specific ideas with principals for improving instruction within certain grade levels, departments, or the school as a whole—ensuring that principals' informal and formal feedback is aligned with coaching work. As mentioned previously, however, coach comments to principals should not be specific to an individual teacher unless there are unusual circumstances where teacher behavior is detrimental to the welfare of children.

- **Provide a clear agenda when meeting with the principal.** Coaches should, whenever possible, provide a tight, clear agenda for meetings with the principal so that time is used wisely. The agenda might begin by highlighting positive examples of teaching and learning in the school (e.g., the interactive read-alouds in first grade are really helping students develop their listening and reading comprehension skills) before moving on to raise questions about possible concerns (e.g., the middle school social studies team is looking for suggestions about how to hold effective small-group discussions) and, finally, identifying ways in which the principal can directly support next coaching moves (e.g., it would be incredibly helpful if you could attend the fifth-grade team meeting where we are going to review work samples; we are going to need to make some instructional changes, and this may affect scheduling).

- **Be honest with the principal about your needs as a coach.** Regular communication with the principal should also surface any immediate coaching concerns, especially noting the support needed to coach more effectively. For example, perhaps you are being taken away from your coaching responsibilities in ways that reduce your effectiveness (e.g., entering data results for all students). Ask the principal if there are ways to address this problem, and be prepared to suggest possible solutions, such as asking a paraprofessional to assist in organizing student data. In other words, the principal might not be aware of the problem and how it is affecting your work; it is important to raise the issue rather than stew about it.

- **Don't break confidentiality unless necessary.** Coaches often ask what to do when they have tried, over and over, to work with a specific teacher or group and have had little or no success. The teacher's or group's negativity may have affected student learning and progress toward meeting school goals. There is no perfect solution for situations like this, and although they aren't necessarily frequent, they can be detrimental to any school change efforts. Given the impact of this negativity, the coach might decide, as a last resort, to have a private conversation with the principal to discuss the situation and generate possible next steps. Most frequently, the principal is aware of the situation and can be helpful; it also requires the principal and coach to design a plan for addressing the problem in ways that don't sabotage the work of the coach. This type of situation highlights the importance of the coach and principal having a relationship of trust, understanding that addressing an issue like this is a delicate process that can only be successfully resolved when the two work together.

### • • • • • • • • • • Put into Practice • • • • • • • • • • •

Meet with a small group of coaching colleagues (in person or online) to discuss how they might address a situation in which a teacher's lack of response to coaching is affecting student learning in her classroom. The coach has tried to work with this teacher in many ways, but there has been no change in

> teacher behavior or attitude. Should the coach talk with the principal? If she does, how might the principal and coach address this issue together? Think about this as requiring a number of steps: What might be causing this sort of response? What could be done first? If little success, what next? In what ways can coaches reduce this reluctance to engage with coaching? In partnership with the principal, what can be done to improve the overall culture of coaching in the school?

## Partnering with Allied Professionals to Support a Culture of Collaboration

Given the complexity of schools in today's world, there are many more opportunities, and needs, for coaches to work collaboratively with various teams of educators beyond classroom teachers. Often coaches serve on leadership or data teams with allied professionals such as interventionists, special educators, librarians, school counselors and psychologists, or speech and language pathologists. The principal and/or assistant principal may also be members of the wider team. These teams may be responsible for analyzing data and making decisions about instruction or discussing the needs of specific students identified as having difficulties with mathematics, reading, writing, speech, and so on. They may also be responsible for discussing the implementation of intervention systems such as Response to Intervention (RtI), multi-tiered systems of support (MTSS), or similar systems designed to differentiate instruction to meet student needs.

In fact, in a study focused on successful implementation of RtI in several schools (Bean & Lillenstein, 2012), principals took the "lead role in establishing conditions for effective implementation . . . being on the sidelines was not an option" (p. 497). Those who were interviewed in that study highlighted the importance of learning to work as team members and indicated that they appreciated the opportunity to listen to and learn from colleagues with different expertise. The psychologist in one school talked about how much he had learned about literacy by working with the reading specialist and coach. Reading specialists and special educators were excited about opportunities to exchange ideas about instruction. Meanwhile, reading specialists and coaches appreciated the opportunities to use a team approach to coaching, with each of them, based on their experiences, working with specific teachers or focusing on a particular area of literacy.

These educators identified the importance of providing constructive as well as positive feedback to teachers and identified three guidelines as important for their work: (1) Treat teachers with respect and value their input, (2) use data to support the message, and (3) focus on student learning. Two major conclusions were drawn from the Bean and Lillenstein (2012) study. First, to implement a program such as RtI, educators in schools need to work collaboratively, to learn with and from each other.

Second, all educators in the school need to develop the leadership skills necessary to work collaboratively.

## Example of a School Change Initiative: The Importance of Systemwide Change

Here we describe an example of a change initiative led by a principal and his colleagues at two underperforming high schools. Note the similarities between the research presented in this chapter and the specifics of this initiative (Reed, 2015). Rather than searching for specific programs or external solutions, these educators decided to build their own capacity and develop the learning environment from the *inside out* (Elmore, 2004) in ways that improved both teacher and student learning. In both schools, student test scores improved in just a few years. Reed (2015) discusses the importance of focus, describing three areas of emphasis:

- **Collaboration.** Informal collaborative meetings held quarterly, called "Coffee and Conversations," provided opportunities for teachers to share their views with the principal and each other. Groups of teachers stopped by during their planning periods to raise issues and suggest solutions. Similar informal conversational meetings were scheduled with parents and students. Other collaborative efforts included teacher leader meetings with the principal to discuss areas of need. Then, teacher leaders would facilitate follow-up meetings with their respective teams. Electronic surveys were also conducted to receive feedback from stakeholders when specific issues arose (e.g., change of graduation venue).
- **Use of data.** Reed (2015) emphasizes the importance of communicating data to teachers in an easy-to-understand form and of discussing what the data mean in terms of improving the system or organization. As a result of data analysis, changes were made in the types of classes being offered, teaching assignments, and the length of the instructional day. The school also implemented a literacy plan that emphasized reading and writing in all disciplines.
- **Building educator capacity.** Coaching became an important approach for facilitating instructional change, with coaches helping teachers reflect on their practices. Teachers participated in informal, voluntary learning walks, facilitated by a colleague or a coach. Following these learning walks, emails with positive feedback about effective strategies that were seen in the classrooms were sent to all educators. These learning walks clearly demonstrated the need for alignment in content and practices across classrooms. Administrators then redesigned the schedule to provide teachers from the same discipline a common planning period to realign the curriculum.

This is only one example of a concerted, long-term school-improvement effort, that is, to change the organizational culture in ways that facilitated learning for both faculty and students. Schools may use different approaches or ways of achieving organizational change, but the broad notions of establishing a mission/vision, collaboration to develop collective efficacy, meaningful use of data, and effective leadership from multiple sources are important foundational elements in building a culture of coaching.

## Summary

In this chapter, we provided a definition of what we mean by "culture" and then discussed evidence about the importance of establishing an organizational culture that promotes shared leadership and collaboration as a means of moving toward a common vision of teaching, learning, and coaching. We provided specific suggestions about shaping the school's culture for improving instruction, followed by a discussion about diversity and equity and ways that instructional coaches might design and facilitate school practices that build on the strength that comes from the diversity in schools and in society. We then discussed ways that coaches can partner productively with principals as well as other allied professionals to collectively shape the culture of a school. We concluded with a specific example of a school remodeling effort at the high school level that emphasized various cultural changes as a means of improving student learning. As Melinda reflected on her own role as a change agent with the responsibility of working with others to initiate school improvement efforts, she realized that she needed to learn more about working at the systems level, thinking more broadly about how she and others could lead change collectively.

## Reflections

- Using the chart found in Appendix A, note ways that coaches can support the development of a culture that is receptive to collaborative learning for both adults and students. How do you as a coach already serve as a change agent, facilitator, designer, and advocate when involved in establishing such a culture in your school? Which activities might you consider adopting that would further these ways of thinking and working?
- In what ways do you, as a coach, work together with your principal to ensure that teachers understand the value of coaching and are receptive to it? In what ways could the relationship be improved? What challenges might exist in this relationship?

## Activities

- With your colleagues, conduct an inventory of the culture in your school, using the CLEE/SRI Professional Learning Communities Survey. What did you find? Which aspects of the inventory might be most important to share with other colleagues and school leaders? What short-term actions might your group suggest? Long-term actions?
- Choose a resource from the Further Readings and Resources list. Read with an individual or group of colleagues, and discuss the ways in which the resource relates to the culture-focused work that you are doing in your school as a coach.
- Discuss the school improvement project described at the end of this chapter (Reed, 2015). Think about the descriptions of these schools and how a group of committed educators, in a shared leadership model, created an environment that produced learning changes for both students and teachers. Would this work in your school or district? What questions or challenges does it raise? What might this suggest about a school's existing culture? What other approaches might be used to achieve the goal of improving student learning at the school or district level?

## FURTHER READINGS AND RESOURCES

### Print Resources

Berger, J. G. (2019). *Unlocking leadership mindtraps: How to thrive in complexity*. Stanford University Press.

Eisenberg, E. B., Eisenberg, B. P., Medrich, E. A., & Charner, I. (2017). *Instructional coaching in action: An integrated approach that transforms thinking, practice, and schools*. ASCD.

Fahey, K., Breidenstein, A., Ippolito, J., & Hensley, F. (2019). *An uncommon theory of school change: Leadership for reinventing schools*. Teachers College Press.

Fullan, M. (2020). *Leading in a culture of change* (2nd ed.). Jossey-Bass.

Gorski, P. C., & Swalwell, K. (2015). Equity literacy for all. *Educational Leadership, 72*(6), 34–40.

Gorski, P., & Swalwell, K. (2023a). *Fix injustice, not kids and other principles for transformative equity leadership*. ASCD.

Gorski, P., & Swalwell, K. (2023b). Moving from equity awareness to action. *Educational Leadership, 80*(8), 20–27.

Nalkur, P. (2024a). The JEDI coach: Embracing inclusivity. *Coaching Today, 50*, 8–13.

Nalkur, P. (2024b). *Stumbling towards inclusion: Finding grace in imperfect leadership*. Amplify Publishing.

Vangrieken, K., Grosemans, I., Dochy, F., & Kyndt, E. (2017). Teacher autonomy and collaboration: A paradox? Conceptualising and measuring teachers' autonomy and collaborative attitude. *Teaching and Teacher Education, 67*, 302–315.

Wagner, T., Kegan, R., Lahey, L. L., Lemons, R. W., Garnier, J., Helsing, D., et al. (2012). *Change leadership: A practical guide to transforming our schools*. John Wiley & Sons.

Walker-Dalhouse, D., & Risko, V. J. (2020). Culturally responsive literacy instruction. In A. Swan Dagen & R. M. Bean (Eds.), *Best practices of literacy leaders: Keys to school improvement* (2nd ed., pp. 304–322). Guilford Press.

Walker-Dalhouse, D., & Risko, V. J. (2024). *Equitable literacy instruction for students in poverty.* Teachers College Press.

Woulfin, S. L., Stevenson, I., & Lord, K. (2023). *Making coaching matter: Leading continuous improvement in schools.* Teachers College Press.

## Web Resources (see www.guilford.com/bean3-materials for live links)

Center for Leadership & Educational Equity and the School Reform Initiative. (2024). *Professional learning communities survey.* www.clee.org/resources/professional-learning-communities-survey and www.clee.org/resources/professional-learning-communities-survey-exercise

Center for Leadership & Educational Equity and the School Reform Initiative. (2024). *Protocols.* www.clee.org/resources

Fullan, M., & Langworthy, M. (2014). *A rich seam: How new pedagogies find deep learning.* Pearson. www.michaelfullan.ca/wp-content/uploads/2014/01/3897.Rich_Seam_web.pdf

InnerDrive. (n.d.). *PISA 2022 results: The influence of parents and guardians on achievement.* https://blog.innerdrive.co.uk/pisa-2022-influence-of-caregivers

National Implementation Research Network. (2024). http://nirn.fpg.unc.edu.

New Leaders. (2023). *3 ways to work towards better implementation in schools and districts.* www.newleaders.org/blog/3-ways-to-work-towards-better-implementation-in-schools-and-districts

# CHAPTER 4

# Introduction to Ways of Working with Teachers

> **GUIDING QUESTIONS**
>
> 1. When beginning to work with teachers, why is it essential to think like a facilitator?
> 2. What do coaches need to know about the power of language and its importance in working with individuals and groups of teachers?
> 3. What are discussion-based protocols, and how can they be useful in facilitating discussions among coaches, individuals, and small groups of teachers?
> 4. In what ways can coaches develop trusting relationships with individuals and groups of teachers?

## Melinda Begins Thinking Like a Facilitator

Melinda knew the teachers she was asked to coach fairly well. She had attended meetings with them, ate lunch with them, and chatted informally with them about school routines, curricula, and policies (in addition to chatting about families and personal lives). But Melinda wasn't quite sure how to begin a more formal coaching relationship with these friends and colleagues. Would these peers bristle at the notion of Melinda coaching them? Should she begin by asking them where they needed support—or was there a better way to begin? What structures and routines might she establish to start her coaching relationships off on the right foot? Should she meet with teachers primarily one-on-one or in small or large groups? While Melinda felt confident about her own content and pedagogical knowledge, was she ready to take on the role of the "expert coach"? Melinda's principal reminded her that becoming a coach didn't mean that she suddenly had to have all the answers. Instead, she should focus on facilitating learning for and with her teacher colleagues. This made sense, but even the idea of becoming an "expert facilitator" left Melinda with some trepidation. How might she best begin her own facilitative leadership journey?

In this chapter, and across Chapters 5 and 6, we directly review the ways in which coaches might think and act as facilitators. We specifically encourage coaches to adopt the stance of "facilitator" rather than "expert," when working with adult learning. We discuss the power of clear and consistent agendas, communicating with teachers in ways that encourage reflection and inquiry, and utilizing discussion-based protocols as ways to support deep individual and group learning. Finally, we conclude with a discussion of coaching activities useful for developing trusting relationships between coaches and teachers—all good places for Melinda to begin her journey.

## Avoiding the Expertise Trap by Thinking and Working Like a Facilitator

Like many educators who step into coaching roles, Melinda might be wondering and nervous about her own areas of expertise. Does she really know enough about the literacy, math, science, and social studies curricula in her school to provide expert answers to her colleagues on all fronts? Does she really have the pedagogical expertise to provide all of her colleagues with advice on how to improve their teaching routines? These are very common and understandable worries that educators face when first taking on coaching work. Peers will be turning to the coach for advice, and what if the coach doesn't know everything about everything?

When we consult with new coaches, who have rightly shared these concerns with us, we often respond with three important suggestions that all relate to thinking and working as a facilitator.

### 1. Focus on Facilitating Teacher Learning (Not Sharing Your Own Expertise)

- One of the first things we say to new coaches is that your real strength as a coach isn't your disciplinary or pedagogical knowledge; your real power is rooted in your skills as a facilitator of adult learning. Each of us leads and coaches from different areas of strength. Certainly, excellent coaches do possess real expertise in their content areas and in pedagogical knowledge about powerful teaching and learning routines. However, no coach can know it all. Over time, we have found that the most effective coaches are those who invite teachers into conversations, drawing out teachers' own disciplinary and pedagogical knowledge. This helps teachers to carefully think through the relationship between their teaching moves, students' responses and data, and the details of the tasks and curriculum that connect them (what might be termed the "instructional core" [City et al., 2009, p. 22]). Much like therapists in a clinical setting, those who coach in schools aren't there to give teachers answer after expert answer. Instead, they are best positioned to help teachers reflect on their practice and become the best versions of themselves. If coaches focus on thinking and working like facilitators, as opposed to living up to the mantle of "expert," then coaches are much more likely to encourage growth in teachers' own mindsets and practices.

### 2. *Focus on Inquiry, Dialogue, and Thought Partnership (Not Pontificating)*

- One of the ways that coaches can position themselves as facilitators, rather than experts, is to focus on being thought partners. When we have asked coaches across districts to describe their roles and craft role descriptions for their work (see Ippolito & Bean, 2024, pp. 119–124), one phrase pops up again and again: "thought partner." Coaches who describe themselves as thought partners help to dispel the myth of expertise. It is perhaps human nature to want an expert, a single individual who knows it all and is able to share their knowledge with us, to suddenly arrive and tell us exactly how we can improve our work on all fronts. But anyone who has worked in schools knows that this is a myth. There are always multiple paths to success, and there is no one individual who knows it all. We call this the "expertise trap," and we encourage coaches not to fall into it! Coaches are often called experts by teachers and leaders, and while that is well intentioned, it can inadvertently place coaches in an awkward position. What happens when the resident expert doesn't know the perfect answer to engaging multilingual learners in math discussions? When expertise is questioned, is credibility lost?

- Instead, we encourage coaches to avoid the expertise trap and position themselves as problem solvers and facilitators of adult learning. Focus on thought partnership. Focus on engaging teachers in conversation about their work, listening and seeking to understand first before diving into making suggestions. Often, the most effective coaches are those who help teachers clarify their own instructional goals, given a specific curriculum and particular group of students. This is not to say that coaches don't have lots of helpful pedagogical and content knowledge to share. We simply suggest that coaches lead from a listening, partnering, and facilitative stance, as opposed to pontificating. If coaches only lead from an expert stance, they will be missing rich opportunities to help teachers surface and refine their own thinking and practice. As a coach, remember what we have learned from our time working with students: Telling isn't teaching; it's better to be a guide on the side than a sage on the stage. The same is perhaps even more true when coaching adult learners.

### 3. Focus on Lifelong Learning (for the Coach Most of All)

- Finally, coaches who think and work as facilitators focus on lifelong learning for teachers as well as themselves. When a teacher asks about best practices, what the research tells us, or what the coach has done previously in their own past classrooms—remember that the focus is on lifelong learning and not always having an answer in the moment. It is perfectly fine for a coach to say some version of: "That's a really good question. I have a few ideas, but I think we both might be best served if we do a bit of reading and exploring of that question together. Let me follow up with you in a day or so with some possible readings and ideas; perhaps we can think about a few that might work for your students." Now, you don't want to always deflect direct questions, but you also don't always need to have an answer at the ready. It is okay to signal to teachers that you are continually learning more too, and perhaps the best outcomes will arise from collaborative inquiry into a specific topic (e.g., productive talk in math classrooms, or connecting hands-on science experiments with text sets of scientific articles offering a range of text complexity). In sum, if coaches focus on lifelong learning for all, then not knowing an answer doesn't have to become a "gotcha" embarrassing moment for a coach. Instead, it becomes an opportunity to engage in more learning together.

We offer these quick suggestions for how to think and work like a facilitator as reminders to all those who coach: The ways in which you position yourself with teachers matters a great deal. We have seen the power in balancing responding to teachers' questions and interests with occasionally directing teachers to try new and specific practices (Ippolito, 2010). When thinking and working like a facilitator, coaches can powerfully support teachers in developing their own mindsets as lifelong learners. Of course, language is the primary tool coaches use to support and facilitate teacher learning. In the next section, we delve further into some of the specific ways that coaches might consider and use language intentionally in their work with teachers.

## The Power of Language: Talking with Individuals and Groups of Teachers

Given that language is arguably a coach's primary tool, and key to the success of any coach–teacher interaction, we begin by describing a few critical notions about language as a tool for thinking and working as a facilitator with teachers.

### First and Foremost, Be an Active Listener

As an active listener, attend to more than the words being spoken and listen for the deeper meaning behind what is being said. Listen for what Heifetz et al. (2009) call the "song beneath the words" (p. 76). A teacher who says, "My students can't work well in small groups" may be expressing frustration, confusion, or anger. They may even be reaching out for help. Likewise, in group settings, listen for the intent of the comments. In conversations we have with coaches, being an active listener is always first on their list of important characteristics of effective coaching. As active listeners, coaches should probably be doing less speaking and more listening in general. Pausing is an important aspect of being an active listener. Before answering a question you have asked, be sure to give teachers time to reflect and respond. For more tools and ideas about listening well, we often recommend that coaches look to Shane Safir's (2017) excellent book *The Listening Leader*, with resources such as the "Mindful Listening Tool" (see Web Resources at the end of this chapter).

### *Be Aware of Your Nonverbal Communication*

Smile, use some humor, or nod affirmatively when others make key points. Too often, coaches are so focused on their goals that they forget to carefully manage their own nonverbal communication (e.g., crossing their arms, frowning, tapping their foot, or otherwise signaling impatience). At times, we look as though we are beginning to think about our next response, a clear indication that we aren't actively listening. Try to maintain a positive or neutral physical presence as much as possible. This is just as (if not more) important virtually as it is in person. Sometimes taking notes during one-on-one and small-group conversations can help coaches to stay in active listening mode and note potential ideas without interrupting teachers. Be careful, however, because sometimes taking notes during a conversation can be a stressor for teachers. This is when it might be helpful to say something like, "I hope you don't mind. I'm just going to take a few notes to help myself hold on to and process our conversation. I'm more than happy to share my notes afterward." This kind of caveat can sometimes put an anxious educator at ease. Remember the old adage that though people may forget what you *said* to them, they always remember *how you made them feel* during the conversation. For a history of variations of this quote, see the article "They May Forget What You Said, but They Will Never Forget How You Made Them Feel" on QuoteInvestigator (see Web Resources at the end of this chapter). Your body language and words should ideally both be suggesting a sense of collaboration and open communication.

### *Use Effective Questioning Techniques*

Although questions are an important tool, be careful to not use them in ways that make conversations feel like interrogation sessions. Rather, they should be used to facilitate or co-construct understanding and build shared meaning so that everyone is on the same page. The following types of questions can be useful when holding conversations with individuals and groups.

- **Focus questions** can highlight the key points or issues in a discussion. They may be generated by the coach or the teacher and are often helpful at the outset of a coaching conversation. Focus questions or statements can also be helpful when a group has moved away from the topic being discussed and there is a need to get back to the intent of the conversation. Examples of focus questions include: "Let's think about the ways in which students were engaged in the lesson. What supported active learning?" and "Let's go back to the original goal of the lesson: In what ways can we make sure to include a follow-up writing assignment to show evidence of student learning?"

- **Clarifying and paraphrasing questions** are helpful for providing a clearer understanding of a teacher's instructional context, the topic being discussed, and testing assumptions. Examples of clarifying questions might include: "What texts are you using to introduce the unit on neighborhood helpers?" and "How many pages are students being asked to read in social studies from the newspaper article on immigration patterns in the early 1900s?" Educators should be able to answer these type of clarifying questions easily, without too much thinking. If anyone has to think too long and hard about a clarifying question, then the question is likely a probing question (see the next bullet point). Paraphrasing can also serve as a clarification tool used to refine thinking. Coaches sometimes use paraphrasing to mirror teachers' words and thoughts back to them in order to surface and check assumptions. Some examples of paraphrasing language include: "In other words, I hear you saying . . . Is that what you mean?" and "I want to be sure I understand—this is what I heard you saying. Is that accurate?"

- **Probing and elaboration questions** are those in which the coach is asking the teacher to say more about a topic, to expand on what was said, or to gently push the teacher to think more expansively about a topic. While clarifying questions help the coach or group of educators understand more about the teaching and learning context, probing questions are often designed to expand the educators' thinking. Probing questions are generally open-ended and elicit slower and often multiple responses. Excellent probing questions may not have ready or right answers, in which case it is important to help teachers understand that the point of the probing question is not to answer it as quickly as possible, but instead to hold on to it and consider it over time. Ultimately, one coaching goal might be to help support teachers in asking their own probing questions as a means of self-reflection. Examples of probing questions include:
    - "Can you say more?"
    - "You indicated students weren't as engaged as you had hoped—what is your hunch about why that might be happening?"
    - "What evidence would convince you that your students understand what you are trying to teach them?"

Such questions, while not always easily or quickly answered, lead to deeper teacher reflection and, ultimately, shifts in thinking and instruction. Over time, teachers can ask themselves these same types of questions, leading to more reflective and meaningful teaching and learning. To read more about crafting and using clarifying and probing questions, consult CLEE/SRI's *Pocket Guide to Probing Questions*, developed by Gene Thompson-Grove (see the Web Resources at the end of the chapter).

In Figure 4.1, we provide a summary of some dos and don'ts of effective communication. You might use this list to briefly reflect on your own communication skills and habits.

Carefully considering and crafting different questions, as described previously, is useful when facilitating both one-on-one and group discussions. While most coaches have no difficulty providing warm feedback to teachers, many experience difficulties

---

**Do:**
- Be an active listener.
- Listen for content and for feelings.
- Use wait time to give speakers opportunities to finish their statements.
- Be aware of your nonverbal communication patterns.
- Listen more than you speak.
- Use questions that are appropriate for the context.
- Use exploratory or focus questions to open the conversation.
- Use clarifying questions that lead to a clearer understanding of the topic or issue.
- Ask questions that invite elaboration.
- Ask probing (often open-ended) questions that extend and deepen the conversation.
- Use summary statements that help synthesize ideas and focus the conversation.
- Paraphrase and mirror others' words to check for understanding.
- Ask group participants for feedback about your message or to summarize what they heard.
- Be quick to praise and show appreciation.
- Find at least one aspect of the teacher's or group's work to praise in each session.
- Thank the teacher or group for their time, flexibility, efforts, and so on.
- Let teachers know what you learned from working with them.

**Don't:**
- Interrupt the speaker.
- Practice internally what you are planning to say in response (this can prevent active listening).
- Make snap judgments about the messages of others.
- Turn the discussion or conversation into a "blame game."
- Monopolize the conversation.
- Focus on what you personally would have done in a specific situation.

**FIGURE 4.1.** Dos and don'ts of effective communication.

when providing cool feedback designed to help a teacher or teachers understand where there is a mismatch between their goals and their instructional actions or where there is simply room for improvement and change. It's often difficult to address topics that might be hurtful; consider how hesitant we are to tell a friend that their outfit doesn't look good on them. Effective questioning can facilitate collaborative inquiry and move a group to deeper, more honest discourse, or as Benson and Fiarman (2020) put it in their excellent book *Unconscious Bias in Schools*, it lets us "move beyond the typical 'culture of nice' . . . to reach a 'culture of brave'" (p. 73).

Here we want to also note that coaches, while focusing on leaving teachers with positive feelings about coaching interactions, should not always end simply by confirming educators' past practices and assumptions. Rather, there should be ample opportunity in coaching sessions, often through skillful facilitating and questioning, for all participants (including coaches) to question their own and others' beliefs, assumptions, and practices. In some cases, coaching work may need to focus more on bolstering educators to keep tinkering and trying new instructional solutions, knowing full well that we are rarely able to *solve* instructional dilemmas completely or quickly. As McDonald et al. (2013) describe in their now classic facilitative book, *The Power of Protocols*, one of the goals of excellent facilitative work is to

> help educators sustain courage in the face of predictably chronic problems . . . The point [of facilitated conversations] is to gain the benefit of others' perspectives and thereby inform one's own, to draw on others' creative resources and thereby replenish one's own, and to experience in the process the encouraging effects of sharing one's burdens. (pp. 27–28)

For all those who coach and take on facilitative work in schools, particularly those interested in practicing different types of questioning, it is wise to study and have at your fingertips a wide variety of discussion-based protocols. We explore this idea further in the next section.

---

**STOP AND REFLECT**

As coaches, we need to be aware of how others interpret what we say and the impact it has on them. After holding a conversation with a teacher, think about the suggestions described in this chapter, and consider these questions: How successful were you in being an active listener? Were you able to elicit positive responses from the teacher in terms of moving forward (e.g., the teacher acknowledging that some of the decisions made would be helpful to their work)? Then consider, how might you improve the ways in which you communicate with teachers? Remember—this is a lifelong endeavor! We each will always have successful conversations, and there will always be times when we think, "I could have done better." Continual reflection and refinement is key.

## Discussion-Based Protocols as Critical Coaching Tools

Throughout this book, we reference discussion-based protocols; therefore, as part of this overview chapter on working with teachers and attending to coaching language, we want to elaborate on the nature and utility of these tools. Protocols can mean different things to different educators, but we think of them as an "agreed upon set of discussion or observation rules that guide coach/teacher/student work, discussion, and interactions" (Ippolito & Lieberman, 2020, p. 79). Importantly, some educators bristle at the term *protocols*, perhaps because they associate protocols with medical terminology or believe discussion-based protocols to be overly prescriptive. This can occur if educators are introduced to discussion-based protocols in inappropriate or slapdash ways. In such instances, we are careful to use different terminology—*structures, tools, routines,* or *agendas*. Ultimately, the terminology we use is not as important as the underlying principle that coaches who plan a structure for their coaching conversations *before* having the conversations often fare much better than those who simply try to navigate the conversation in the moment.

Protocols are sometimes deceptively simple, with just a handful of steps that ask a facilitator (i.e., coach) and teacher presenter or participant to work together to define, consider, and begin to solve an educational dilemma. Consider the steps in the classic Consultancy protocol (a CLEE/SRI resource developed by Faith Dunne, Paula Evans, and Gene Thompson-Grove), used as a tool for helping a group of teachers discuss a dilemma identified by one of their peers. The steps in this protocol are as follows:

1. A teacher describes a particular instructional dilemma or piece of work, ending with a focus question.
2. The coach and group ask clarifying questions (i.e., those that are factual and have clear answers to help a coach and group better understand the context).
3. The coach and group ask probing questions (i.e., those deeper questions that broaden thinking and do not have ready answers).
4. The presenter sits quietly while the coach and group discuss the matter at hand, mirroring back what they have heard and sometimes offering concrete suggestions for next steps.
5. Finally, the teacher or presenter is invited back into the conversation to have a "final word" before the entire group debriefs the conversation in order to improve the group's process (see the Web Resources at the end of the chapter).

Note that these simple steps are not so simple. Skilled facilitation is needed to help individuals and groups understand the power of each of these steps, negotiate the differences between clarifying and probing questions, and wring the most value out of brief conversations. What does this look like with groups versus one-on-one conversations between a coach and teacher? How and when do you move a group to the next question, step, or phase of a conversation? When might you shift gears entirely? What might you do when challenged by a group member publicly in the middle of a coaching session?

One of our favorite tools to help coaches consider what they might do in different real-life coaching situations, related to the use of protocols, is David Allen and Tina Blythe's "Facilitation Scenarios," hosted by CLEE/SRI (see Web Resources at the end of the chapter). These vignettes are focused specifically on the facilitation of professional learning community discussions; however, we have used these with all those who coach (as well as asked them to write their own) to help them reflect on their own larger set of facilitation skills.

Another consideration is the selection and creation of protocols and collaborative structures. In fact, often the most powerful protocols that coaches use are those that they create themselves, because they are authentic and specific to the school context. But it does take practice to be able to do this. Reviewing already published resources can help coaches learn more about how to create their own. On this point, we often recommend Allen and Blythe's (2004) *Facilitator's Book of Questions* and their companion book *Facilitating for Learning* (2015). Both books include a number of excellent resources for coaches thinking about the purpose of protocols and how to select, refine, and even design them. However, two of our other favorite freely available tools related to protocol selection are the *Guide to Using 7 of the Student Work Problem Solving Protocols* and the *Continuum of Discussion-Based Protocols* (see Web Resources at the end of this chapter). The *Guide*, revised by Gene Thompson-Grove, Amy Schuff, and Diane Leahy, is designed to help coaches consider which of the classic discussion-based protocols (e.g., consultancy, Issaquah, tuning, collaborative assessment conference, ATLAS [learning from student work], describing students' work, and charrette) might be most appropriate for a given coaching conversation. Note that each of these protocols is freely available at the CREE/SRI website (see Web Resources at the end of this chapter).

As always, the purpose of the conversation needs to drive the decision for which protocol or structure to use. The *Continuum*, designed by Jacy Ippolito, suggests that there are some protocols that are best introduced early to teachers because they help groups get to know one another as well as learn how protocols work. Two examples of these "early" protocols are the Microlab, with its focus on reflective writing and conversation in trios, and Compass Points, in which group members reflect on and share their own collaboration styles and preferences when entering a new group. Over time, as comfort levels and trust increase within a group, new protocols can be introduced that push everyone to share more of their own work, their students' work, and, eventually, their own deepest beliefs and values related to teaching and learning. For example, if sequenced and facilitated well, such a series of protocol-based discussions might help a group of educators dive down through Schein's (2010) three levels of culture discussed in Chapter 3 (e.g., artifacts, espoused values, and underlying assumptions). Specifically, this *Continuum* is important for the following reasons:

1. It helps those new to protocols consider the purposes and timing of when different protocols might be used. Hundreds of protocols can be downloaded and adapted from the CLEE/SRI website, the Harvard Graduate School of Education's Instructional Moves website focused on facilitating discussions, and Harvard's Project Zero Visible Thinking Routines repository (see Web Resources at the end this chapter). However, to the uninitiated, the long lists of protocols might seem overwhelming. Where do we start? The *Continuum* provides a reasonable guide.
2. The *Continuum* is important because we often see coaches and districts download and use the riskiest, most sophisticated protocols with brand-new groups of teachers, without consideration of first developing teachers' relational trust. When groups are asked to take risks that they aren't yet ready for, they (by and large) walk away frustrated, vulnerable, and disinclined to work with protocols again. The *Continuum* helps coaches make better decisions about which protocols might be best introduced early versus later in coaching work, given teacher comfort levels and experience.
3. The *Continuum* also maps onto our own Levels of Intensity model (introduced in Chapter 2), and can be a concrete way for coaches to consider how they might grow their own facilitation skills over time, as group comfort and levels of intensity increase.

A final caveat: The more closely a protocol relates to the needs and interests of teachers in a specific school, the more receptivity there will be to participating in structured discussions. Again, when protocols are seen as contrived or irrelevant, group members may see them as inauthentic and not useful. As a result, teachers will be less willing to participate.

## Coaching Activities for Developing Relationships with Individuals and Groups of Teachers

Many coaches, like Melinda, often wonder how they can promote teacher involvement in the coaching process, and often, they are encouraged to start by working with volunteers. Yet, according to Timperley (2008), volunteering does not necessarily lead to change. Timperley (2008) identifies two important questions that identify whether teachers will engage in a meaningful and deep way: Are they learning key content by participating in meaningful activities? And is there a rationale for the activities based on identified student needs (p. 16)? Meaningful engagement, in our view, begins with establishing a relationship of trust between coaches and teachers.

As literacy coach Shauna Magee mentions in the following Voices from the Field, and as we have mentioned previously (see Chapter 1), developing such relationships with teachers is foundational work for all who coach.

> **VOICES FROM THE FIELD**
>
> As an extension of our interactive read-aloud study group, teachers co-planned lessons and scheduled classroom observations. While I did the majority of observations and demonstrations, a few brave teachers opened up their classrooms to their colleagues to watch lessons. At the conclusion of the study group, a teacher who had been previously resistant to coaching approached me to ask about what she and I could focus on for a one-on-one coaching opportunity next year! Slowly but surely, people are becoming more comfortable talking about their teaching and watching each other teach.
>
> —Shauna Magee, Literacy Coach

Moreover, many instructional leaders who coach worry about working with so-called reluctant or resistant teachers. This is a legitimate concern, and all with coaching responsibilities have at times found themselves faced with a teacher hesitant to dive into a coaching relationship. However, we find that it does not help to frame the situation as "working with a resistant teacher." Instead of asking "What can I do to reach resistant teachers?" coaches might reframe and ask, "How can I encourage teachers to welcome me into their rooms? To respond in a positive way to my suggestions? To consult me when they are experiencing difficulties?" Always begin by asking yourself why a teacher might be hesitant to become involved in coaching. They may be dealing with personal issues (e.g., health, family), or there may be professional issues (e.g., lack of understanding about the non-evaluative nature of coaching). Ultimately, we view issues of resistance more as issues of trust and credibility, of consistency between coach and teacher beliefs about teaching and learning. Building any relationship takes time, and establishing a coaching partnership with teachers requires coaches to work slowly and thoughtfully in ways that are comfortable for the teachers being coached. Being able to demonstrate to teachers that you value their beliefs and respect the difficulties they face as classroom teachers can go a long way toward building strong coach–teacher relationships.

Although we certainly recognize that not all teachers will greet a coach with open arms, and that there will be varying degrees of receptivity to coaching, our rules of thumb are that coaches need to convince (i.e., show) teachers that they can provide valuable support and that differentiating the ways they approach teachers is key. Moreover, teacher receptivity often increases over time when coaches and principals are on the same page and working collaboratively to message that coaching is a critical part of everyone's ongoing professional learning (not simply for teachers who need help the most). In the following Voices from the Field, Linda DiMartino talks about how she works with teachers who may be somewhat hesitant to participate in coaching activities.

> **VOICES FROM THE FIELD**
>
> I sometimes encounter the challenge of veteran teachers who say, "I'm all set," as they figuratively shut the door. I am aware that change is difficult, and I respect the knowledge and experience they have acquired. Their years of experience speak volumes. The words "This is against my philosophy" ring loud in my ears. My approach in a situation like this is to offer a reflective statement, let them know that I hear and recognize how they feel. I provide more information, such as "Research shows that . . ." I tell the teacher that I would like to try something out, and I'd like to use his or her class as a trial run for a lesson. I place the focus on me and what I'm doing as a teacher. I ask for more opportunities to model lessons or co-plan as I work my way in. I verbalize the benefits of what I'm doing and focus on student work. I ask for questions or concerns to keep communication open and positive. I offer to get a unit or practice up and running and model the steps to success, while always maintaining a no-judgment stance. This approach works well, because the focus is not directly on the teacher.
>
> —LINDA DiMARTINO, Literacy Supervisor

What is evident in the way that Linda DiMartino works with a teacher is her respect for their views and experience, her willingness to try various coaching activities that may increase the teacher's receptivity, her focus on student learning, and ultimately, her willingness to keep trying. We think this is good advice for all coaches faced with nearly any issue that could be labeled as "resistance." Often, when teachers see the success that others are having, they become more willing to collaborate with coaches. This leads us to also suggest to coaches that sometimes the best way to manage resistance is to coach *around the resistance*. Focus on doing good work with more-willing teachers who may be on the same team or in the same department as the more-reluctant teacher. In this way, coaches can build credibility and slowly bring even the most reluctant teacher into the work by way of their teammates and colleagues. Additionally, remember that reluctance to engage in one particular coaching initiative or activity (e.g., coaching cycles) may not necessarily suggest hesitancy about all coaching activities—this might be a time to introduce a menu of services and suggest other less-intensive options. For more strategies focused on gaining entry into teachers' classrooms, we recommend the excellent research and writing of Jen Munson and Stephanie Saclarides, including their 2023 *Kappan* article "How Coaches Get In" (see Web Resources at the end of this chapter)

Be patient, be tenacious, and be flexible when building relationships with all teachers, and especially those who are somewhat reluctant to participate in coaching activities. Ultimately, our best advice about working with reluctant teachers is to become more diligent and deliberate in the ways you establish coaching relationships. Here we provide several ideas useful for all who coach, but especially for those new to a school or coaching role:

- **Explain your role.** As we have described before (Ippolito & Bean, 2024, pp. 119–136), coaching responsibilities can differ from school to school and year to year and thus are incredibly important to describe, both in codified role description documents and when chatting with teachers and leaders. Take the time to talk with teachers about what your role is and is not (e.g., with a teacher: "I'm not here to evaluate you in any way"; with a principal: "I'm so sorry, but I'm not able to substitute today because of my coaching caseload"). The best-case scenario is for the principal and coach together to discuss the coaching role with the whole school, and to share both a coaching role description and menu of services (see Ippolito & Bean, 2024 for examples).

- **Be available and accessible.** All coaches, especially those new to the school or to specific teachers, must make their presence known. Sitting with teachers at lunch, connecting in common spaces, posting your coaching calendar publicly (hard copy as well as digitally), and setting up a clear communication system (e.g., a Google Form for teachers to book time with the coach; a way for teachers to add themselves virtually to the coach's calendar) establishes the coaches' availability. Coaches often deploy a variety of strategies for managing their time. Some coaches hang a physical weekly calendar outside their office for teachers to sign up to meet with the coach. Others use virtual sign-ups, forms, and calendars. Still others ensure that coaching cycles with specific grade-level teams or departments are put on the calendar at the very beginning of the school year, to provide a general idea of where the coach will be spending dedicated time each month (while still allowing for flexibility day to day and week by week). Finally, in addition to all these options, holding open office hours on a weekly basis lets both teachers and leaders know when might be best to engage in an impromptu conversation. When receiving email or cell phone messages, effective coaches respond as quickly as possible, generally during the day they receive the message, while also still maintaining boundaries during evenings and weekends.

- **Be credible.** When making a commitment to a teacher, honor that commitment. For example, if you experience a schedule change, perhaps because of an unexpected but important meeting at the district office, teachers who are affected should be notified and informed of the reason, and every attempt should be made to reschedule as soon as possible. Also, keep to a minimum the number of times that you cancel appointments with teachers.

- **Begin immediately, but go slowly.** Coaches new to the role often ask what they are supposed to do in the beginning months of a coaching initiative, especially in September when teachers are busy organizing their classrooms and getting to know their students. As a coach, this is a great time to be helpful to teachers: Volunteer to find or develop resources for them, set up or refresh a professional resource room with books organized by level or genre, write one or two brief flyers describing several techniques or strategies that teachers might use in their classrooms at the beginning of the year (e.g., setting guidelines for small-group discussions, reviewing key classroom management techniques, introducing vocabulary routines, suggesting ways to learn more about students and their families). Volunteer to go into classrooms to get to know the students (e.g., in the elementary grades, volunteer to lead a read-aloud with each class with the caveat that the teacher remains in the classroom to observe students' participation; in a high school history class, volunteer to be a discussion leader for a small group working with document-based questions). Importantly, get to know the school and the teachers. Arrange to meet and have brief conversations with teachers about their students and their instructional goals. Figure 4.2 describes some ideas for these initial conversations.

---

Schedule a time to meet with each teacher individually in a comfortable situation and when it is convenient for the teacher to talk. Below is a suggested framework for the conversation.

**Breaking the ice.** Share with the teacher some information about yourself—your goals as a coach, your background (if new to the school). Talk with the teacher about their background and interests. Sometimes there are pictures of children, vacation trips, or pets that can spark a short conversation.

**Setting a goal.** Establish the reason why you are holding these conversations: Get to know the teacher's goals for the students; learn more about the students in the classroom and their strengths and needs.

**Suggested questions:**
- What are your goals for your students this year? (Think about broad goals related to curriculum.)
- What are the skills and abilities of students in terms of achieving the goals? What skills and knowledge do they bring to your classroom? Where might they experience some challenges?
- How can I help you learn more about your students?
- What strategies and approaches seem to work for you and help you achieve your goals?
- What resources would be helpful to you?
- In what ways can I be helpful?

---

**FIGURE 4.2.** Questions for an initial conversation with teachers. Adapted from Bean and Goatley (2021, p. 184). Copyright © 2021 The Guilford Press. Adapted by permission.

Even in the early stages of coaching, when developing a relationship of trust, coaches can begin helping teachers think more deeply about their work and help them tackle instructional issues. Most importantly, the nature and timing of coaching activities is perhaps the coach's best offense (and defense) when trying to overcome reluctance toward coaching. The type and timing of coaching activities should be carefully designed to build trust, credibility, and rapport. Moreover, as instructional coach Marsha Turner-Hall emphasizes in the following Voices from the Field, each individual teacher might need a slightly different sequence of coaching events and varying amounts of support.

> **VOICES FROM THE FIELD**
>
> A one-size-fits-all coaching model isn't effective for classroom teachers, nor does it work for instructional coaches. Coaching teachers is much more impactful when it occurs consistently throughout the year in various formats. I have found coaching support during professional learning community meetings and through one-on-one coaching sessions helpful. I have also found offering practice clinics useful. Practice clinics are brief (25–30 minute) professional development sessions when one specific instructional move is discussed, modeled, and practiced. Beyond the benefit of providing brief, more frequent professional development sessions, the value of the clinic lies in the majority of the session time being devoted to practice and feedback, the heart of improving instructional practices. Together, offering a variety of these coaching formats across the year results in the most growth in teachers' instructional practices.
> —Marsha Turner-Hall, Teacher and Instructional Coach

## High-Leverage Facilitative Coaching Moves

Finally, we end this chapter by sharing several high-leverage, low-risk, and low-intensity facilitative coaching moves. These moves all support coaches in building strong relationships with teachers and foundational coaching routines to then use again and again over time. Note, readers should consider variations on and different possible sequences for the activities described here to maximize success within specific school contexts (see also our Levels of Intensity model in Table 2.1).

### *Using an Agenda for Individual and Group Coaching Sessions*

While it may sound like a simple recommendation, so much good coaching work goes awry because the coach didn't plan and provide an agenda ahead of time. While agendas can be simple and flexible, by always showing up with a clear agenda to coaching sessions, the coach signals preparedness and planning. For one-on-one coaching sessions, a simple list of topics to discuss might be enough to carry the day. For small-group and certainly for larger-group coaching sessions, agendas are critical to success. We greatly appreciate Boudett and City's (2014) excellent resource guide *Meeting Wise* as an essential tool for helping coaches match purpose with specific facilitative steps in an agenda to meet that purpose. While Harvard's freely available *Meeting Wise* agenda template (see Web Resources at the end of this chapter) may be a bit overwhelming for one-on-one coaching sessions, it could be perfect for small-group and large-group meetings. Moreover, simply consider Boudett and City's (2014) 12 elements for a meeting (i.e., the *Meeting Wise* checklist); they can spur coaches to consider which elements they would like to include in a given coaching session. Agendas also allow coaches to introduce steps for a discussion-based protocol without using the word *protocol* and unnerving teachers who may be a bit reluctant to jump into formal protocol discussions (e.g., coaches can include warm and cool feedback steps, without necessarily naming it as a Tuning protocol). By using agendas consistently, coaches can help themselves and teachers make the most of their time together, which ultimately builds strong coach–teacher relationships.

## *Facilitating Initial Problem Solving*

During the day-to-day interactions that coaches have with teachers, specific questions may arise (e.g., "Would you take a look at Tamika's writing sample; I'm not sure what to make of her limited response?"). Teachers may stop by the coach's office to talk about an upcoming conference with a parent or ask the coach to look at test data from students' work with fractions. All these instances are great problem-solving opportunities for coaches and teachers (i.e., opportunities to think like a designer). Problem solving can serve as an initial step for developing a trusting relationship between coach and teacher. Moreover, when coaches and teachers work together collegially to solve a problem, they are engaged as professionals who recognize the complexity of teaching and learning dilemmas and the need for adaptive thinking related to individual students, individual classrooms, and their relationship to the larger grade level, content area, and school (thinking like a change agent). Many issues and concerns arise in schools that can serve as the basis for problem-solving discussions. These concerns might include the following:

- Student-based dilemmas (e.g., "I'm not sure how to help Joaquin, a new student who is having difficulty reading the biology textbook.")
- Curriculum- or instruction-based dilemmas (e.g., "As a world history teacher, I'm supposed to be introducing vocabulary in rich, robust ways; I'm just not sure how to do that.")
- Classroom environment or management dilemmas (e.g., "This class just doesn't seem to be able to work independently in math centers—any ideas?")

- Professional learning dilemmas (e.g., "I'd like to learn more about how to integrate technology into my teaching of writing—do you have any resources or suggestions?")
- Assessment dilemmas (e.g., "Here are the test results for the unit I taught on ecology. Students did well on the multiple-choice questions but really had difficulties answering open-ended questions. I'm wondering whether it relates to their knowledge of the subject or their difficulties with expressing themselves in writing. What are your thoughts about how to address this?")

> • • • • • • • • • • • **Put into Practice** • • • • • • • • • • •
>
> Think about each of the teacher concerns identified in this section. Select one and role-play a problem-solving conversation you might have with a teacher. You might ask a colleague to observe and provide feedback about your conversation.

## Co-Planning

Some teachers are comfortable sitting with a coach, looking at a lesson that is about to be taught, and discussing how modifications can be made for the students in their classrooms. By facilitating co-planning conversations, coaches position themselves to raise questions related to students: "Which of the suggested steps or procedures in this lesson might be problematic for all or some of your students?" "Which might not be necessary, given what your students bring to the lesson?" "What adaptations might be made in the lesson?" Questions relative to teacher comfort and understanding of how to teach the lesson can also be shared: "Is there anything in the lesson that seems confusing to you?" "Do you have the materials and resources you need to teach the lesson?" "How can I be helpful?" Co-planning can lead to coach observations of the lesson, co-teaching, or teacher–coach conversations about the success of the lesson. Part of the goal of co-planning is to support more in-depth coaching down the line. Essentially, it can be an initial step for developing a relationship of trust between coach and teacher. Remember, because you genuinely want to know, talk with the teacher after the lesson has been taught to get their reactions to what went well or whether there were any challenges. As part of co-planning conversations, teachers deserve a chance to share their feedback, both warm and cool.

## Facilitating Assessment and Data-Based Conversations

Often, coaches can help teachers by assisting with assessment tasks (e.g., screening or progress monitoring) required by the school. They can be part of a team of educators who enter the classroom to assess all students. Coaches can also discuss assessment results for instructional decision making, lead conversations about looking at student work, and facilitate larger grade-level or cross-grade (and content-focused) sessions in which larger samples of student work are analyzed for similarities and differences that might lead to new instructional decisions. Much more about data-focused coaching work is discussed in Chapter 7.

### *On-the-Fly Coaching*

In general, coaching work with teachers should be intentional, focused, and planned ahead of time (hint: this is partly why crafting agendas can be so helpful!). However, coaches should also certainly take advantage of coaching opportunities that arise spontaneously. Sometimes, teachers will mention an issue in an informal situation (e.g., at the copy machine, in the hallway, during lunch duty), and the coach can use the opportunity to talk briefly with this teacher and then schedule additional time to address the issue more fully. Be prepared to follow through on these serendipitous opportunities; they can often lead to further productive coaching experiences.

### *Making the Rounds (Informally)*

Visiting classrooms, informally and for short periods of time, with or without students present, can be incredibly beneficial for several reasons. Brief visits can lead to discussions about necessary resources or specific student needs. Teachers can become more comfortable with having a coach in their classrooms, and the visits might provide an impetus for more in-depth coaching with specific teachers. Such visits can be made before classes begin in the morning, after classes end in the afternoon, or sometimes during teachers' prep periods. One elementary coach made it a rule to see each teacher in the building at least once a week, stopping by before classes began and chatting informally about the students or the math program, being sure to ask whether she could be helpful in any way.

At the secondary level, coaches might rotate classroom visits, alternately focusing on teachers in a specific discipline or at a common grade level to learn more about how students respond to the disciplinary literacy instruction being used to enhance content learning. In elementary schools, coaches might visit during the literacy block, talking with students at their seats to get a better sense of what they are doing and whether they seem to understand the goals of instruction. Coaches can also work quietly with students who might be experiencing difficulties with a task. When visiting classrooms, we encourage coaches to establish a routine. The following questions might be helpful:

- What is the instructional environment in the room (e.g., evidence of student work, books, and other materials)?
- What are students doing, and can they talk about their work? (Do they

understand the task and reason for it? Are the activities meaningful ones, and are students engaged in their work?)
- What is the teacher doing to implement effective instruction (questioning, fostering peer-to-peer discussions, opportunities for feedback)?

When leaving the classroom, consider leaving a short note on the teacher's desk with a few positive comments about their teaching and their students (e.g., "I loved watching your students tackle that difficult question about the differences between 'equal' and 'equitable'"). As a coach, it might also be helpful to jot down a few notes or questions for later reflection about a particular teacher's instruction, or more generally, about the instruction of several teachers so you can analyze patterns across classrooms. Often these notes can indicate whether there are some common issues or even some common positives occurring across settings.

## *Facilitating or Participating in Group Meetings*

Schools host a wide variety of group meetings, from professional learning community (PLC) meetings, to data meetings, to grade-level team meetings, to instructional leadership team (ILT) meetings. All these meetings are generally scheduled on a routine basis, and they provide great opportunities for coaches to get to know individual teachers and how they function within groups. They also allow coaches to become working members of various teams, helping them to accomplish a specific task, establishing positive working relationships, and even generating possible follow-up coaching opportunities with individual teachers. Also, coaches can quickly tell which groups are working well as teams and which are experiencing difficulties. As one coach stated, "I love working with every grade-level team, except for the second-grade group. They spend their time complaining about their students, the materials they are using, and even the fact that the meeting is a waste of time!"

This team might benefit from creating community agreements for group work and then evaluating the use of those agreements at each meeting (for more on creating norms and community agreements, see Chapter 6 and Ippolito & Bean, 2024, pp. 240–241). These ideas provide coaches with multiple ways to develop relationships that promote openness and honesty. They also foster conversations in which coaches and teachers engage in meaningful discourse so they can identify preconceived views, understand the disconnects between those views and new learning, and apply what they have learned to inform instructional practice.

Once again, while the coaching activities reviewed thus far have all been shown to support both teacher and student learning, the sequencing and intensity of activities will necessarily vary depending on contextual factors. Moreover, the focus of individual versus group coaching meetings will often shift depending on coach and teacher needs. We delve into some of these differences in the next two chapters, where we specifically address individual and group coaching.

## Summary

In this chapter, we discussed the need for coaches to think and work as facilitators. We reviewed the importance of avoiding the expertise trap. We then examined the power of language in coaching work and identified key notions about how coaches can use language effectively in working with both individuals and groups of teachers. We also described the value of discussion-based protocols and gave some examples of those that might be useful in coaching work. Finally, we identified facilitative ideas for working with teachers to establish a relationship of trust. We elaborate on many of these ideas, providing further examples, in the next two chapters: working with individuals (Chapter 5) and working with groups (Chapter 6).

As Melinda began to consider her own experiences in meetings and working with groups of teachers, she was comforted to remember that facilitators don't need to have all the answers; rather, they are charged with supporting adult learning and collaboration. As she reviewed a number of discussion-based protocols and agenda examples, she became less nervous about her own areas of expertise and growing edges. In fact, she was now more excited about the ways in which she might be able to support her colleagues in growing their own practices. For her, thinking like a facilitator began to shift her mindset away from her own knowledge base and toward building a sense of collaborative inquiry and problem solving.

## Reflections

- Using the chart found in Appendix A, note ways that coaches can function as change agents, facilitators, designers, and advocates when attempting to develop a relationship of trust between themselves and the teachers with whom they work. Which activities might you consider adopting that would further these ways of thinking and working?
- When thinking about your own experiences participating in school-based groups and meetings, when have you experienced excellent facilitation? What factors contributed to the group's and/or meeting's success? What moves did the facilitator make that kept student learning and work front and center?
- As you reflect on the chapter, which of your own facilitative skills are you most excited to grow (e.g., more intentional use of questioning and coaching language, use of discussion-based protocols, design and use of agendas, and so on)?

## Activities

1. Download and review one of the protocols described in this chapter. Talk with a colleague about its potential for facilitating conversations with teachers. When would you use it? What benefits do you see in its use? Any concerns? As a next step, use one of the protocols with a group of teachers, and seek their feedback about the ways in which the protocol helped the discussion.
2. Partner with a coaching colleague, with each of you using one of the prompts listed below. The other person should serve as facilitator, asking questions that move the conversation along. Tape this short three- to five-minute conversation. Then go back and analyze the type of questioning that was used to facilitate the conversation. You may generate your own prompts, but here are a few to get you started:
   a. Talk about a recent trip you have taken, what you enjoyed, and any unusual experiences you had.
   b. Talk about a book you read recently, your views about it, and why you would or would not suggest reading it.
   c. Talk about one of your favorite hobbies, how you became interested in it, what your goals are, and so on.

### FURTHER READINGS AND RESOURCES

**Print Resources**

Allen, D., & Blythe, T. (2018). Aesthetics of facilitation: Cultivating teacher leadership. *International Journal of Teacher Leadership, 9*(2), 48–68.

Allen, D., Blythe, T., Dichter, A., & Lynch, T. (2018). *Protocols in the classroom: Tools to help students read, write, think, & collaborate.* Teachers College Press.

Blythe, T., Allen, D., & Powell, B. S. (2015). *Looking together at student work* (3rd ed.). Teachers College Press.

Bocala, C., & Holman, R. R. (2021). Coaching for equity demands deeper dialogue. *Educational Leadership, 78*(6), 66–71.

Boudett, K. P., & City, E. A. (2014). *Meeting wise: Making the most of collaborative time for educators.* Harvard Education Press.

Ippolito, J., & Bean, R. M. (2024). A reminder: All coaching is mediated and supported by language. In J. Ippolito & R. M. Bean, *The power of instructional coaching in context: A systems view for aligning content and coaching* (pp. 136–143). Guilford Press.

Jacobs, J., Boardman, A., Potvin, A., & Wang, C. (2018). Understanding teacher resistance to instructional coaching. *Professional Development in Education, 44*(5), 690–703.

Kaner, S. (2014). *Facilitator's guide to participatory decision-making* (3rd ed.). Jossey-Bass.

McDonald, J. P., Zydney, J. M., Dichter, A., & McDonald, E. C. (2012). *Going online with protocols: New tools for teaching and learning.* Teachers College Press.

Pierce, J. D. (2019). How good coaches build alliance with teachers. *Educational Leadership, 77*(3), 78–82.

Robertson, D. A., Ford-Connors, E., Frahm, T., Bock, K., & Paratore, J. R. (2020a). Unpacking productive coaching interactions: Identifying coaching approaches that support instructional uptake. *Professional Development in Education, 46*(3), 405–423.

Van Soelen, T. M. (2021). *Meeting goals: Protocols for leading effective, purpose-driven discussion in schools.* Solution Tree Press.

**Web Resources (see www.guilford.com/bean3-materials for live links)**

Center for Leadership & Educational Equity and the School Reform Initiative. (2024). *Consultancy.* www.clee.org/resources/consultancy

Center for Leadership & Educational Equity and the School Reform Initiative. (2024). *Continuum of discussion-based protocols.* www.clee.org/resources/continuum-of-discussion-based-protocols

Center for Leadership & Educational Equity and the School Reform Initiative. (2024). *Facilitation scenarios activity.* www.clee.org/resources/facilitation-scenarios-activity

Center for Leadership & Educational Equity and the School Reform Initiative. (2024). *Guide for using 7 of the student work problem solving protocols.* www.clee.org/resources/guide-to-using-7-of-the-student-work-problem-solving-protocols

Center for Leadership & Educational Equity and the School Reform Initiative. (2024). *Pocket guide to probing questions.* www.clee.org/resources/pocket-guide-to-probing-questions

Center for Leadership & Educational Equity and the School Reform Initiative. (2024). *Protocols.* www.clee.org/resources

Harvard Graduate School of Education. (n.d.). *Facilitating discussions.* Instructional Moves. http://instructionalmoves.gse.harvard.edu/facilitating-discussions

Harvard University. (n.d.). *Meeting Wise resources.* DataWise. http://datawise.gse.harvard.edu/meeting-wise-resources

Munson, J., & Saclarides, S. (2023). How coaches get in. *Kappan.* http://kappanonline.org/how-academic-coaches-get-access-munson

Project Zero. (n.d.). *Project Zero's Thinking Routine Toolbox.* Harvard Graduate School of Education. http://pz.harvard.edu/thinking-routines

Quoteresearch. (2014). *They may forget what you said, but they will never forget how you made them feel.* Quote Investigator. http://quoteinvestigator.com/2014/04/06/they-feel

Safir, S. (2024). Listening leadership tools. http://shanesafir.com/resources

Thompson-Grove, G. (2024). *Pocket Guide to Probing Questions.* School Reform Initiative. www.newenglandssc.org/wp-content/uploads/2016/11/Pocket-Guide-to-Probing-Questions.pdf

# CHAPTER 5

# Working with Individual Teachers to Analyze and Transform Practice

> ### GUIDING QUESTIONS
>
> 1. What is the rationale for coaching individual teachers?
> 2. What are key guidelines for using the coaching activities of modeling, co-teaching, and observing?
> 3. In what ways do coaches think like designers and facilitators when working with individual teachers?
> 4. In what ways can coaches facilitate post-observation conversations so that they encourage teacher inquiry and problem solving?

## Melinda Begins to Work with Teachers One-on-One

When Melinda stopped by the classroom of one of the third-grade teachers in her school, she saw Janice peering at the new math curriculum's teacher guide and shaking her head. She looked at Melinda and said, "There's just too much in here. I don't know where to begin. Help!" Melinda rightly recognized this as an important "coaching moment," a time to both build a stronger relationship with Janice and provide the just-in-time support her new role was designed to offer. However, Melinda wondered about the most productive way to start. Should she volunteer to sit with Janice and co-plan the next few instructional lessons? Should she take more time to observe in Janice's classroom to gain a better sense of the students and their needs? How could she strike a balance between providing support and not overstepping?

Working with individual teachers is, for many, the heart of coaching. It facilitates teachers' professional learning in ways that help them become reflective problem solvers who address instructional dilemmas as design problems. In this chapter, we describe activities specific to analyzing and transforming the instructional practices of individual teachers (Levels 2 and 3 of our Levels of Intensity; see Chapter 2). To illustrate what we mean by an "observation cycle of coaching," we include a vignette of a coach and teacher working together during each step of the cycle. We conclude by discussing post-observation conversations as a means of developing teacher inquiry and problem solving.

## Powerful Ways of Coaching Individual Teachers

In some ways, coaching in schools is similar to coaching sports—attempting to teach specific technical skills and, in team sports, encouraging and motivating individuals to work together. Coaching in schools also requires a focus on developing technical skills and on encouraging teachers to work as a team. However, coaching in schools is somewhat different from coaching on the field. Specifically, the key roles of the instructional coach are to facilitate teachers' reflective thinking and help them analyze their own instructional practices, generate ideas for how to address instructional issues, and grow as professionals to *then* support their own students (a layer of learning and focus less common in sports coaching). Coaches provide another set of eyes and ears, helping teachers move outside their comfort zone to better support their students. Given that quality teaching makes a difference in student learning (Opper, 2019), investing in learning experiences that help teachers think about, analyze, and transform their practice is a key part of a school's comprehensive teaching and learning plan.

Moreover, emerging research has begun to inform our thinking about the most powerful ways for coaches to engage with both groups of teachers and individuals (Gibbons & Cobb, 2017). While a number of coaching activities have been reviewed for efficacy, two coaching practices related to working with individuals have surfaced as particularly effective: modeling instruction and co-teaching. Therefore, in the following sections, we describe these individual coaching activities (as well as others that are "potentially productive" [Gibbons & Cobb, 2017]) wherein coaches have some of the best opportunities to help teachers analyze and transform their instructional practices.

Across these activities, coaches must think like designers (about content) and like facilitators (about coaching processes). By reflecting with teachers about design problems, we focus on how a lesson could better meet student needs (rather than highlighting "what went wrong"). Framing issues as design problems resonates with teachers who, as professionals, can reflect on what they already know, need to learn, and need to do to improve instruction for their students. In terms of facilitation, coaches need to consider how much direction or guidance is necessary to enhance teacher problem solving and reflectivity. Is it better to co-plan with the teacher, co-teach, watch the teacher in action, or model? Furthermore, it is often important for coaches to consider how they might layer and sequence different coaching activities to provide a fuller menu of professional learning experiences that solidify teacher thinking and action.

Although there are many coaching activities that support one-on-one work with teachers, an important point to remember is that changes, whether in performance or beliefs, require intentionality and planning and often necessitate ongoing interactions with a single teacher. Across the literature the notion of "coaching cycles" is frequently used to describe coaches' one-on-one work with teachers. These coaching cycles may occur over a set period of time (e.g., anywhere from a few meetings to a number of meetings across a handful of weeks). They, of course, include coach–teacher conversations, as well as various coaching activities such as modeling, co-teaching, observing, and so forth, described in this chapter. For example, a coaching cycle might include an initial conversation with a teacher that results in the coach modeling a specific strategy in the classroom, followed by a debriefing conversation, a follow-up observation of the teacher implementing that same strategy, and another debriefing conversation. But other variations in coaching cycles are possible, depending on various factors (e.g., student needs; teacher choice, knowledge, and skill). In other words, we think of coaching cycles simply as a series of coach–teacher connections that are intentionally planned, not random or ad hoc, to support teacher inquiry and refinement in instruction. They require coaches to think and act like designers as they craft cycles that meet the specific needs of individuals with whom they are working.

For instance, a coach might begin by modeling ("I teach"), move to co-planning or co-teaching ("we co-plan and co-teach"), and then progress to observing ("you teach") to see and support the teacher applying what has been learned from the previous activities. Although such a continuum can be useful, this full sequence may not always be possible or necessary. For example, a coach might first observe and then decide upon next steps, perhaps modeling or co-teaching. With another teacher, the coach might model and then observe, skipping the co-teaching altogether. Coaching strategies can and should differ based on several factors, including students' needs, teacher experience and receptivity to coaching, and the multiple time challenges that coaches and teachers face when trying to engage in adult collaborative work during the school day. In the following Voices from the Field, instructional coach Marsha Turner-Hall describes the ways in which she worked with an experienced teacher who was initially somewhat resistant to schoolwide efforts to change literacy instruction. We then delve into three specific coaching activities (modeling, co-teaching, and observing), suggesting guidelines for each activity.

> **VOICES FROM THE FIELD**
>
> Throughout the course of the school year, a classroom teacher participated in my classroom "learning lab" and expressed her surprise at the depth of the students' conversations, some of whom were in her classroom the prior year! Soon after, I modeled a literacy lesson in her classroom, in which students began practicing skills similar to what we had observed in the learning lab. The classroom teacher was amazed at what the majority of her students were able to do. After a little encouragement and support, she agreed to co-teach a literacy lesson with me. During this lesson, the classroom teacher would catch herself, look over at me, and laugh, knowing that she was saying or doing what we were trying to change. She explained to her students that she was learning something new and that it was hard!
>
> —Marsha Turner-Hall, Teacher and Instructional Coach

As you read about the suggested coaching activities that follow, think back to Marsha Turner-Hall's experience described in Voices from the Field and consider how she layered different coaching moves to support this classroom teacher over time. Think also about Melinda and how she might use the following activities in her work with teachers.

## Modeling

Many of us need to see something before we understand it, let alone before we can do it ourselves. That's why instructors show us how to do something, or we watch videos to see how something is done. The coach who models instruction provides a visual example that often helps teachers reach an aha moment. Modeling is helpful when a practice is new to teachers, when a practice is complex, or when teachers remain uncertain about how to implement a specific strategy after an initial introduction. Modeling is also a powerful coaching move to make when teachers are unsure of whether a particular practice will work for their students, or when teachers are having specific difficulties with implementation. Guidelines for modeling follow (adapted from Bean & Goatley, 2021).

### *Establish Goals*

Talk with the teacher about the goals for the modeled lesson. What are the expected outcomes for students? What are the goals for the teacher (the teacher's expectations for learning)? Be sure the modeling is focused—for example, the coach could agree to model for a second-grade teacher how to use strategies for helping students who continue to struggle with decoding multisyllabic words.

### *Involve Teachers as You Model*

In a modeled lesson, the teacher can assist in management of the lesson, distributing materials and manipulatives, redirecting students, and so on. Teachers can also monitor the work of specific students, especially those who may have some difficulties with the lesson content. If students spend some time working in small groups, the teacher can work with one group while the coach works with another. The teacher and coach can also agree upon some "look-fors," and teachers can record their observations and questions on a tool similar to the one in Appendix B.

### *Talk and Reflect with the Teacher Soon after the Lesson*

Were goals achieved? If not, why? The fact that some goals may not have been achieved is often a great talking point. No coach is perfect! Each student group is different, and it is important for teachers to recognize that coaches aren't perfect. Both teachers and coaches can learn a great deal by discussing challenges, and teachers often breathe a sigh of relief when they see that coaches too can experience teaching dilemmas.

### *Follow Up*

What are the next steps? Do you move to co-teaching? Should the teacher now try to use what has been learned and then talk with you as the coach? Together, the coach and teacher can make decisions about activities that make the most sense.

### *A Few Cautions*

While modeling is a powerful coaching activity, there are a few cautions to consider when modeling or demonstrating. First, teachers can become reliant on modeling—they may be very willing for *you* to model, but they don't necessarily want you to watch *them* teach. To avoid this very understandable scenario, it is important to establish some ground rules up front, so that teachers can expect only a certain amount of coach modeling before they leap back into the lead instructor position.

Second, when you return to observe in the teacher's classroom, you may see very little application of what was originally modeled showing up in classroom instruction. There may be several reasons for this. Teachers may not have fully understood or valued what was modeled, or perhaps they worry that they cannot replicate what the coach modeled. This is an opportunity for a conversation. Talk with the teacher about what additional supports might be needed. Perhaps there are additional possibilities for improving classroom instruction that could act as bridges to the target practice. Keep asking the teacher what might help them the most. For example, instead of modeling again, the two of you might co-plan the lesson or co-teach it.

A third caution: The experienced teacher may be less receptive to modeling than the novice who appreciates seeing a specific strategy or approach in action. The experienced teacher, on the other hand, may be somewhat resentful about being told or shown how to teach. In fact, the savvy coach is always attending to power dynamics within coaching work, particularly when age, seniority, or power imbalances are in play (Rainville & Jones, 2008; Roberston et al., 2020b). At the same time, in our work with teachers, we note that they identified modeling as the most valuable activity. Likewise, modeling has also been recently highlighted as one of the most powerfully productive coaching moves with individual teachers (Gibbons & Cobb, 2017). Modeling, then, can be useful, but as with all coaching activities, decisions about when, how, with whom, and for how long are important to consider, with special attention to the content being taught and the larger school context within which both coaches and teachers are working.

> • • • • • • • • • **Put into Practice** • • • • • • • • • •
>
> Ask a teacher if you can model a specific instructional strategy or approach in their classroom to learn more about their students and how they respond to the strategy being modeled (in a pre-observation conversation, identify the purpose and teacher activities for the modeled lesson). Hold a debriefing conversation with the teacher to discuss the lesson, reflecting on what made the modeling experience a valuable one. What might you, as a coach, do differently next time?

## Co-Teaching

Co-teaching is often considered a bridge between modeling and observing—a bridge that can lead in either direction, with either the modeling or observing coming first. Co-teaching is not always necessary, but it is useful in many ways. First, it promotes teachers and coaches working together as colleagues to address a particular instructional dilemma or focal area. Coaches can use co-teaching to learn more about teachers' planning and teaching processes, as well as develop a better understanding of teachers' beliefs, values, and content knowledge. Second, co-teaching helps coaches and teachers to continue building the trusting and collaborative relationships that are so important to coaching work. Sometimes co-teaching is even seen as less threatening than the coach simply observing in the classroom. Third, coaches can learn much about the students in teachers' classrooms, to gain a better sense of what they need to be successful learners. Co-teaching, in essence, helps to establish the coach as a partner in the teaching experience.

Additionally, some coaches (whether coaching is their full-time or part-time role) may be assigned instructional responsibilities; therefore, co-teaching may be an important way to directly support students as well as continue to build credibility and keep honing their own teaching skills. Many full- and part-time coaches take on some teaching responsibilities for part of the day, whether whole-class, small-group, or supporting individuals as part of intervention work. Further, some specialists, interventionists, or special educators working within a multi-tiered system of support may be responsible for both providing coaching support to colleagues and also providing tier 2 interventions for students in classrooms. In a recent U.S. national survey of specialized literacy professionals, for example, we found (as expected) that many respondents, even those who did not specifically identify as coaches, had various coaching responsibilities (Bean et al., 2024). Thus, adopting a co-teaching model allows teachers, specialists, and coaches opportunities to support and learn from each other. In the points that follow, we share some possible approaches to co-teaching.

### *Teaching and Assisting/Monitoring*

In this scenario, one educator acts as the lead teacher, presenting a lesson (e.g., teaching ratios, a phonics lesson, or a specific note-taking strategy in a history lesson). The second educator serves as a monitor, observing and supporting students as they work. The coach or classroom teacher could assume either role, depending on whether coach modeling or coach observing/supporting is desired. For example, in the early grades, when students are being asked to practice blending and segmenting words using letter tiles, the educator in the monitor role could quickly and efficiently provide needed support. In the later grades, especially with project-based content-area learning, having two educators in the classroom can be quite helpful. For example, after a middle school social studies teacher introduces a text set including a variety of primary sources related to the American Revolution, a coach could assist individuals or small groups of students in beginning to close-read the primary sources and take notes, perhaps as part of a larger interdisciplinary research-writing project.

### *Parallel Teaching*

In this scenario, both teacher and coach are responsible for teaching the same lesson to a small group of students in the classroom. Each educator differentiates instruction by providing more or less scaffolding or modifying instructional techniques (e.g., in one group, students read segments of the selection silently, stopping to discuss at specific points; in the other group, students read aloud to a partner). Given the smaller number of students in the group, there is more opportunity to focus on students' individual needs and to modify the lesson. This would work well with other disciplines, for example, in math classes, given that some students need additional scaffolding, more direct instruction, and/or practice.

### *Station Teaching*

In this scenario, students are learning at centers or stations, and the coach and teacher develop goals and activities for specific stations. In a middle school science classroom, for example, there may be four stations, and students rotate from one to another during an extended block of time to experience hands-on learning coupled with a variety of reading, writing, and mathematical/scientific tasks. While some students might be working independently at writing and reading stations, the teacher at the third station might be working with a group on content-area vocabulary activities specific to a textbook chapter focused on cell biology. Meanwhile, the coach might be working at the fourth station with a small group, supporting students' use of microscopes and diagramming cell structures in their science journals.

### *Turn Taking or Team Teaching*

The teacher and coach plan a lesson that requires each of them to assume teaching responsibility in the lesson. In some cases, there may be turn taking. For example, the coach might introduce and explain a vocabulary word, using the notion of student-friendly definitions (Beck et al., 2013); the teacher might do the same with another word. There may also be more sophisticated uses of team teaching, where both teachers introduce concepts and then lead students through the various steps of a lesson (e.g., reviewing different ways to consider and convert fractions into decimals or percentages). Some colleagues have indicated that this sort of teaching works best when coaches and teachers know each other and their styles well. In the words of one coach, "I can finish the sentence of my teaching partner."

### *Final Thoughts on Co-Teaching*

Co-teaching might also be used as an optional or ad hoc coaching activity, perhaps focused on helping a teacher understand how to implement a specific new instructional strategy or approach. In one situation, three days a week for a month, a coach and teacher taught together during the elementary math block; the teacher had been transferred from the middle school to the elementary grades and was still making sense of the transition. According to the coach, the time was well spent because the teacher, by the end of the month, was able to effectively manage the entire extended math block independently (i.e., more easily toggling between whole-group, small-group, and independent practice chunks of the lesson).

At the secondary level, co-teaching might be an effective way of helping content-area teachers as they learn to use various disciplinary literacy strategies appropriate for developing students' content knowledge. The coach and teacher can co-plan and then co-teach a lesson in which students are asked to work collaboratively in small groups. This provides ample opportunities for coaches to learn more about discipline-specific content and habits of mind (e.g., in a chemistry class, how to think about similarities and differences between covalent versus ionic bonds), while the classroom teacher learns more about literacy- and strategy-focused instruction (e.g., modeling word-learning strategies in dense, technical texts). Again, the key to successful co-teaching is for the coach to reflect with the teacher after the lesson to discuss its effectiveness, talk about what each educator learned about their own instructional practice, and note the effects for students to unearth next steps for instructional refinement.

> • • • • • • • • • • • **Put into Practice** • • • • • • • • • • • •
>
> Ask a teacher with whom you are working if you can co-teach with them. Think about which of the co-teaching configurations described earlier might work best and plan the lesson with the teacher. After co-teaching the lesson, take time to talk about what went well and what might be improved. Possible questions to discuss include the following:
>
> - Were the students able to achieve the goals of the lesson?
> - Did co-teaching lead to more student engagement in the lesson?
> - In what ways did co-teaching contribute to those goals?
> - What worked effectively? What changes might be made?

## Observing

Observing teachers as they work with students provides information about whether teachers can "walk the talk." That is, to what extent can teachers use specific strategies or approaches, manage classrooms, or provide a classroom environment to support learning? Periodic observations can help coaches pinpoint what feedback would be helpful to individual teachers in making changes in their instruction. Sometimes observations can be useful when coaches want to learn more about specific students who may be experiencing difficulties (e.g., engaging in lessons, responding to various levels of questions, and so forth). Teachers often appreciate it when coaches are focusing their attention on student learning rather than on their teaching. At times, observations may be used to determine the extent to which a specific strategy or instructional approach is being implemented appropriately in classrooms.

For example, a coach might observe in all fifth-grade classrooms to get a better sense of how teachers are implementing a newly adopted writing curriculum. Results of the observations can help coaches plan for upcoming large- and small-group, coach-led professional learning. Also, observations may be used as a follow-up after modeling or co-teaching sessions to support teachers in their efforts to transform their instruction. Coaches may also observe in classrooms where student performance, perhaps on progress-monitoring tests, has been low and there is a need to gain a better sense of the instruction in that classroom. Here we present some key notions about observing.

### *Observations Should Assist in Improving Instruction*

Coaching observations are not conducted for evaluation purposes, and results are not to be shared with principals or supervisors. What coaches see, and the feedback they offer, should be confidential and shared only with the teacher being observed. In fact, we suggest that coaches closely monitor the ways in which they observe to de-emphasize any potential evaluative messages. To what extent does the coach focus on describing rather than evaluating or making judgments about what they see? We encourage coaches to observe in a descriptive mode, taking low-inference notes (taking note of what is happening and sharing it with teachers, without adding any inferences or value judgments/statements). Note this example:

> A 10th-grade history teacher, during a lesson, asks individual students to read aloud paragraphs of a specific chapter in the textbook one at a time (i.e., round-robin reading). This goes on for the entire period. The coach, in a debriefing conversation, is careful to stay in "descriptive mode," describing the activity and lack of student attention in purely factual terms. For example, the coach might say, "During a 15-minute reading time, eight students were called upon to read. Each student read for less than two minutes. Seven other students were observed reading something other than the textbook or looking at other papers on their desks. Twelve additional students were observed interacting with each other, nonverbally or quietly, but not with the text." The coach is cautious not to immediately criticize such round-robin reading as an instructional practice. Instead, when the teacher indicates that the students can't read the book on their own as a rationale for asking students to read aloud, the coach could suggest some other research-based alternatives to round-robin reading, such as partner reading, that might be more effective. The coach might also volunteer to model or co-teach a lesson using such a practice.

### *A One-Time Observation Is Just a Snapshot*

An observation reflects just one moment in time of both teachers' and students' actions. Many things can affect what is seen: the topic or skill being taught, the behavior of a specific student during one particular point in time, activities going on in the school (e.g., a pep rally later that day), and so on. Also, the coach doesn't have as much information as the teacher about the purpose of the lesson, particular classroom dynamics, or the attributes of specific students that may affect instruction. Thus, pre-observation conversations help coaches obtain a better understanding of the lesson's context.

Working with Individual Teachers

> **STOP AND REFLECT**
>
> Before we unpack the observation cycle, take a few moments to reflect on the activities that you use as part of your coaching repertoire. Which activities are most comfortable for you? For the teachers whom you support? In what ways do you think you can improve your coaching practices, and how would you start? (Consider whether you might want to talk with some of your coaching colleagues as you reflect on these questions.)

## Unpacking the Observation Cycle

Implicit in much of what we have written so far is the foundational observation cycle that many coaches use across all of their activities and work. Remember, the observation cycle we outline here is just one specific, intensive example of the larger category of "coaching cycles" that all who coach might design and engage in (see Figure 5.1).

We recognize that both coaches' and teachers' schedules may limit the degree to which coaches can implement this cycle fully; further, it may not be necessary to go through the entire cycle for all observations. When working with a single teacher over time, the pre-observation conversation (often used for planning) can occur during the post-observation conversation (i.e., teachers and coaches can plan what to do next). In the sections that follow, we discuss the four steps in more depth, illustrating the work of a fictional elementary instructional coach (Paul) and a fourth-grade teacher

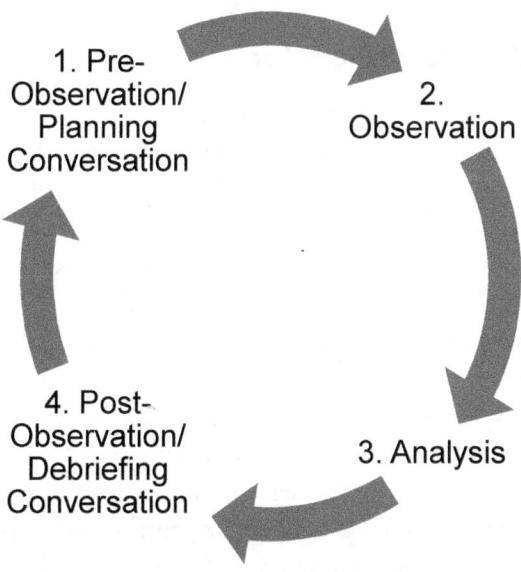

**FIGURE 5.1.** The observation cycle.

(Maria) through a series of vignettes revealing their interactions during each phase of the process (note: while Paul and Maria are fictional, they have been created as "composite" cases from multiple coaches and teachers with whom we have worked in the past). We begin with an example, which sets the context for the observation. Think about yourself as the coach and how you might move through this observation cycle.

> **PAUL AND MARIA:**
> **PRE-OBSERVATION/PLANNING CONVERSATION**
>
> The Miller Elementary School recently reviewed and changed its K–5 literacy curriculum. In the early grades, there are now many opportunities for direct instruction in phonics as well as plenty of authentic language, reading, and writing opportunities. In the later elementary grades (fourth and fifth), classroom teachers are piloting vocabulary, fluency, and comprehension instructional practices across all disciplines, helping students to prepare for a disciplinary literacy-focused curriculum in middle school and high school.
>
> Maria, a new fourth-grade teacher, was having difficulty understanding how to explicitly teach vocabulary within her science units. She asked Paul, her building's K–5 coach, if he would observe a lesson and provide her with feedback. As they finished their initial planning conversation, Paul reminded Maria that he would be taking notes during the observation to help him remember important points. He also encouraged Maria to reflect on the lesson and jot down a few thoughts and questions immediately after teaching. Paul and Maria then agreed on both a time for Paul to observe, and a time for the pair to debrief the following day.

### *Pre-Observation/Planning Conversation*

The goal of meeting with a teacher before an observation is to develop a focus or goal for that observation and possible subsequent coaching conversations. Because Maria requested the observation and identified the focus, most likely the post-observation conversation and follow-up will be positive. In other instances, the coach may be the one to suggest the observation and the focus, such as observing a specific strategy required by the school or conducting a routine observation to see teachers' implementation of a newly adopted core curriculum. At times, the coach and teacher together may decide on the focus. What is important is that *there is a focus*. Trying to observe all that is going on in a classroom during a single lesson is difficult (if not impossible). This pre-observation conversation can also serve to reinforce the notion that the coach and teacher are co-learners and have the same goal or focus in mind. The teacher and coach can also talk about the protocol to be used for taking notes, if any are to be taken. This conversation does not have to be lengthy, especially if the teacher and coach have participated in an observation cycle previously.

## Observation

Before observing, the coach, perhaps with the teacher, should develop or select a tool or strategy for collecting data as a source of evidence for discussion after the observation. Coaches may design or propose a particular protocol (e.g., a checklist, a rubric, or even an open-ended procedure). We review each method briefly here:

- Checklists that include a scale can be useful (e.g., a three-point scale ranging from "evident to some degree" to "not all all"). Such checklists provide coaches with direction and enable them to be consistent in how they think about what they see. A coach may choose to address only one or two sections of the checklist if a specific focus has been selected. Alternatively, coaches and teachers may jointly develop or select a checklist and scale that is aligned with a particular instructional strategy (e.g., the school has selected a systematic decoding strategy to be used in each first-grade classroom, and coaches have developed a checklist to remind teachers of the various steps). Or, for example, a template that addresses only one aspect of a specific initiative or program could be used (e.g., expectations for encouraging active engagement and high-level thinking during a discussion). Appendix C provides an example of a checklist that could be used for observing in content-area classes (adapted from Bean & Goatley, 2021, pp. 195–197). Note how the observation tool addresses three specific areas: classroom environment, instruction, and engagement.

- Descriptive or scripting approaches are also helpful. Coaches using this approach write down as much as they can of both the teacher's and students' words and actions. An important advantage of this system for coding an observation is that results can be shared with teachers to provide evidence of what the teacher and students said or did. Thus, in many ways, this type of coding can be more objective than checklists. Data from the notes can be readily used to describe what went on in the lesson and identify discussion topics. Some guidelines that may help when using a descriptive approach follow (see the example in Figure 5.2):
    - Develop abbreviations or create symbols to represent words (e.g., "OB" for "observed," "NE" for "not engaged," "OC" for "observer comments").
    - Use a T-Chart to indicate the teacher's and students' words and actions.
    - Draw a line to indicate a change in activities or a specific time period (e.g., draw a new line after every five minutes).

Often, teachers who see the results of this sort of observation are amazed, surprised, or stunned. For example, sometimes they don't realize how much talking they do during class, while others are pleased to see improvements in areas they've been working on in their instruction. This type of data lends itself well to a descriptive or low-inference approach to observation, as opposed to a more judgmental approach that can sometimes produce resentment or resistance. In place of this type

| Teacher | Students |
|---|---|
| 10:30 A.M.—*Okay, friends. Today we're going to be learning more about converting energy from one form into another. I want you to turn to a partner and talk about the three words I have up on the board.*<br><br>[T. points to three words on whiteboard: *circuit*, *convert*, and *passive*.]<br><br>10:33 A.M.—*In pairs, talk about what you already know about these words, both in your own lives and also when thinking about what we have been studying in science class. Jot down some ideas on scrap paper, and be ready to talk about what you discussed in five minutes.*<br><br>10:35 A.M.—*Please start chatting with your partner, and I will be walking around the class to make sure that we are all staying focused!* | Most students are looking at and listening to T.<br><br>Two students are whispering to each other.<br><br><br><br>Many students are scrambling for pencils and paper. |
| 10:36 A.M.—T. walking around the classroom, listening to student conversations. | Students begin talking in pairs. Three students raise hands to ask for pencils and paper; clarify who their partner should be.<br><br>Few (<6) are jotting ideas. |
| 10:40 A.M.—*Okay, everyone, eyes back on me! Let's have some volunteers tell us what they discussed as they talked about these words.*<br><br>10:40 A.M.—*Okay. I know that some of these words can be intimidating. Why don't I help out by giving some quick definitions . . .*<br><br>[T. begins to write short definitions on whiteboard.] | [silence]<br><br><br><br>Students watch T. write definitions. Can't see any students copying definitions on their own papers. |

**FIGURE 5.2.** Partial example of descriptive coding.

of scripting, the coach and teacher may decide to video or audio record part of the lesson and obtain similar information. One of the advantages of video/audio is that it can be shared with the teacher and, if the teacher grants permission, used for a discussion with peers. Additionally, given the benefits of making teaching public or visible (Grossman, 2020), video or audio recordings of classroom instruction can be especially helpful to guide coach–teacher debriefing conversations (Gillespie & Amador, 2024). Note, however, that the use of video/audio as a coaching tool can be intimidating, and we consider it to be Level 2 or 3 on our Levels of Intensity (see Chapter 2, Table 2.1).

Sample observation protocols can be downloaded from the CLEE/SRI website (see Web Resources at the end this chapter). In addition, we often share with coaches two broad guidelines for observing:

1. Make arrangements with the teacher before entering the classroom about where you will sit and the degree to which you will be an unobtrusive observer. The two of you may decide that you will not interact at all in the lesson, or, if there is an appropriate time (and a request from the teacher), you might be able to participate in the lesson. Regardless, the decision should be one that helps both of you address the goals of the observation, and it should be agreed upon before the observation.
2. When leaving the classroom, thank the teacher for letting you visit. If possible and appropriate, thank the class and indicate how much you enjoyed being there; be as specific as you can (e.g., "I really enjoyed hearing everyone read aloud; you are really wonderful readers").

In the next part of Maria and Paul's journey, Paul observes Maria's lesson and takes explicit notes, using a descriptive approach.

### PAUL AND MARIA: LESSON OBSERVATION

Maria began her fourth-grade science lesson about converting energy from one form into another by asking students to turn-and-talk about three vocabulary words that were essential to understanding the science texts for the day: *circuit*, *convert*, and *passive*. She asked the student pairs to jot down quick thoughts about the possible definitions of each word. Had students heard or read these words before? Could they have different meanings in the scientific texts they were about to read, as compared to everyday meanings? Students began chatting, but very few wrote anything down. Paul sat in the back of the classroom taking notes. Maria asked for all eyes to focus back on her, and then she asked for volunteers to share some of the definitions they had crafted. No one raised their hands. Paul looked at his watch, and before 5 seconds passed, Maria announced that she completely understood that these words could be challenging, and she proceeded to provide quick definitions of her own on the whiteboard behind her. Students watched and listened, but they did not copy down Maria's definitions nor ask any questions.

Next, Maria announced that students would be rotating across four stations during today's lesson, at each station reading a small snippet of scientific text about different ways that energy can be converted (e.g., passive solar heaters converting light into heat, circuits converting electrical energy into motion within a car). Maria asked students to take notes in their science journals as they moved from station to station, recording

> words they thought were important. Students would spend 10 minutes at each of three stations (understanding that not all students would visit all stations), and then come back to the whole group to share what they had learned and wondered.
>
> When Maria asked students to grab their science journals and begin to rotate through stations, some of the children scattered to corners of the room, some leapt for backpacks to find their journals, and others seemed to sit and chat with their tablemates before moving. Maria raised her voice: "You need to start working in your stations *now* or you will run out of time!" Some students stood with their journals staring at Maria, not quite understanding where to go or what was being asked of them. Maria walked past Paul as she steered a student into his assigned station. "I'm so sorry that the kiddos seem a bit discombobulated today," she said. "I don't understand, because we've done science stations in the past!" "Hang in there," Paul whispered. "We've all had days like this!"

## *Analysis of the Observation*

This step is a key one in that it enables the coach and teacher to individually think about and reflect on the lesson. Always, the goal is to refer back to the pre-observation/planning conversation: What was the focus of the observation, and in what ways did the lesson address that focus? In Appendix D, we provide a Lesson Analysis Guide to help coaches reflect as they prepare for a post-observation debrief. The guide can be used for both preparing for and facilitating the conversation with the teacher. The coach can also ask the teacher to analyze the lesson, using a similar protocol. Two key points to think about when analyzing the lesson are: How can the data (checklist, scripts) be used as evidence to identify essential elements of the lesson? Are there any critical or pivotal incidents that warrant discussion, such as good use of an open-ended question or a student raising a question about another student's comment?

The teacher can often, but not always, identify a problem and assist with the solution. Consider the following questions in making decisions about the follow-up conversation:

- How can the coach work with the teacher to co-construct and develop a shared understanding of the observations?
- What changes do the teacher and coach view as most important for student learning? Which changes do the teacher and coach see as most urgent? Most doable?
- What resources or supports does the teacher need to make changes?
- What were the effective elements of the lesson? In what ways did the teacher achieve the goals?
- What are possible alternatives or options to address any difficulties (generated by the coach and teacher)?
- What are the key points for discussion with the teacher? (Identify only two or

three to increase the likelihood of follow-up and implementation. Make sure to include points that reinforce positive aspects of the lesson.)

The coach should also carefully consider their opening statement in the conversation. It can often set the tone for the entire discussion. It may be problematic to begin by asking the teacher, "What do you think about the lesson?" Teachers may think the lesson was great, which puts the coach in an uncomfortable position if they have quite different views about the success of the lesson. Some alternative possibilities for an opening statement include the following:

- **Responsive coaching:** "I appreciated having an opportunity to visit your classroom. Let's use this opportunity to review the goals for the lesson, think about those aspects of the lesson that helped you achieve the goals, and raise questions about anything that you think might need to be changed. Perhaps you can share your thinking first?"
- **Directive coaching:** "I really enjoyed being in your classroom today. I jotted some notes about aspects of the lesson related to the goals we set. I tried to identify what seemed to really work well for you in achieving your goals—and raised some questions for you to think about. Let me share a few of those with you."

### PAUL AND MARIA: ANALYSIS OF THE LESSON

After leaving the room, Paul sat down in his office to reflect on the lesson design, thinking about what appeared to work well and what could be changed to meet students' needs. He also thought about how to approach his conversation with Maria, scheduled for the next day. In other words, Paul was thinking like a designer ("How can this lesson be improved for these students?") and as a facilitator ("How can I work with Maria to elicit her ideas, learn more about her students, and collaborate in ways that support Maria's learning and enhance students' science and scientific literacy learning?").

Paul realized that there were several design elements to consider. In reviewing his notes, he identified three possible focus topics: direct vocabulary instruction (how was Maria encouraging students to be word-curious and fostering independence in word learning?); disciplinary literacy skill instruction (how was Maria supporting students' reading and note-taking in ways that encouraged them to think like scientists?); and classroom management (setting up the stations, delivering clear instructions to students, helping students take ownership of the routine). As he reflected, Paul identified some specific questions:

- Why did Maria choose to introduce those particular three vocabulary words, and did her vocabulary instruction meet her stated content and literacy goals?
- What other possibilities existed to involve students in the discussion of key vocabulary?

> - Would asking students to adopt a specific vocabulary strategy (e.g., a Frayer model, defining words in their science notebooks) have helped them internalize a way of tracking words in the whole-class mini-lesson and in and across the stations?
> - If Maria adjusted her mini-lesson to focus more on how students tracked words in their science notebooks, would they have been better prepared to move into stations?
> - Could she have organized the stations a bit differently so that she would be able to provide additional direct instruction and/or assistance to the small groups as students rotated?
>
> Paul's goal was to work collaboratively with Maria to think about the lesson and possible options for improving its effectiveness. He wanted to capitalize on Maria's willingness to learn and reinforce what she was doing well. Paul made notes about the possible content of the post-observation conversation, using a protocol similar to the one in Appendix D.

## *Post-Observation/Debriefing Conversation*

This conversation requires perhaps the deftest facilitation skills of the entire cycle. The points raised about urgency and feasibility are key; coaches need to help teachers focus on important issues. Simultaneously, coaches need to consider which changes in teacher beliefs and knowledge are necessary and possible at this point in the teacher's professional learning process. Next, we provide some general guidelines for the post-observation conversation:

- **Make the setting a comfortable one.** If possible, sit next to the teacher rather than across a desk from them, to develop an atmosphere that establishes the two of you as co-learners. It's also easier to review data when sitting side by side.
- **Establish the goals of and purpose for the conversation.** Understand the limits of time, making certain that important items are addressed first.
- **Provide balanced feedback.** Help teachers understand what was effective and where changes might have a positive influence on lesson outcomes. This example illustrates what we mean by balanced feedback:
  - "Giving students opportunities to talk with others about their views about fracking and its effect on the environment is an effective approach for encouraging active involvement and high-level thinking. I wonder whether the conversations might be more productive if initially some of the pros and cons had been identified by the group and perhaps written on the SMART Board. What do you think?"
- **Make plans for next steps.** What will the teacher plan to do? What does the coach need to do to support the teacher's efforts? Again, recognize the

importance of selecting priority goals, perhaps only one or two so that the teacher will be successful in these change efforts.

Providing feedback can be difficult for coaches, and receiving feedback can be equally difficult for teachers. At times, coaches find themselves focusing on the positive, minimizing teachers' need to address specific areas of concern, or dominating the conversation. Too often, the common pattern for feedback is to first provide positive feedback and then to *tell* teachers what is wrong or ineffective. Instead, Timperley (2010) suggests that feedback sessions be seen as learning conversations in which the coach and teacher collaboratively design solutions for identified problems. Peterson et al. (2009) and Duncan (2006) both provide examples of such conversations, notably guided by simple discussion protocols. These conversations are demanding (not demeaning), and there is respect for each other's views and a focus on developing reflectivity and inquiry as habits of mind.

Further, in planning these conversations, coaches must consider each teacher's ways of knowing and leadership stances (Breidenstein et al., 2012; Drago-Severson & Blum-DeStefano, 2017; Fahey et al., 2019), as identified in Chapter 2 (i.e., instrumental learning, socializing learning, self-authoring learning). The savvy coach will listen carefully to the kinds of questions the teacher is asking and identify which stance they might be adopting, and try to respond in ways that both support teachers' current thinking and nudge them toward new and more complex ways of understanding their work.

- Is the teacher asking for quick, concrete solutions and looking to the coach for explicit, expert advice (suggestive of an instrumental learning approach)?
- Is the teacher asking for support from colleagues, thinking about ways to bring a dilemma to the weekly PLC meeting, or perhaps asking to observe others in action (suggestive of a more socializing learning approach)?
- Is the teacher asking for the coach to listen as they talk through a few different ways that they are already thinking of solving the dilemma, wanting the coach to act more as a sounding board or extra set of eyes (suggestive of a more self-authoring stance)?

Which of these ways of knowing and learning might be in play during the post-observation conversation? What kinds of coach responses might help the teacher feel most heard and validated? What might the coach do to help create an environment in which the teacher can safely stretch a bit? (For example, the coach could, rather than simply giving a teacher an answer, instead suggest that they observe a colleague or talk with their instructional team. Or the coach could ask the teacher who is quick to lean on their team to instead suggest a few alternatives that they imagine their team might provide.) It is always important to take into consideration the skills and knowledge of each teacher as well as the goals for student learning.

> **VOICES FROM THE FIELD**
>
> My role is vital to improving student achievement. It's difficult enough to teach, but then to self-evaluate one's effectiveness and make necessary corrections while doing so is next to impossible. By providing real-time feedback, teachers can make the necessary adjustments to their instructional moves and see immediate results in their students' behaviors.
> —MARSHA TURNER-HALL, Instructional Coach

In the paragraphs that follow, we describe three particular stances toward providing feedback that can be useful in conversations between coaches and teachers (adapted from Ippolito, 2010; Robbins, 1991; Robertson et al., 2020b), when to use them, and examples of language that illustrates each. Again, selecting a stance (or multiple stances) is dependent on the teacher's knowledge, experience, and disposition, as well as the strength of the relationship between the coach and teacher. Also, a conversation is often a mix of the various stances, with a coach moving from one stance to another as needed.

### *Coach as Expert, or Directive Stance*

While we generally caution coaches to be wary about adopting the mantle of "expert" (see Chapter 4), there are times when coaches can and should take a more directive approach when working with teachers. When adopting such a stance, coaches bring their expertise to the conversation by providing concrete ideas, suggestions, resources, and materials that teachers might find helpful. This stance can be helpful when engaging with teachers who are interested in a more instrumental learning experience. The directive approach is useful when teachers lack the knowledge or experience of a specific strategy or approach, or when they are seeking immediate information (e.g., "I need to try something different *tomorrow* to help four of my students who are struggling with creating number sentences after reading word problems").

Coaches may also use this stance when a teacher asks, "What do you think?" or, "How would you handle Sammy, who is disrupting my lessons by getting out of his seat and refusing to participate?" This reply is an example of a coach adopting a more directive stance: "You asked about how to help a child become more fluent in his reading. There is research evidence suggesting that lots of practice reading and rereading connected text really helps. Here are some specific ideas that seem to have worked well for other teachers. Might any of these work for you and your students?"

Note that a coach, even when adopting this directive stance, can still provide options for the teacher and solicit teacher input about the feasibility of those options. Again, with any design problem, there are always a number of ways to solve it. Serving as an expert, or responding in a directive manner, may be useful when addressing technical issues but less advantageous when dealing with changes that require adaptive thinking.

### Coach as Peer, or Balanced Stance

When using this stance, the coach uses language that enhances the ability of both the coach and the teacher to work collaboratively to identify and solve problems. This stance is useful for promoting teacher reflectivity and for addressing changes that require adaptive thinking about specific and often complex classroom problems (as well as potential solutions). This stance might be more commonly used with teachers when engaging in socializing or self-authoring learning. When there is a high level of trust and a low-risk environment, the teacher will most likely be willing to talk openly. An example of the language in such a conversation follows:

- **Teacher:** "What would you think about me trying to use more informational texts in our upcoming unit about families and communities, using the approach discussed in the article by Nell Duke? I know my third-grade students need more opportunities to read informational texts."
- **Coach:** "Let's think about what that approach means in terms of putting it into practice. What specific ideas is Duke recommending? What are your thoughts about how you might start? What questions do you have, and how can I help? Do you need some suggestions for informational texts across a range of complexity? I might suggest you begin with a few familiar nonfiction picture books to start the conversation about both the topic and genre features."

### Coach as Mirror, or Responsive Stance

The metaphor of a mirror is one that illustrates the key role of the coach as a listener or as someone to draw out, organize, and generally facilitate reflections made by the teacher—that is, to encourage teachers to think in more complex and nuanced ways about teaching and learning. This stance is often associated with a cognitive coaching approach to the work (Costa & Garmston, 2015). This stance can be used with a teacher comfortable with a more self-authoring learning stance (or a teacher the coach is trying to encourage to become more self-authoring). This stance is perfect for those who can self-reflect and who want the opportunity to talk through a lesson with a knowledgeable peer; the coach can help by asking probing questions that raise the level of thinking. Such questions provide guided-inquiry experiences that help develop reflective thinking. In a conversation using this stance, a coach might say, "You've identified the goal of increasing student engagement by asking questions that require higher-level thinking. As you look at the transcript of the lesson, where do you see that goal being met? Where do you see room for tweaking? How might I help you get to the next level regarding your goal?" Notably, this stance may be less effective with a novice teacher (or a teacher more interested in instrumental learning), someone who is eagerly seeking a concrete answer from the coach. Instead, the teacher might potentially find this line of guided questioning evasive and frustrating. Again, it is very important for the coach to gauge what the teacher needs both substantively and procedurally during these conversations.

### Final Coaching Stance Considerations

Remember that all three of these stances may be used in one conversation, and, in fact, often should be (Ippolito, 2010). Also note that these stances can be adopted and enacted any time that a coach is talking with a teacher or group (not just within the post-observation conversation). Think about each conversation as an intricate dance—one with many steps, with participants moving forward, backward, and sideways. Every conversation is an opportunity to encourage different ways of learning and knowing, with both the coach and the teacher pushing each other to adopt more complex stances toward reflecting on their practice. The key is the ability of the coach to listen to the response of the teacher, feed off that response, and provide comments or questions that facilitate thinking for both parties. Of course, using note-taking guides or protocols (like the one in Appendix D) can help guide your thinking.

In the final "Paul and Maria" installment, we summarize Paul's post-observation conversation with Maria. As you read the text, think about how they work together to solve the design problems in the lesson. Also, note how Paul's questioning and comments help facilitate the conversation.

---

**PAUL AND MARIA:
POST-OBSERVATION/DEBRIEFING CONVERSATION**

In their post-observation conversation, Paul began with a comment about how this fourth-grade content can be quite difficult to teach, as it often can seem quite abstract to students. There are also a ton of new vocabulary words introduced that will feel unfamiliar to students. He asked Maria to talk a bit about the students in the class and their familiarity with the vocabulary routines she was trying to introduce, as well as the format of learning via stations.

Using a set of focus questions he had crafted ahead of the debrief, Paul asked Maria to talk a little about the vocabulary words she chose to highlight, the texts she had chosen for the stations, and how she ideally envisioned students using their science notebooks. Paul applauded Maria's focus on introducing fourth graders to robust vocabulary routines that they could use as they encountered increasingly complex historical and scientific texts in the coming years. He listened to Maria describe how she really wanted the science notebooks to become tools for students to use in discovering and

> documenting new scientific words, and Paul emphasized how powerful a routine that could be for students, now and in the future. Paul reminded Maria of the Frayer model vocabulary routine that had been discussed in last month's grade-level team meeting, and he also suggested that a bit more modeling of how to construct and use the Frayer model might be helpful.
>
> They both agreed that students would need additional support with these types of lessons, and Maria then asked Paul for some suggestions. Paul and Maria discussed possible options for improving the lesson design—Maria illustrating a Frayer model with one of her chosen words on the whiteboard, before asking students to practice the routine with three or four words in their science notebooks as they rotated through stations; Maria practicing simple management routines with students to pick up their notebooks from four designated spots around the classroom, always rotating stations in a similar pattern—to help create more time for students to engage deeply with the texts at each station. Although Paul offered some possibilities, Maria added ideas about how she might reduce the number of stations and texts that each group of students might encounter, instead focusing on depth over breadth. Maria also described how she might divide the lesson into two shorter lessons taught over two days, to increase students' opportunities to practice, and to ensure that all students encountered all stations and texts.
>
> Paul and Maria then discussed the connection between instruction and classroom engagement. Were there elements that could be changed to increase student engagement? Maria and Paul together identified two possible instructional changes: partner reading of texts instead of small groups rotating through stations, and initially providing students with a list of vocabulary words that she would then expect them to see and define during the lesson.
>
> Together, Maria and Paul summarized what was discussed and formulated next steps. They agreed that the two of them would co-plan and co-teach a similar lesson in the coming week.

Note that both directive and responsive coaching (i.e., balanced coaching) was used in the post-observation conversation just described. Paul shared his expertise while also asking clarifying and probing questions that required Maria to think critically about disciplinary literacy instruction. In many ways, the conversation leaned a bit toward an instrumental learning focus to support Maria as she learned new strategies for adopting (what were for her) new practices. At the same time, Paul asked questions that required Maria to take an inquiry stance, encouraging a bit more of a socializing learning or self-authoring learning stance. We can imagine Paul suggesting that Maria bring these same issues to her weekly grade-level team meeting for further discussion and reflection, or to engage in a bit of self-study by keeping a journal of instructional results and writing her own reflections at the end of each day. These coaching moves are designed to help edge Maria, bit by bit, into more socializing and self-authoring ways of working.

In the observation cycle described in the preceding sections, Paul and Maria collaborated to address an instructional issue of importance to Maria and to develop a shared understanding of both identified problems and potential solutions. Further, Paul used his facilitation skills of active listening and questioning to learn more about the students, the lesson, and the teacher, recognizing that teachers themselves bring their own funds of knowledge (Moll, 2000) to the conversations. These coaching moves are critical, as classroom teachers often have a deeper understanding of the specific classroom context and students than does the coach. As one teacher talking about the differences between herself and a reading specialist said, "*She's* a reading specialist; *I'm* a kid specialist!"

## Summary

In this chapter, we discussed the rationale for coaching teachers one-on-one and then described the coaching activities of modeling, co-teaching, and observing. We delved deeply into an illustrated example of the coaching observation cycle (including pre-observation/planning conversations, observation, analysis, and post-observation/debriefing conversations). We also provided specific guidelines about how coaching can promote teacher learning and an inquiring habit of mind. We concluded by discussing the importance of providing feedback in ways that show respect for teachers' views and knowledge, while challenging them to adopt more and different ways of reflecting on how to improve learning for their students. Returning to the case of Melinda from the outset of this chapter, we can imagine that some of the suggestions and examples in this chapter might help Melinda find a few productive ways of launching a coaching cycle with Janice about the new math curriculum, interweaving modeling, co-planning and co-teaching, and observing as she supports Janice in learning and implementing the new curriculum.

## Reflections

- Using the chart found in Appendix A, note the ways that coaches function as change agents, facilitators, designers, and advocates when working with individual teachers. List some possibilities that you might consider in your current position.
- Consider the three main individual coaching moves outlined in this chapter: modeling, co-teaching, and observation. With a coaching colleague or on your own, reflect on when each of these three coaching moves feels most productive to you. When might each feel challenging or less productive? What further relationship-building with teachers or additional partnering with a principal or curriculum director might further support your ability to engage in each of these coaching moves?
- Reread the case of Paul and Maria as they collaboratively engage in an observation

coaching cycle. How did Paul facilitate the conversations? In what ways did Maria and Paul work together to solve instructional design problems? In what ways does this coaching cycle mirror ones that you have engaged in? What new ideas or questions arise? How might you use some of what you read in the next coaching cycles that you plan and enact?

## **Activities**

1. Watch a video of a classroom lesson, either by yourself or with some coaching colleagues. (Many sample videos, across grade levels and disciplines, can be found on the Teaching Channel [*www.teachingchannel.org*] and YouTube [*www.youtube.com*].) Assume the teacher is a coach modeling instruction. Identify some prior look-fors and then take on the role of the teacher who is watching this modeled lesson. When you finish, think about your experience watching this lesson. What did you learn by watching this modeled lesson that can help you develop your ability to model and talk with teachers after the lesson? If you are watching with coaching colleagues, discuss what you learned and compare your experiences.
2. Read one or all of the following articles (see Web Resources at the end of this chapter). Consider and/or discuss with colleagues further ideas and takeaways that may support the coaching of individual teachers:
    - Gibbons & Cobb (2017), "Focusing on Teacher Learning Opportunities to Identify Potentially Productive Coaching Activities"
    - Vanderburg & Stephens (2009), "What Teachers Say They Changed because of Their Coach and How They Think Their Coach Helped Them"
    - Bean & DeFord (2012), "Do's and Don'ts for Literacy Coaches"

### **FURTHER READINGS AND RESOURCES**

#### **Print Resources**

Haneda, M., Teemant, A., & Sherman, B. (2017). Instructional coaching through dialogic interaction: Helping a teacher to become agentive in her practice. *Language and Education, 31*(1), 46–64.

Hu, Y., & Tuten, J. (2017). Literacy teachers' learning through a recursive coaching cycle. *The Reading Professor, 40*(2), Article 18.

Knight, J. (2016). *Better conversations: Coaching ourselves and each other to be more credible, caring, and connected.* Corwin Press.

Knight, J. (2017). *The impact cycle: What instructional coaches should do to foster powerful improvements in teaching.* Corwin Press.

Knight, J. (2019). Instructional coaching for implementing visible learning: A model for translating research into practice. *Education Sciences, 9*(2), 1–16.

Russell, J. L., Correnti, R., Stein, M. K., Thomas, A., Bill, V., & Speranzo, L. (2020). Mathematics coaching for conceptual understanding: Promising evidence regarding the Tennessee math coaching model. *Educational Evaluation and Policy Analysis, 42*(3), 439–466.

Saclarides, E. S. (2022). Reflecting on the past and looking ahead: An exploration of coach–teacher talk during reflection meetings. *School Science and Mathematics, 122*(4), 195–208.

Sweeney, D., & Harris, L. S. (2016). *Student-centered coaching: The moves*. Corwin Press.

**Web Resources (see www.guilford.com/bean3-materials for live links)**

Bean, R., & DeFord, D. (2012). Do's and don't's for literacy coaches: Advice from the field. *Literacy Coaching Clearinghouse.* http://files.eric.ed.gov/fulltext/ED530365.pdf

Center for Leadership & Educational Equity and the School Reform Initiative. (2024). *Protocols.* www.clee.org/resources

Gibbons, L. K., & Cobb, P. (2017). Focusing on teacher learning opportunities to identify potentially productive coaching activities. *Journal of Teacher Education.* http://journals.sagepub.com/doi/10.1177/0022487117702579

Learning Forward. (2015). 3 steps to great coaching: A simple but powerful instructional coaching cycle nets results. *The Learning Professional.* https://learningforward.org/journal/february-2015-issue/3-steps-to-great-coaching

Saclarides, E. S., & Munson, J. (2021). Exploring the foci and depth of coach–teacher interactions during modeled lessons. *Teaching and Teacher Education, 105,* 103418. https://doi.org/10.1016/j.tate.2021.103418

Vanderburg, M., & Stephens, D. (2009). What teachers say they changed because of their coach and how they think their coach helped them. *Literacy Coaching Clearinghouse.* http://files.eric.ed.gov/fulltext/ED530297.pdf

# CHAPTER 6

# Working with Groups to Build a Culture of Adult Learning

> **GUIDING QUESTIONS**
>
> 1. Why and when is group coaching effective?
> 2. What do coaches need to know about facilitating small-group meetings? Making presentations to large groups?
> 3. In what ways can coaches help build a wider culture of adult learning through group coaching?

## Melinda Begins to Consider Group Coaching and Facilitation Skills

Melinda, in her new role as a coach, has now been asked to serve as a facilitative leader for the second-grade team of five teachers, two special educators, and two interventionists (one for literacy and one for math). This group of experienced and novice educators has varying views about literacy, math, and content-area instruction, not to mention divergent views about classroom management and supporting students' social-emotional learning. A few teachers are wedded to the older core literacy program, moving through it with little variation, while two of the more novice teachers are eager to adopt a newer model with more direct instruction. They also see lots of opportunities to work as a team, regrouping students across classrooms to best serve students' specific math and literacy needs. Melinda knows that she needs the facilitation skills that will help her work effectively with this team of teachers, but which routines and structures might prove most successful? How can she make sure to start out on the right foot? In what ways can she help the group navigate differences of opinion and potential conflicts, ultimately helping the group move toward consensus?

To begin to address Melinda's questions, in this chapter we focus on how coaches can work productively with groups of teachers. First, we discuss the rationale for working with small groups, present related guidelines, and share specific strategies and routines for coaches working with small groups. Next, we present ideas for working effectively with large groups, including making schoolwide presentations. Finally, we end with a section on developing and facilitating professional learning communities (PLCs), and suggest specific approaches for developing a wider culture of learning for both adults and students.

> ### VOICES FROM THE FIELD
>
> My thinking on how best to provide coaching support has changed over the years. I used to think coaching was best in a one-on-one format. I still support some teachers independently; however, my coaching support has evolved into that of a facilitator in a group setting. Due to the volume of teachers needing instructional support and finding adequate time for the one-on-one coaching sessions, I moved to coaching during professional learning community (PLC) meetings. I still ask the same reflective questions and push everyone's thinking just like I did in an individual format—I'm just doing it with groups of teachers rather than one-on-one. I have found that when working with a group, the conversations are richer, the thinking is deeper, and teachers value the time spent with their colleagues. I'm introducing structures, such as peer coaching, classroom learning labs, and instructional rounds, as ways for teachers to support one another in daily job-embedded professional learning, resulting in learning that continues without my presence. Recently, I added practice clinics [a specific form of coaching labs] as a way for teachers to learn and practice impactful instructional moves.
>
> I find the implementation of all these structures has made the biggest impact on my teachers' instructional practices. Teachers still need the individualized support one-on-one coaching provides, but they also benefit from the collaboration and rich discussions provided in PLCs and practice clinics. Coaching teachers with a variety of instructional needs demands a multidimensional approach. I then follow up with individual teachers as needed. As I reflect on my support, I always ask the same question: "Do my words and actions promote dependence or independence?"
>
> —MARSHA TURNER-HALL, Teacher and Instructional Coach

## Why Coaches Work with Groups

For most instructional coaches, working one-on-one with teachers is the heart of their work. However, recent evidence (Gibbons & Cobb, 2017) reminds us that some of our most effective coaching work occurs when facilitating group experiences. In their study of the existing coaching literature focused on improving math instruction, Gibbons and Cobb (2017) identify four potentially productive group coaching activities that seem to outperform other coaching actions. The four most potentially effective group coaching activities include analyzing classroom video, engaging directly with disciplinary content, examining student work, and engaging in lesson study. Notice how each of these four activities specifically increases joint coach–teacher reflection on the instructional core (City et al., 2009) or the interaction of teachers and students with content and curriculum. This study of potentially productive coaching activities is notable, in part, because it reminds readers of the power of group coaching (i.e., only two individual coaching activities—coach modeling and co-teaching—were found to be as potentially productive as the group coaching activities). For us (Jacy and Rita), as both producers and consumers of educational research focused on coaching, this is an important finding. Of course, we look forward to new and emerging research that continues to shed light on the ways in which group coaching and one-on-one coaching vary in efficacy according to contextual factors.

While many coaches spend much of their time working with individual teachers, we want to invite readers to consider the ways in which individual work may not quite lead to larger systemic shifts in teaching and learning. As Mangin and Dunsmore (2015) suggest, when we focus only on one-on-one coaching, we might be assuming that the "the sum of individual changes across teachers [will be] equivalent to systemic reform" (p. 203), but this is not necessarily the case. In fact, if we wish to make larger shifts in teaching and learning within and across schools, then we must be cognizant of the value of group coaching, as opposed to coaching only individuals. When we do focus on group coaching, then we position ourselves to collaboratively discuss the vision and goals for instructional programs for each grade-level, specific subject area, school, or district. We can analyze data to inform instruction and collaboratively develop curriculum, and we can make large-group presentations to develop background information about instructional topics (e.g., SEL to support literacy learning, peer-to-peer conversations to deepen mathematical reasoning). The reasons for working with groups of teachers, from just a few to an entire faculty, are many and multifaceted—in fact, you can likely think of multiple ways in which you have already been involved in productive group work during the school year. Some of the core reasons for working with groups are detailed in the following sections.

### *Working with Groups Can Spur Change*

By working with groups of educators, changes in school culture can be more easily facilitated (Bryk et al., 2015; Donohoo et al., 2018; Dumay, 2009; Hattie, 2012, 2016; Leithwood & Mascall, 2008; Printy, 2008; Vescio et al., 2008). Coaches can spur change by leading efforts to develop an organizational environment—a learning community—that promotes social interaction focused on improving both teacher and student learning. Moreover, when the culture is such that teachers *as a group* share a similar vision and a sense of responsibility for all students, believe that students can learn, hold high expectations, and are committed to school improvement, it is much more likely that there will be overall improvement in student learning (Donohoo et al., 2018; Hattie, 2012, 2016; Leana & Pil, 2006). A toxic environment diminishes the possibility of larger school change. Think about the need for enough effort, enthusiasm, and belief in an initiative to make a difference, what Gladwell (2000) calls a "tipping point." We have seen this in schools where reform or remodeling efforts have resulted in an overall change in the school's orientation toward ongoing professional learning. When teachers are collectively excited about an initiative, they talk about it and share their ideas with others in ways that support coaching work.

### *Group Coaching Is Connected to Targeted Coaching with Individuals*

By working effectively with groups of teachers, coaches can also enhance and differentiate the coaching of individual teachers. Grierson (2011), in her study of coaching, discusses the value of group coaching as a means of identifying which follow-up coaching activities would be best for individual teachers. She found that group coaching was necessary but not sufficient. Follow-up individual coaching was an essential aspect for improving teacher practices. During group meetings, individual teachers may share their instructional experiences, positive and problematic, with group members. Follow-up individual coaching, using some of the ideas discussed in Chapter 5, can then be differentiated to better meet the needs of individual teachers. Alternatively, some coaches begin with coaching individual teachers, but then find it critical to bring a group together to share what is being learned across classrooms. The exact order of individual and group coaching may be less important than the notion that the two activities feed into each other. Importantly, teachers in small groups begin to see each other as rich resources and supports, instead of simply looking to the coach for advice. This can potentially free the coach a bit to focus more specifically on those who might want or need more intensive individual coaching.

### *Working with Groups Increases Efficiency*

Coaches can reach more teachers when they work with groups, thereby increasing the likelihood of large-scale or schoolwide change. This is especially true when most teachers in a school are involved in a specific initiative (e.g., implementing a new literacy curriculum across a K–5 school; piloting project-based learning across a sixth- to eighth-grade middle school; experimenting with flipped classrooms across a ninth- to twelfth-grade high school). Too often, coaches work with only a small percentage of teachers in a school, and sometimes only with those teachers who volunteer to be coached or who have been identified as "needing support" by an administrator. In these latter cases, serial one-on-one coaching can lead both coaches and teachers to feel as though their efforts aren't building toward a larger shared understanding of improved teaching and learning within and across grade levels.

Furthermore, working with small groups of teachers can allow coaches to harness the power of the group to encourage shy or reluctant colleagues. Where an individual teacher might balk at a suggestion from a coach in a one-on-one meeting, sometimes that same teacher might be more willing to try something new when an entire group of colleagues is taking on the same challenge (e.g., all second-grade teachers engaging in lesson study within a new math unit). Working with groups of teachers can result in a much more efficient route toward adopting and adapting new practices than does persuading and cajoling one-by-one.

In other words, while individual coaching is critical, coaches need to be able to work with groups in ways that help teachers learn from and with each other. By working effectively with groups, coaches can build on notions of social capital and collective efficacy (see Chapter 3) to increase the overall capacity of the school as a learning organization. Thinking like a facilitator is one of the keys to successfully coaching both small and large groups; therefore, in the next sections, we detail some of the highest-leverage group facilitation moves coaches can make.

## General Guidelines for Working with Groups of All Sizes

For coaches wishing to think and work as facilitators, especially those new to their roles like Melinda, it is important to keep in mind a handful of basic principles. Below, we outline what we consider to be essential ways of thinking about and working with groups of various sizes.

### *Craft Community Agreements for Participation and Review Them Periodically*

As one of our coaching colleagues says often, "All groups have norms. It's just that some groups name them, and thereby take ownership and control of them!" Taking a few minutes to talk about and set norms, or agreements for participation, either when a group first forms or when a coach begins working with an already established group, can allow a facilitator to avoid pitfalls later in the group's working life. Community agreements also provide a starting point for the facilitator (and group members) to then revisit and address any group-dynamic issues that may arise over time.

Of special note, while many coaches use the word *norms* for talking about and setting group guidelines for participation, we have recently shifted to using the phrase *community agreements* with the groups we coach. We see community agreements as hyperlocal, context-specific agreements that coaches can set with educators, focused on productive ways of working given the identities, values, and goals of the members of each community; whereas, we see the term *norms* as unintentionally signaling that there is a monolithic "right way" to engage with one another. We encourage coaches to use whatever terminology works best for them and their groups; however, we encourage coaches to consider how a term like *community agreements* might be more inclusive and equitable over time.

When setting community agreements, consider that some will likely be technical/logistical—such as arriving on time, limiting cell phone and laptop use, and so on—while other agreements may focus more on ways of productively collaborating (e.g., posing suggestions as "I wonder . . ." statements; always beginning with descriptive language and clarifying questions before making inferences). Finally, some agreements may touch on cultural aspects of the work such as remembering to connect instructional suggestions to student learning outcomes, always remembering to consider students with different learning needs, and so on. In Figure 6.1, we identify a few steps a coach might use when working with a group to quickly establish community agreements.

Several other recommended protocols from CLEE/SRI (see Web Resources at the end of this chapter) can assist in the establishment of strong community agreements:

- Compass Points (good for larger groups)
- Forming Ground Rules (good for smaller groups)
- Norms Construction (good for smaller groups)

One final note related to setting community agreements. In some cases, particularly when coaches are facilitating conversations related to equity and social justice, it might be advantageous to have groups begin with an already established list of agreements. This "straw man draft" of agreements can then be discussed, refined, and adopted as a first-draft set of agreements for a group to use and live with for a while. In these instances, if we do not start with a sample list of agreements that nudge us toward creating brave spaces, then our groups may not spontaneously generate the agreements that are most needed. Thus, starting with a predetermined list of agreements can be important. To begin, we recommend the four agreements from Singleton's (2014) *Courageous Conversations about Race:* stay engaged, experience discomfort, speak your truth, and expect and accept nonclosure. However, many facilitators have expanded on these basic four agreements over time—to learn more, we

> - Ask group members individually to make a T-Chart identifying characteristics of effective groups and ineffective groups.
> - Share with the entire group the results of the individual work, listing characteristics of effective groups on chart paper or a SMART Board. Discuss the need to establish community agreements for working together so that the group can effectively accomplish goals.
> - After the bulk of items have been listed, we often ask, "Is there anything qualitatively new or different that hasn't yet been added?" to ensure that all voices have been heard.
> - Then, ask the group for help in synthesizing and combining items, or collectively making decisions about the top five characteristics that the group believes will be essential to their work. Whittling the list down to a manageable number of agreements will help the group hold on to, apply, and reflect on them. Post the list for all to review before each meeting.
> - Let the group know that these agreements will be revisited in the near future, with a goal of creating space for reflection on group processes and progress. This allows the group to correct course and further revise agreements as needed.

**FIGURE 6.1.** Coach-led process for developing group community agreements.

recommend Googling "norms" or "agreements" related to "brave" and "courageous conversations" for a wide array of examples. When thinking like designers, coaches also sometimes utilize Stanford University's D.School (2024) design thinking process for setting group intentions and norms that support equity-focused work (see Web Resources at the end of this chapter). Finally, for guidance in establishing community agreements and facilitating critical conversations with students, we recommend the *Let's Talk!* tool from Learning for Justice (formerly Teaching Tolerance; see Web Resources at the end of this chapter). For further advice on setting community agreements, see Ippolito and Bean (2024, pp. 240–241).

### Be the "Guide on the Side"

Beyond establishing community agreements, one of the best pieces of advice we can give to coaches working with small groups is to be the "guide on the side." Although coaches may at times need to convey specific bits of knowledge or content, one of the major goals of group facilitation is to elicit the knowledge, beliefs, and perspectives of group members. Therefore, we recommend that coaches truly lean in to the notion of thinking and working as facilitators and co-learners when working with groups. The goal is for teachers to see coaches as colleagues—as "lead learners"—whose focus is student success. Provide opportunities for group members to share their expertise, raise questions, and participate in design thinking and problem solving.

Coaches who spend more time talking (or lecturing) than they do listening are not building the capacity of group members. Such behavior lessens teacher ownership and may generate resentment or resistance from colleagues who feel as though they are being talked at or that their beliefs and knowledge have little value. Here are three quick ways to ensure that you don't inadvertently monopolize the conversation and that you're also building facilitative capacity in teachers:

1. Establish a clear agenda (Harvard's *Meeting Wise* website offers agenda suggestions; see Web Resources at the end of this chapter) or use a discussion-based protocol with rounds of noticing, questioning, and interpretation where all voices can be heard.
2. Solicit suggestions for agenda items before each meeting, perhaps over email or in person, depending on participants' preferences, so that the agenda is never *entirely* coach-driven.
3. Rotate the facilitation of group meetings so that you (as coach) are not the only one leading the group meetings.

### *Remember That Engagement Is Important*

Coaches must understand that not all adult group members are engaged in the same way or ready for the same kinds of learning experiences (see Chapter 2 for more on this notion). Some group members take an active role, raising questions and making comments. Other participants are less vocal but still may be mentally involved. Effective facilitators aim to hear from all members of the group in each meeting. The following strategies can help increase participation:

- Ask those who haven't said anything to respond. For example, "I'd like to hear from those who haven't said anything yet about this issue, to make sure that all views are heard."
- Initiate a "whip-around," either written or oral, urging everyone to reply to a specific question or prompt. For example, "Let's begin with Laurie. What is one challenge that you might experience if we decided to shift toward more small-group learning experiences in class?"
- Call for a simple thumbs-up / thumbs-down / thumbs-sideways. For example, "Do you agree, disagree, or feel neutral in response to this statement?"

Soliciting insights and contributions from those who might naturally tend more toward silence often contributes greatly to a conversation, and the coach has a responsibility to encourage and draw out this participation. Coaches might increase engagement by first asking teachers to share classroom success stories before sharing specific difficulties or problems. For example, each teacher can be asked to share work samples from a specific student who has made great progress and describe factors contributing to that success. Other group members can then follow up by asking questions or making comments. One way to guide this kind of conversation is to use a Success Analysis or Gap Analysis protocol from the CLEE/SRI website (see Web Resources at the end of this chapter).

### *Balance Routine and Repertoire*

Wasley et al. (1997) talk about the importance of balancing routine and repertoire in teaching students, and we recommend the same advice to all those who coach groups. Coaches can introduce groups to powerful routines for collaborative learning, mechanisms that will be used in every meeting, such as a five-minute whip-around asking everyone to check in and talk about one successful teaching moment in the past week, a weekly check-out where everyone states one thing they're going to try in their classrooms before meeting again, and so on. However, excellent facilitators also have a wide repertoire of facilitative moves that they employ so that groups do not sink into a slump, always feeling as if they are using the same protocol or structure to learn together. The book *Facilitator's Guide to Participatory Decision-Making* (Kaner, 2014) is filled with suggestions for facilitating group learning and decision-making processes.

> • • • • • • • • • • **Put into Practice** • • • • • • • • • •
>
> - Record a portion of a group session that you are facilitating (or one in which you are participating). Listen to the recording to answer the following questions:
>   —Did all members of the group have an opportunity to talk?
>   —How much of the conversation was directed by the coach/facilitator?
>   —To what extent were all members of the group positively involved in the conversation?
> - Visit YouTube or the Teaching Channel website. Watch a video clip of a coach working with a group of teachers. What is the coach doing to support group learning? What community agreements seem to already be in place? How would you characterize the levels of engagement and active listening?

## Strategies for Working with Small Groups

There are many reasons for working with teachers in small groups. Small-group meetings can include teachers from one grade level or content area, teachers from across grade levels or content areas in a school, or, at times, teachers from across several schools in a district who share a similar focus (such as teacher representatives from schools across a district, each of whom is implementing a new district-selected curriculum). At times, small-group meetings may follow large-group presentations provided within schools or at the district level. In such cases, a coach assigned to a school may meet with teachers to better understand what follow-up steps are needed: Would teachers appreciate seeing a specific strategy modeled in their classroom? Do they need clarification about specific ideas? What have they attempted in terms of implementation? Most importantly, how can the coach be helpful?

Facilitating small-group learning is different from large-group facilitation in several important ways. Although it requires some of the same skills (e.g., connecting with participants and acknowledging and respecting the audience), generally speaking, small groups often meet on an ongoing basis and require a clearer set of agreements, goals, and routines. Therefore, small-group work requires coaches to learn more about each group member, to facilitate in ways that promote active engagement of members over time, and to craft (or co-craft) each agenda to accomplish goals. Hersey and Blanchard (1977) call for attention to both "task actions" (how can goals be achieved?) and what they call "maintenance actions" (in what ways can relationships be built to facilitate member involvement?). In Figure 6.2, we identify examples of how group leaders and participants contribute to the functioning of a group.

All the actions described in Figure 6.2 are important ones, but some become more important than others in specific group situations. When a group is excited and motivated by its task, there may be less need for maintenance activities, as group relationships appear to be positive and members are eager to work on the task at hand. Conversely, when group members don't understand the goal or are unhappy about being in this setting, relationship or maintenance actions are extremely important. Ultimately, the actions in Figure 6.2 are positive ones that can be developed and practiced by both coaches and participants in the group.

> • • • • • • • • • • **Put into Practice** • • • • • • • • • •
>
> Think about each of the actions associated with coaching small groups, as well as others you may have taken in the past. Below are three options that may help you observe more closely how individuals behave in groups, including which roles they assume, how they engage in positive or negative behaviors, and how they influence the work of the group. Which actions do you engage in regularly? Which may you want to try next?
>
> - Observe a group (either by yourself or with a coaching colleague), and identify the actions taken by individuals in the group. You might be able to attend a grade-level or team meeting at the school or even a school board meeting. What do you notice? How might you facilitate differently to accentuate positive behaviors and minimize the negative?
> - Ask one of your coaching colleagues to observe you as you lead a group; have them look for examples of positive actions exhibited by various group members—including you! What is noticed? What might be done differently in the future to better support group interactions and learning?
> - Find examples of small-group educational meetings on the internet (e.g., the Teaching Channel, YouTube); view these meetings for examples of group members' behaviors. Your interest in viewing these videos is not in the content, but in the processes used to facilitate group work. Which coach/facilitator "moves" do you already make? Which moves might you want to add to your own repertoire, and why?

**Task Roles**

*Presenting or Seeking Information*

- "I read an article that gives great ideas for how to help students analyze websites more critically. It introduces multiple strategies to help students check for authenticity."
- "I'd like to know more about what Susan is trying with project-based learning."

*Elaborating on the Contributions of Others*

- "In the article that Carlos mentioned about analyzing websites for authenticity, there are also great ideas for specific close-reading lessons; for example, . . . "

*Presenting the Opinions or Seeking the Opinions of Others*

- "I think the notion of sharing our learning center materials is an excellent one. I'd really appreciate getting some new ideas about writing instruction."
- "What do you think, Helena, about forming a committee to begin looking at how we can integrate math goals and assignments with those expected in science classes?"

*Synthesizing the Contributions of Others*

- "It's exciting when you think about how the ideas expressed by Frank and Alicia fit together. It seems as though we could move quickly if we . . . "

**Maintenance or Relationship-Building Roles**

*Encouraging Others to Participate*

- "Zach, what do you think? You ask your students to work in small groups a lot; so, what strategies do you use to help them learn how to do that? To keep them focused on the task?"

*Providing Ideas for Compromise*

- "It seems as though we have two ideas, each of which requires lots of work. I wonder whether we could divide into two smaller groups, and each group could address issues related to one of the ideas?"

*Gatekeeping*

- "Whoa! It appears that we are straying away from the topic. Why don't we finish discussing this topic and then move on to the new topic? We could use our 'parking lot' to hold on to the new idea for later. We are so close to a decision; let's not lose the opportunity to finish our work."

*Using Humor to Move the Agenda*

- "Speaking of students and their ability to work in small groups, Lucille, why don't you share that story about how you got your rowdy group to work together!"

**FIGURE 6.2.** Roles of group members. Adapted from Hersey and Blanchard (1977) and Johnson and Johnson (2003). Copyright © 1977 Prentice Hall and Allyn-Bacon. Adapted by permission.

Small-group dynamics can be complex, evolving over time in ways that require instructional leaders to continually take stock and change direction. Facilitating small groups requires certain skills and strategies to ensure efficiency, progress, and a healthy group culture. Additional strategies for facilitating the work of small groups are discussed in the following sections.

### Don't Forget the Power of an Agenda

As mentioned briefly in Chapter 4 and earlier in this chapter, it is critical to develop (or co-develop) an agenda for each small-group meeting. Whether your agenda is independent for each meeting or part of a longer "running agenda" that is updated for each new meeting (e.g., a running Google or slide document that is simply added onto for each meeting), the key is to ensure that each small-group coaching session has an articulated goal, activities that engage teachers in authentic collaboration/learning, and clear takeaways with next steps. Again, we often refer coaches to the *Meeting Wise* (Boudett & City, 2014) checklist for meeting agendas to remind them of the variety of components that excellent meetings might include. (Harvard's *Meeting Wise* website offers an agenda template and checklist of meeting elements; see Web Resources at the end of this chapter.) Note that you may not include every element in each meeting, but the checklist can support overall meeting design.

Plan your small-group meeting agendas in ways that designate a specific amount of time for each topic or activity to be addressed, with important topics or essential questions at the top of the agenda. The final item on the agenda might include a summary of what has occurred, tasks to be accomplished before the next meeting, and identification of who is responsible for working on those tasks. It is also helpful to take time to reflect on what went well in the meeting and what might be improved. Ask, "What did the group appreciate about our work today? How did we do with our community agreements? How can we improve our collaborative work over time?"

Finally, the more that coaches can invite participating teachers into the work of co-creating and co-facilitating agendas, the more the group's capacity to facilitate its own collaborative inquiry work will grow. As a coach, you may slowly transfer agenda creation and facilitation responsibilities to group members, perhaps beginning by designating specific roles to lead teachers (e.g., note-taker, timekeeper) to start building the entire group's capacity to both participate in and lead small-group work. As Marsha Turner-Hall suggested in Voices from the Field earlier in this chapter, think about whether your words and actions promote teacher dependence or independence.

### Make Decisions in a Group-Appropriate Way

Groups can make decisions in different ways, and the coach's approach to decision making depends on many factors, including, but not limited to, school culture, the content of the decision, and the time available to make the decision. Questions that coaches may want to consider as they guide group decision making include:

- To what extent do teachers have the authority to make policy decisions?
- Is this decision about classroom practices, policies, or procedures?
- Is this an important decision that can be made over time with careful study, or one that needs to be made immediately with the best information available?

When decisions are important ones affecting the direction or goals of the group, use approaches that involve all members, both for improving the quality of the decision and enhancing the commitment of the group to the decision. Groups can come to a consensus (everyone agrees), or they can vote (either in writing or by hand). At times, the coach or an expert member of the group may decide and then simply ask the group to respond or support the decision. Alternatively, if the group has talked extensively about a specific issue without a resolution, the facilitator may suggest that the group table that issue and move to the next item on the agenda. All group members should have the information they need to make specific decisions. A series of decision-making steps should be identified so that the group members, at any given point in time, understand the extent to which they are involved in decision making and the amount of time and input they have. We particularly appreciate the decision-making options outlined by Kaner (2014), which include the person in charge deciding without group discussion, the person in charge deciding after group discussion, majority vote, and unanimous agreement. As a coach leading small-group decision-making processes, it is imperative to let the group know ahead of time which decision-making rules will be used so that everyone is clear on their role and the nature of their participation.

Coaches often play important roles in facilitating decision making and can build collective capacity by not rushing groups into technical, superficial responses to complex questions. An interesting approach to decision making that builds groups' reflective and decision-making skills is the one called 10-10-10, outlined by Suzy Welch (2010) in a book by the same title. Group members are asked to think about the impact a specific decision might have on teaching and learning within the school in 10 minutes, 10 months, and 10 years. Such a process enables the group to step back from the immediate question at hand (and perhaps related high emotions), and instead prompts thinking about long-term impact. Individual group members can jot down their ideas, and then the group can share, or participants can work in pairs or trios before a full-group discussion. A similar process can be found in the CLEE/SRI's Future (aka Back to the Future) protocol (see Web Resources at the end of this chapter), which allows groups to discuss an ideal vision of their work five years from now and then backward-plan steps to reach that more ideal future.

### Manage Group Dynamics

Life would be grand if all groups were composed of positive, supportive individuals focused on achieving the same goal. But many groups have one member (or perhaps a few!) whose participation is not as positive as we would wish. These individuals may monopolize the conversation, make negative comments, or even attempt to shift the direction of the group through confrontational comments about the topic or about other group members. As a coach, how might you navigate these difficult group dynamics?

First, dig into the reasoning behind difficult individual and group dynamics. Members of groups don't behave randomly—there are always underlying reasons for negativism or conflict that must be surfaced to solve or curtail them. Consider the following when thinking of individuals: Is conflict arising because of a difference in how they view the topic, a misunderstanding, or even some personal or personality issues between or among members? Taking time to think about why individuals and groups behave as they do will help coaches manage their own frustrations and better consider how to address the issue. Sometimes, the coach needs to redirect a conversation so that the same group member is not always talking, such as simply suggesting: "Okay, let's hear what others think!" Using some of the statements in Figure 6.2 can help coaches facilitate group interactions. Also, at times, the coach may need to speak to an individual privately to discuss specific behaviors. You may not always be successful, but with the help of other group members, you can often minimize the negative effects of specific members.

• • • • • • • • • • **Put into Practice** • • • • • • • • • • •

Download the Facilitation Scenarios Activity from the CLEE/SRI website (see Web Resources at the end of this chapter). With a partner or group of coaching colleagues, review some of the difficult group dynamics detailed in each scenario. What might you do as a coach/facilitator "in the moment" to best support group learning? What might you do ahead of time to prevent each of the difficult situations from arising?

### Remember That Differences Are Inevitable

Kaner (2014) describes how groups proceed from "divergent thinking"—through a "groan zone"—to "convergent thinking" (p. 20). Part of the excitement of working with groups is observing and facilitating their progress as they learn to work together, learn more about the tasks at hand, and determine how to reach their final goals. Sometimes excitement about co-creating a final product (e.g., a polished curriculum guide, codified modifications for small-group tier 2 interventions, a YouTube video sent to the community that describes the school's new approach to math instruction, and so on) can also motivate group members to work well together. Supporting groups as they make their own decisions builds the capacity of the group to engage independently in collaborative inquiry work and, ultimately, is the key to forming long-lasting collegial relationships.

In sum, small-group decision-making and facilitative work takes time—much longer than it might take for a coach or school leader to simply decide on their own. However, on the other hand, groups that are invited, as professionals, into teaching- and learning-focused decision-making and inquiry work can often accomplish so much more than simply announcing a new mandate. Moreover, as previously stated, the results decided upon by a group are far more likely to find life in the classroom or the school than decisions that are handed down or assigned. In the next Voices from the Field, we provide an example of how coach Linda DiMartino worked with teacher leaders in group settings to implement their coaching initiative.

> **VOICES FROM THE FIELD**
>
> Our school has a coaching model that is unique and similar to moving a barge slowly but consistently forward. We have 73 teachers from kindergarten through grade 4, across four buildings. There is one tugboat moving this barge of amazing teachers, and that would be the fearless coach (or captain). With the support of administration, we have one teacher leader at each grade level within each building. Additionally, we have a Reading Recovery teacher who joins the grade 1 team.
>
> The coach meets with each teacher-leader team once a month by grade level. One month the meetings are held after school for two hours, and the next month for a half-day during school with substitutes provided for classroom teachers. After-school meetings are for looking at data, discussing a book we are using, examining curriculum maps for pacing and revision, reflecting on strategies, or problem solving. The half-day meetings are more direct training sessions, for example, a workshop on a particular topic. The coach has provided in-depth training on a topic (e.g., poetry) and then launched it in a classroom where others observed. The coach supported the leaders through modeling and coaching, and then the teacher leaders presented this topic during professional development for their grade-level colleagues.
>
> This professional development model has grown because we have maintained the same teacher leaders over the past five years. They support moving the barge forward because they participate in goal setting and share the vision of the district and coach.
>
> —LINDA DiMARTINO, Literacy Supervisor

## Strategies for Working with Large Groups

In addition to small-group facilitation, coaches are also often asked to facilitate large-group meetings. The most common form this large-group facilitation takes is making presentations to large groups of teachers, administrators, or even the school board. Coaches may be asked to review instructional strategies, a new curriculum plan or program, school-level achievement data, and much more. Such large-group presentations have their place. They provide an opportunity for all to hear the same message at the same time. They are efficient. However, they also have limitations. Teacher participants are nearly always at different stages of learning—some know a lot about the topic, and others do not. They may have different perspectives about the importance of the topic. Further, as is evident in studies of professional learning initiatives (Darling-Hammond et al., 2017; Guskey & Yoon, 2009), such introductory presentations alone are rarely sufficient to guarantee effective implementation in classrooms. Here we present several ideas for how to make large-group presentations more efficient and effective:

- Making a presentation to a large group requires close attention to both content and process. The presentation should be focused, address the needs of the group, and flow in a coherent and consistent manner. At the same time, opportunities for active group participation to maintain attention and engagement are important. A simple turn-and-talk (perhaps after 10 minutes of speaking, or after a specific topic has been discussed) can greatly increase the power of a large-group presentation. For example, after describing key ideas about the importance of equitable instruction, ask individuals to talk with a partner for two minutes, each discussing what that term means to them. This is also an opportunity for a coach to model group facilitation moves, which can be replicated by teachers in PLCs or in classrooms with students.

- To the extent possible, make certain that large-group presentations are planned in ways that anticipate and honor the learning needs of adults. As we described in Chapter 2, building on adult development theory, educators have different ways of knowing and learning. Considering potential differences between instrumental, socializing, and self-authoring ways of learning can help a coach better plan for a large-group presentation. The following questions may guide you in planning large-group presentations:

    o Is the environment one that is conducive to active learning? (For example, does it have round tables, which increases the possibility of small-group interaction?) Carefully plan for and set up the physical learning environment so it facilitates interaction between peers or small groups.

    o Will participants have opportunities for choice of learning activities, such as small-group breakout sessions, different readings and resources, stations, or flexible pairings/groupings? Plan for variety in the presentation so that individuals are involved and able to collaborate. Even a brief opportunity to choose one reading or resource over another, coupled with an opportunity to chat with colleagues about what was found, can help break up lengthier large-group presentations.

○ Is there a "hook" that captures the attention of participants? Is there a clearly articulated goal or rationale for the session, clarifying how the session can help teachers improve student learning? Be sure to identify your purpose and your agenda (i.e., naming the goals of the presentation). Remember the importance of the first few minutes spent with the audience. Consider how you can generate interest and engagement with the topic. Think about ways to connect with the audience—share common experiences or interest in the topic. (For example, you might talk about the challenges you had getting home from school during the recent blizzard or your experience watching the total solar eclipse.) If you are the second speaker, think of ways you can relate your remarks to what has been said before; that is, show relationships between the previous presentation and yours (e.g., "As Melinda said, classroom observations and achievement data indicate that our intermediate-level students would benefit from more emphasis on vocabulary development").

○ Use the right tools for delivering the presentation. Presenters may use videos that they have developed or obtained from online sources to show examples of specific instructional strategies or approaches. Many develop PowerPoint slides to organize their remarks. We all know that when technology works, it is great; if not, it can be a disaster. Having a plan B is essential; if the video doesn't work, what options do you have? Note that PowerPoint presentations, although popular, can be extremely problematic if they are poorly done. See Figure 6.3 for ideas about how to develop effective PowerPoint presentations.

○ As a test of whether you are ready to make a large presentation, practice summarizing your major points to determine if they flow well and are consistent

---

- Use only a few words on each slide to make a key point—keep text to a minimum, just to remind you and your audience of main ideas.
- Keep the overall number of slides to a minimum.
- Make sure the font is large enough for the group to read (size 24 at least).
- Combine text with visuals to hold the attention of the audience.
- If accessing the internet, sound, or videos during your presentation, test your multimedia components as you are setting up, and be prepared to skip them or use local copies on your computer (as opposed to streaming or clicking on embedded multimedia in your presentation).
- If presenting to a large audience in a well-lit space, consider using a dark background and lighter text, as this is often better for viewing in such cases.

**FIGURE 6.3.** Tips for creating effective slide presentations.

with your goal or purpose. Too often, speakers try to put too much into a presentation. Remember, focus on your goal(s) and the ideas and activities that will help you accomplish it.

## *Making a Virtual Presentation*

There are times, especially in large districts, when coaches may be asked to make a presentation to a large group via Zoom, Google Meet, or another virtual platform. Many of the ideas presented previously apply: Provide time for audience participation, make the visuals interesting and readable, and include ideas for follow-up, especially if you are presenting in your own district (e.g., in what ways can the coaches help teachers implement specific instructional strategies?). Both of us (Rita and Jacy) have worked with and across districts and have found that virtual presentations can hold participants' attention and provide an efficient way of meeting with a large group if carefully constructed with multiple opportunities for participant involvement (e.g., utilizing the chat box, raising hands, breaking into smaller groups via breakout rooms, and so forth). In fact, when we have worked virtually with a group of educators over time, we actually feel as though we get to know them *almost* as well as if we were with them face-to-face.

## *Suggestions for Follow-Up*

Whether in-person or virtual, consider which follow-up activities might be helpful after a large-group presentation so that participants will think about how they can use what they have learned. Garmston (2005) suggests that presentations end with a call to action rather than a summary. In other words, how might participants use information from the presentation immediately? For example, participants might be invited to select specific instructional strategies from the presentation to try in their classrooms.

Also, coaches/facilitators can plan for small-group meetings in each school to address questions identified by teachers and provide essential follow-up support within more specific school, grade-level, or content-area contexts. Coaches who are presenting across schools or at the district level can provide their contact information, encouraging participants to get in touch if they have questions. Providing participants with handouts (or a link to an online repository of files) to which they can refer is also helpful, as it is easy to forget or misinterpret what has been heard.

Finally, make sure to provide opportunities for participant feedback. Such feedback can provide the coach/facilitator with information about what went well and how to improve the presentation. At the same time, such feedback can also help participants identify and remember what is important to each of them and how they might use what they learned in their classroom instruction. One useful strategy is the 3-2-1 exit slip (via paper or Google Forms), in which participants are asked to identify three points they are going to remember, two ideas they plan to use in their work, and one question that remains for them.

> **STOP AND REFLECT**
>
> Now that you have read about working with small and large groups, think about your own strengths. Ask yourself: What makes me successful as a facilitator of small-group meetings? How might I improve? Then consider your facilitation skills when working with large groups. Are there ways that you wish to improve, and if so, how? Consult the Further Readings and Resources at the end of this chapter as a starting point.

## Group Activities That Support the Development of Professional Learning Communities

Professional learning communities have endured across decades in U.S. schools and beyond. PLCs have been used to support grade-level, content-area, and departmental work, as well as a wide variety of task-specific purposes (e.g., curricular review, equity and justice work in schools). In fact, the term *PLC* has been used so ubiquitously that, as stated by DuFour (2004), "it is in danger of losing all meaning" (p. 6). As DuFour explains, there are three big ideas that represent the core principles of PLCs: ensuring that students learn (teachers focusing on student learning), a culture of collaboration (teachers working together to improve classroom practices), and a focus on results (assessing whether professional learning is improving teaching and learning). We think of PLCs as "initiatives by schools for all staff members to work collaboratively as learners to achieve a common goal, that of improving student learning" (Swan Dagen & Bean, 2020, p. 430). Therefore, many different group activities can be useful in promoting such collaboration.

Although coaches often play an important role in facilitating PLC work, the effort requires principal support and leadership; in other words, as expanded upon in Chapter 3, coaches must work closely with principals to establish such collegial environments. Vescio et al. (2008) provide evidence that when schools function as learning communities, there is a positive impact on teacher classroom practices and student learning. They identify five key notions critical for establishing such efforts in schools: shared values and norms, a focus on student learning, reflective dialogue among teachers, teaching made public, and collaboration. For those interested in assessing the degree to which effective PLCs exist in their school or district, consult the collaborative environment assessment tools mentioned in Chapter 3 (the CLEE/SRI Professional Learning Communities Survey).

> **VOICES FROM THE FIELD**
>
> A large part of our journey in becoming a true professional learning community (as a school) has to do with establishing a culture of trust where teachers feel safe saying what they're good at, where they need help, and where they also feel safe watching each other teach. This trust exists in pockets but is certainly not the norm.
>
> —SHAUNA MAGEE, Literacy Coach

Coaches should be thoughtful about which group formats and processes will best serve teachers' needs at particular junctures, refining and expanding traditional PLC formats. For a quick review of some of the most common options, we turn to *Best Practices of Literacy Leaders: Keys to School Improvement*, in which Swan Dagen and Bean (2020) describe various activities that are effective in promoting collaborative work in schools. We highlight a few of these activities in the following sections and provide additional suggestions.

### *Book Clubs or Study Groups*

These can build teacher knowledge about a topic and, at the same time, help teachers become more reflective in their work. Risko and Vogt (2016) highlight the rationale for using book study groups, provide ideas about how to implement such professional learning activities, and discuss the challenges of such discussions. Walpole and Beauchat (2008) identify two important criteria for instituting such study groups: providing opportunities for choice and making connections to classroom practice. We have recently worked with groups reading Ippolito et al.'s (2019, 2024) *Disciplinary Literacy Inquiry and Instruction* to support middle and high school educators in reviewing and revising their discipline-specific literacy instruction across content areas. We also know of districts that have read books such as Knight's (2017) *Impact Cycle* and Aguilar's (2016) *Art of Coaching Teams* to build a collective understanding of how coaches and school leaders can collaborate to build cultures of continuous learning in their schools. In some schools, coaches choose to use short texts, articles, or digital "briefs" (e.g., International Literacy Association's Digital Resources; see Web Resources at the end of this chapter) to prompt group discussion. Shorter texts can be especially helpful for introducing teachers to new information without committing them to a task that requires a long-term responsibility. Whether using books or shorter texts, all worked well because the *groups* chose the texts—then each resource was strategically read for high-leverage strategies and routines to implement. Later, each text served as a reference guide once the formal study groups had ended.

## *Lesson Study*

The lesson study format (Collet, 2019; Risko & Vogt, 2016) is a process that enables teachers to study their own work collectively and systematically. Teachers, as a group, plan a lesson, and then one teacher volunteers to teach that lesson, which is observed by others or video recorded. The group then holds a follow-up discussion of the lesson and its effects on student learning. The lesson is revised and retaught, and the process continues. In one school, the principal agreed to teach a lesson that was video recorded for follow-up discussion. Anxiety about videoing was reduced, and, as you can imagine, teachers enjoyed providing feedback to the principal.

## *Data Meetings*

These meetings are held to discuss the results of assessment measures (both formal and informal) and can serve as a source of learning for teachers. In such meetings, the focus should be twofold. First, what do the data tell members about the strengths and needs of students? Second, what do the data suggest in terms of the need for instructional changes in classrooms? For coaches delving deeply into facilitating data meetings, we always recommend the *Data Wise* series of books as excellent guides. (More about assessment and coaching work can be found in Chapter 7.)

## *Grade-Level Meetings*

Productive grade-level meetings provide opportunities for discussion about substantive issues in addition to addressing more logistical items, such as scheduling or test administration details. Teachers can sign up in advance to make brief presentations on a student about whom they have concerns or a strategy or approach that has or hasn't worked well. Teachers can be asked to bring documentation (student work or assessment data) for the group to see and discuss. Discussion-based protocols are often an effective means in situations such as this for helping teachers work effectively and efficiently.

## *Classroom Learning Walks*

Another useful approach is for coaches and teachers to establish learning walks as a means of teacher learning. Note that different districts talk about these activities and engage in them in slightly different ways. You might hear these referred to as "data walks," "instructional rounds," or "walk-throughs." While there are differences in terminology and procedures, the key is to make sure that everyone in your community knows both the purposes and the rules of engagement *before* beginning. In Figure 6.4, we identify key steps for coaches involved in facilitating learning walks

- **Discuss the purpose of the learning walk** (e.g., improvement of instruction), the nature of the activity (e.g., descriptive, not evaluative), and the content focus (e.g., observing student engagement or teacher levels of questioning).
- **Decide on who will be observed** (ask for volunteers, or invite teachers with specific expertise or experience to volunteer).
- **Develop a learning walk guide with specific questions or look-fors that address the focus of the observation** (e.g., effective teacher questioning, student grouping options, and so on). Sample questions that might guide observations include: What is the learning environment in the room (e.g., evidence of student work, books and other materials available)? What are students doing, and can they talk about their work (e.g., do they understand the task and reason for it)? What is the teacher doing to encourage effective student participation? Instead of a specific guide, you may also use a note-catcher that tracks several overarching questions: What I noticed? What I wondered? Positive feedback? (This sort of note-catcher can be useful when coaches are introducing learning walks to teachers.)
- **Establish procedures for the learning walk.** Observers should stand to the side, but if students are working at seats, observers can talk informally with them. Observers should not talk with each other as they observe. Again, the learning walk is not for evaluative purposes.
- **Schedule walks.** Generally, teachers may be able to observe in at least two classrooms during one of their planning periods. The coach and at least two teachers should observe so a team of teachers can learn from each other.
- **Spend 10 minutes or so in the classroom and then debrief in the hallway.** If possible, include the classroom teacher in this debriefing. Address the focus of the learning walk. What questions do you have for the teacher? In a later group or grade-level meeting, there can be more extensive discussion of the observation with a focus on application. What can teachers take back to their classrooms?
- **Leave a thank-you note for each teacher who was observed.**

**FIGURE 6.4.** Steps in initiating learning walks.

in their school. (See also Ippolito & Bean, 2024, Chapter 4, for further information and related resources.)

### *Collaborative Cycles of Inquiry*

Finally, one of the most sophisticated yet powerful activities for small groups to undertake is that of collaborative inquiry (Cochran-Smith & Lytle, 2009; Ippolito et al., 2019, 2024; Risko & Vogt, 2016). A coach can support small teams as they first identify their own inquiry goals, such as learning more about teaching peer-revision processes, discipline-specific vocabulary strategies, or crafting high-quality responses to document-based questions. Then the coach supports team members as they find resources, read about their intended areas of interest, synthesize findings, and begin to adopt and adapt new classroom practices. When each member is ready, teachers volunteer to try new practices in their respective classrooms and then bring the results back to the group for discussion and reflection. Ultimately, the group assesses the effects of the new work and begins the cycle of inquiry over again, sometimes digging deeper into the same topic and sometimes deciding to leave a topic for a while and begin a new cycle of inquiry focused on a related or entirely new topic. We find that CLEE/SRI's two graphics about collaborative cycles of inquiry are helpful in presenting this idea to teams of teachers: Cycle of Inquiry and Cycle of Inquiry for Professional Learning Communities Activities (see Web Resources at the end of this chapter).

Although scheduling collaborative work often requires creativity (e.g., during shared planning periods, before-school breakfasts or coffees, after-school study groups) and support from administrators (e.g., flexible scheduling, professional development days, use of substitutes), these activities can take place for short amounts of time, such as one class period, or for more extended stretches, such as two-hour blocks or one afternoon every other week. The key to any of these formats is forming ground rules when starting and sustaining the work long enough for teachers to see the effects of their collaborative efforts, reinforcing that collaboration is important and should continue.

## Summary

In this chapter, we have outlined some of the major ways of working with teachers in groups, both small and large, and have discussed the importance of establishing community agreements, carefully selecting collaboration formats, and ensuring engagement in every coaching interaction. We then offered suggestions for presenting to large groups of teachers. Finally, we highlighted several specifics of what group coaching typically entails, including an array of PLC collaborative inquiry formats. Ultimately, Melinda might find the ideas in this chapter useful in beginning her work with the grade-level team, both in *starting* (e.g., establishing community agreements, crafting clear agendas, considering routine and repertoire) and in *sustaining* the work (e.g., engaging in classroom learning walks, lesson study, collaborative inquiry).

## Reflections

- Using the chart found in Appendix A, identify ways that coaches can support teachers through small-group and large-group work. How do you as a coach serve as a change agent, facilitator, designer, and advocate when working with teachers in groups? Which activities might you consider adopting that would further these ways of thinking and working?
- In rereading the sections of this chapter that focus specifically on facilitating

small-group learning experiences, which coaching moves most closely mirror work you have previously undertaken? Now consider large-group coaching. Which ideas and moves seem new and important to try next? Based on what you read in this chapter, what changes might you now make when facilitating for groups?

# Activities

- Discuss the ideas in this chapter with a coaching colleague. Identify some of your own and each other's strengths and areas of growth related to small- and large-group facilitation. What are your current coaching "superpowers" when it comes to facilitating group work (e.g., clearly articulating meeting goals)? What might be your "kryptonite" (e.g., navigating difficult group dynamics)? How might you best support one another in growing your facilitative skill set?
- Choose an article or resource from the list of Further Readings and Resources. Make a connection between the new resource, this book chapter, and your own work. What new questions arise for you? What new coaching moves might you want to try?
- Observe two different team meetings, and note the following: role of the facilitator, distribution of work and participation across the group, focus of the work, and agenda and protocol usage. As you compare the two observations, what did you learn that you would like to use in your own work? What might you offer as suggestions?

## FURTHER READINGS AND RESOURCES

### Print Resources

Adams, S. R., & Breidenstein, A. (Eds.). (2023). *Exploring meaningful and sustainable intentional learning communities for P-20 educators.* IGI Global.

Dana, N. F., & Yendol-Hoppey, D. (2008). *The reflective educator's guide to professional development: Coaching inquiry-oriented learning communities.* Corwin Press.

Kaner, S. (2014). *The facilitator's guide to participatory decision-making* (3rd ed.). Jossey-Bass.

Kaner, S. (2014). Introduction to the role of facilitator. In S. Kaner (Ed.), *The facilitator's guide to participatory decision-making* (3rd ed., pp. 31–40). Jossey-Bass.

Risko, V. J., & Vogt, M. E. (2016). *Professional learning in action: An inquiry approach for teachers of literacy.* Teachers College Press.

Shand, R., & Batts, J. (2023). Toward more inclusive professional learning communities. *Journal of Education Human Resources, 41*(1), 110–141.

Venables, D. R. (2017). *Facilitating teacher teams and authentic PLCs: The human side of leading people, protocols, and practices.* ASCD.

**Web Resources (see *www.guilford.com/bean3-materials* for live links)**

Center for Leadership & Educational Equity and the School Reform Initiative. (2024). *Protocols.* www.clee.org/resources

Conyers, T. (2023). Engagement matters: Tips for facilitating large groups. Medium. https://medium.com/@tricia.conyers/engagement-matters-d0250aa9bf02

Harvard University. (n.d.). *Meeting Wise resources.* DataWise. http://datawise.gse.harvard.edu/meeting-wise-resources

International Literacy Association. (n.d.). Digital resources by topic. www.literacyworldwide.org/get-resources/resources-by-topic

Learning Forward. (n.d.). *Featured coaching resources.* https://learningforward.org/coaches

Miller, A. (2020). *Creating effective professional learning communities.* Edutopia. www.edutopia.org/article/creating-effective-professional-learning-communities

PowerSchool. (2023). *The PLC handbook for educators: Unlocking professional learning communities.* www.powerschool.com/blog/plc-handbook

Spangler, D. (2023). *PLC coaching: 12 ways to achieve effective results.* SmartBrief. www.smartbrief.com/original/plc-coaching-impact-cycle

Stanford D.School. (n.d.). *Setting group intentions for brave spaces.* http://dschool.stanford.edu/resources/norms

Teaching Tolerance. (2019). *Let's talk! Facilitating critical conversations with students.* Southern Poverty Law Center. www.learningforjustice.org/sites/default/files/2019-12/TT-Lets-Talk-December-2019.pdf

We and Me. (n.d.). *Chad Littlefield: Co-founder, speaker, author, and creator of We! Connect Cards.* https://weand.me/chad-littlefield

# CHAPTER 7

# Using Assessment to Guide Student Learning and School Improvement

> **GUIDING QUESTIONS**
>
> 1. What are the major purposes of assessment, and what sources of data are available to assess student learning?
> 2. In what ways can large-scale assessment measures be used effectively, and what are their limitations?
> 3. In what ways can coaches partner with teachers to help them use data to effectively inform classroom instruction?
> 4. What are key considerations for schools and districts in developing a comprehensive assessment system, and how can coaches facilitate the development of such a system?

## Melinda Wades into Assessment Work

The superintendent and district leadership team, because of their concerns about low test scores after the pandemic, and noting that a percentage of their students are "opting out" of taking standardized tests, have decided that it's time to reconsider how to improve their current district assessment plan. The superintendent and Melinda's principal have asked Melinda and a small group of teachers across elementary schools to serve as a task force to explore and recommend changes that might be made to the district assessment plan. Team members were excited about designing an assessment plan that would help teachers in making instructional decisions. Melinda was pleased to be asked to lead the task force, but a bit nervous about this large district-level responsibility.

At the first team meeting, Melinda facilitated a discussion that focused on the team's thoughts about the current district plan. Members agreed that assessment data were important in helping teachers plan instruction, and in addition, they felt as though much of their district assessment plan was congruent with both state goals and their own district expectations. At the same time, they had several concerns about current assessment tools. First, the team felt that more attention should be given to developing and using assessment tools that would help teachers identify more than students' academic learning—what tools would help teachers learn more about how students' social, cultural, and personal needs and strengths affect learning? Second, they were concerned about the cumulative time spent on assessment work and wanted their district comprehensive plan to be "lean and mean," assessing priority student skills, behaviors, attitudes, and perceptions. This meant thinking about tools whose results could be used soon after administration, and which assessments might be eliminated, thus providing more time for instruction. Finally, although Melinda and her team recognized the importance of assessment for accountability purposes, they wanted to focus on assessments that would provide the data teachers need to make appropriate instructional decisions for all students.

They began their work by reading several articles about assessment, including excerpts from the book *The Perfect Assessment System* by Stiggins (2017). In a follow-up discussion, team members identified three key points that they wanted to share with all teachers:

- Addressing the need for a new vision for assessment, given the new mission identified by their school district
- Focusing on the need for all students to succeed, that is, developing an assessment plan that would address issues of diversity and equity
- Improving their system of communicating assessment results to various stakeholders, including teachers, administrators, and families/caregivers (adapted from Stiggins, 2017)

This team of educators then began thinking about an action plan that could be used to plan professional learning that would increase teacher knowledge and understanding of assessment, its value, and its limitations. They wanted to be certain that, in addition to the required standardized measures, teachers would be involved in co-designing other tools that they could readily interpret and use in their instructional planning. A key revelation for this small group of planners was that what teachers believed about their own subject area would influence what they viewed as important to measure. Therefore, one of the task force's first steps would be to facilitate school-based and cross-school discussions to help teachers think about their own views about the content areas they taught and how to measure student learning.

## How This Chapter Can Help Melinda and All Coaches to Think about Assessment

Across schools and districts, all educators who coach eventually must wrestle with issues of assessment, both at the micro classroom level and often (as Melinda is facing) at the macro school or district level. Therefore, to support coaches in thinking and working like a designer and tackling assessment work, in this chapter we address the issues that Melinda and her teacher team identified as important in their planning. We begin by providing a definition of assessment and describing sources of data important for making decisions about student, classroom, and school performance. We then provide foundational information about large-scale measures used to make judgments about schools and school systems, identifying the potential uses and limitations of these measures. This is followed by a discussion of formative assessments and their usefulness in helping classroom teachers understand how to work with data to improve instructional practices and student learning. We conclude by discussing the need for a well-conceived assessment system as a means of analyzing and improving whole-school performance.

As mentioned in Ippolito and Bean (2024), working at both the individual and the system levels simultaneously is especially important for coaches when designing plans for selecting assessment tools and for applying their results, given data's potential for shaping instruction for individuals, classrooms, and systems. Because our focus is on the process and use of assessment, rather than on specific measures, see Further Readings and Resources at the end of this chapter for suggested references for instructional coaches to consult for more detailed information about assessment and specific assessment instruments, their applicability, and usefulness in assessing student learning.

## Assessment of Student Learning: The What and Why

When individuals are asked to define or describe assessment, they often respond with some version of the following terms: *testing, tests, examinations, evaluation, judging,* and *measuring*. We appreciate Stiggins's (2017) definition of assessment: "the process of gathering evidence of student learning to inform educational decisions" (p. 5). Such decisions can be made about individuals or groups of students, as well as about schools, districts, states, and countries. "Such data are multidimensional, encompassing more than just standardized tests" (Bean & Goatley, 2021, p. 254). They can be retrieved from many different sources, from tests to observations of students, samples of student performance (e.g., writing), inventories of motivation, or surveys of attitudes about instruction, schooling, and so on (see Figure 7.1 for examples of data sources).

***Tests***

- Standardized tests (statewide or district), given annually
- Interim assessment measures, screening measures, or benchmark tests, administered at multiple times during the school year
- Teacher-developed tests for groups of students (end-of-unit or end-of-course)
- Diagnostic tests for individual students to obtain additional information about their strengths and needs (reading or math inventories, language assessment)

***Student assignments or work samples***

- Class projects or writing samples. When viewed by the classroom teacher, these work samples can yield key pieces of information about multiple factors, including content knowledge, writing and spelling skills, and even motivation to learn.

***Classroom observations***

- Classroom teachers can learn a great deal from the attitudes and responses of students to the lessons being taught.
- They can also learn much when watching students in the classroom environment; are they participating in classroom activities? Responding to questions?
- Teachers might also watch video of lessons they or other teachers have taught to obtain valuable information about a specific student or students.

***Portfolios***

- Teachers who keep portfolios of student work over time can learn a great deal about the progress or lack of progress of students.
- Portfolios are important sources of information for caregivers or family members.
- They also serve as a valuable resource for teachers in providing additional materials and activities for specific students.

***Teacher conferences***

- Interviews with individuals or groups of students (focus groups)
- Much can be learned when teachers take the time to talk with students about their perceptions of their experiences in the classroom. Teachers can also talk with parents/caregivers and other teachers. These conferences or conversations can provide important information, yielding a more holistic view of the student and their needs.

***Attendance records, surveys, and inventories***

- If students aren't in school, there is little opportunity to learn. Instructional leaders can learn a great deal by looking at which grade levels, subject areas, and lengths of time students may have been absent (e.g., did a student miss portions of first grade when teachers were emphasizing phonics?; did a student miss a portion of third grade when fractions were introduced?).
- Surveys of parents, teachers, and students
- Surveys can provide useful information about perceptions of various groups, student backgrounds, and student knowledge. See Elish-Piper et al. (2022) for examples of assessment surveys and inventories.

**FIGURE 7.1.** Sources of data.

Assessment results have three important uses or purposes: (1) Assessment *for* learning relates to the uses that teachers make of formative tools to inform their teaching, (2) assessment *as* learning refers to the ways that students use assessment results to monitor their own learning, and (3) assessment *of* learning relates to the judgments or comparisons that teachers can make to determine whether students have achieved desired outcomes or goals (think summative assessment) (Brookhart, 2023; Chappuis et al., 2012; Stiggins, 2017).

Stiggins (2014) suggests that given the importance of assessment in instructional decision making, teachers must be "assessment literate" (p. 67); that is, they must understand assessment, what it is, its limitations, and how student performance on different measures might affect teaching and learning. Thus, one of the important roles of coaches is to support school personnel in gaining the knowledge and understanding to be able to use assessment results to inform instruction and, ultimately, to improve student performance overall.

Assessment in today's schools is undergoing a transformation, with Miguel Cardona, U.S. secretary of education, calling for states to develop more innovative and high-quality assessment models to replace current ones that have considerable limitations (Tomasic, 2024). In the following sections, we identify in more detail summative assessments, their strengths and limitations, and then formative assessments, which can be especially useful to teachers in shaping their instruction. As Grose (2024) indicates, many students are opting out of taking standardized tests, calling into question their validity, especially for underserved and minority populations. However, Grose goes on to suggest that efforts be made to fix these tests rather than discard them.

### *Summative Assessments*

First, assessment results can be used for accountability, that is, to determine whether schools or districts are achieving their goals and where they might need to improve. These outcome measures, known as summative measures, serve as assessments *of* learning, and evaluate whether students have learned what they were expected to learn. They can be used for grading purposes (of a student or school), and results can be shared with various stakeholders (e.g., families and the school board). Summative measures, as designed or selected by teachers (e.g., end-of-term examinations, end-of-unit tests, and student-developed portfolios), can be useful in determining whether students have achieved specific classroom or even school goals. Some even suggest that these standardized assessments (e.g., SATs) can serve as a better measure than grades to identify the potential success of underrepresented minorities for college (Leonhardt, 2024).

However, summative assessments, in the form of large-scale, high-stakes measures (standardized tests given by the school district or state exams), are often controversial in many ways, including for the time they take from instruction, the validity of their results given the diversity of students in schools, and even the nature of the tests, which often focus on multiple-choice, low-level responses. As mentioned previously, there are efforts at both the federal and state levels to make changes in standardized tests that will make them more valid and useful.

### Large-Scale, High-Stakes Measures: Potential and Pitfalls

Large-scale measures, generally standardized instruments required by the individual states, if selected carefully for their technical robustness, provide results that enable comparisons among schools and, if data are disaggregated, generate information about the performance of various subgroups being tested. Certainly, the results have made clear the educational gaps in the performance of various subgroups (e.g., multilingual learners, students with learning differences, those who are economically disadvantaged, racial and ethnic subgroups, and so on) and have led to more focused attempt to improve equal educational opportunities for all students (Darling-Hammond, 2010). Also, results can be useful at the school level for identifying various areas of strength or weakness in curricular areas. In other words, instruments that provide summative data can be useful for taking an overall look at the school or district. They can provide information about groups of students that can be shared with various stakeholders, including families, school boards, and legislators responsible for funding schools.

However, there are several problems that arise when these tests and their results are used inappropriately. First, results of a single measure are too often used to make high-stakes decisions (retention and graduation) that affect the lives of individuals and groups of students. Yet, as indicated in the position statement of the International Literacy Association (then the International Reading Association) on using high-stakes literacy assessments (Hall, 2014), a single measure does not adequately assess the literacy competencies of an individual. In the position statement, it is recommended that high-stakes decisions be based on multiple assessments that include teacher judgment as well as student and family input, in addition to test results, when making decisions about grade retention or graduation. This is especially important given that a single test result may misrepresent the learning of historically minoritized students in schools.

Second, these tests do not provide much useful information for the classroom teacher (Brookhart, 2023; Hess, 2023). The tests are generally given infrequently or at the end of the year and don't provide results at a useful time to guide instruction, nor are the results specific enough to set instructional learning targets for classroom instruction. As an example, in a landmark study by Buly and Valencia (2002), results of students' reading scores on a high-stakes measure were compared with results of additional diagnostic testing. Several distinctive and different patterns of reading ability were found that were not evident on the large-scale measure. In other words, two students receiving the same score (e.g., reading at the third stanine or at the

45th percentile) on a standardized large-scale measure may have different literacy strengths and needs.

Third, given the format of most of these high-stake measures, there tends to be more of an emphasis on recall and recognition rather than on more high-level skills such as problem solving, evaluation, and drawing inferences. Furthermore, they are often not aligned with the curriculum; that is, there may be little overlap, and therefore, the results provide little useful data for improving instruction.

Fourth, high-stakes measures have influenced curriculum and instruction in negative ways. Too often, there is a focus on teaching to the test, which can narrow the curriculum and reduce time spent on subjects such as social studies, science, or the arts. Moreover, too much time may be spent on preparing students for the tests. We have all heard tales of schools preparing for the large-scale measures that take place each year, with time spent motivating students to do well, helping them to become familiar with various test formats or answering specific types of questions. Some schools hold motivational "testing parties" or "assemblies," or they provide incentives for those classrooms with 100% attendance on testing day. Parents are sent flyers or emails in which they are given suggestions for how they can best prepare their children for test days (e.g., make certain they get enough sleep and eat a good breakfast). Often, teachers are asked to provide students with "test prep" activities long before the tests are administered.

Ultimately, we think it is important for coaches and school leaders (in conversation with teachers) to keep considering how much emphasis is placed on test preparation and success. How much is helpful, and how much can be detrimental to the emotional states of students and their families? In some schools, pressures to do well have influenced educators to ignore students who score the highest and the lowest on these high-stakes measures. Teachers are asked to concentrate their instructional efforts on students labeled as "bubble children," those who score just below the proficiency cutoff, with the expectation that it is more likely that these students will improve and the overall scores for the school will be higher.

Fifth, both parents and teachers have criticized the amount of time devoted to assessment and the stress generated by these time-consuming measures. As mentioned previously, some parents across the country are "opting out" of testing for their children, indicating their displeasure with these large-scale measures. And during the 2020 COVID-19 global pandemic, many educators were concerned about the validity of test scores, given that students were taking the tests online—and in some instances receiving additional support from families!

Finally, coaches can have a positive influence on helping teachers navigate the often narrow focus of high stakes testing on basic skills by working collaboratively with teachers to develop various alternative and effective instructional approaches. Zoch (2015), for example, discusses the ways that a coach, with her principal's support, worked to develop a sense of community and collective efficacy that enhanced literacy instruction in the school. In this study, the coach was able to serve as a mediator to help teachers meet accountability requirements and at the same time implement evidence-based instructional strategies. But there are cautions that must be considered. See the following Voices from the Field for ways that the focus on assessment can take coaches away from their essential work.

> **VOICES FROM THE FIELD**
>
> Another challenge for many of our coaches is the administration of standardized tests. In several schools, coaches are the test coordinators, monitors, makeup administrators, and general proctors when teachers are absent. Some are also charged with pulling out the "bubble" students and tutoring them in effective test-taking strategies so they can help raise the school's scores and positively impact the school's report card, taking them away from their coaching responsibilities.
> —Ellen Eisenberg, Executive Director,
> The Professional Institute for Instructional Coaching

Currently, large-scale assessment measures are part of the fabric of life in today's schools, although there appears to be more recognition that the overemphasis on large-scale testing, accountability, and punitive measures against schools and teachers have not been productive in improving student learning (Stiggins, 2017). Thus, it is exciting that across the country, there is an emphasis on making changes that might improve these state assessment measures (Tomasic, 2024). Florida and Texas, for example, have replaced current end-of-year assessments with progress-monitoring models that assess students three times a year (Tomasic, 2024).

The bottom line is that school leaders and coaches, to be effective, must think and operate like designers. They must carefully match assessment measures (both large- and small-scale) with inquiry questions about students, teaching, and learning. Collectively, we must understand what large-scale measures can and cannot provide. Coaches and leaders can *facilitate* reflective discussions with teachers about data from these measures and assist them in making decisions about what those data suggest about instructional practices. Further, coaches can be *advocates* for teachers and for students by providing school boards, families, and the community with accurate, up-to-date information about what the results of these measures really mean. In the following section, we discuss the use of formative assessment to improve classroom instruction—critical work in aligning coaching efforts with content and context.

## Formative Assessments

A second purpose of assessment is to provide formative information about how to improve learning for students. Formative measures are useful for planning instructional activities, screening student performance, monitoring student progress, designing and implementing metacognitive tasks, diagnosing learning problems, and providing feedback to students about their performance. Often, these measures are "process" strategies or approaches used during instruction (e.g., oral questioning, think-alouds, every-pupil-response techniques such as "thumbs up" or "thumbs down," or student-developed graphic organizers or conceptual maps). Measurement tools, such as benchmark or progress-monitoring tests, can also provide formative information to teachers; results can be readily attained and may be useful for modifying instruction. The remainder of this chapter delves specifically into the ways that coaches can use and support formative assessments to directly improve classroom instruction.

## Ideas for Coaches: Using Data to Improve Classroom Instruction

Coaches can have an enormous influence on instruction in the classroom if they help teachers use data to identify specific needs and strengths of the students with whom they work and use those results to inform instruction. Such data can be used to make decisions about how to prioritize instructional time, to identify individual student strengths and needs, to identify specific instructional interventions, to target supplemental instruction for students who are struggling, to judge the instructional effectiveness of specific lessons, and to refine instructional methods (Hamilton et al., 2009). Yet, often teachers who are responsible for using such data do not believe that they have the necessary professional skills that enable them to interpret and then apply the results (Elish-Piper et al., 2022; Stiggins, 2017). Thus, there is great need for coaches to help develop teacher capacity to understand and use the data available to them.

As Melinda thinks about how best to support her team in providing professional learning for teachers about assessment issues, she might do well to start with Figure 7.2. The figure contains a checklist adapted from Hamilton et al. (2009, p. 9) that identifies recommendations for using data for classroom, school, and district decision making. In the next section, we discuss Recommendations 1 and 2, which highlight data use by teachers in their classrooms and ways that coaches can work with teachers to put these recommendations into practice. Subsequently, we discuss more fully Recommendations 3 and 4.

### Recommendation #1: Make Data an Essential Aspect of the Instructional Improvement Cycle

Too often, schools are inundated with data that are not used or useful. Teachers complain about having too much data and little time to do anything with them, and as mentioned previously, they may lack the expertise to understand what the data mean for instruction. Other teachers are concerned that although they can analyze the data, they aren't sure how to use the results in making instructional decisions. We suggest that coaches implement an assessment cycle as described in Figure 7.3. This

> **Recommendation 1: Make data part of an ongoing cycle of instructional improvement.**
> \_\_\_\_\_ Collect and prepare a variety of data about student learning.
> \_\_\_\_\_ Interpret data and develop hypotheses about how to improve student learning.
> \_\_\_\_\_ Modify instruction to test hypotheses and increase student learning.
>
> **Recommendation 2: Teach students to examine their own data and set learning goals.**
> \_\_\_\_\_ Explain expectations and assessment criteria.
> \_\_\_\_\_ Provide feedback to students that is timely, specific, well formatted, and constructive.
> \_\_\_\_\_ Provide tools that help students learn from feedback.
> \_\_\_\_\_ Use students' data analyses to guide instructional change.
>
> **Recommendation 3: Establish a clear vision for schoolwide data use.**
> \_\_\_\_\_ Establish a schoolwide data team that sets the tone for ongoing data use.
> \_\_\_\_\_ Define critical teaching and learning concepts.
> \_\_\_\_\_ Develop a written plan that articulates activities, roles, and responsibilities.
> \_\_\_\_\_ Provide ongoing data leadership.
>
> **Recommendation 4: Provide supports that foster a data-driven culture within the school.**
> \_\_\_\_\_ Designate a school-based facilitator who meets with teacher teams to discuss data.
> \_\_\_\_\_ Dedicate structured time for staff collaboration.
> \_\_\_\_\_ Provide targeted professional development regularly.

**FIGURE 7.2.** Using data for decision making. Adapted from Hamilton et al. (2009). Copyright © 2009 Institute of Education Sciences. Adapted by permission.

cycle is iterative and requires the team working with data to reflect on whether decisions made were useful in promoting student learning. Meetings about data should be focused, with most time spent on interpretation and development of instructional plans.

As described in Figure 7.2, Recommendation 1, data must be collected, organized, interpreted, and then used in making instructional decisions. Data-team meetings have become commonplace in schools today, especially since the implementation of MTSS (a framework for improving academic, behavioral, and social-emotional outcomes for all students). Generally, school leaders such as principals, teacher leaders, and various specialists, including coaches, are given the task of collecting and organizing the data for discussion and analysis by grade level or academic department teams; frequently, they also lead the meetings. Often, these meetings are focused on the results of interim or benchmark assessment measures, but in some schools, teachers are asked to analyze the results of performance measures, such as

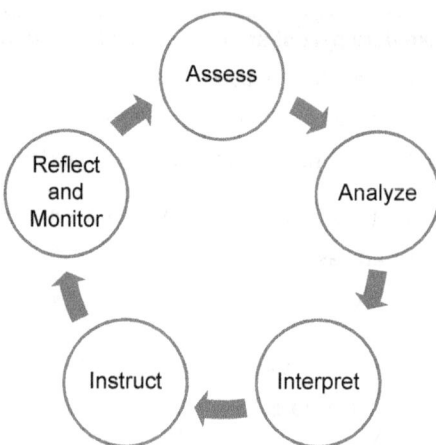

**FIGURE 7.3.** Assessment cycle. Adapted from Pennsylvania Department of Education (2019, p. 126). Copyright © 2019 Pennsylvania Department of Education. Adapted by permission.

writing samples or class assignments that provide direct evidence of students' skills, knowledge, or understanding. One of the greatest teaching and learning tools for teachers is the analysis of the work of their students and others in their school at the same grade level or in the same academic department. (See Figure 7.4 for a protocol that could be used for a 30-minute data meeting; timing can be adjusted depending on the length of the meeting.)

| Steps | Comments/Questions |
|---|---|
| **Guiding questions (4–5 minutes)**<br>What are the key points to consider today? | |
| **Data analysis (8–10 minutes)**<br>What do the data say or suggest? | |
| **Group interpretation (10–15 minutes)**<br>What do the data mean for instruction, grouping, additional assessments? | |
| **Next steps (5–8 minutes)**<br>Who will do what and when? How?<br>How can the coach/teacher leader be helpful? | |
| **Follow-up for next meeting (2–4 minutes)**<br>Expectations for following meeting? | |

**FIGURE 7.4.** Protocol for a 30-minute data meeting. Adapted from Pennsylvania Department of Education (2019, pp. 127–128). Copyright © 2019 Pennsylvania Department of Education. Adapted by permission.

## The Specifics of Data-Team Meetings

Often, results from benchmark or progress-monitoring tests are an important focus of discussion in data-team or problem-solving team meetings, and generally, the goals of the meetings are to decide upon changes in instruction, grouping, or even which teachers might have responsibilities for working with specific students. These meetings, which call for collaborative problem solving, may occur frequently, perhaps once a week; however, in some schools, such data meetings are scheduled once a month or even four to six times a year. One of the major hurdles to be addressed by schools is scheduling the time for these meetings. Next, we identify some possible approaches for scheduling meetings for such collaborative problem solving (schools have become ingenious in developing schedules that enable teachers to meet in meaningful groups):

- Include discussion of data in weekly or biweekly planning meetings that teachers have as part of their schedules.
- Begin or end a school day one or two hours later, perhaps once or twice per month.
- Hire substitutes to cover the classes of teachers at a specific grade level for a 45- to 60-minute period (e.g., four substitutes are hired to cover the classes of four teachers at a grade level, and meetings of teachers from grades 1 to 5 could be held in one day). Such meetings might occur once each grading period.
- Have teachers meet after school for one or two hours every six weeks and receive compensation for these meetings.

Generally, in a data meeting, teachers are presented with a data sheet with up-to-date information about students from their grade level, generally compiled by a coach or teacher leader. The coach or teacher leader might then facilitate discussions and analysis of the strengths and needs of individual students, with the group then making recommendations for changes in instructional approach, grouping, or teacher assignment. Discussion results can be summarized on a sheet designed to capture notes or a Google spreadsheet for later distribution to the group. Recommendations should be specific and indicate who is going to do what, how, and when. For example, the fourth-grade classroom teachers might focus on helping students learn key words essential for the text they are going to read, not only in their reading text but across subject areas, while the Title I teacher might provide supplemental instruction for specific students that focuses on how to use morphological analysis to decode and understand the meaning of words. The coach might agree to obtain additional resources or materials for teachers. These collaborative meetings not only facilitate the interpretation of data but also promote a greater degree of understanding among teachers about possible changes in expectations, assessment, or instructional practices. Further, the meetings provide for alignment in instructional practices and goals across teachers, a key factor in helping students, especially those who experience learning difficulties, receive the coordinated instruction they need to make sense of their learning experiences.

This same approach can be used to analyze student work. For example, teachers could examine student writing samples from a group of sixth graders in a social studies class, in which they have been asked to write a persuasive essay about the most important innovations of ancient Egypt. At a grade-level team meeting focused on team understanding of writing expectations and students' current strengths and weaknesses, a coach might facilitate an ATLAS protocol from the CLEE/SRI website (see Web Resources at the end of this chapter) to guide the group in looking deeply at student work. The group would first be asked to describe the student work: "What do you see?" Next, the group would be asked to make preliminary interpretations: "From the student's perspective, what is the student working on?" Finally, after describing and interpreting the work, the group is asked to reflect on implications for practice: "What are the implications of this work for teaching and assessment?"

Many student-work and data-focused protocols follow a similar pattern, supporting educators as they continually refine their skills in describing and interpreting student work and data sets and then translate their observations into implications and actions for classroom instruction. (See Chapters 4 and 5, as well as Further Readings and Related Resources at the end of this chapter, for more on this topic.)

### Recommendation #2: Teach Students to Self-Assess and Set Their Own Goals

As mentioned in Figure 7.2 (Recommendation 2), students play an important role in evaluating their own work (Afflerbach et al., 2011; Brookhart, 2023; Elish-Piper et al., 2022; Morrow et al., 2023; Torgeson & Miller, 2009). As Stiggins (2014) indicates, students should be players, not victims or beneficiaries, in the testing game. Being able to assess one's own work is a hallmark of independent learners, strongly emphasized as an important trait in today's state standards. Stiggins (2014) identifies what he calls a student's Bill of Assessment Rights that calls for students to understand the following: the purpose of each assessment and how it will be used, the learning target of an instructional exercise and the scoring guides to be used, and how to self-assess their progress. He also indicates that students are entitled to reliable and valid assessment of their achievement, which highlights the importance of high-quality assessment measures. Finally, he notes the importance of effective communication of assessment results to students, families, and other stakeholders. When teachers adhere to these recommendations, students are provided with a sense of control over their own outcomes. Coaches can share the ideas in the Bill of Assessment Rights and use them as a discussion tool for promoting better use of data by teachers.

> **• • • • • • • • • • Put into Practice • • • • • • • • • • •**
>
> Discuss the student Bill of Assessment Rights (Stiggins, 2014) with teachers, asking them to consider which of these are evident in their classroom or school practices, or how such ideas can be implemented in the school. Discuss ways that data results are shared with families and what the roles of each educator, including the coach, might be in collecting, analyzing, and sharing assessment outcomes.

Teachers working in teams can develop common rubrics that can be given to students when an assignment is introduced (e.g., writing a persuasive essay, solving word problems, or conducting a science experiment) and then used to provide feedback when the assignment has been completed. Students can also use the rubric to reflect on their work themselves or participate in a peer-assessment process. Providing specific, timely, and constructive feedback to students is an important means of helping students learn how to improve. Involving students from elementary through high school grades in the assessment process can help them develop independence and self-assessment strategies. Even in the early grades, students can be asked to self-assess their work with a simple scale (e.g., Circle one of the following: This is my very best work :) I know I can do better :( I'm not sure :|).

## Recommendation #3: Use Data to Establish a Vision for School and District Improvement

In this section, we look at data and their usefulness in overall school and district achievement results. In too many districts, decisions about the assessment tools used to measure student learning are made idiosyncratically. Often, there are overlaps in these measures (i.e., several measures assess the same skills), or some elements of the curricula may not be measured at all. In some grades, there are many different assessment measures, and in other grades, perhaps not enough. At the time of this writing, end-of-year testing (in language arts and math) is required by the federal government in grades 3 through 8 and once at the high school level. However, the focus is on providing summative information; individual districts will need to develop or select measures that can provide data for formative use. In the points that follow, we identify important questions for coaches, and the teams they support, to consider when developing a systemic or comprehensive assessment system for a district or school:

- Are the assessments at various grade levels consistent with the goals and outcomes identified as most critical for student learning at those stages? Is there redundancy in measures, and if so, which can be eliminated? Are important components of student learning represented?
- What purposes do each of the assessment measures serve? Do they serve

accountability purposes (summative assessment)? Or do they assist teachers in planning for student learning (formative assessment)? Do teachers view assessment measures as useful for making instructional decisions?
- Do the measures provide a longitudinal look at student learning? In other words, can educators track the growth of students over time?

Afflerbach (2014), who has written extensively about literacy assessment (see also Afflerbach, 2018, 2022; Afflerbach & Cho, 2011), provides helpful information for those responsible for developing a comprehensive assessment system. Despite Afflerbach's specific focus on literacy, we have found his framework useful for considering assessment systems across content areas. Inspired by Afflerbach's literacy-specific lists of assessment possibilities across his publications, here we have broadened the lists to apply to all disciplines more generally. When devising or revising an assessment system, there is a need for balance among the following:

- Assessment of skills and how students apply those skills (e.g., measuring specific decoding skills and students' ability to use those skills when reading text)
- Measurement of basic skills and higher-order thinking
- Ability to retrieve information from a single test as well as multiple texts, including the internet
- Cognitive and affective learning outcomes
- Summative and formative assessment

• • • • • • • • • • **Put into Practice** • • • • • • • • • • •

This notion of balance when building and refining assessment systems is important for all teachers across subject areas and grade levels to consider. With a group of teacher leaders, coaches might discuss the need for balance among the five assessment dimensions identified in the previous bullet points. In what ways has your school attempted to balance the assessment focus? Where might there be need for improvement?

Recommendation 3 in Figure 7.2 highlights the importance of establishing a clear vision for schoolwide data use and identifies the importance of a data team that provides input about which data are to be gathered and used in the school. In some schools, the instructional leadership team (ILT) may have the responsibility of setting the tone for ongoing data use and supporting teachers in using data for improvement in learning at the individual, classroom, and school levels. This team can assist in several ways: identifying and clarifying the school's data vision, providing teachers with a written plan that articulates the ways in which data are to be used and detailing the desired goals of such use, and helping teachers gain a better understanding of what is meant by "data" and how the information provided can be used to improve classroom instruction. An important role of data teams, and especially coaches who serve on these teams, is to help teachers develop a common language so that there is a shared understanding of the various and varied terms related to assessment.

Another responsibility of the data or leadership team may be to develop a systemic, comprehensive assessment system using the notions just described. Coaches might use a matrix such as the one in Appendix E to lead a discussion about the various assessment tools already used in the district or schools and identify redundancies and gaps in the system. Based on this analysis, the data or instructional leadership team can make recommendations to modify the system so that there is a systemic, comprehensive approach to assessment that provides essential information but is not overwhelming to students, teachers, or parents.

### Look for Relationships Across Data Points to Improve Student Learning

Schools have access to so much data beyond those provided by assessment measures, and to make strides toward school improvement, coaches and their teacher colleagues need to think about the interrelationships among the available data. Bernhardt (2013), in her text *Data Analysis for Continuous School Improvement*, highlights the importance of data as a means of focusing the work of schools and reducing the random nature of school improvement. She identifies four categories of data that school personnel can consider as sources for improving teaching and learning. (See additional information about these four categories in Ippolito and Bean, 2024.)

1. Demographics (students and their families [diversity], enrollment, attendance)
2. Student learning (formative and summative assessment measures)
3. Perceptions (attitudes, values, and beliefs of teachers, families, and students)
4. School processes (programs, organizational, instructional processes) (Bernhardt, 2013, p. 17)

Bernhardt also describes the importance of analyzing the interactions among the various data sources to make decisions about school improvement efforts. Instructional leaders, for example, can look at the relationship between demographics (e.g., multilingual learners or economically disadvantaged students) and performance on various student learning measures: Are specific groups doing better than others? Leaders can also look at multiple relationships; for example, do students from specific subgroups (demographics) perform better on the standardized achievement test (student learning) when they receive supplemental mathematics instruction from math specialists (processes)? This type of deep analysis can provide schools with a better understanding of how to focus their energies and plan systematically to improve learning in the school overall. Coaches can facilitate efforts to involve teachers in analyzing data and designing curriculum and instruction that meets the learning needs of the students in the school.

> **STOP AND REFLECT**
>
> Looking back at the data sources identified in Figure 7.1, consider which data sources might fit into each of Bernhardt's (2013) categories. Which data sources would be better for accountability purposes? Which would best serve as sources of information for instructional decision making?

### *Recommendation #4: Develop a Culture That Uses Data for Instructional Decision Making*

Recommendation 4 in Figure 7.2 highlights the importance of facilitators, collaboration time, and regular professional learning to support a data-driven culture. The goal in schools should be to develop an *assessment culture*, in which educators understand the basic principles of sound assessment practices—that is, how to gather reliable and valid evidence of student learning and to use the process and results appropriately (Stiggins, 2014). Coaches may be responsible for serving as the data facilitators who meet with teachers individually or, more frequently, with teacher teams. Their role is one of helping teachers interpret data and providing the professional learning experiences teachers need to make meaningful use of data. Although coaches are present to provide support, one of their important roles and goals is to build the capacity of teachers to become "assessment literate." Further, as mentioned earlier, those responsible for developing school schedules need to provide the structured time for teachers to collaborate about assessment and instruction and to make these collaborative meetings a priority.

Providing professional learning experiences about assessment is key, and such experiences should be developed based on the specific needs in the school or district. In some instances, teachers are novices and need entry-level information about assessment. In other schools, the focus might be on interpretation and use of multiple data sources, or in still other schools, the focus may be on data technology systems and how they can be useful in schools. In Appendix F, we describe a series of steps that a coach, along with other instructional leaders, can use to develop a comprehensive assessment system for a district.

## Summary

After defining assessment as a process used for purposes of accountability and improving student learning and overall school performance, we discussed large-scale measures, their potential uses, and their limitations. One of the major foci of the chapter was on how instructional coaches and teacher leaders can work with classroom teachers to help them understand how to work with data, especially formative data, to improve instructional practices. We concluded with a section that addresses the need for a coherent, systemic, and comprehensive assessment plan that enables coaches to think about a school's goals and vision, and how assessment will help guide efforts to achieve desired outcomes. The resources and guidelines provided in this chapter should be helpful to Melinda and her team as they forge ahead to make changes in the current assessment system in ways that will provide more insightful and comprehensive information about student learning.

## Reflections

- Using the chart found in Appendix A, note the ways that coaches function as change agents, facilitators, designers, and advocates when working on assessment tasks. List some possibilities that you might consider in your current position.
- As a coach, think about your own role in supporting teachers' use of assessment data. After reading and reflecting on this chapter, what do you believe has been working well for you? What possible changes might you make in your work?

## Activities

- Using Appendix E, analyze the assessment measures used in your school or district. Consider whether the current assessment measures are consistent with the vision and mission of the school or district. Is there a need to make changes in the overall assessment plan?
- Visit the CLEE/SRI's repository of protocols focused on data and looking at student work (see Web Resources at the end of this chapter). Review the protocols focused on data analysis and learning from student work (e.g., Data Driven Dialogue, Looking at Data Sets, the Collaborative Assessment Conference, the Slice). Which of these protocols are already part of your coaching and assessment tools? Which protocols might best serve your immediate purposes when leading your school's and system's assessment work?
- Read Jennifer Borgioli Binis's article "Standardized Tests Aren't Going Anywhere. So What Do We Do?" from the *Cult of Pedagogy* blog (see Web Resources at the end of this chapter). Discuss with colleagues as you continue to consider ways to support teachers and students in managing standardized testing procedures and anxieties. Consider reading and discussing other assessment-related blog posts (see the Cult of Pedagogy link in the Web Resources at the end of this chapter) as part of your assessment-team, data-team, or teacher study group activities.
- Choose an additional resource from the Print Resources that follow as a possible source for a book study with a group of teachers. Focus on the connections that can be made between the ideas in the reading and current assessment practices in your school.

## FURTHER READINGS AND RESOURCES

**Print Resources**

Bernhardt, V. L. (2017). *Data analysis for continuous school improvement* (4th ed.). Routledge.

Blythe, T., Allen, D., & Powell, B. S. (2015). *Looking together at student work* (3rd ed.). Teachers College Press.

Brookhart, S. (2024). *Classroom assessment essentials*. ASCD.

Chappuis, J., & Stiggins, R. J. (2019). *Classroom assessment for student learning: Doing it right—Using it well* (3rd ed.). Pearson.

Datnow, A., & Park, V. (2018). Opening or closing doors for students? Equity and data use in schools. *Journal of Educational Change, 19,* 131–152.

Elish-Piper, L., Matthews, M. W., & Risko, V. J. (2022). *Reading assessment to promote equitable learning: An empowering approach for grades K–5*. Guilford Press.

McTighe, J. (2019). *Designing authentic performance tasks and projects: Tools for meaningful learning and assessment*. ASCD.

Schildkamp, K. (2019). Data-based decision-making for school improvement: Research insights and gaps. *Educational Research, 61*(3), 257–273.

Stiggins, R. (2017). *The perfect assessment system*. ASCD.

**Web Resources (see www.guilford.com/bean3-materials for live links)**

Borgioli Binis, J. (2024). Standardized tests aren't going anywhere. So what do we do? *Cult of Pedagogy.* *www.cultofpedagogy.com/standardized-tests-what-to-do*

Center for Leadership & Educational Equity and the School Reform Initiative. (2024). *ATLAS: Learning from student work.* *www.clee.org/resources/atlas-learning-from-student-work-protocol*

Center for Leadership & Educational Equity and the School Reform Initiative. (2024) *Tag: Data* [list of protocols]. *www.clee.org/resources/?_resource_goal=learn-from-data*

Center for Leadership & Educational Equity and the School Reform Initiative. (2024). *Tag: Student work* [list of protocols]. *www.clee.org/resources/?_resource_goal=learn-from-student-work*

Cult of Pedagogy. *Assessment.* *www.cultofpedagogy.com/tag/assessment*

Long, C. (2023). Standardized testing is still failing students. *NEA Today.* *www.nea.org/nea-today/all-news-articles/standardized-testing-still-failing-students*

Nelson, N., Cook, S., Caudle, T., Orozco, K., & Graupman, K. (2020). *Comprehensive assessment plan*. Coeur d'Alene Public Schools. *www.cdaschools.org/documents/departments/assessments/welcome/607050*

Visscher, A. J. (2021). On the value of data-based decision making in education: The evidence from six intervention studies. *Studies in Educational Evaluation, 69,* Article 100899. *www.sciencedirect.com/science/article/pii/S0191491X20301474*

# CHAPTER 8

# Developing, Implementing, and Sustaining Schoolwide Instructional Programs

### GUIDING QUESTIONS

1. What are the key roles and responsibilities of coaches in collaboratively crafting a clear instructional mission and vision in schools and districts?

2. How can coaches facilitate a needs-assessment process that provides comprehensive information about curriculum and instruction in a school or district, one that inspires learning for all?

3. What key notions are important for the development, implementation, and sustainability of an action plan that builds upon and addresses the goals/priorities of a needs-assessment process?

4. In what ways can coaches facilitate the selection and development of materials, including new technologies, essential to the success of effective instructional programs?

## Melinda Tackles School-Level Work with the Instructional Leadership Team

As a member of the school's ILT, Melinda was beginning to think about the big picture, considering what might be necessary for improving student learning across all grades and curricula in her school. Were there certain groups of students who were not achieving, and if so, why? Moving beyond her earlier considerations of individuals and groups of teachers, she was now beginning to focus on the importance of identifying the strengths and needs of the school overall. Melinda was wondering about how best to involve teachers in developing an action plan that would enable them to collectively achieve schoolwide goals. Looking at current research about school-level planning, she and others on the ILT began to talk about first conducting a needs assessment, and then, based on findings, developing a school action plan. But how might she and others begin this work? What steps would need to be taken in the short term? In the long term?

To support Melinda, and all who are wrestling with similar systems-focused coaching questions, in this chapter we discuss some of the potential roles of coaches on schoolwide ILTs as both participants in, and leaders of, schoolwide change efforts. We then describe a needs-assessment process that can lead to the development of an action plan that will guide schools in developing, implementing, and sustaining effective and equity-based instructional programs. We then review the importance of selecting high-quality materials that include both print and nonprint options. We conclude with suggestions about how coaches can work effectively at both individual and system levels simultaneously. Not all coaches will be involved to the same extent in overall school or district change initiatives. However, given that growth in student performance is closely related to schoolwide efforts, all coaches must consider how they can influence and even shape schoolwide change (Bryk et al., 2015).

## The Role of Coaches in Improving Schoolwide Learning

We appreciate the following quote, which highlights the importance of school leadership and, in our view, reinforces the important role of coaches: "Leaders that dig deep to update strategic plans, improve school climate, and foster equity and inclusion will be strongly positioned to navigate the years ahead" (Hanover Research, 2023, p. 20). Coaches can focus on leadership efforts at one level (e.g., elementary) or in one discipline (e.g., math, science), or they can address frameworks for effective instruction across the board from PreK through grade 12. This type of work requires collaboration and teamwork to develop the collective efficacy necessary for school change (Donohoo et al., 2018; Hattie, 2023) that will enable students to meet the increasing demands in this ever-changing, challenging world.

Often, for coaches, an important aspect of any school improvement initiative is the development of an action plan that includes professional learning to support teachers as they work together to make large-scale changes in teaching and learning. The results of research over the past two decades have identified critical elements of effective professional learning, which include ongoing, sustained experiences; active learning that involves inquiry, practice-focused materials, and opportunities for collaborative problem solving; meaningful adult learning experiences that focus on content-specific practices and allow for follow-up opportunities with teachers; and ongoing supports such as coaching (Hill & Papay, 2022; Hill et al., 2021; Risko & Vogt, 2016). Also, Learning Forward's revised Standards for Professional Learning provide a useful tool for educators who want to know more about key factors that influence teacher learning (see Web Resources at the end of this chapter).

To provide the most appropriate PL experiences, coaches can lead or be involved in two essential, schoolwide efforts: first, developing and implementing a needs-assessment process at the school or district level, and second, developing an action plan based on the findings of the needs-assessment process. Such an action plan might include a systematic, long-range program of professional learning; recommendations for selecting or developing materials for various instructional programs; leading professional learning activities to support implementation of new programs or approaches; and an assessment system for monitoring and/or evaluating implementation efforts.

Here we describe a few examples of schoolwide projects or initiatives in which coaches might be involved. Think about how you could approach each of these important and possibly urgent tasks. What are the key questions and issues to consider when responding to each of these tasks?

- The superintendent calls you into her office and indicates that the district has received money from the state to upgrade the technology resources in the middle school. Decisions must be made about the selection of specific hardware and software by the end of next month. She is concerned about how to involve teachers in the decision-making process, but she also wants to make certain that the school gets the funding. The job is yours. Congratulations! What might be your first step?
- Elementary teachers are concerned about the alignment between recently updated state standards, policies about the need for evidence-based reading programs, and the core program that has guided reading instruction for the past six years. The district has agreed to allot funds to purchase a new program. The assistant superintendent for curriculum has appointed a committee charged with curricular review and selection. You have been asked to chair the committee. What might be your first steps (other than holding a committee meeting)?
- The principal at the high school has volunteered the school to be part of a professional learning effort to integrate disciplinary literacy instruction across all academic subjects. Because you are the department chair for English, he thinks you would be a great coach to lead this project. Your responsibilities include helping all content-area teachers understand, accept, and become excited about participating in this endeavor in general. The project sounds exciting, ambitious, and ambiguous. What exactly will be your new responsibilities? And how will you balance your new and current roles?
- The district leadership team agrees that all schools need to improve their efforts to provide equitable opportunities for students across all subject areas. The team's goal is to develop a well-structured series of workshops at the district level to help teachers better understand what it means to provide equitable instruction for all, and then to begin revising curriculum and instruction

to address this. As a coach and member of the team, you will be responsible for following up with teachers at your school. You know the next step is to talk with your principal about this upcoming initiative, but how will you begin the conversation?

> **STOP AND REFLECT**
>
> Think about the ways in which you have been involved in schoolwide initiatives. Can you connect to any of the dilemmas described in the previous section? Or, are there other schoolwide initiatives in which you have played a leadership or facilitation role? What skill sets have you brought to such initiatives? What skill sets do you think you might still need to develop?

It is evident that coaches must be able to multitask. At times they will be involved in working with individuals or small groups of teachers, addressing specific classroom or grade-level needs. At other times, they will be involved in larger-scale projects, ones that require working at the systems level and requiring more complex skills and knowledge (see Ippolito & Bean, 2024). For example, in this chapter, we highlight the ways in which coaches think and act as designers and change agents as they support schoolwide and systems-level work related to assessment, curriculum, and instruction. At the same time, advocacy becomes especially important if school change processes are to be successful. The key is to balance the competing commitments of urgent new requests with current and long-term efforts. In the following section, we begin to support coaches in taking on and managing this complex work by discussing the importance of an ILT as one of the most important drivers for reviewing and improving teaching and learning in a school.

## How Coaches Can Support Instructional Leadership Teams

School and district ILTs can serve many purposes: determining whether a school is meeting the academic and social-emotional needs of all its students, supporting teachers in engaging students in active learning, developing professional learning experiences for teachers, developing (with teachers) ways to partner with communities and families, making decisions about how best to integrate technology more seamlessly into instruction, and so on. An ILT can generate a sense of shared ownership of a school's programs—it can help teachers develop common understandings and language about instruction and assessment. The primary focus of the ILT might be different year by year, however, depending on where a school finds itself within the change process. In some schools, the yearlong focus might be on the development of a comprehensive action plan that addresses the overall mission/vision and goals for all levels and disciplines and the steps for achieving them (e.g., increasing student engagement), while other schools might be involved in investigating a single topic (e.g., selecting assessment tools that provide for systematic, reliable evaluation PreK–12); still other schools might be developing or selecting curriculum for one or more disciplines. The team might also be responsible for monitoring the efforts of the school as it continues its journey toward equitable instruction and student learning.

Several key notions for the development of an ILT include:

- The ILT leader/facilitator should be someone who has the leadership and facilitation skills that inspire and persuade others to work collaboratively. At times, a principal or another administrator might serve as leader of the team, but in many schools, coaches have been asked to lead such efforts. Often, the coach can obtain or provide important information about current instructional activities and facilitate team efforts.

- The team should include a representative group of teachers, including those from different grade levels, those who teach various subgroups of students (e.g., multilingual learners, students with special needs), teachers of the disciplines (e.g., English language arts, history, math, science), and representative special educators, specialists, and interventionists. Teachers on the team might serve for several years and then rotate off to allow others in the school to be involved in the in-depth work of school change. Involvement creates ownership—and ownership creates a willingness to apply what has been developed. (See also Ippolito & Bean, 2024, pp. 74–81, for more information about forming an ILT.)

- Although the team may begin by working as a whole group, subgroups can be formed as a means of moving forward quickly and efficiently. For example, groups might meet by level (e.g., early childhood, elementary, and so on), by discipline (e.g., math, English language arts, social studies, science), or even by program (e.g., special education, Title I, and so on) to discuss current curriculum, needs, and strengths. Or, each subgroup might be asked to focus on a specific demographic group needing attention (e.g., multilingual students, newcomers, students with special needs, and so on). The groups can work separately on their tasks and then report back to the full ILT. Teacher ILT representatives or subgroups can also talk with other teachers in the school to seek and share information. The leader should work with the team to establish timelines and work schedules and to assume responsibility for sharing information across the entire group (see Chapter 6 for further ideas about working with small groups of educators).

- Working effectively as a team is not easy (see Ippolito & Bean, 2024 and Chapters 4, 5, and 6 in this text). We appreciate the work of Lencioni (2002), who identifies five characteristics of what he calls "dysfunctional teams," each one building on the critical first characteristic of trust (pp. 188–189). As Lencioni puts it, "Like a chain with just one link broken, teamwork deteriorates if even a single dysfunction is allowed to flourish" (p. 189). We think it is worth considering these five characteristics and even asking groups to discuss them, not only at the outset of their work, but periodically as they continue working together. Coaches might consider posting these questions where groups can see them.

- Is there an absence of trust among group members? In other words, are team members willing to be vulnerable and to share their ideas openly with others?
- Do individuals fear conflict? Are they hesitant to speak freely? That is, are they unable to engage in a "passionate debate of ideas" (Lencioni, 2002, p. 188)?
- Is there a lack of commitment to the goals of the group? Given the absence of open discussions, team members may not truly commit to decisions being made.
- Do group members avoid accountability for the goals of the project? Members must be committed to the goals and decisions of the group, or they might not follow through and may hesitate to ask their peers to commit.
- Do individuals disregard the desired outcomes or goals of the team, focusing instead on their own individual needs and goals?

• In the initial stages of any effort to make changes in a school, gathering input from colleagues is important. The leader/facilitator of the ILT may want to first survey or hold a discussion with the entire group of educators to discuss perceptions about the issue at hand. The questions in Figure 8.1 are examples of what teachers might discuss in person (or, with a bit of modification, might be offered to teachers via an online survey or discussion forum before discussing in person). These questions can be modified or supplemented to reflect each school's specific context more accurately.

Additionally, there can be adaptations in the size, structure, and responsibilities of an ILT depending on school size and whether the ILT is school- or district-based. There may be a district-level ILT whose responsibilities are to conduct a districtwide needs assessment and develop a comprehensive action plan across schools. Members on the team may represent specific schools and may have responsibilities for leading efforts in their own schools or working with smaller school-based teams. Such a district-level team might also include representation from community entities (e.g., libraries, universities), families/caregivers, and students. Ultimately, alignment of efforts within and across schools is key to producing schoolwide and districtwide plans that serve all students. And whether working with a school-based or district-based ILT, often the best starting point for both is a well-planned needs-assessment process.

- What are our academic goals for students at specific grade levels in English language arts, math, science, social studies, and so on? What are our more global academic and social-emotional learning goals for this school? To what extent are we accomplishing these goals? Where are we experiencing difficulties? (Each grade level can address such questions.)
- Are we meeting the needs of all students, especially those identified as multilingual learners, students with special needs, and so on? If not, any thoughts as to why?
- To what extent are students able to read, write, and communicate in discipline-specific and age-appropriate ways, across all grade levels, in preparation for the demands of college and the workplace (e.g., lab-report writing in science, analyzing primary sources in social studies, translating a word problem into a figure and then into an algebraic expression in math class)?
- Are the materials we use adequate for helping us to accomplish our goals? If not, what materials might be needed? In what ways are we preparing students to use technology as a resource for learning?
- What assessment tools are used to inform instruction? Are they useful in planning lessons?
- In what ways do we involve families and the community in our instructional efforts? What improvements may be needed?
- How can the school better support each of us as adult learners? What additional professional learning experiences would be useful?

**FIGURE 8.1.** Schoolwide instructional programs—questions for discussion.

## The Needs-Assessment Process

For many schools and districts, involving representative educators in conducting a needs assessment of instructional programs to discern how they support student learning is an important first step. The questions in Figure 8.1 can be used to generate in-depth thinking and help the ILT consider upcoming work.

### *What Is a Needs Assessment?*

A needs assessment is a process whose purpose is to: identify gaps between current and desired practices, prioritize identified needs, implement data-informed changes related to needs, and ensure appropriate resources to achieve goals (Cuiccio & Husby-Slater, 2018). Needs assessments with slightly different focal points are often called by different names, such as equity audits or quality school reviews (Corbett & Redding, 2017). Schools and districts may undertake a *comprehensive* needs assessment, in which they choose to look at overall organizational goals and strategies, or a *segmented* needs assessment, in which there is a targeted or focused look at a specific aspect of school programming (e.g., assessment practices, math curricular alignment across grades, and so on). Currently, many schools have identified a need to focus on

- Goals and vision for learning (What are the district's core beliefs about students and what they will need to know and be able to do as future citizens?)
- Standards as a means of identifying outcomes
- Curriculum and instructional materials that address standards in various subject areas (e.g., consider the core curriculum, approaches, and materials for differentiating instruction, or the role of technology in the curriculum)
- Specific interventions for various subgroups
- Assessment tools
- Time allocations for areas of instruction and instructional design
- Professional learning opportunities and commitment
- Partnerships with families and communities
- Leadership responsibilities
- An action plan
- Plans for dissemination

**FIGURE 8.2.** Components of a comprehensive needs assessment.

addressing issues related to equity, and the goal of the needs assessment is to examine data to understand "where gaps to access and challenges to educational equity exist" (Pendhankar, 2023, para. 10). In developing a needs-assessment plan, whether in one area or in several, the elements identified in Figure 8.2 might be considered.

### *Stages of the Needs-Assessment Process*

Figure 8.3 identifies five important stages of any needs-assessment effort. We explain each part of the process more fully in the sections that follow.

#### *Identify Goals*

The rationale for a needs assessment is an important consideration. As previously stated, is this needs-assessment effort designed as a comprehensive view of all instructional programs in a school or district, or is it a targeted effort? For example, is it focused on teachers' knowledge and application of the state standards for a specific subject (e.g., math, science). Or is it focused on assessment, or perhaps the

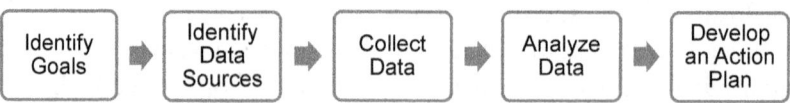

**FIGURE 8.3.** Stages of a needs-assessment process.

professional learning experiences necessary if teachers are to become proficient using technology within a newly selected math program?

Often a school is involved in focusing on only one or maybe two academic areas. A school may decide where the focus should be, perhaps based on the results of teacher discussions (see Figure 8.1), current test data, surveys, and so on. Often, it is better to start small and "drill down" rather than trying to attempt too much initially and, perhaps, superficially. When data are available (e.g., classroom teaching practices, test data, and perceptions of teachers, families, and students), they can be used to describe where the needs might lie, and the ILT, with the leadership of the principal and coach(es), can move quickly to determine "where we want to go" and "how we can get there." If specific data are missing, arrangements can be made to obtain them (e.g., data about current practices to assure a successful transition from elementary to middle school). We recommend the following two resources to coaches who are facilitating needs-assessment efforts (see Web Resources at the end of this chapter):

- Cuiccio & Husby-Slater (2018), *Needs Assessment Guidebook: Supporting the Development of District and School Needs Assessments*
- Corbett & Redding (2017), *Using Needs Assessments for School and District Improvement: A Tactical Guide*

As we have stated before, "the process of engaging in needs assessment work is as important as the final product!" (Ippolito & Bean, 2024, p. 82). Such work tends to generate a sense of shared ownership. At the same time, findings of the process matter and should be used to make decisions about change, short- and long-term. After identifying goals, a framework or system for guiding the process must be developed or selected. See the bulleted resources in the previous paragraph.

After crafting goals and a plan for moving ahead, decisions must be made about identifying the data necessary to address identified concerns or issues.

### *Identify Data Sources*

As described in Chapter 7, the four sources of data described by Bernhardt (2013)—demographics, student learning, perceptions, and school processes—can provide critical information for conducting a needs assessment, identifying the gaps between expectations and current status, and making decisions about an action plan for moving ahead.

Bernhardt (2013) suggests that schools consider the following four questions as they proceed with their needs-assessment work: "Who are we? How do we do business? How are our students doing? What are our processes?" (p. 15). Each of these questions helps to identify important sources of data to collect. For additional information about the multiple measures that schools might consider using when collecting data, see Chapter 7; also see Chapter 3 in Ippolito and Bean (2024).

### Collect Data

Three powerful data-collection tools are available to help schools obtain the data they need: document analysis, surveys, and interviews (both individual and focus groups). When developing tools for collecting data, we remind readers of the importance of focus and priority. Those being asked to respond or participate in a data-collection process are more likely to participate if they aren't overwhelmed with the request and recognize the importance of their voice being heard. Below we offer advice and possible tools for collecting data that can provide useful information.

- **Document analysis.** Often data are relatively accessible to schools (although at times, not well organized). These include rich information about student, family, and educator demographics, student absenteeism, standardized test scores, and so forth. These data should probably be analyzed first, given that they are readily available for educators to review. Even lesson plans, as well as assignments across classrooms for a specific unit of study, can be revealing. How similar are these assignments, and do they all help students to think and perform at high levels? Pictures or videos of classrooms to illustrate the access that students have to materials, the grouping patterns, and whether student work is displayed can be helpful in thinking about the status of instruction in the school. Teachers can be asked to keep logs of their instruction. For example, how much time did they allow students to engage in small-group experiences that required active learning? To include writing in all the content areas? Results of these simple logs can be discussed, and often, these results can be eye-opening for teachers and reveal differences as well as similarities in the emphasis given by teachers to various practices or even to specific groups of students (e.g., those who are underperforming as compared to those who are performing well).

- **Surveys.** These are useful for seeking input from larger groups of various stakeholders (e.g., parents/caregivers, teachers, administrators, students) to gain their perspectives. Digital survey tools (SurveyMonkey, Google Forms, etc.) can be especially helpful for collecting and analyzing survey data. Some important points to consider include the time it will take participants to complete the survey; the clarity of the questions; and, of course, whether the questions, the focus, are of interest and concern to the responding group. So, for example, family members and caregivers might be eager to participate in surveys that ask them questions about whether their children enjoy school, are engaged, and feel safe and what (if any) concerns they have. In Appendix G, we include an example of an adapted survey that assesses perceptions of teachers about their professional learning experiences (from Bean & Goatley, 2021, pp. 230–231). Remember, keep it simple!

- **Interviews (individual and focus groups).** Individual interviews and focus groups can provide powerful complementary data to document analysis and survey data. Interview and focus groups can provide incredibly rich data; however, they can also take much more time to conduct and interpret. Teachers within specific grade levels or departments can be interviewed individually or in focus groups for their perspectives on various topics (e.g., availability of resources, time for instruction, student engagement). Focus group sessions can often provide a more systematic and expedient approach to gathering data from various stakeholders. They can contain similar questions to individual interviews (e.g., what are your thoughts about the amount of time devoted to standardized testing?) as well as questions more specific to the group being interviewed. For example, groups of parents representing specific grade levels—primary, intermediate, secondary—can be asked to participate in an hour-long session to discuss specific aspects of the instruction received by their children. Literacy or math specialists who provide interventions for struggling students might discuss their perceptions of the effectiveness of instructional approaches, grouping, scheduling, and so on. Teachers at the secondary level might be asked to discuss their perceptions of what they see as challenges to engaging students in disciplinary work or how to integrate disciplinary literacy practices into their curriculum. Coaches too might participate in a focus group with an emphasis on determining whether they believe they are receiving the appropriate support to be effective in their positions (e.g., time to coach, opportunity to meet with administrators, alignment of their role with district goals, availability of a district mentor or champion of coaching).

More broadly, and most importantly, ensure that information is being collected from all audiences who need to be consulted. There must be a systematic plan for who will collect what data, when, and from whom. Strategic ILTs often divide and conquer, discussing target audiences together and then collecting data from separate audiences in small groups. The ILT and various coaches might be responsible for collecting the data, keeping them in a secure place, and preparing them for data analysis. At times, districts might employ an outside consultant to lead or participate in the development, collection, and analysis of data.

### Analyze Data

Without analyzing the collected data and using findings in an action plan, little will be gained. Strengths, needs, and priorities (short-term and long-term) for change must be identified. The analysis should be a team effort, and it requires excellent facilitation by coaches and other leaders and members of the ILT. One of the key aspects of analysis is to identify the gaps between current practices and outcomes and the goals set for the school or district. Then, based on this gap analysis and identification of key priorities, probably not more than two to five, the ILT should work "full speed ahead" to accomplish the identified priorities. In too many instances, school leaders, including coaches, are attempting to do too much in a short amount of time. Schmoker (2011) says it well: Keep in mind "the power of simplicity, clarity, and priority" (p. 12). Multiple and scattered initiatives frustrate and confuse everyone. By establishing priorities, being clear about how you are going to achieve them, and developing a simple but focused plan, there is much more likelihood that you will achieve your goals.

*Develop an Action Plan*

The results of a needs-assessment process, with its identified priorities, should lead to the writing of an action plan for the district and/or school. If a district action plan is written, then each school can use the broad plan to further develop their own school-based action plans connected to the district framework. Again, processes for achieving priority goals should be described. Who will do what, when, and how (what processes and resources are needed to achieve the goals)? Again, it is critical to identify and collect evidence that goals have been accomplished. One possible way to think about this is to distinguish between short-term and long-term goals (see Appendix H for an example of an action-planning guide). In the section that follows, we identify some general ideas that coaches might consider when they are leading or participating in writing an action plan.

## Moving from Needs Assessment to Action Planning

As the needs-assessment process comes to a close with the analysis of data and initial crafting of an action plan, a number of additional considerations arise. Coaches and school leaders, working collaboratively with their ILTs, must be thoughtful about how they initiate and facilitate the action-planning process. In the sections that follow, we provide guidance for the action-planning part of the process.

### Crafting the Action Plan

The written action plan document should be reader-friendly and accessible, and should provide a useful guide for leading instructional efforts, often for several years. Coaches, collaborating with their ILTs, can serve an important role here: They can summarize findings from the needs assessment that lead to specific recommendations for action. There may also be a need for editing, often done by a coach or multiple leaders, so that there is coherency in the document. In our recent work with districts supporting the development of needs assessments and action plans, most were available electronically as well as in print, and teachers could access those sections most critical for them.

## *Disseminating the Action Plan*

One step, often neglected, is "getting the word out." Even though there is an ILT and teachers have been involved, to a lesser or greater degree, some in the district or school will have little or no awareness that there is an action plan designed to guide instructional efforts.

Designing a dissemination plan that includes ideas for sharing the document with teachers and the community is key to implementation efforts. Some districts have developed videos that highlight ideas in the plan. In other districts, the plan serves as the professional learning focus for the year; specific sections are "unpacked" and elaborated on in mini-workshops. Think about the authenticity of such workshops, where the focus is on genuinely improving instruction and assessment based on the analysis of current efforts in your specific school.

## *Implementing the Action Plan: Managing Change*

As is all too familiar, school improvement initiatives come and go. An all-too-often accurate statement made by teachers is that they can wait out the current program or change initiative because surely there will be another one the following year. As one participant in a study of teachers' reflections of professional change indicated, "Seems like a freight train coming through . . . last year it was math, this year it's writing, and now all of a sudden it's the six-trait writing model . . . what happened to math?" (Nielsen et al., 2008, p. 1294). Coaches, then, must be aware of the many factors that can influence implementation efforts in positive and negative ways. They must also be thinking—from the beginning—about ways that they can monitor and evaluate what they are doing and make changes necessary to ensure sustainability. The action plan, with its recommended set of priorities, activities, and time line, can assist in guiding school efforts.

Readers who want to become more knowledgeable about implementation and school change processes can access modules and lessons from the website of the National Implementation Research Network (see Web Resources at the end of this chapter). The website provides in-depth information about implementation issues and how to address them. In Figure 8.4, we highlight some roadblocks that may arise and possible ways to address these barriers.

> • • • • • • • • • • **Put into Practice** • • • • • • • • • • •
>
> Talk with teachers, coaches, and other leaders about a specific implementation effort at your school. Use Figure 8.4 to discuss roadblocks that your school has experienced and how you overcame those barriers. What might you have done differently?

| Roadblocks | Possible Solutions |
|---|---|
| • Lack of understanding (knowledge) of the vision and goals<br>• Difficulty accepting notions of the initiative (not consistent with current ideas) | • Communicate the vision consistently and with all stakeholders.<br>• Involve teachers from the very beginning (not just to gain buy-in but to encourage shared ownership).<br>• Provide the necessary professional learning experiences, not just for building knowledge, but also for applying in classroom instruction (informational sessions plus ongoing practice and coaching).<br>• Be willing to live with "growing pains."<br>• Recognize that there will be some critics (at least at first) and a possible implementation dip.<br>• Support by monitoring and celebrating small positive steps. |
| • Lack of support and resources for initiative (time, funding, personnel, materials) | • Involve school leadership in the implementation efforts.<br>• Restructure the school schedule to provide necessary professional learning experiences.<br>• Work with district leadership to obtain necessary funding, resources, and support. |
| • Lack of long-term effort to achieve goals<br>• Lack of a reasonable road map | • Celebrate short-term successes.<br>• Monitor efforts to determine any needed modifications and adaptations.<br>• Recognize the need for long-range planning and implementation. |

**FIGURE 8.4.** Possible implementation roadblocks and solutions. Adapted from Jerald, (2005). Copyright © 2005 Center for Comprehensive School Reform and Improvement.

Developing or creating an action plan is important, but the implementation part of the process is perhaps most difficult given that it often involves addressing adaptive challenges and transformational change (Bryk et al., 2015, 2021; Jerald, 2005). These are two important points about implementation:

**1.** Teachers need to be provided with adequate support and recognition for their efforts, even small ones, as they move through the implementation process. Because teachers are faced with many demands and responsibilities, helping them understand the initiative and its importance to student learning is key. Coaches and other teacher leaders must encourage, nudge, and motivate teachers, providing them with needed resources and the professional learning experiences that enable them to implement an initiative as designed. At the same time, keeping those involved in implementation accountable is also a necessary ingredient. Administrators and coaches, including other teacher leaders, should monitor change efforts and provide feedback that includes ideas for improvement.

**2.** Regardless of how prescriptive or well-defined a project initiative is (e.g., a state mandate that all districts implement MTSS initiatives in their schools), implementation is complex, and local schools and educators in them will shape how the program unfolds (Coburn & Woulfin, 2012; Woulfin, 2020). McLaughlin (1990), in discussing implementation, describes this as "mutual adaptation"—that is, the ways in which organizations make modifications, based on "local expertise, capacity, and sophistication in project implementation, as well as local motivation and management style" (p. 12). Districts have a responsibility to think about their specific contexts and how a specific implementation effort might be adapted to fit the needs of that district. As an example, think about the implementation of coaching in a specific school. In some schools with experienced and knowledgeable staff, coaches may spend more time working with groups and encouraging shared leadership by others. They may be more involved with adaptive change efforts. In schools with many novice teachers or those new to the initiative, coaches may spend more time helping teachers develop the technical skills they need to implement the program rather than focusing on problems that require adaptive thinking.

### *Shifting from Initial Implementation to Sustainability*

Implementation is not a short-term effort; it requires ongoing attention over a long period of time. Fixsen et al. (2006) describe five stages of implementation leading to sustainability: exploring and installing, initial implementation, full implementation, adaptations, and sustainability. Schools will need different amounts of time to go through these stages, and those who write about implementation and sustainability often talk about the need for a three- to five-year process for full implementation (Bryk et al., 2015; Fullan, 2015). In a study of sustainability of Reading First in two states, Bean et al. (2015) found many factors that contributed. These included leadership of principals and their belief in and support for the initiative; ongoing professional learning experiences and support for teachers, including coaching; the need for adaptations for their school context; a commitment to using data to inform instruction; and stability in students and staff. Also, there was evidence of increased student learning in schools where there were greater degrees of implementation and acceptance by teachers of the instructional approaches about teaching literacy.

An essential aspect of sustainability is ongoing monitoring and evaluating to obtain evidence about the process of implementation and impact (outcomes) of the initiative. Plans for such evaluation should be part of the action plan (see Appendix H) and should include both formative and summative data. Again, the four sources of data—demographics, student learning, perceptions, and school processes—and the interactions between and among them can provide schools with useful information about program effectiveness. In sum, evaluation should be an essential aspect of any programmatic initiative, addressed on an ongoing basis, so that appropriate modifications or adaptations can be made.

> **VOICES FROM THE FIELD**
>
> Knowing what I know now, I would have collected data not only on how coaching impacted student achievement, but also on how it impacted the correlates of student achievement like collective efficacy, school culture, and social capital. Transforming low-achieving, high-risk school systems takes time, but that is no excuse for not measuring incremental growth. When it comes to evaluating coaching programs, I believe we should spend as much attention measuring the invisible impacts, such as changes in collective efficacy and social capital, as we do measuring the visible impacts like student achievement.
>
> —Christina Steinbacher-Reed,
> Executive Director, BLaST Intermediate Unit 17

## Guidelines for Developing or Selecting Curriculum and Materials

The selection of materials is one of the very important tasks that coaches can be asked to undertake as part of (or separate from) needs-assessment and action-planning work. The choice of materials affects instruction in classrooms, often for five or more years. In fact, in many districts, the materials *become the curriculum*! By "materials," we mean all resources, digital and print, used to support effective instruction, including those used for whole classes, small groups, and individual instruction. As stated by Steiner et al. (2019), quality curriculum and associated materials, along with effective teaching, influence student learning. Teachers benefit when provided with materials that contain evidence-based ideas about instruction and encourage attention to student differences and needs. Currently, many more states are getting involved in defining what they mean by high-quality instructional materials (HQIM) and developing policies about the selection of materials. In Ippolito and Bean (2024), we provide an in-depth discussion of the importance of selecting curricula and materials that are evidence-based and that are consistent with the vision, standards, and goals identified by the district. Here, we provide two brief reminders that coaches might consider as they undertake a process to review and/or select materials.

1. Curricula should "have a well-developed, evidence-based scope and sequence that provides for coherence within and across grade levels and includes meaningful pedagogical strategies and aligned assessment tools" (Ippolito & Bean, 2024, p. 54).

2. Materials and instructional activities must provide for access to "rigorous grade level experiences for all students," ones that help develop a "robust and equitable education for all" (Ippolito & Bean, 2024, p. 55).

Although criteria for the selection of materials, and even the process for selection, may be dictated by state policies, districts should also identify their own standards for materials selection, within the parameters of state policy. Three important considerations include the content (what is being taught), the processes (how it is being taught), and the focus and clarity of the strategies included. Districts therefore should identify their goals and vision for learning as a lens through which to evaluate whether materials under consideration are aligned with them. Second, districts must determine whether the materials address the needs of students—that is, does the curriculum include materials that meet the needs of multilingual learners, those who experience difficulty with reading and writing, those students identified as proficient or advanced, and so forth? Districts often grapple with the demand to include more complex text in the curriculum and what that means for instruction. We suggest that coaches go first to the national organizations in various disciplines (e.g., math, literacy, and so forth), as they often provide helpful information about evaluating materials. In addition, coaches and teachers together should review information from current research and literature. Moreover, it is wise for coaches leading curricular review and selection processes, to develop, in collaboration with teachers, context-specific rubrics to guide their work. Here are a few examples of checklists and ideas that will be helpful to districts reviewing various materials:

- Association of Science and Technology Centers (n.d.). "Professional Competencies for the Informal STEM Learning Field."
- Briars (2014). *Curriculum Materials Matter: Evaluating the Evaluation Process.*
- Foorman et al. (2016). "Foundational Skills to Support Reading for Understanding in Kindergarten through 3rd Grade: Educator's Practice Guide."
- Johnson et al. (1995). "Science Curriculum Review: Evaluating Materials for High-Ability Learners."
- Meader (2019). *9 Tips for Textbook Adoption.*
- National Council for the Social Studies (n.d.). *NCSS social studies standards.*
- National Council of Teachers of Mathematics (n.d.). *NCTM standards.*
- National Science Teaching Association (n.d.). *Science standards.*

## Technology as a Tool to Support Student Learning

Given the influence of technology in our world and in today's schools, here we discuss the importance of providing students access to digital learning tools and knowledge about how to use these tools critically. We also provide some cautions for coaches and other school leaders to consider as they move forward with technological initiatives. Technology has made a dramatic difference in how we communicate and learn in and out of schools—even more so after the global COVID-19 pandemic and the emergence of widespread use of artificial intelligence (AI) tools. In fact, the pandemic not only increased interest in using technological tools for instruction and assessment, but reinforced the need for it. Teachers were forced to learn new ways of instructing (e.g., Zoom, Google Classroom) as more and more schools were closed for long periods of time. Indeed, this phenomenon occurred internationally, and according to the 2022 report from PISA that assesses the reading, science, and math skills of 15-year-olds across the world, "the COVID-19 pandemic was a stress test for education systems" (OECD, 2023, p. 23). Results of this large-scale assessment revealed that some schools and countries did better than others in responding to the pandemic, especially those with fewer obstacles to remote learning. The PISA results also indicate, on average across OECD countries, that almost one in two students frequently had difficulty understanding their assignments and motivating themselves to complete them.

Today, many young students come to school with much experience using tablets, smartphones, computers, and a wide array of touchscreen devices, while most older students will have spent a great deal of their free time engaged in gaming, social networking, and texting. They have experience playing games on their iPads and using Skype, FaceTime, Zoom, and Google Meet to communicate with friends and family, and they often have their own cell phones. Increasingly, students are also savvy about creating and modifying content (both text and visuals) using various AI tools (e.g., Google's Gemini). Ultimately, as schools wrestle with how much to embrace the use of cell phones, computers, and AI in and out of school as learning tools, coaches must stay in conversation with teachers and leaders about best policies and practices.

At the same time, a gap exists between those who have access to technology and those who don't. For example, as cited in the *Pittsburgh Post-Gazette*, "42 million citizens still lack broadband connectivity and 35% of Americans remain digitally illiterate" (Mindlin, 2024). In other words, the increased investment in technology in schools has also "fueled educational inequality" (Mindlin, 2024). Moreover, while many students have experience using the internet, too many do not know how to use it effectively or critically. Thus, more schools are focusing on students' critical consumption of online text and media in addition to engaging students in content creation and computer programming. Many teachers, across grade levels, are focusing on how to help students to use the internet and a wide number of personal devices as learning tools, especially as they provide students with opportunities to engage in rigorous and authentic assignments, mirroring the multimodal and discipline-specific work of college and the workplace. Coaches can do a great deal to support a community of educators learning together about best teaching practices that include technology, especially to address high-level, rigorous standards.

### *Considering Uses of Technology across Classrooms*

As described in a report by the Brookings Institution (Ganimian et al., 2020), educational technology can serve at least four different purposes in schools and classrooms. At the same time, careful thought should be given to which of these purposes might be necessary and most effective for students and teachers.

- **Encouraging consistency.** Think about schools in locales where teachers lack knowledge or expertise in teaching specific topics and where there is a need to provide consistency in both instruction and professional learning. Likewise, consider schools in rural or remote areas where it is difficult for coaches or other support personnel to provide face-to-face support frequently and easily. In these instances, technology can certainly provide a means for all teachers to receive shared professional learning supports (e.g., models of prerecorded lessons), ensuring that teachers and students are receiving similar professional learning and instructional experiences.
- **Differentiating instruction.** We know the importance of providing more than "one-size-fits-all" instruction, given the increased variability in students' skills, knowledge, and cultural backgrounds in schools today. Various tutoring programs designed to both diagnose students' needs and assign students to appropriate instructional exercises can be especially helpful both for students experiencing learning difficulties and those who would benefit from enrichment programs.
- **Providing practice.** In many schools, students are assigned computer-based activities that provide them with the opportunity to practice what they have learned via teacher instruction. Such activities can be completed during the school day, after school, or even at home. As states move toward more online assessment tools, such practice becomes essential.
- **Engaging students.** Students today are accustomed to—and often expect to be involved in—activities that include some sort of visual support (e.g., laptops, iPads, and so forth). Often computer-accessed lessons can provide students with such visual aids, making them more appealing (e.g., gamelike activities) and permitting students with opportunities to correct errors on their own.

Having acknowledged these benefits, as was found during the pandemic, educational technology was not always the solution to all school challenges. Not all students had access to computers. Not all teachers were aware of how to use various devices effectively. Not all students found online instruction stimulating. They missed the social interactions and relationships present in face-to-face learning. We still have much to learn about not only what is best for students but also how to help teachers best use technology. According to Ganimian et al. (2020), "there is no single 'ed-tech' initiative that will achieve the same results everywhere, simply because school systems differ in students and teachers, as well as in the availability and quality of materials and technologies" (p. 62).

> • • • • • • • • • • **Put into Practice** • • • • • • • • • • •
>
> Talk with several of your grade-level or department colleagues about Ganimian et al.'s (2020) description of how schools can embed technology learning into the instructional program. How has this integration been tackled at your school? What improvements might you suggest?

### Coaches' Role in Developing Teachers' Ability to Use Technology Effectively

As recently reported (Ippolito & Bean, 2024; Ippolito et al., 2023), and based on research conducted across the COVID-19 pandemic, virtual learning has had some clear benefits and challenges, as has virtual coaching, in supporting teachers' use of technological tools. One interesting outcome of pandemic virtual coaching was that coaches could easily access the classrooms of teachers and observe instruction; further, coaches reported having more flexibility in meeting with teachers across schools and the district. Elish-Piper et al. (2016) provide several key ideas for how disciplinary coaches who work at the secondary level can connect virtually with teachers to leverage various technology tools to provide coaching "beyond time and location constraints" (p. 78). They suggest that coaches might maintain a blog as a means of sharing resources or use Zoom, Google Hangouts, or Google Meet to connect virtually with teachers across grade levels, subjects, or schools and even develop a community of coaches in their district or across districts.

For coaches wishing to improve teachers' use of technology, it is not sufficient to simply make technology available; rather, teachers need to be supported in their efforts to embed technology in their instructional practices, when appropriate. In other words, technology should not drive instruction—it should be a tool that helps teachers reach their identified goals. Given that technology, and its use in schools, is evolving so rapidly, we often refer coaches to the work of Julie Coiro (2005, 2021) for guidance about leading tech-related professional learning. Based partially on her work, and our own hard-learned lessons over the years, we suggest that coaches consider the following:

- Recognize that teachers are at different stages as users of technology. Some use technology to teach in traditional ways, while others are willing to embed technology in their current practices, making adaptations in how they teach. Other teachers use technology in new, creative ways. In other words, in all schools, there will be a range of expertise from novices to sophisticated users, and thus coaching support will almost necessarily differ.
- Teachers will have different perspectives about technology, its value, and their willingness to use it. These perspectives can range from "I don't see a need for it" to "Technology has made a difference in how I teach and how students learn." Also, perspectives will affect the specific recommendations made by coaches and school leaders and the success of those recommendations.
- Authentic, classroom-based learning that includes opportunities for collaboration is essential in advancing teacher learning and enthusiasm for technology in the classroom. (See Chapter 6 for more ideas about working with small groups.)

While there is much more that could be said about the role of technology in a modern, effective instructional program, this is still an emerging field, and coaches can certainly become involved by working collaboratively with teachers. We suggest consulting the latest standards of the International Society for Technology in Education, which provide guidance for students, teachers, leaders, and coaches (see Web Resources at the end of the chapter).

## Advocating for Programs or Materials

Changing materials can become a controversial issue, with teachers taking sides, some of them defending current programs while others criticize them. It can also become a political issue, especially if the process for materials selection is not well defined or described. Therefore, any advocacy work must be undertaken collaboratively and cautiously, with administrators and teachers fully engaged in the conversation and decision-making process. While not all stakeholders may see eye to eye at first, creating a shared understanding of students' needs and what programs or models can (and cannot) offer students is an important step toward aligning practices with needs.

### *Maintaining a Dual Focus on Individuals and Systems*

As a quick review, at the end of this chapter on thinking about schoolwide programs, we provide a few possible moves that support coaches' and other instructional leaders' dual focus on individuals and systems simultaneously. As you read the following list, consider how each of the actions requires thinking and acting as change agents, facilitators, designers, and advocates:

- Hold regular conversations with school and district leadership about the larger vision for school and district instructional change, focusing on change goals and action steps along the way. When formal and informal leaders develop a shared understanding of desired learning instructional goals and reasonable action steps to achieve those goals, then coaches and teacher leaders are better positioned to see and communicate how individual work aligns (or doesn't) with the larger vision.

- Keep individuals in mind during larger vision conversations to mentally test the validity of larger school change policies and procedures. As a thought exercise and validity check, coaches might spend a few minutes during regularly scheduled conversations with school and district leaders, asking, "How does this vision of change map onto my experiences working with teachers?" Coaches might raise concerns if there appears to be too big of a gap between administrators' and teachers' expectations of change. In other words, how prepared are teachers to adjust to proposed changes? Do they have the resources and support they need to move forward? Have they been involved in discussions about the proposed changes? Coaches and other teacher leaders can be helpful in bridging the gap between administrators and teachers.

- Link individual practice and dilemmas to larger change initiatives so that conversations with individual teachers are never *just* about one particular teacher's students or classroom. Effective coaches can frame and reframe individual classroom dilemmas as part of larger school- and districtwide efforts to support students. If a teacher is concerned about ensuring that students' academic discussions are truly supporting instruction, then a coach might use this as an opportunity to connect the teacher's concerns to larger schoolwide initiatives about productive classroom talk. If such a larger initiative doesn't currently exist in the school (or if the schoolwide focus is slightly different), then this might be an opportunity to test whether other individuals are wondering about the same instructional moves. We are not suggesting that coaches twist every conversation to suit larger school or district goals; however, we invite coaches to consider the power of helping teachers connect individual efforts to larger group initiatives and existing supports.

- Plan carefully for meetings and conversations with teachers and leaders so that each of these interactions with large groups, administrators, and individual teachers touches briefly on the concerns of the system and the concerns of individuals. This does not mean the rigid or lockstep use of formal written agendas or discussion-based protocols as scripts; instead, just a bit of planning ahead for meetings can help coaches ensure that both system and individual concerns are represented in decision-making conversations.

## Summary

In this chapter, we have discussed the key roles and responsibilities of coaches in the schoolwide change process and the important role of the ILT. We described two processes for leading various schoolwide efforts: conducting a needs assessment and crafting an action plan. After describing important notions about implementation issues and sustainability, we have provided information about the selection or development of instructional materials, both print and electronic. We concluded with a brief review of the importance of the dual focus of coaches and other instructional leaders: working with individuals and systems simultaneously.

As Melinda began her collaborative efforts related to managing a needs-assessment process and following up with action planning, she noted how these activities influenced the balance of her time commitments. Suddenly, she found herself with less time to meet individually with teachers. However, she also realized that the time spent on whole-school processes and related small groups (including her school's ILT) gave her a deeper understanding of teacher knowledge, beliefs, and skills. In the long run, she knew her schoolwide work would have a positive influence on the relationships she was continuing to forge with teachers, ultimately enabling her to address issues of teaching and learning more effectively.

## Reflections

- Using the chart found in Appendix A, note the ways that coaches act as change agents, facilitators, designers, and advocates when involved in schoolwide instructional programming. List some possibilities that you might consider adopting in your current position.
- Consider the ways that you as a coach engage in schoolwide or districtwide efforts to enact change. What challenges have you faced? What successes have you had? What factors have influenced you in your work? Share your thoughts with a colleague, and discuss strategies that you have found successful.
- Read one of the resources mentioned in the Further Readings and Resources section at the end of this chapter (or one of your choice), and consider what you can apply in your own work as a coach involved in schoolwide programming.
- If you are involved in a schoolwide initiative, keep a simple journal describing your work. This provides you with opportunities to reflect on successes and challenges, as well as important collaborations. It may also help to reduce and manage stress that you experience in your role as a change agent.

## Activities

1. Searching online, locate two different needs-assessment documents (if possible, one from your own state). Compare and contrast the documents: In what ways are they similar and different? Which would be most helpful to you and your school?
2. Using Figure 8.1, facilitate a discussion with teachers about the array of instructional programs in your school (or the instructional program in one specific area) and their perceptions of it. Use the results of the discussion to analyze the current strengths and needs of the program, as perceived by teachers. Talk with colleagues about these results and possible next steps.
3. Discuss with a colleague one of the scenarios at the beginning of Chapter 8, in the section "The Role of Coaches in Improving Schoolwide Learning," that describes a task that may be assigned to a coach. How would you address this leadership task? (Think about possible steps or a process.)

## FURTHER READINGS AND RESOURCES

**Print Resources**

Coiro, J. (2021). Toward a multifaceted heuristic of digital reading to inform assessment, research, practice, and policy. *Reading Research Quarterly, 56*(1), 9–31.

Fisher, D., & Frey, N. (2023). The technology-enhanced school. *Educational Leadership, 80*(6), 76–77.

Ippolito, J., Bean, R. M., & Sacha, K. (2023). Innovations in elementary literacy coaching: Sustaining coaching practices in virtual spaces. In D. Robertson, L. A. Hall, & C. Brock (Eds.), *Innovations in literacy professional learning: Strengthening equity, access, and sustainability* (pp. 213–239). Guilford Press.

Kiili, C., Lakkala, M., Ilomäki, L., Toom, A., Coiro, J., Hämäläinen, E., & Sormunen, E. (2021). Designing classroom practices for teaching online inquiry: Experiences from the field. *Journal of Adolescent & Adult Literacy, 65*(4), 297–308.

**Web Resources (see www.guilford.com/bean3-materials for live links)**

ASCD & ISTE. (2023). Deepening learning with technology [Special issue]. *Educational Leadership.* www.ascd.org/el/deepening-learning-with-technology

CAST. (2018). *Universal design for learning guidelines* (Version 2.2). http://udlguidelines.cast.org

Corbett, J., & Redding, S. (2017). *Using needs assessments for school and district improvement: A tactical guide.* Center on School Turnaround at WestEd and Council of Chief State School Officers. www.adi.org/downloads/NeedsAssessment-Final.pdf

Cuiccio, C., & Husby-Slater, M. (2018). *Needs assessment guidebook: Supporting the development of district and school needs assessments.* American Institutes for Research. http://oese.ed.gov/files/2020/10/needsassessmentguidebook-508_003.pdf

Ganimian, A. J., Vegas, E., & Hess, F. M. (2020). *Realizing the promise: How can education technology improve learning for all?* The Brookings Institution. www.brookings.edu/articles/realizing-the-promise-how-can-education-technology-improve-learning-for-all

Gray, L., & Lewis, L. (2021). *Use of educational technology for instruction in public schools: 2019–20* (NCES 2021-017). U.S. Department of Education, Institute of Education Sciences, National Center for Education Statistics. https://nces.ed.gov/pubsearch/pubsinfo.asp?pubid=2021017

Hanover Research. (2023). *2023 trends in K–12 education.* www.hanoverresearch.com/reports-and-briefs/2023-trends-in-k-12-education

International Society for Technology in Education (ISTE). (2024). *ISTE standards.* https://iste.org/standards

Learning Forward. (n.d.). *Standards for Professional Learning, revised.* https://standards.learningforward.org/standards-for-professional-learning

National Implementation Research Network. (n.d.). http://nirn.fpg.unc.edu

Ross, E. M. (2023, July). *Embracing artificial intelligence in the classroom. Usable knowledge.* Harvard Graduate School of Education. www.gse.harvard.edu/ideas/usable-knowledge/23/07/embracing-artificial-intelligence-classroom

Wiener, R., & Pimentel, S. (2017). *Practice what you teach: Connecting curriculum and professional learning in schools.* The Aspen Institute. www.aspeninstitute.org/wp-content/uploads/2017/04/Practice-What-You-Teach.pdf

## CHAPTER 9

# Working with Families and Communities

### GUIDING QUESTIONS

1. Why should coaches promote family and community engagement?
2. In what ways can coaches work with teachers to promote family and community engagement?
3. In what ways can grants support the school's various learning initiatives? What are some key guidelines for writing grants?

## Melinda Begins to Look Beyond the School Walls

As part of their needs-assessment process and newly drafted schoolwide action plan, Melinda and her teaching colleagues identified a great need to build stronger partnerships with the community, not only with families but with the agencies and organizations in the local region. Given the increased student diversity in their school, which necessitates greater attention to issues of equity, the team wanted to include a number of concrete steps in their schoolwide action plan focused on improving school–community relationships. As the team looked to Melinda for suggestions, she felt the need to learn more about productive school–community partnering strategies. What might she recommend? Where might she turn to learn more?

In this chapter, we focus on the importance of developing strong links to the external community—families, community agencies, businesses, libraries, universities, and so on—for improving student learning. We address several ways that coaches can facilitate efforts to build meaningful relationships with these entities. We also describe ideas for how to obtain external funding to support important instructional initiatives. This chapter highlights the many ways that coaches are involved as change agents, facilitators, designers, and especially advocates as they work with families and communities.

## The Importance of Engaging Families and Communities

Research points to the positive relationships that exist between higher levels of family involvement and student achievement, motivation to learn, higher rates of graduation, and even higher secondary school grade point averages (Bryk et al., 2010; Burton, 2013; Henderson & Mapp, 2002; Jung & Zhang, 2016; Paratore et al., 2020). This engagement is important for all students, yet at times family situations prohibit or limit involvement. Factors that affect family engagement may include language or cultural barriers, financial constraints (parents working multiple jobs or single-parent households), or negative experiences with schooling that affect families' willingness to participate in school activities (Edwards, 2016; Edwards et al., 2014). Moreover, too frequently, traditional models of family engagement, such as volunteering at the school, chaperoning field trips, or attending parent–teacher association (PTA) meetings, exclude parents who don't have the resources or time for such activities. We encourage coaches to think broadly about parental engagement, and especially to consider ways that technology can assist schools in increasing parent involvement. Epstein et al. (2009, 2018), for example, identify six general categories of parental involvement:

1. **Parenting.** Working with parents in ways that help them establish effective home environments for learning (e.g., opportunities for conversation, availability of reading materials).
2. **Communicating with families.** Designing effective modes of home–school communication that includes the use of technology.
3. **Volunteering.** Providing opportunities for volunteers in the school. Such volunteers can include family members, senior citizens, members of local service organizations, university students, and so on.
4. **Learning at home.** Developing families' ability to support student learning at home (e.g., helping with homework, reading to and with children).
5. **Decision making.** Involving families in decision making at the school (e.g., deciding how and when to schedule events, the best ways to communicate).
6. **Collaborating with the community.** Developing partnerships with various community organizations and providing services to the community (e.g., adult literacy, family math programs).

What is key here is the importance of a systematic, intentional program across the school. Efforts by individual teachers are nice but won't suffice! That is why the work being done by Melinda and her team is so important. For additional information, see the Partnership Schools website (see the Web Resources at the end of the chapter), Soo Hong's (2019) book, *Natural Allies: Hope and Possibility in Teacher–Family Partnerships*, and Ippolito and Bean (2024) for additional ideas and resources.

> • • • • • • • • • • **Put into Practice** • • • • • • • • • • • •
>
> Discuss with teachers the six types of family involvement just described. How does your school enact each of these? What are your school's strengths in this area? Weaknesses? Needs? Develop an action plan for improving family involvement by identifying two or three priority items that could serve as goals for your school over the next two years.

Next, we expand on some of Epstein's major points and identify strategies that can be used by coaches to support teachers in their efforts to work effectively with these external communities. In many cases, teachers can take the lead in developing and facilitating these activities while coaches provide additional support and encouragement. Many of the ideas were inspired by multiple sources, including the Henderson and Mapp report (2002) and the PTA's (2021) National Standards for Family-School Partnerships (see the Web Resources as the end of the chapter).

## Ideas for Developing a School Culture That Understands, Values, and Celebrates the Diversity of Its Communities

Building school capacity so that all staff members in the school (e.g., teachers, administrators, staff, custodians, and so on) work effectively with families and community members is a first, and challenging, step. Individual teachers in the school may work well with families, but the goal of this book is to promote both individual *and* systems-level change—that is, to create a schoolwide or districtwide climate that respects, values, and appreciates cultural diversity and the need for equitable experiences and outcomes for students. Coaches have many opportunities to think and work as change agents and advocates as they help to develop such a culture. Suggestions include:

- Develop awareness of the existing school and community cultures related to family engagement. Is there an understanding by educators of the challenges that families face, and in what ways parents can be supported in understanding how and why the school operates as it does? Staff can respond to the questions in Figure 9.1 individually and then discuss responses as a group. They can describe ways that teachers individually and as a group provide for active engagement of families. All staff members, from those who sit in the reception area to those responsible for maintaining the environment in and around the school, can be asked to participate in this activity. Based on the results, ideas for improving faculty and staff receptivity to family and community involvement can be generated.

- Create a welcoming environment for those who enter the school. Possible ways of doing this include posting welcome signs, invitations to visit classrooms, and designated parking spots for guests (all in multiple languages to reflect the linguistic

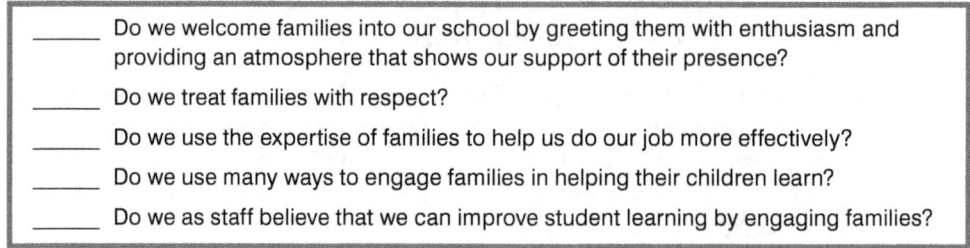

**FIGURE 9.1.** Discussing family and community involvement. Adapted from Constantino (2008). Copyright © 2008 Engage! Press.

diversity of families and community members). The front office makes an important first impression—family members should feel welcome (e.g., pictures of student work can be posted, and staff can quickly and pleasantly welcome those who enter).

• Provide staff with related professional learning experiences. Such learning experiences can focus on the importance of developing a school community that respects and values the diversity of families. Further, these experiences should include opportunities for staff to think about their own backgrounds and how their perceptions and possible biases can influence the ways in which they treat others. Staff can be asked to read and discuss materials related to working effectively with students and their families. (A possible text might be Patricia Edwards's [2016] book, *New Ways to Engage Parents: Strategies and Tools for Teachers and Leaders, K–12*.)

• Celebrate the diversity that exists in the school (among the staff as well as in the community). Students and teachers can design posters that identify traits of their respective cultures (e.g., foods, traditions, and activities). Family members can be invited to talk with students about their heritage, their jobs, and so on. Students at the secondary level can interview family members or write their biographies. Remember that just as individual students differ, so do their families; each family brings unique skills and talents that need to be taken into consideration as schools work to develop positive relationships with them (Edwards, 2016).

• Assist teachers in selecting materials (print and nonprint). Classroom and library materials should reflect the diversity that exists in the school and community. At this time, there is concern in some communities about the nature of books that are included in classroom and school libraries, often with strong feelings among various groups of citizens. We encourage coaches and other school leaders to work closely with community leaders to discuss this important issue. In some schools, leaders have started "book clubs" in which community members and educators together read books that have been identified as questionable for placement in school libraries. Resources such as the following many be helpful to educators who face this issue in their communities (see Web Resources at the end of this chapter):

  ○ American Library Association's "Banned and Challenged Books"
  ○ Vanderbilt University's Banned Book Initiative

As Emily Veader writes in the next Voices from the Field, coaches and school leaders have a responsibility for working with teachers to help them recognize what students *can* do, to have high expectations for all, and to plan instruction that enhances learning through recognizing and celebrating diversity in the school and community. We encourage schools to include books in their classrooms and libraries that provide students with "mirrors, windows, and sliding glass doors" (Bishop, 1990), to help students see themselves and others in books, as well as to have opportunities to visualize new and different people and places across all subjects and curricula.

> **VOICES FROM THE FIELD**
>
> This year, with the support of our principal, we were able to revive two prepandemic events: Math Morning and Math Evening. For Math Morning, we invited first-grade parents in at the beginning of the day. They spent 15 minutes in the library listening to us share some of the strategies that first graders tend to use when solving addition and subtraction problems. We taught them two games that encourage students to add and subtract. Then, the parents joined their children in their classrooms for half an hour to play the games with them. As we walked around, it was clear that parents were just as excited as we were to notice first graders' math thinking. One parent said, "I just saw what you were saying. My daughter said I know 5+5=10, so 5+4 must equal 9." Math Evening took place a week later and was just for the parents. We spent time solving two-digit addition and subtraction problems using strategies that their children would start using at the end of first grade and would continue for years to come. A parent said she was so happy to finally understand what her older child had been doing in math. She said she hoped we would continue to hold these evenings. During the presentation, our principal said, "We have spent the past year really looking at these strategies during grade-level meetings and in classrooms. I am realizing that what we are really doing is providing students opportunities to become flexible thinkers." It makes my job as a coach so much easier when parents and my principal understand and encourage the same goals for our students.
> —EMILY VEADER, Elementary Math Instructional Coach

## Build Two-Way Communication Channels to Enhance Family Understanding and Involvement

Make efforts to inform families and seek information from them; that is, obtain feedback that can influence various decisions about curriculum, school events, scheduling, and so on.

## Find Ways to Communicate with Families

Design, with teachers, simple practices for reaching out to parents. In one school, teachers were asked to make four phone calls a month: two positive ones and two addressing needs of students about whom they have concerns. In another school, teachers selected three or four students per month and sent written certificates that identified these students as honor students to their families. Each certificate had one or two sentences describing the accomplishments of that student.

Develop and use multiple means of communication to increase family involvement. Electronic communication can be especially helpful for working parents who might have limited time to visit the school. Consider the following: Communicate electronically, given that so many families now have email capability, but hold realistic expectations about receiving responses. Develop and maintain a school or district website. Write and distribute electronic newsletters (secondary students could be responsible for writing these newsletters or updating classroom blogs with student work or reports of class activities). Provide families with online access to their child's data (using password-protected websites). Use a classroom management app that enables parents to obtain access to feedback about the behavior of their children (e.g., ClassDojo). Surveys can be used to seek family opinions about possible school events or activities while brief descriptive flyers can be sent to inform parents about upcoming events or to provide information about ways that parents can support their child's learning, and so forth.

## Provide Activities and Programs That Support Families in Their Efforts to Guide Their Children's Learning

Continue efforts for family involvement throughout the grades. Although secondary students may not need direct assistance with their schoolwork, proactive communication between home and school and a focus on helping students and their families think about academic achievement (and its relationship to future success) is important.

Hold sessions to describe important initiatives or instructional efforts for families and explain how important they can be in assisting schools in achieving their goals. For example, coaches or other school leaders might explain the standards-based curriculum that requires students to engage in high-level learning tasks. However, explanations should be audience friendly, and families should be provided with specific examples that illustrate what is meant. To the degree possible, don't use educational jargon, and make sure to explain what a specific term means. Parents may not understand terms like *disciplinary literacy, phonemic awareness, counting on, factoring*, and so forth. Parents may even be asked to participate in a learning activity that their children might experience (e.g., they can participate in a lab experiment in a science class, attempt math problems that students are currently tackling in class, or be asked to look at several anonymous student writing examples and consider which they think best describes a character or takes a stand on a specific issue). (For an example of this in a math coaching/teaching context, see Emily Veader's extended case in Chapter 11.)

Remember that open houses and parent–teacher conferences are informal learning opportunities for parents to engage not only with faculty and staff but also with materials and content that their children are learning. Parents who learn something during an open house are often better prepared to help their children at home. Student-led conferences are another mechanism for connecting teachers, students, and families in meaningful ways.

Be specific with parents about educational requirements for students. How long should a homework assignment take? How can parents best support their children? How can families contact teachers? Requirements differ for various levels, of course. At the preschool level, parents may be provided with information about how they can develop the oral language of their children by holding dinnertime conversations or reading to them. At the elementary level, parents may be given suggestions for what they need to do when they listen to their child read. At the middle school level, parents may be asked to collaborate with their children on homework assignments. At the high school level, parents may attend meetings or receive information electronically about various program options, career choices, and graduation requirements.

Create a family resource center where families can find information about student learning or supporting students at home. Such a place can also provide opportunities for adult learning (e.g., learning English). For example, parents in the Springfield, Massachusetts school system who want to help their children with the college-application process, figure out how to balance the family budget, learn to knit, or even become a certified lifeguard can take a class through the district's Parent Academy (see the Web Resources at the end of the chapter). The Parent Academy, a collaborative effort of community agencies, businesses, and schools, focuses its work on helping parents understand their importance as role models for their children. Workshops for parents are focused on needs that have been identified.

Seek volunteers from the community to work in schools. Volunteers may be college students, senior citizens, or even high school students wishing to learn more about becoming a teacher or fulfilling teacher preparation requirements (e.g., tutoring children for a requisite number of hours). Volunteers may tutor children, perform clerical tasks that assist teachers in their work (duplicate necessary material, make materials for learning centers, and so on), or work informally with the teacher to manage classroom activities (e.g., putting on a classroom play or going on a field trip). In all cases, volunteers need to be prepared for the tasks they are being asked to do. For example, those tutoring students should be given specific instructions about how to use instructional materials and how to address any specific behavioral issues. Volunteer tutors often need help in understanding the culture of the school (the "dos and don'ts" for each classroom and for the school in general). In the America Reads program (Bean et al., 2002), in which college students tutored students in inner-city schools, we had to address questions related to the clothing tutors wore to school, teachers' approach to discipline, and ways tutors could effectively manage students presenting behavioral challenges.

## *Involve Families in Decision Making and Encourage Their Participation as Partners in Efforts to Educate Their Children*

Families can be partners in the educational enterprise in many ways. Educators can consider how to involve families in decision making so that agendas are mutually determined and beneficial. In other words, families can be empowered to work *with* schools to develop programs that meet the needs of students. Suggestions include:

- Support the development of various parent organizations or advisory councils (e.g., parent–teacher associations and organizations, safety committees, or curriculum committees).
- Offer training that assists parents in learning how to serve as representatives of the school, including how to reach out to other families in the school, especially those new to the community.
- Provide information about school processes and events to all families so that they are informed about school programs, challenges, and concerns.
- Share issues of concern with parents to help them understand the views of educators, and also to seek their advice about possible solutions (e.g., whether particular books are appropriate for students at specific grade levels).
- Consider involving parents in decisions about homework assignments, school priorities, and so on.
- Ask parents to lead informal after-school clubs or to work with teachers on such clubs (e.g., a book discussion group only for boys or girls, a Shakespeare club, or a science club).

## *Help Develop Teachers' Understanding of How to Talk with and Support Families*

It's common for teachers to reach out to their colleagues, or to coaches or other leaders, about individual students who may be experiencing difficulties, either with behavior or with academic subjects, not only to seek advice about how to help that student, but also for advice about how to talk with the family about the student's difficulties.

In addition to providing specific advice, coaches can also develop mini-workshops that focus on this topic. Various scenarios, based on actual events in the school, might be used in these sessions as seeds for discussion. Some examples include a parent being concerned about the instruction that her child in first grade, who already knows how to read, is receiving; or a science teacher meeting with the parent of a middle school student who has not been turning in assignments and has difficulties responding to writing tasks. Other suggestions for these meetings include: share examples of student work to illustrate what the child can and cannot do, talk only about a specific child rather than making comparisons with others in the classroom, listen more than you talk, refrain from using jargon, and *show* more than you *tell* what may be difficult for the student (Bean & Goatley, 2021). Another way to help parents feel more comfortable is to sit at a table next to them rather than behind a desk.

To develop teachers' ability to communicate effectively with families, work internally in ways that establish connections among all professionals in the school. Although coaches might have awareness of the academic needs of specific students or families, collaborating with other school professionals, such as social workers, guidance counselors, and teachers, can be helpful in identifying more specifically the reasons students might be experiencing difficulties and the type of support needed. For example, although the teacher may notice that a student has been sleeping in English class, it may take a conversation with the social worker to identify the cause (e.g., the father is now unemployed, and the family is living with cousins in an overcrowded apartment). Schools that have leadership teams, with representation of specialists from various fields, are better able to communicate with each other about specific students and their needs.

> **STOP AND REFLECT**
>
> In what ways has your school systematically made efforts to develop school–community partnerships? What has made these efforts successful? Which activities or initiatives might you and other coaches consider to enhance current partnerships? Perhaps it would be wise to consider whether all parents/caregivers are involved in these partnerships. In what ways can you ensure that all groups feel as though they are important to the school community?

## Capitalizing on Community Resources by Establishing Relationships

Educators are well aware that "student success requires attention to the needs of the whole child" (National Education Association, n.d., p. 1). Thus, we see a recent emphasis in some underserved communities on the establishment of full-service schools that provide comprehensive "wraparound" services. Such services often include health care, family engagement and learning experiences, expanded after-school learning and summer programming, and even opportunities to discuss postsecondary education and career options. Coaches may find themselves advocating for such services and leading efforts to develop them. (See the Web Resources at the end of the chapter.)

Even if a district is not involved in a comprehensive effort to establish a full-service school, it must consider ways that it can involve community partners to educate the students it serves. Schools are affected by, and affect, the organizations around them. Businesses expect schools to produce employees who can communicate effectively, are able to work well with others, and have well-established work habits. Libraries can support the work of the school by housing books and resources that align with the curriculum of the school. They can also provide summer (as well as year-round) programming that supports the work of the school. Universities can learn from schools, getting a better idea of how research is affecting practice; at the same time, they can help enhance educational programs in the school by their involvement. Another important partnership is that of schools with preschool providers in the district. Given the emphasis on early childhood education, schools need to learn more about what is provided in these contexts and, just as important, share with their preschool partners key instructional practices and expectations.

In the paragraphs that follow, we provide some examples of our work with schools in establishing school–community relationships. At the same time, the local context and availability of specific partners should guide school efforts to develop, maintain, and sustain such partnerships.

### *Working with Local Preschool Providers*

Given the emphasis on early childhood education and research evidence that points to its positive effects on behavior and later success in life (Gray-Lobe et al., 2023), schools would be well advised to partner with preschools that exist within their community. Some possible efforts include:

- Coaches and teachers of young children can meet and collaborate regularly with preschool educators and administrators (e.g., meeting with them to discuss school initiatives, expectations, and so on).
- Schools can invite early childhood educators to attend workshops at the school that are relevant to beginning literacy or math instruction. Even if only a few teachers can attend, those who do participate can share information with their colleagues when they return to their preschools.
- Schools can provide opportunities for early childhood teachers, kindergarten, and first-grade teachers to meet and discuss questions: What are the expectations and goals for each level? How can we make certain that students entering kindergarten or first grade are prepared to succeed? What are the goals and programs in preschools that are important to students' developmental literacy, language, and academic growth?
- Coaches or teachers can volunteer to talk with parents of preschool children to describe expectations and assist early childhood teachers in discussing how parents can help support literacy and language learning.

## Working with Local Libraries

As Bean and Goatley (2021) describe, there are many ways that schools can partner with the community library:

- Given that students, especially those from low-income families, may suffer from the lack of learning experiences during the summer (Alexander et al., 2007; Schwartz et al., 2018) and benefit from structured summer programming (Kim et al., 2017), encouraging students to participate in school-related and community library offerings during the summer is important. Meeting with librarians to discuss offerings and collaboratively brainstorm ideas can also be helpful.

- In my (Rita's) former community, the library, in partnership with the local Lions Club, a service organization, provided programming that encouraged students to read actively (e.g., Book Walks, Read to the Dogs, Book Bingos, and Reading with the Stars, where local celebrities, including the mayor, read to children). Library programs that build parents' and children's enthusiasm for reading and learning are important to the work of the school, and we encourage schools to promote student attendance at these events.

- In this same community, the library and the school district participated in an adult literacy program for refugee adults from Nepal who lived there. The adults were transported to the library on a bus called the "Learn Bus," supplied by the school district. They attended classes at the library to improve their ability to speak and read English.

- In a large urban school district, the community library developed a program in which librarians went into the school to read and discuss books with third-grade children. The students learned more about the community library and its resources and enjoyed listening to librarians read from quality books—informational and fiction. Teachers appreciated the opportunity to learn about new trade books. In fact, the books were then given to the teachers to use in their classrooms (Genest, 2014; Genest & Bean, 2007).

- And remember, libraries are able to support students' and families' literacy and knowledge development across domains, including all subject areas, technology, and information literacies. Partnering with libraries can be a foundational support for all disciplinary literacy work in schools across content areas.

## Working with Local Universities

School–university partnerships are win-win situations. Schools benefit from the infusion of additional personnel and ideas from university students and faculty. Universities benefit because they can place their teacher candidates or graduate students in real-life situations where they have authentic problems to solve. Further, such partnerships enable university faculty to test their ideas and beliefs and keep them apprised of current school efforts and initiatives. How often do we hear that university faculty have an "ivory tower" mentality? Working in school settings prevents that sort of thinking and provides ongoing learning for all involved in teacher education or educational research.

For the past 25 years or so, the Reading Department at the University of Pittsburgh has placed candidates for the reading specialist certification program in local school districts. These graduate students serve as reading specialist interns who work with struggling readers and writers, with the guidance of district reading specialists and classroom teachers. This yearlong internship has been invaluable: It provides support to young readers and writers, energizes classroom teachers who are exposed to new ideas from university students, and provides the university intern with real-life experience as a reading specialist. The longevity of the program speaks to its value, and even faced with funding or other difficulties with implementation, it has stayed the course. We encourage school districts to seek out interested university or college partners as they move forward with various initiatives such as this one.

## Grant Writing: Accessing Resources from External Sources

Although some coaches may not view grant writing as one of their primary responsibilities, many will have the opportunity or need to write a proposal at some point. Community organizations or foundations, for example, often provide teachers with opportunities to write mini-proposals to fund special projects (e.g., writing oral histories of senior citizens; purchasing books related to a special theme; or purchasing digital tools, such as iPads or digital cameras). The state may have special initiatives that require proposals (e.g., upgrading school technology resources or hiring technology coaches to help teachers integrate technology into their instruction). Lastly, a local foundation may be eager to fund special summer programs to support young students' literacy or math learning. In other words, external funding can often provide the impetus for a school to implement initiatives that it can't fund itself.

Funding can jump-start important initiatives. In large school districts, there may be a dedicated district-level grant writer who can help with this sort of task; in smaller districts, teachers or school-based coaches with creative ideas may write the proposal. We provide some key ideas for proposal writing and recommend several resources that may be helpful to those involved in such efforts:

- **Take the risk!** There is a trite but true expression that says, "If you don't put your foot in the water, you won't get wet." Be willing to write and submit a proposal. Even a rejection can provide feedback that can be helpful for the next submission. And contact the funder before you begin writing if you have questions. Funders *want* to give away money and generally they are

very willing to answer questions you may have about writing the proposal, its appropriateness for your idea or initiative, and so on.
- **Work collaboratively with others in your school.** Develop ideas together and share the proposal with others to get feedback about its clarity. (Is it convincing? Do you have a good idea that will intrigue the funder?) Funders also appreciate (and sometimes require) group involvement in and support of proposals. Such proposals are much more likely to be granted funds, implemented, and sustained in schools.
- **Find the right match for your proposal.** At times, you may be writing to the state or responding to a call for proposals, but at other times you may be looking for an agency interested in your specific idea or program. Find an agency interested in that specific problem. Make your case with a local nonprofit for why this idea is critical now. Create a sense of urgency, and connect your ideas clearly to teacher- and student-level outcomes.
- **Write clearly and succinctly.** A well-written proposal is a must. A proposal that contains grammatical errors, or one that is difficult to understand, will not likely be funded. It sounds simple, yet so many proposals are compiled quickly, by multiple authors, that they aren't coherent or polished. Take the extra time to reread your proposal, ask someone else to read and provide feedback so that the final submission is one that represents your thoughts clearly and concisely.
- **Follow the guidelines.** Be certain that you address all elements required by the funder. Almost all funders ask for goals or objectives, a description of project activities, a list of personnel to be involved, a rubric for how the project will be evaluated, a time line, and a budget. Some larger and lengthier processes will also include space for you to write a summary of related research or evidence supporting the idea. See the end of this chapter for a list of Further Readings and Resources.

One final caveat about grant writing: All too often, we have seen excellent teacher leadership and coaching initiatives begin with grant seed money, only to disappear completely two years later when the grant money has been spent. If grants are being sought and secured to begin a coaching or teacher leadership project, we suggest that sustainability and long-term feasibility be considered up front.

One recommendation in cases like this is for a school or district to reevaluate and edit its current budget to create a teacher leadership or coaching role from sustainable funds (e.g., creating a coaching line item), and then seek and secure grant money to pay for other aspects of the initiative (e.g., books, technology, and teacher stipends for participation in related professional learning experiences). This allows the school or district to directly manage the leadership and coaching work, assess the ongoing success of the project, and not be suddenly surprised when grant funds come to an end and a key leader (i.e., the coach) disappears!

## Summary

In this chapter, we discussed the importance and responsibilities of parents in promoting children's learning (including being a cheerleader, teacher, enforcer, and advocate). We also described ways that schools can support parents—and parents can support schools. We also highlighted the importance of local service organizations, libraries, and universities as key partners in educating students and in facilitating whole-school improvement. We concluded with a section on grant writing as a source of additional and needed funds. Finally, we encouraged coaches and other teacher leaders to use their creative and problem-solving skills to collaboratively write grants that address special goals or initiatives.

As a result of their reading and follow-up discussion, Melinda and her team generated a proposal for a schoolwide parent involvement program that included a plan for a professional learning initiative for teachers. Further, they secured funding from a local foundation to purchase children's books to give to the families and to support the development of a video that could be used for the professional learning of teachers.

## Reflections

- Using the chart found in Appendix A, note the ways that coaches function as change agents, facilitators, designers, and advocates when working to establish relationships between the school and community. List some possibilities that you might consider adopting in your current position.
- Talk with colleagues about the ways in which your school works with community agencies, and discuss the ways in which school leaders might seek out some new possibilities with businesses, universities, or community libraries. Which ideas and resources from this chapter might spark new ideas?

## Activities

1. Hold meetings with other specialized professionals, such as a school psychologist, librarian, guidance counselor, or special educator, to discuss ways in which they develop and establish connections between families and the school. Ask these professionals to share their ideas with classroom teachers and administrators.
2. Ask teachers to write a brief scenario describing a dilemma or problem related to family–school relationships. Use these scenarios as the basis for a larger discussion, asking participants to talk about possible solutions to the identified dilemmas. Hold workshops with teachers about how to facilitate effective parent–teacher

conferences. Role-play various scenarios, with teachers and coaches assuming the specific roles of parents or teachers.

## FURTHER READINGS AND RESOURCES

### Print Resources

Edwards, P. (2016). *New ways to engage parents: Strategies and tools for teachers and leaders, K–12.* Teachers College Press.

Hong, S. (2020). *Natural allies: Hope and possibility in teacher–family partnerships.* Harvard Education Press.

Paratore, J., Steiner, L. M., & Dougherty, S. M. (2020). Developing effective home–school literacy partnerships. In A. Swan Dagen & R. M. Bean (Eds.), *Best practices of literacy leaders: Keys to school improvement* (2nd ed., pp. 346–363). Guilford Press.

Rothstein, A. L. (2019). *Creating winning grant proposals: A step-by-step guide.* Guilford Press.

Thiers, N. (2017). Unlocking families' potential: A conversation with Karen L. Mapp. *Educational Leadership, 75*(1), 40–44.

### Web Resources (see *www.guilford.com/bean3-materials* for live links)

American Library Association. (n.d.). *Banned and challenged books.* www.ala.org/advocacy/bbooks

Coalition for Community Schools. (2020). *Institute for Educational Leadership.* www.communityschools.org

Cooper, J. (2023). 7 tips for improving parent engagement in schools. *SchoolNow.* www.schoolnow.com/blog/parent-involvement-school-another

Harvard Graduate School of Education. (n.d.). *100 stories of impact: Improving our schools, one family at a time.* www.gse.harvard.edu/hgse100/story/improving-our-schools-one-family-time

Jakob, E., Porter, A., Podos, J., Braun, B., Johnson, N., & Vessey, S. (2010). How to fail in grant writing. *The Chronicle of Higher Education.* www.chronicle.com/article/how-to-fail-in-grant-writing

Mapp, K. L., & Bergman, E. (2019). *The dual capacity-building framework for family–school partnerships* (Version 2). www.dualcapacity.org

National Education Association. (n.d.). *95 ways to engage members through family and community engagement.* http://www.nea.org/sites/default/files/2021-01/NEA%20Calendar%20(1)

National PTA. (2021). *National Standards for Family-School Partnerships.* www.pta.org/home/run-your-pta/family-school-partnerships

Springfield Parent Academy. (2024). *Parent academy.* http://springfieldparentacademy.com

Vanderbilt University. (n.d.). *Banned book initiative.* https://researchguides.library.vanderbilt.edu/c.php?g=1241477&p=9146774

Warren, M. R. (n.d.). *Books, published articles* [books and articles on school–community connections]. www.mark-warren.org/books-1

# CHAPTER 10

# Coaches as Lifelong Learners

> **GUIDING QUESTIONS**
>
> 1. In what ways can coaches maintain a focus on their own lifelong learning, while simultaneously maintaining a focus on leading learning for colleagues?
> 2. What is the knowledge base for those seeking to become coaches?
> 3. How can coaches use reflective practices and evaluation tools as guides in their own ongoing professional learning?

## Melinda Considers Her Own Ongoing Professional Learning

As Melinda slowly but surely becomes more confident in her new coaching role, her mind next turns to a final important question: How might she both maintain and grow her own coaching knowledge and skill set over time? Melinda is keenly aware that she still has much to learn about curricular content, related instructional practices, and a wide variety of coaching practices. How might she ensure that she is practicing what she preaches and continually growing as a coach and educator herself?

In this chapter, we review some of the broad categories of knowledge, skills, and dispositions that coaches often possess and acquire slowly over the course of their careers. Our argument throughout the chapter is that working as a coach requires adopting the stance of lifelong learner. In fact, we have found that the best coaches are often those leaders who position themselves alongside colleagues as *co-learners*. We expand on the notion of *leaders as learners* throughout the chapter. Finally, we end with a list of concrete strategies for maintaining a focus on learning and leading simultaneously.

## A Reminder about Adopting an "Expert" Stance

We circle around again (see Chapter 4) to provide an important reminder about the issue of adopting an "expert" stance as a coach. If you're anything like us when we worked full-time as teachers and coaches in schools, you probably think to yourself on a regular basis: "I'm not so sure I'm expert enough to *really* help my colleagues transform their practice and meet all students' needs." In fact, anyone who is paying attention to the growing number and range of student needs today might be living in a constant state of low-level panic, because the needs are many, and research-based answers are (relatively) few. In the midst of the maelstrom of standards, accountability (for students, teachers, coaches, and leaders), the aftermath of the COVID-19 pandemic, class and socioeconomic disparities, ongoing racial inequities, and day-to-day dilemmas that arise in all schools, a coach might be singled out by colleagues as the lone hero (or sometimes villain!) because after all, you're the expert, right? And if you're like us, there is a small part of you that takes great pride in being an expert. Then there is likely a larger part that might be quite nervous that all your colleagues have gotten it wrong—you might wonder, "How can *I* really be the expert? What exactly is expected of me, after all?"

When we look across relevant books, articles, and national policy documents, we find a wide variety and large number of areas in which coaches are often expected to be experts. For example, Elish-Piper and L'Allier (2011), in their study of literacy coaching, found a relationship between advanced literacy preparation of coaches and student reading performance. Documents of professional organizations and states (e.g., ILA, 2018; Learning Forward, n.d.; New Teacher Center, 2018; Pennsylvania Department of Education, 2016) recommend that coaches have specialized knowledge about their discipline (e.g., literacy, math, science, social studies, social emotional learning, technology, and so on), assessment, adult learning, leadership, and school change. At the same time, those who coach need to know how to wield their expertise in ways that honor and value what others bring to the table: the principal with special leadership skills, the teachers with their knowledge of classroom instruction, the school psychologists, special educators, librarians, and so on. Although a coach's knowledge of their discipline, leadership skills, and experience will guide and influence them in their work with others, *how* they use that expertise will make a difference in whether there are systemic changes in teaching and learning in a school.

The notion of expertise can create a dynamic, which we see too often and which even the best of us can become mired in, where teachers, administrators, and parents will turn to you—the expert—for a quick and authoritative (perhaps technical) answer to whatever might be the most pressing instructional or assessment issue at hand. Of course, this can create tension and is sometimes dangerous, for if we give in to the temptation to always provide a quick, technical answer, we run the risk of never reaching those deeper, adaptive, transformative solutions that are successful in part because they were crafted by a larger group and thus have earned widespread support. This is yet another version of the myth of heroic leadership (Eisold, 1997) that we see operating in schools, where we pin all our hopes on a savior (a new leader, a new program, a new building) and then attribute any subsequent successes (or failures) to the appearance of that hero (Bradford & Cohen, 1998).

Schools rarely transform in positive, sustainable ways as the result of single heroic acts; instead, they transform slowly because of concerted group efforts, or what Bradford and Cohen (1998) term "post-heroic leadership," in which leaders operate as developers who support teams who share responsibilities. When faced with the "expert" label, perhaps it is better to try to reframe the conversation by saying something like this: "Well, remember that true expertise resides in us as a group—our ideas, strategies, and plans are always better when we create them together, because each of you knows your students and classrooms best." While Holden Caulfield might cry "Phony!," we would argue that this is one of the more powerful leadership moves one can make. The more carefully coaches manage their own and their community's understanding of expertise by distributing that expertise across groups of teachers, specialists, and leaders, the better positioned coaches will be to build widespread, shared understandings of what it means to effectively teach and learn.

As we wrote in Chapter 2, we urge coaches to adopt the mindset of advocate, wielding their expertise to improve teaching and learning methods in schools. However, we have rarely seen coaches make great changes in schools by leading with the "I'm the expert, so just follow my advice" model. Instead, the most powerful models we have witnessed all share a common principle: working as a facilitator and leading individuals and teams to review, discover, adopt, adapt, and invent practices that will work best for their students. When operating with the mindset of a change agent (who instead of dictating is interested in building capacity and supporting communities who are ready for change) and the mindset of a facilitator (concerned with helping others have rich conversations and reflect deeply on their own work), coaches can wield their expertise deftly. Coaches can have a loud voice, not because they are talking over others, but because others know that their own viewpoints are valued and therefore are willing to listen to a coach's viewpoint. It is in this delicate space that coaches are able to connect individual adult learning to larger group learning and to the learning of the school as an organization. It is this kind of relational and facilitative expertise that we end up prizing in coaches, just as much as any particular content knowledge. With this caveat out of the way, we now turn to some of the other domains of knowledge necessary for coaches to acquire over time to be truly effective.

> **VOICES FROM THE FIELD**
>
> Several years ago, I was hired as a District Literacy Coach / State and Federal Programs Coordinator for a rural school district. This was a new experience for me. Instead of being part of a team of coaches, I was *the* coach for the district. . . . I was also responsible for their Title I program, an area I had zero experience in, so I had a steep learning curve. Both parts of my position required new learning and adjustments to what I knew before. With that being said, I wouldn't trade it for the world. I love the challenges that being the district coach offers, including how to be a more effective and efficient coach, and I have learned so much about federal programming. Both positions have allowed me a district-level view into providing on-the-job professional development and federal support.
> —Marsha Turner-Hall, Teacher and Instructional Coach

## Knowledge That Supports Coaching Work

As Marsha Turner-Hall states in her Voices from the Field above, her role as a coach has changed over the years, requiring a great deal of "new learning" along the way. As we have written about elsewhere (Ippolito & Bean, 2024), one way to think about the lifelong learning of an effective coach is to consider the different domains of knowledge that directly relate to the work of leadership and school change. We have identified seven domains of knowledge, skills, and dispositions that seem most relevant for both those preparing to become coaches and those engaging in ongoing professional learning while in their professional roles (Ippolito & Bean, 2024). These domains include disciplinary knowledge, adult learning, organizational leadership and school improvement, professional learning, facilitative leadership, assessment, and coaching processes and approaches. (For a full description that can be used as a self-assessment tool, See Appendix I.) These domains certainly do not represent the totality of what a coach may want or need to know, but we would argue that a coach with a working knowledge of these seven domains is well positioned to operate as a lead learner within almost any school setting.

While at first it might seem overwhelming to read over these domains and consider your own degree of familiarity and comfort with each, we want to reiterate that these domains represent a wide range of knowledge and skills that are best acquired over the length of a professional career. A graduate preparation program or coaching endorsement program might do well to touch on each of these domains lightly, but deep expertise in each will only come from practice in a professional role over time and adoption of the lifelong learner stance. We acknowledge that each coach will likely come to their position with different skills, knowledge, and dispositions. The key, then, ultimately, is to continually identify professional learning goals and spend some time each academic year investigating (ideally as part of a network of coaches) the targeted domain. Here we highlight a few practical ways to manage the professional learning process.

### *Keep Apprised of National and State Standards*

First and foremost, we recommend staying apprised of national and state standards for professionals in your discipline, as well as standards outlining skill sets related to coaching specifically. These include position statements on the work of coaches, recent surveys of professionals holding these positions, and instructional standards around which coaching work will focus. Note that most standards directed at coaches (e.g., ILA, 2018) include deep knowledge of disciplinary content as one of the primary areas of expertise for coaches; understandably, without knowledge of the discipline, it is difficult, if not impossible, for coaches to be able to see, understand, and shape what is occurring in classrooms.

### *Find or Form a Professional Network*

Next, we recommend finding or forming a professional network of colleagues with whom you establish and explore professional learning goals. Both from research (Bean et al., 2015; Bean et al., 2018) and our own work in schools, coaches widely report that networking with peers is one of the most beneficial means of their ongoing learning. Whether talking with a few colleagues once a month as part of an after-school study group, connecting with role-alike colleagues across the district monthly, or meeting with colleagues farther afield in a monthly online webinar or social media chat, it is important to be able to reflect on and discuss professional dilemmas and successes with colleagues (see Messina, 2013, for a rich description of just such a network of coaches and secondary teachers across a district that formed a "disciplinary literacy network." See also the cases in Chapter 11 for further examples).

Some coaches have indicated that they appreciated being assigned to a mentor or lead coach who would work with them as they began their role in the school. Often these mentors served as champions for coaches and for the coaching program. For more on this idea, look to Chapter 11, including the case written by Ellen and Bruce Eisenberg, with an example of a statewide project that highlighted the work of mentors who supported the work of coaches. See also the case written by Kristi Sachi, who served as a leader of a districtwide coaching initiative, and the case written by Christina Steinbacher-Reed, who champions the cause of coaching in an technical support agency (i.e., an intermediate unit in Pennsylvania). All three cases provide concrete examples of how those in leadership positions can support the development, refinement, and ongoing work of coaching programs.

## *Keep a Journal*

We always recommend that coaches keep a professional reflective log or journal (or online blog) tracking major lessons learned, effective practices, and reflections on professional texts they have read. Although this is one of the toughest pieces of advice to follow (at least for us!), coaches who regularly write about and reflect on their work, their dilemmas, and their successes find themselves better equipped to respond effectively to future professional challenges. The brief Voices from the Field scattered throughout this book, as well as the case examples in Chapter 11, highlight the insights of coaches and leaders as they reflect on their own role evolutions. Self-reflection remains one of the primary paths to professional growth and improvement, and we find that regular reflective writing about your own role helps enormously. (Remember to consult the Further Readings and Resources at the end of each chapter in this book to find lists of various books, articles, and online resources that coaches have made available to foster coach growth.)

## *Join a Professional Learning Organization*

Joining and actively participating in a professional learning-focused organization allows you to regularly skim their publications, as well as attend their online events and annual conferences. This can become one of the easiest and most effective ways to stay up to date about emerging trends in your discipline and related coaching practices. Moreover, state-level affiliates offer regular publications for their members and conferences that can be attended by colleagues from your school or district. National and international organizations that can deepen your thinking about coaching within your discipline include ASCD, ILA, and Learning Forward, the last of which focuses exclusively on supporting high-quality professional learning for educators across disciplines.

## *Strive for a Balanced Professional Reading Diet*

We encourage coaches to balance their investigations of popular press, research journals, and online offerings, perhaps seeking to read one resource from each category every month (or at whatever interval makes the most sense for you). Just as students need to consume a balanced diet of literary and informational text, along with easy readers and more complex text, we recommend that coaches balance their diet of professional texts. Don't double-down on dense research articles and then grow quickly jaded about how to implement research findings. Try to find one or two research pieces that fit your targeted professional learning goals, and then branch out to shorter, digestible pieces from sources such as *Phi Delta Kappan*, *Ed Leadership*, *Ed Week*, or *Edutopia*. Note that many of these publications can be read digitally, which is often our preference for skimming and saving our favorite articles quickly into folders associated with different topics.

### *Keep an Eye on State and National Education News and Policy*

Because we now know much more about how context can influence coaching work (Ippolito & Bean, 2024; Woulfin et al., 2023), we strongly suggest that coaches keep apprised of local, state, and national news and policies that affect coaching as well as curriculum, instruction, and school programming. Such policies may directly affect your work in schools. We find the webinars and papers of the National Alliance for Excellent Education (see Web Resources at the end of the chapter) helpful, as they address national topics of importance (e.g., reforming high school instruction, digital learning).

Furthermore, we encourage coaches to read state and national education-related news in online platforms such as *Education Week, The 74, Educational Leadership,* and *The Learning Professional* (see Web Resources at the end of the chapter). Make time to read publications and to attend webinars offered by these organizations, sometimes hosted via social media outlets, featuring nationally known researchers and speakers talking about current topics related to both coaching and your discipline.

### *Take "Lifelong" Seriously*

Most importantly, remember the "lifelong" component of the "lifelong learner" title of this chapter. We cannot overstate the point that it can take a lifetime to master just one of the domains in Appendix I, let alone all seven! Focus on becoming an *expert learner,* and content and coaching expertise will naturally follow.

## Self-Assessment and Reflective Tools to Encourage Lifelong Learning

As a lifelong learner in the realm of coaching, consider the importance not only of self-assessment but of seeking feedback from those with whom you work—teachers, administrators, and so forth. Note, this isn't about conducting a formal evaluation; rather, it is important for coaches to gain a more objective understanding of "where they are" in their own work and career paths, and to determine what they want and need to learn next. In Ippolito and Bean (2024, Chapter 10), we discuss the importance of evaluating a coaching program (not just individual coaches). In this book, our focus is on how individual coaches can reflect on their own individual performance and seek feedback from colleagues. Here we identify a few ideas and resources that might be helpful to coaches in this pursuit, including both self-assessment tools and tools that can help coaches solicit feedback about their work.

## Self-Assessment

The tool in Appendix I (described earlier in this chapter) can be used by individual coaches as a means of thinking about individual strengths in the various domains shared across this book, with the 24 items "mapped" onto those domains. We ask coaches to reflect on whether they see themselves as "emerging," "developing," or "proficient" across domains. Responses can help determine areas of strength as well as future needs. The tool can also be useful as a means of prompting the need for (and developing) professional learning experiences for groups of coaches in a district or school. Several other sources for such tools include the following (see Further Readings and Resources at the end of this chapter for more publication details):

- Brieske-Ulenski & Kelley, "Development and Validation of the Literacy Coach Self-Efficacy Scale," 1–22. Although specific to literacy coaching, this tool contains items that apply to all coaching roles.
- The Center for Strengthening the Teaching Profession, *Working with Adult Leaders: Teacher Leader Self-Assessment*. The self-assessment tool developed by this center for assessing skills, knowledge, and dispositions of teacher leaders is organized into five categories: working with adult learners, collaborative work, communication, knowledge of content and pedagogy, and systems thinking. The tool identifies key questions related to teacher leadership and provides coaches with a comprehensive assessment of their own competencies. This tool can also be used as the beginning template for designing a coaching evaluation system. A coach- and principal-modified self-assessment could be completed individually by both the coach and principal, and then discussed.
- New Teacher Center, *Continuum of Instructional Coaching Practice*. This resource allows coaches to consider their developing knowledge and skills along a continuum of practice, from "establishing" to "applying, integrating" and then to "innovating," across foundational, structural, and instructional domains.
- Thomas, Knight, Harris, & Hoffman, *Evaluating Instructional Coaching: People, Programs, and Partnerships*. Appendix 4 has a self-evaluation form that instructional coaches can use to reflect on their performance.

### • • • • • • • • • Put into Practice • • • • • • • • • •

Take some time to review one or more of the self-assessment tools listed in the previous section. Which tool might connect most directly with your particular coaching content and context? Take time to review coaching strengths and growing edges, according to the self-assessment tools, individually and with colleagues. What next steps might arise related to your own professional learning?

| Date / Time | Activity | With Whom | Comments | Next Steps |
|---|---|---|---|---|
| 3/25/24, 9–10 A.M. | Data team meeting, reviewing grade-level math benchmark assessment scores | 5th-grade teachers at Green School | Ts discussed benchmarks. Noticed differences across classrooms. Discussed instructional changes. | Asked me to share some instructional ideas at next meeting. |
| | | | | |
| | | | | |

**FIGURE 10.1.** Example of simple coach log.

We also encourage coaches to keep a simple log of their activities as a means of assessing how they are spending their time. Often, districts or schools require that coaches complete such logs as a means of evaluating the coaching program. In Figure 10.1, we show an example of such a log.

Finally, a district might encourage groups of coaches to complete a self-assessment individually and then discuss the results with each other as a means of addressing the following questions: What do I see as my strengths? My needs? What are my goals for improvement, and what can I do to achieve them? Are there any collective goals that we would like to focus on? What support and resources can the school or district provide? For more self-assessment ideas, see the Voices from the Field from Dr. Adam Brieske-Ulenski.

> **VOICES FROM THE FIELD**
> *Helping Coaches Determine the Focus*
> *of Their Own Professional Learning*
>
> Instructional or discipline-specific coaches have a wide range of tasks and responsibilities to take on in their educational setting. It is of great value and appreciation for those that regularly step up to take on this multifaceted role. One common responsibility that coaches provide is learning opportunities or professional development to colleagues. Many of them do this beautifully because they know their teachers, the students, and both of their needs. This is how many coaches build relationships and

establish themselves as someone that their colleagues can go to for support or trust.

While it is important for coaches to deliver professional learning, it is equally important that the coach continues to learn too. This can take on many different forms. Some useful tools to support coaches in determining their own professional learning are the Elementary Literacy Coach Self-Efficacy Survey (ELCSE; Ulenski et al., 2019) and the Literacy Coach Self-Efficacy Scale (LCSE; Brieske-Ulenski & Kelley, 2023). The ELCSE Survey was developed using ILA's 2010 standards (ILA, 2010) and the LCSE scale was developed using ILA's 2017 standards (ILA, 2018); therefore, once coaches have rated their confidence for specific coaching tasks, they can use the ILA standards as a resource to refine their coaching.

Coaches can then find articles, videos, webinars, and professional literature that reflect their needs based on their survey responses. Coaches that have used the survey or scales have indicated that they like the idea that they take the survey alone and identify their own professional learning topics. Others have shared their results with their administrator to discuss opportunities to travel to attend workshops or conferences to learn more about the task(s) they felt less confident in performing. It can be empowering for a coach to identify their own needs and set their own professional learning pathway, similar to how they coach their teacher colleagues around a particular practice or problem.

Professional learning can reinvigorate a coach, inspire new ways of coaching, and enable coaches to feel as if they are part of the learning process, especially when the coach has autonomy over their professional learning decisions and pathways. It is necessary that coaches have the time, space, and resources to engage in reflection about their coaching work and set professional goals that are meaningful to them and their colleagues and profession.

—ADAM BRIESKE-ULENSKI, Associate Professor of Reading Education

Each of the aforementioned documents and tools are merely beginning places for coaches to consider their current knowledge and skill base, as well as which domains might be the focus of targeted future inquiry. The real power in any of this work is in the selection of a focus area for personal and professional growth and the adherence to a system (e.g., monthly study groups, discussions with a coaching network, weekly journaling) by which you plan to grow your own coaching toolbox.

## *Seeking Feedback*

We end by noting that coaches can also generate their own powerful tools for seeking feedback. For example, they might ask teachers with whom they have worked to respond in writing on a regular basis to two or three questions about their work: (1) Which recent coaching activities have been most useful to you? (2) Is there anything that you would like me to focus on in the near future? (3) Do you have any other feedback? They can also, as part of their individual coaching conversations, ask teachers to respond to these sorts of questions, especially if they have a strong partnering relationship with them. The Thomas et al. (2022) book mentioned previously in the chapter also has assessment tools that principals and teachers can complete; however, we see those as being more appropriate for use in evaluating a coaching program.

## Self-Reflection Related to Our Coaching Mindsets

As we conclude this chapter about coaches as lifelong learners, we wanted to return to the four major coaching mindsets that we introduced in Chapter 2: thinking and working like a change agent, facilitator, designer, and advocate. The degree to which any coach (regardless of discipline, grade level, etc.) can balance thinking and working like a change agent, facilitator, designer, and advocate might determine both professional success and job satisfaction. Here we list a few guiding questions for self-reflection related to these habits of mind, which coaches might use as a quick self-check.

- In what ways have you provided colleagues with low-risk opportunities to be co-learners, to reflect on their practices with you and others? What might you do to facilitate this in the future?
- In what ways have you helped teachers adopt a co-learning stance, recognizing that there are few "right" answers, and that productive problem solving requires thinking as a designer to solve both technical and adaptive challenges?
- In what ways have you worked collaboratively with others (e.g., shared leadership) to develop a comprehensive vision of learning and a plan that enhances quality teaching and student learning?
- In what ways have you served as an advocate for students, teachers, and community partnerships and for specific practices, models, and programs?
- In what ways have you helped to shape the system or context in which you work by assuming leadership positions in the school or district? In these roles, how have you served as an agent of change?

## Summary

In this chapter, we discussed ways that coaches can maintain a focus on lifelong learning, reflected on the term "expert," and considered the danger of being viewed as the superhero in the school. We described seven domains that serve as a knowledge base framework for those who are coaches. Then, we described ways in which coaches can reflect on their work and seek feedback from others to generate ideas for self-growth. Melinda, as she progressed through her first year, was pleased that she was a member of a coaching network in the district, supported by a lead coach who championed the cause of coaching in the district and served as a mentor and advocate for both individual coaches and the coaching program. She knew that the reflective practices in which she had engaged had been helpful to her growth as a coach and was thankful for the resources provided by the district.

## Reflections

1. Review the reflective chart (from Appendix A) that you have been referring to throughout this book. Use the questions from the previous section, "Self-Reflection Related to Our Coaching Mindsets," as self-reflection questions, in conjunction with reviewing your notes across Appendix A.
2. In what ways has your thinking changed as you have read and thought about the chapters in this book? In what ways are you considering changing your coaching work as a result?
3. As you near the end of this book, do a bit of reflective writing in your coaching journal or log, using one of our favorite end-of-session prompts: "I used to think . . . And now I think . . ."

## Activities

1. Complete the self-assessment tool in Appendix I and answer the questions at the bottom of the protocol. Think about how you might be able to obtain the professional learning experiences that would help you become better at your role.
2. Read Emily Veader's case in Chapter 11 with the self-assessment from Appendix I in mind. What can you learn from Emily's work that you can relate to your own experiences? Where do you see similarities between Emily's strengths and yours? Similar challenges and growing edges that you both might face?
3. Read Mike Henry's case in Chapter 11 about working part-time as a secondary coach. What strengths does Mike bring to his role? What dilemmas do you see Mike facing? What could Mike's school leaders do to better support his work? What advice might you give him about continuing his own professional learning, in support of increasing the efficacy of his work?

## FURTHER READINGS AND RESOURCES

### Print Resources

Brieske-Ulenski, A., & Kelley, M. J. (2023). Development and validation of the Literacy Coach Self-Efficacy Scale. *Literacy Research and Instruction,* 1–22.

Thomas, S., S., Knight, J., Harris, M., & Hoffman, A. (2022). *Evaluating instructional coaching: People, programs, and partnerships.* ASCD.

Ulenski, A., Gill, M., & Kelley, M. (2019). Developing and validating the Elementary Literacy Coach Self-Efficacy Survey. *The Teacher Educator, 54*(3), 225–243.

Woulfin, S. L., & Rigby, J. G. (2017). Coaching for coherence: How instructional coaches lead change in the evaluation era. *Educational Researcher, 46*(6), 323–328.

### Web Resources (see www.guilford.com/bean3-materials for live links)

ASCD. (2024). *El Magazine: By educators, for educators.* www.ascd.org/el

Center for Strengthening the Teaching Profession. (n.d.). *Working with adult leaders: Teacher leader self-assessment.* http://cstp-wa.org/cstp2013/wp-content/uploads/2013/11/CSTP_self_assessment.pdf

Education Week (2024). Education week. www.edweek.org

International Literacy Association. (2010). *Standards 2010: Role 5: Reading specialist/literacy coach.* www.literacyworldwide.org/get-resources/standards/standards-for-reading-professionals/standards-2010-role-5

International Literacy Association. (2018). *Standards 2017: Standards for the preparation of literacy professionals.* www.literacyworldwide.org/get-resources/standards/standards-2017

Learning Forward. (2024). *The Learning Professional: The Learning Forward Journal.* www.learningforward.org/the-learning-professional

National Alliance for Excellent Education. (2024). *What's new at All4Ed.* http://all4ed.org

New Teacher Center. (2018). *Continuum of instructional coaching practice.* https://newteachercenter.org/wp-content/uploads/2021/07/Cont-of-IC-Practice_RB21.pdf

Spangler, D. (2023). *7 ways to measure instructional coaching for impact, not activity.* SmartBrief. www.smartbrief.com/original/7-ways-to-measure-instructional-coaching-for-impact-not-activity

The 74 Media. (2024). *The 74.* www.the74million.org

# CHAPTER 11

# Coaching Cases: Stories of Coaches and Coaching

> **GUIDING QUESTIONS**
>
> 1. In what ways do the stories in this chapter connect to the work you do? What lessons can you learn from the stories?
> 2. What are the similarities and differences in these stories (e.g., how coaching is defined and operationalized; differences in support structures for coaches)?
> 3. In what ways are all those who share their stories "instructional leaders"?

Over the years, we have met many effective coaches who have described their work and the ways in which they have supported and coached educators in schools. Some of their voices are included in the short vignettes provided throughout the book. Here, in this final chapter, we include five longer stories of coaches and coaching initiatives, each one demonstrating a different aspect of instructional leadership, but none "finished"—each story is ongoing and continually evolving. Like the Voices from the Field vignettes across the book, the stories that follow were written by coaches/leaders to illustrate various aspects of their coaching journeys. By providing these stories, we hope to illustrate the many different pathways into coaching, the many ways in which coaches function, and the evolution of coaching over time. We provide several guiding questions before each narrative to help readers consider what they might learn from each story.

## Case 1: The Evolution of a Coach

*Source: Christina Steinbacher-Reed, Executive Director, BLaST Intermediate Unit 17, Williamsport, PA*

In the following case, Christina Steinbacher-Reed talks about her 20-year journey, beginning as a new coach in a single school, moving to a supervisory role in which she supported the work of multiple coaches, and then taking on the role of external coach coordinating professional learning across districts. In her current position, she is executive director of Intermediate Unit 17, where she serves as the chief school officer for an education service agency serving over 4,000 students and 19 school districts in the northeastern region of Pennsylvania.

> ### QUESTIONS TO PONDER
>
> - What were the greatest challenges for Christina in her first coaching position?
> - Why does Christina think that external coaches can be helpful to school districts or schools?
> - How does Christina apply a coaching mindset to executive leadership?
> - After reading about Christina and her views about coaching, what do you see as three important "takeaways"?

### *School-Based Coach (2003–2005)*

I became an instructional coach in 2003 in a school district plagued by generational poverty and labeled as a "failing school district." Prior to becoming an instructional coach, I was an elementary classroom teacher in a high-performing, suburban school district. Going into this new position, I only had five years of successful teaching experience under my belt, coupled with graduate work in school leadership. I tried to convince myself that I was ready for such a position—but to be honest, I was not. I was terrified and consumed with self-doubt. The work awaiting me as a coach in a high-needs district was in stark contrast to my teaching experience.

I will never forget the lump in my throat on my first day. The school was nestled in the center of the most violent community housing development in the city. When I pulled into the parking lot, I noticed the tall metal fence that enclosed the lot and wondered if it would eventually make me feel safe—because at that moment, I felt vulnerable. I feared the uncertainty that lay ahead of me. The uncertainty of not knowing simple things like where to find the bathroom or how to find that secret stash of chart paper when you need it. The uncertainty of not knowing the important things, like a single student or a single teacher—or how to be a successful coach in one of the lowest-performing schools in the state.

When I walked through those doors and saw the students, I was quickly reminded that I did know some important things. I knew how to immediately connect with kids, and I knew how to build relationships with teachers. So that's what I did, and it got me through week 1. Then I wondered, "What should I do for the next 44 weeks?" Here's what I learned not to do:

- Do not give a teacher who expresses frustration with classroom management an article entitled "Classroom Management for Literacy." (That resulted in tears.)
- Do not say, "I'm here to help you." (That resulted in a flood of copy requests.)
- Do not have my office anywhere near the principal's office. (That resulted in many thinking I was an administrator, and the administrator constantly asking me to proofread his parent letters.)
- Do not assume that teachers are waiting for me with open arms, eager and ready to expose all of their vulnerabilities. (That results in delusional thinking.)

While I was quickly learning what *not* to do, the fact remained that I needed to know what *to* do. Thankfully, I had a network of internal and external support. Our district team of 10 coaches met once a month to work with an external consultant on developing coaching skills and knowledge. This was also a time to build strong partnerships with other internal coaches who understood the complexities and challenges of working in a high-needs district. Our external consultants worked individually with coaches at our school two to four times a month for the specific purpose of "coaching coaches." During our consultant's first visits, I would shadow her while she coached teachers. This included observing her doing in-class demos, co-planning, and building relationships. Eventually, I would engage in coaching activities while the consultant observed me and provided feedback. This type of job-embedded support was the single most important layer of support that I received as a coach. Not only did it provide me with essential coaching strategies, but it also allowed me to understand what it felt like to be coached. It was important for me to feel the same anxiety, vulnerability, trust, and success that many teachers would experience when working with me as a coach.

## *A Change in Direction*

After I survived my first year, I was starting to feel like I was finally figuring out this coaching thing. I was building trusting relationships and designing my coaching based on teachers' individual needs. Then I was anointed a "Reading First coach," and it seemed like everything changed. This transition was first described to me by my administration as "no big deal; we just need to change the title for funding purposes." I quickly learned that, as a recipient of over 6 million dollars in federal funding, Reading First was *indeed* a big deal.

In that first year of Reading First, I was supposed to become an expert in DIBELS (Dynamic Indicators of Basic Early Literacy Skills), uninterrupted 90-minute reading blocks, the five essential elements of reading, research-based core reading programs, progress monitoring, and effective interventions. There was no longer time to work with our external consultants, as they did not meet the Reading First criteria of being "scientifically based"—so out went my job-embedded coaching support. Instead, I was assigned a "technical assistant" who asked to see my logs and wanted to visit classrooms with me to complete "fidelity checklists." During that year, my role significantly shifted from confidential coach to Reading First compliance officer. I was frustrated with my new role, and so were our teachers. They were used to me "meeting them where they were at," and now my approach prioritized the grant's needs over their needs.

Looking back on those two years, I now realize that my first year of coaching was based on a purely responsive model, while in my second year as a coach, I was asked to assume a directive approach to coaching. My first year of responsive coaching provided me with an opportunity to really get to know the individual needs of teachers. At the same time, the challenge of that first year was that while I felt like I met the individual needs of some teachers, I didn't feel like I was impacting the system. For example, some teachers improved in their reading instruction while others enhanced their writing workshop. But I was left wondering how random acts of improvement would ever result in systemic reform.

By the end of my second year, I started to notice that my most successful coaching experiences were when I was intentional about my coaching. Knowing when to use which approach, and being aware of why I was using that approach, made all the difference. Oftentimes it wasn't one approach over the other, but rather a balance of both responsive and directive coaching. My first two years of coaching were the most difficult years of my career, but I embraced those challenges as opportunities to deepen my understanding and craft of coaching. And as a result, those two years were filled with some of the most rewarding experiences to date.

I often think back to my first day when I was sitting in the fenced-in parking lot, scared of the uncertainties. I now have many more years of coaching experience to draw from, and this is what I know—there will be uncertainties. The truth is, coaching is filled with uncertainties—we never quite know what approach will work with any given teacher at any given time. Skilled coaches have a repertoire of skills and strategies that can balance the needs of individual teachers with the needs of students in ways that impact the entire school or district.

### *Supervisor of Coaches (2006–2010)*

In 2006, I transitioned from a coaching role into an administrative role, where I was responsible for supervising a team of 10 district coaches. Supervising coaches came with its own set of challenges and rewards. One of the first challenges I experienced was that our team was not "walking the walk" when it came to coaching. We focused so much attention on coaching our teachers that we neglected our own coaching needs. One of my first challenges of supervising coaches was to build a system in which coaches would have opportunities to coach each other.

When entering a "coach the coach" partnership, I quickly realized that coaches felt the same level of vulnerability as our teachers. This process also uncovered some hard truths about our coaching model—we didn't all share the same beliefs about effective coaching. I committed to creating a system of professional learning for our coaches that was responsive to their individual needs while also trying to adhere to established criteria of "best practices" for coaches. Although we were still funded by Reading First, the coaching guidelines of the grant did not align with our district philosophy on coaching. We believed our coaching should reflect a balanced approach that would give us opportunities to be directive and responsive. I focused much of my work that year in working with coaches to develop self-assessment tools, a differentiated supervision model, lab classrooms, and criteria for effective coaching. I felt that as a team, we were building a shared mental model of effective coaching.

In my last year as supervisor, the Reading First grant had expired, and the district did not have the funding to sustain full-time coaches. I desperately wished that I had some solid evidence to demonstrate the impact that coaches had on our system. I wanted the board to have tangible evidence about what could be eliminated. I doubt it would have saved coaching positions, but it would have at least provided evidence of their impact.

My experiences as a coaching supervisor provided me with a systems perspective on coaching. Over time I realized the value of a more systemic approach to coaching. I began understanding that a strategic approach to coaching could yield a greater return systemically. One of my mentors often reminded me, "If you put a good person in a bad system, the system will win every time." The work I do now centers on building good systems that focus on developing the capacity of each individual to work collaboratively to support the system.

## *External Coach (2010–2015)*

In 2010, I had an opportunity to apply my interest in building coaching systems to a new role serving as the coordinator for professional learning and curriculum development for BLaST Intermediate Unit 17, a regional education service agency serving 19 school districts in Pennsylvania. One of my responsibilities was to serve as an external coach to a number of districts across our state. School districts contracted with me for a specific number of days to provide job-embedded instructional coaching in a very specific strategy. At first, I found this coaching model to be incredibly challenging because I was walking into a coaching partnership "cold." I did not have preexisting relationships with the teachers or administrators, and I had very limited experience with their school system. I wondered how I could possibly be effective without having time to build trusting relationships. To my surprise, I discovered that many of the challenges faced by external coaches may also contribute to successful coaching partnerships.

- **Objectivity.** Not having preexisting relationships with staff made it easier for me to enter partnerships with total objectivity. My only focus was to work with the teacher in that moment. I was removed from the school politics that often pose challenges for school-based coaches.
- **Credibility.** Because we did not have any shared history, teachers needed to know quickly that I had something of value to offer. Teachers did not care about my degrees and certifications, and rightly so. I needed to build instant credibility, and to do this, I built modeling or demonstration lessons into one of my first school visits.
- **Focus.** Administrators and teachers held our time together sacred. Schedules were made months in advance, substitutes were secured, and there were no interruptions. I had the luxury of engaging in highly focused and engaging coaching activities.

External coaching can add value to a system only if the purpose is to create sustainable school improvement. With this goal in mind, districts should not be dependent on external coaches. Instead, external coaches and school teams need to work together to determine how the coach's impact will improve the system, not just individual teachers. For example, when a school is adopting new standards or learning a new pedagogy, the use of external coaches who hold expertise in these areas is beneficial. In this case, the external coaches would work specifically with select coaches, teacher leaders, or specialists to build their capacity in the new strategy. The external coach can focus on building a cadre of local experts who can then sustain and support the new implementation in the entire school or district. The ultimate goal of external coaching is to support the district in developing its internal capacity to sustain the improvements over time.

### *Executive Director (2017–Present)*

In 2017, I became the executive director for the intermediate unit. This role was not in my professional plan, and truth be told, I really struggled with the decision. I felt like I was abandoning my coaching work and pivoting away from my work on teachership, a new type of school leadership (Steinbacher-Reed & Rotella, 2017). It wasn't until a trusted mentor helped me to realize that my commitment to developing systems for empowerment is exactly why I needed to take this new position. My mentor was right, and eight years later, I'm still driven by a coaching mindset, albeit in new ways.

Executive leaders that have a coaching mindset have a superpower that sets them apart from other leaders. We know what meaningful effective professional learning looks like, we understand the return on investment, and we are in a position of authority to make decisions that support coaching and remove barriers. Coming from a career in coaching, at first I was not comfortable with positional "authority" and "power." As a coach, I knew real change didn't follow an organizational chart. As a new executive leader, I had to reconcile the differences between the influence of coaching and the authority of an executive leader—and understand how the two could complement each other.

Over my first few years, I learned to carefully balance a coaching mindset and director mindset. My coaching mindset focused on creating the culture, whereas my "authority" mindset created opportunities and removed barriers. For example, in my past coaching roles I had plenty of opportunities to create professional learning lab classrooms, but I lacked the authority to pay the lead teacher a stipend. In my current role as executive director, I now have the authority to do exactly that. I have exercised that authority because my coaching mindset recognizes the importance of building career ladders for teacher leaders. Leaders in positions of authority who apply a coaching mindset can remove barriers that I often encountered when I was in my coaching roles. They also can support work that creates a culture of coaching. Over the last several years, we have been intentional in creating conditions and opportunities that support a culture of coaching and empowerment. Below are a few examples of our work:

- **Strategic planning.** After a year in the position, I began leading the collaborative development of our new strategic plan. With only three priority areas, this was my opportunity to signal to the organization the most important goals over the next three years. One of those goals was to "empower staff, develop educator agency and leadership capacity, and distribute leadership across the organization." Committing to this goal in writing was a way of communicating the importance of empowerment, while also holding myself and our board of directors accountable to fulfilling this goal.

- **Lab classrooms.** A lab classroom is "a fully functioning classroom taught by an exemplary teacher which also doubles as a hands-on professional learning environment" (Steinbacher-Reed & Rotella, 2017, para. 12). The purpose of a lab classroom is to provide multiple opportunities for teachers and aspiring teachers to work side by side to learn and improve teaching practices in the context of functional classrooms. To be most effective, lab classrooms need to be part of a comprehensive professional learning system that provides educators in all roles with opportunities to bridge theory to practice.

- **Micro-innovations.** Micro-innovations are new practices and innovations that take place at a grassroots, organic level and serve as a critical component to advancing school change in both pedagogy and culture. Through our educational foundation that solicits private donations to fund special projects and events, we have dedicated mini-grants to teachers who want to create innovative special projects for their students or colleagues.

• **Ignite sessions.** In lieu of a keynote speaker for our opening in-service, we invited key stakeholders to the stage to share their five-minute powerful message on how our staff and agency are transforming their lives. Imagine the impact on our staff when they hear from a parent about how we are impacting the lives of her children!

• **Spark sessions.** Throughout the year, I meet directly with small groups of "job-alike" staff for *spark sessions*. Sparks are anything the staff think I need to know to "spark my thinking" about the organization. Sparks can include what they are most proud of, recent accomplishments, and areas where we need to improve. Spark sessions are a way for me to stay connected to the context in which our staff are working.

As I look back on my many roles, I can see clearly how coaching has contributed to my leadership identity in three major ways:

• **Intention.** Know the difference between responsive and directive approaches, have the skills to assume both roles, and have the wisdom to determine when to use which approach. There is a time to influence a system or person, and a time to exercise authority. Don't confuse the two, but stay committed to using both in harmony with each other.

• **Systems.** Whether the system is a classroom, school, or an entire organization, maintain the ability to remain objective so that you know how it works or doesn't work. Only then, can one begin the work of creating systems to support agency and empowerment.

• **Context.** Step back from the action of what is happening as a means of gaining a better understanding of the context of the system. Context is the Velcro, and without it, new learning or change will not stick.

Sometimes it's not until we look back on our career that we can connect the dots to understand our leadership identity. The same is true for me. Almost eight years later, I am grateful to that mentor who encouraged me to carry a coaching mindset into an executive leadership role and who supported me along the journey.

## Case 2: School-Based Elementary Math Coach

*Source: Emily Veader, Math Instructional Coach,*
*Bishop Elementary School, Arlington, MA*

In this case, we hear from Emily Veader, the lead math coach in a K–5 elementary school. Emily describes both the evolution of her role as a building-based math coach, as well as the many relationships that support her work (e.g., connecting with teachers, interventionists/specialists, her principal). Across the case, we encourage readers to notice ways in which Emily is thinking about her coaching and leadership work within a systems perspective, describing the interconnectedness of coaching with other school systems and structures.

> **QUESTIONS TO PONDER**
>
> - Who does Emily connect with regularly in her school and district to support coaching work and to bolster the work of teachers?
> - How are the relationships Emily describes, and the alignment of purpose across roles in her school, essential to buoying coaching work?
> - What does Emily's principal do to support coaching directly and indirectly?
> - How does Emily use both assessment data and classroom video footage to help focus her coaching work with teachers?

This is my 11th year as a school-based math coach in Arlington, Massachusetts. It is also my third year as the district lead math coach. In this role, I support both the math coaches and math interventionists across our seven elementary schools. This is the best year I have had so far. I believe this is because a number of things have come together for me. First and foremost, it comes from the leadership in the school in which I coach. I feel supported by my administration in my work and feel we are starting to have the type of collaboration that I have always envisioned. Teachers, coaches, administrators, and parents are all starting to pay attention to the same aspects of student thinking, which means we are all beginning to share the same expectations.

As a lead coach, I have worked with the coaches, math interventionists, and teachers to create a system of collecting assessment data to support students across all tiers of instruction. I enjoy being able to make a change at the district level and then experience the impact of those changes firsthand. I can see how it affects my school in individual classrooms and with specific students. From my weekly conversations with the math coaches and interventionists, I can hear how the changes are impacting teachers and students across the district. We then can use this information to continue to adjust our practice.

For example, over the past several years, a group of math coaches in my district became interested in creating a system for teachers to follow how their students are thinking about fact fluency. We developed a series of short addition/subtraction and multiplication/division interview screeners. Teachers use the screeners not only to keep track of students' answers, but also to understand the way that they solve those problems. Teachers now give these fluency screeners in grades K–4 three times a year. Teachers at my own school have asked me to video record students who have struggled with fluency in class. The recordings have provided many benefits. When we first started this work, we just used the videos to calibrate teacher, coach, and administrator thinking. Were we all scoring the assessment the same way? Then we started focusing on strategies students were or were not using. In first grade, students often count back to solve a subtraction equation, but they do not always know which number to start with. If a student is subtracting 9 – 4, they might say "9, 8, 7, 6, the answer is 6." Seeing this happen both in their own assessments and the ones that I recorded led teachers to start focusing some of their discussions on modeling how to count back. In another example, fourth-grade teachers were concerned about a student's progress, but then in the video we heard the student solve 8 × 7 by saying "Well, 8 × 5 = 40 and then I just needed to add two more 8s to make 56." We realized that, in fact, this student had made significant improvement and that he only needed to focus his attention on a few remaining facts. Listening to students and keeping track of their thinking both helps us know what they are and are not understanding and gives us concrete evidence of their progress.

Now that we have a system for collecting fluency assessment data, we are starting to pilot the collection of unit assessment data. We use these two data sources, as well as classroom observations, to select students who may need more support through our pre-teaching program. Our interventionists use the data from earlier assessments on a particular concept to select a small group of students who have struggled in the past. The interventionists then use a targeted intervention assessment to narrow the group to four or five students. They work with this group for six to eight weeks during "What I Need" (WIN) time, months before students start working on the same concepts in tier 1 instruction. The interventionists pull students out during WIN. They also push in during math to support students with what they worked on during the pre-teaching. For example, in third grade our first addition/subtraction unit is in November. The interventionists can use the data from second grade to select a group of students to pre-teach. In September and October, they focused on place value, addition, and subtraction skills. When the class got to addition/subtraction, teachers reported that students who were in the pre-teaching group were suddenly raising their hands and volunteering to share their thinking. One student proudly explained to her class when they were stumped, "I know how to do this. My math teacher showed me."

In our interventionist meetings, each week I ask one interventionist to bring a short video of their work with students in their pre-teaching groups. Because they are all using the same assessments and working on the same pre-teaching ideas, the interventionists offer each other wonderful support. Sometimes the person whose turn it is to make the video that week is hesitant beforehand because it is hard to be vulnerable, but then they find the feedback from their peers helpful. And it is usually valuable to the rest of the team as well. As one interventionist said, after watching someone else's video and hearing the comments, "Great, now I have my whole next week planned!" Each of the seven schools operates somewhat differently, so this work is not seamless, but because the coaches and interventionists each meet weekly in job-alike groups, and because coaches and interventionists meet with each other in each school, we are able to support and problem solve as an elementary math team.

Not all struggling students receive pre-teaching. Most support for students happens in tier 1 instruction. Some of the planning for this support happens through coaching during grade-level team meetings. For example, this year at my school, a grade-level team wanted to focus on hearing the voices of our struggling students during their math discussions. To figure out what students were struggling with, we needed to be able to observe how students were making sense of the math. Listening to 20 to 25 students in a classroom can be daunting for a classroom teacher when they are the only person in the room. When I join teachers in classrooms, we divide up which students we check in with. I video record the students on my list and then share the recordings with the teacher to watch outside of class time. I also bring some of the videos to our weekly grade-level meetings.

I am very fortunate that our principal and assistant principal attend these meetings. Being able to watch a short video together gives us an opportunity to really focus on what students are saying. We can listen more than once to students' thinking if we didn't catch something the first time. We can try to model with cubes or ten frames what we thought the student was saying. Having my principal, classroom teachers, and me all model a student's thinking has led to great discussions. We often find that we are modeling in different ways or that we may not have originally understood exactly what a student was saying. As we get better at understanding the different strategies students use, a goal for next year might be to select particular student ideas to highlight in the discussion, but the first step is just listening to them!

In the years to come, I will continue to advocate for us to take time to listen to what students have to say. In our School Improvement Plan, we are focusing on giving voice to our students of color, multilingual learners, and special education students. Our ILT is also beginning to work on "empathy interviews" and "equity learning walks." I feel this is directly connected to the work in our grade-level meetings of listening to student math thinking. Our district is beginning to focus on giving a voice to all students, and I feel this can only improve their experience as learners.

## Case 3: A Coaching Mindset in the Classroom

*Source: Michael P. Henry, EdD, High School Instructional Coach, Burbank, IL*

In this case, Michael Henry, a high school instructional coach, describes his part-time coaching role, his relationship with administration, and the ways in which his coaching and teaching interact and inform each other. Being a part-time coach is not easy, and Michael has developed a system that helps him function efficiently and effectively.

> **QUESTIONS TO PONDER**
>
> - What do you see as the strengths of this model of coaching? Which coaching activities seem to work well for Michael, enabling him to work productively as a coach?
> - What do you see as the challenges of the part-time coaching position? What questions would you want to ask Michael about his position, including aspects he would change?
> - Michael talks about having a coaching mindset—and that this mindset influences his own classroom instruction. What do you think Michael means when he says "coaching mindset"? How does this connect to, and differ from, the coaching mindsets outlined in this book?

How did I become a high school instructional coach? For 20 years, I was an English teacher at a large, diverse high school just outside Chicago. For the past 15 years, I have been splitting my days as a coach and teacher. In 2007, I received my master's degree with a reading specialist certificate. I began working as a part-time literacy coach at my school the following year. In 2017, I completed my doctorate in curriculum and instruction with a specialization in literacy. While my title is "literacy coach," the needs of teachers have expanded my role beyond literacy coaching into the more appropriately named "instructional coach." As a part-time instructional coach, I work with over 75 teachers, 20 administrators, and countless students, who have all taught me so much about what it means to be an effective coach and teacher.

### *Coaching as a Part-Time Responsibility*

Presumably, many high school instructional coaches, like me, spend a part of their day coaching and a part of their day teaching. I work with individual teachers and also have small-group responsibilities to assist with curriculum development. At my school, I teach five periods a day. Two periods are dedicated to coaching teachers. When I work with individual teachers, we schedule one day a week for me to work with teachers and their students in their classrooms while they are teaching. This is where the important work occurs. We confer and have conversations in brief moments during class, quickly between classes, and over email and phone calls. Opportunities for extended conversations are rare.

The school also has dedicated PLC time, during which I am scheduled to meet with teams of teachers and administrators about curriculum development, but not necessarily with the teachers with whom I am regularly working that semester. In other words, I work very closely with four to six teachers per semester in their classes, one day per week. And I work each semester with another 10 to 15 teachers and administrators in groups focused on curriculum development.

## *Importance of the Relationship with Administrators*

Without the trust and support of my administration, it would be difficult to navigate my dual role. It is important that they give me freedom to work with teachers where we are finding success, sometimes for multiple semesters or years. It is important that they allow me to be in classrooms with teachers and not pull me for other duties. I value their patience and the fact that my administrators trust the findings and data that I share with them regarding my work with teachers. Above all, I value that they give me space without administrative mandates on my time or practice, which has allowed me to learn, on my own, how to be the best I can be in both of my roles.

## *Mindset Is Key*

One very important lesson I have learned is that coaching has changed my mindset. This daily shift in responsibilities can be tricky. As a coach, my job is to get experienced teachers to voluntarily shift their mindsets and make pedagogical and instructional changes in their classrooms. This is no easy task. So how do I do it? With the teachers, together we create frameworks that reflect the real-world application of the skills being taught and assessed. Then we create protocols for the students to guide them there—wherever "there" is for the class. I then work with teachers in their classrooms applying our frameworks and protocols as a team for at least the entire semester or longer. This has worked so well that I have "coached" myself into following the same blueprint to teach my own classes.

## *Frameworks*

Frameworks form the foundation of my work as an instructional coach with teachers in their classrooms. The frameworks that the teachers and I design together guide us in facilitating the discipline-specific behaviors and processes we wish to see from students. They provide a common structure and set of instructional routines enabling teachers and me as coach to best support student learning. Teachers answer the question, "What should students be able to do and produce?" Frameworks provide the base that allows for a potentially endless list of possibilities for guiding students along their way. They are the foundation that the teachers and I fall back on when learning gets messy. The frameworks we use are anchored to reading, writing, listening, and speaking like historians, mathematicians, kinesiologists, scientists, and even cooks and seamstresses. As a high school instructional coach, I am only with teachers in their classrooms once a week. With such gaps in our time together, we rely on our frameworks to keep us and the students grounded.

After meeting with teachers and understanding their goals for our work together, I develop frameworks using the teacher's input, research about the field in which the concepts are applied, and my preparation in literacy leadership, learning, and pedagogy. Once outlined, I then add what's necessary to ensure that students are reading, writing, listening, speaking, and practicing like professionals in the field, all while staying in the comfort zone of the teacher. The framework tells us that when we work together, we need to see students accessing and producing in the ways that we have outlined. Once our framework is created, we use it for the entire semester, only making small changes when necessary.

When our work with students begins, I am in the classroom with the teacher and their students every week on the dedicated day of the week that we selected. I observe how the framework plays out in the classroom, not being afraid to make changes along the way, while being able to explain to the teacher which evidence shows that a change is necessary. Was it something students said? Or the way a teacher struggled to get students to seek out understanding? As the coach, I can point to the framework as the reason for asking the teacher to make changes, not because I think they should change or because they're doing something wrong. In my experience, teachers are much more receptive to suggested changes to the framework than they are to suggested changes in their teaching.

## *Protocols*

Once the teacher and I agree on the tenets of the framework, we work together to design application protocols that tell the students what they should be doing, how they should be doing it, the key terms that they should be using, and how long each piece of the production process should take them. Teachers answer the question, "How will students access the appropriate information, and how will they show that they understand?" The protocols provide the students with step-by-step procedures to help guide them through their reading, writing, speaking, and listening experiences. Teachers then ask students to follow specific processes, to use specific terminology, and to report their learning in ways specific to the field of study. Once protocols are created, we stick to the same ones for the entire semester, only making minor changes in order to make them better when our work with students unfolds. But asking teachers to make changes is difficult. So, like with the frameworks, because we can revise by changing the protocol, not the teacher or the teaching, teachers are much more open to suggestions.

Because I generally can only work with teachers during one class period per week, we work with the same protocol structure throughout the semester. With limited time, it's important for the students to know what they are going to be asked to do when the teacher and I are working together. We do this to avoid the back-and-forth of "What are we doing today?" Having the students know the expectations for the day and having them familiar with the protocols allows the teacher and me to use the entire class period to focus on students' thoughts and applications of the content. This also allows both the teacher and me to be equal resources to the students as they work through their protocols. By doing this, as the coach, I am a valuable resource to both the teacher and the students, making my time coaching more fruitful. (For two examples of disciplinary literacy protocols from Henry, see Appendix J.)

## How This Has Changed Me as a Classroom Teacher

Because I am also a classroom teacher, and have seen great success with this approach to coaching teachers, I have carried these strategies over into my own classes. As a reading intervention teacher and writing teacher, I have developed my own frameworks and protocols for the two different classes that I teach. I have found that my teaching experiences make my coaching more credible, while my coaching experiences make my teaching more confident.

### Reading Intervention Design

The framework that I designed for my reading intervention class consists of the behaviors exhibited by readers. Like in my work as a coach, I dedicated specific days of the week to focusing on specific behaviors. This allows students to know what our focus will be based on which day of the week it is. Throughout the week, I look for students selecting free-choice reading materials from the school library that are a good fit for them. I'm looking for students to read silently and consistently during reading time. I'm looking for students to write letters about their reading, to generate quality visual aids for describing their reading, and to talk about their reading in thoughtful, reflective ways. Each day of the week has specific class time to complete these activities. They do these things because this is what good readers do.

The protocols help them question and assess their reading and their work output. The protocols push them to focus on literary ideas such as character, setting, conflict, resolution, dialogue, action, structure, and author's choices. The protocols guide them to make connections, to ask questions, and to seek what meaning they can find in the reading. Because students know what they are supposed to do and how they are supposed to go about doing it, I am available to look for the little windows of opportunity to guide my students on their own reading journey. I can focus on the individual reader, not the entire class as a whole. I can do this because each day when they come to class, they know which aspect of the framework we will be focused on and which protocol they will use to guide them.

### Writing Design

The framework I designed for my writing class consists of the behaviors exhibited by writers. As with my reading class, which is taken in addition to this writing class, the framework has specific behaviors that the students should engage in on a particular day of each week. As such, every week I look for students generating writing topics that are a good fit for them. I provide the purpose (e.g., to inform, persuade, analyze, or write creatively) and the form; the students decide the topic and how to make it their own. The framework is built on the concept that students will consistently generate lots of writing for various purposes during the class period.

Protocols focus on grammar, style, and mechanics, with students practicing and using different sentence patterns. They do this because it is what good writers do. As their guide, I question their topics so I can help them get to a deeper understanding of what they want to say. I provide requirements for their writing to push them to use a variety of sentence patterns, punctuation, styles, and mechanics that they would likely not use on their own. I can do this because the students come to understand the expectations for each day based on the framework that we follow and the protocols that we use.

Coaching continues to change my mindset. It has shown me that designing my coaching and teaching around consistent frameworks and protocols helps everyone (i.e., teachers and students) be more consistent and productive with the limited time that we have together in our fast-paced high school environment.

### Case 4: Mentoring Instructional Coaches: An Eight-Year Journey

*Source: Kristi Sacha, Teaching and Learning Consultant, Educational Service Center of Northeast Ohio*

In this case, we hear from Kristi Sacha, who served as an instructional coach liaison (ICL) for eight years in a large urban district before moving to her new role as a consultant for an educational service center in Ohio. In her ICL role, her responsibility was to "champion" the cause of coaching and provide alignment and consistency across the content, the context, and the processes of coaching. In the following she describes her role, and then focuses on five lessons that she believes are important for any individual serving in any sort of coaching role.

> **QUESTIONS TO PONDER**
>
> - What coaching mindsets were especially important for Kristi to be successful in her instructional coach liaison role?
> - In what ways did Kristi assume leadership in creating "bridges" across district and school administration, and coaches?
> - Which of the five lessons identified by Kristi resonates with you in your current role and why?
> - Kristi describes several models of coaching in her discussion of lessons learned. Which of the models is used in your district, and what do you see as the benefits and limitations of your model?

In 2014, I accepted the position of instructional coach liaison in a large urban district in Ohio. My responsibilities were to support 36 instructional coaches, each of whom coached at one or two schools. I helped strengthen, protect, and champion the coaching role in the district. Further, I developed ongoing learning and collaboration opportunities for the coaches. I also provided coaching to the coaches to help them troubleshoot challenges, strengthen their coaching moves, and grow in their coaching practice. Below I describe more specifically some of my responsibilities. I then reflect on what I learned during this eight-year journey.

## *Working at the District Level: Leading and Guiding Coaches*

My days were spent connecting and communicating with the coaches. I would differentiate my support and amount of contact with the coaches based on their needs and years of coaching experience. During site visits, I would give the coaches feedback based on their artifacts, data-collection information, schedules, and conversations about their coaching work and practices. I would watch them in action and provide feedback and opportunities for reflection.

An important part of my responsibilities at the district level was to plan and provide professional learning for coaches. Coaches were expected to write weekly reflections on their work and submit them to me. I would read these reflections to gain a deeper understanding of their challenges and needs. This information would help me identify opportunities for growth and patterns of need, which then guided me in structuring and prioritizing learning for our weekly meetings. During these PLC meetings, coaches came together for professional learning and had an opportunity to share ideas and reflect on their practice. We would practice and learn more about coaching conversations, instructional strategies, engagement structures, and facilitation skills. We would also strengthen our knowledge of district initiatives and curriculum.

Another aspect of my work was to ensure that coaching was connected to and aligned with school and district goals. To do this, I worked with the district leadership team and building leadership teams. I advocated for coaching work and ensured coaching was embedded not only within individual classrooms impacting teachers and students, but also within the larger realm of improvement work in schools and our district.

## *Five Lessons Learned*

Over my many years in this role, I learned a great deal, and all of this knowledge enabled me to work with others to make changes in the coaching program that, in many ways, made it much more effective as a professional learning experience for teachers. Below I highlight five of these lessons.

*Lesson 1*

To ensure success in a coaching program, the coaching role must be clearly defined. Before the coaching model began and coaches were selected, I worked with district leadership to develop clarity on why we had coaches, the content of their coaching, who they coach, and how they coach. We continually communicated this to everyone in the district. In a large district like ours, it was important that there was consistency in the role of coaches across schools. Inconsistency, lack of clarity on what coaches do, and lack of support across schools would break down the effectiveness of our district coaching model. To encourage consistency, we would work with coaches to audit and reflect on their schedules to ensure they spent most of their time partnering with teachers in school improvement efforts and impacting student achievement.

I learned that to have a successful coaching program, coaching had to be acknowledged and understood as an important and integral aspect of a school community. It can be challenging to determine where coaching fits in a district. Over the years, we had many different models of coaching in our district. When we shifted to having embedded coaches in schools rather than coaches as an extension of the curriculum team who go out to visit schools, coaches functioned more strategically, and teachers and principals gained a deeper understanding of and appreciation for what coaches do. Coaches built relationships and trust since they were visible and connected.

*Lesson 2*

One of the most important aspects of developing a strong coaching program is to strengthen the relationships between principals and coaches. Coaches created partnership agreements with their principals outlining roles, responsibilities, goals, priorities, procedures for navigating conflict, and communication preferences. Getting clear on how coaching will be launched and communicated to teachers prior to the start of a coaching program and also at the beginning of each school year was essential. Although the coaches could prioritize their work with teachers who needed more support or classrooms where student data results were declining, teachers needed to understand how coaching could help everyone. The principal needed to communicate that message and advocate for partnering with the coach. Principals and coaches were expected to meet weekly to ensure the coaching was aligned to building goals and so the principal had a clear understanding of the coaching work taking place in the building. Coaches captured their weekly work in a schedule and also communicated with principals about the teachers they were working with, the topics and tasks they focused on, and the amount of time they spent. They also discussed schoolwide issues and challenges. When coaches shared information, it was not evaluative. Coaching conversations with teachers were kept confidential so the coach could maintain trust with teachers.

## Lesson 3

We learned that in order to determine the impact of coaching, we had to develop a system for measuring and monitoring both the work of coaches and the effectiveness of the coaching program. We had challenges in finding an effective way to evaluate the coaches. We learned that it was important to consider evaluation plans prior to establishing a coaching model; further, such a plan needs to be considered and developed thoughtfully and approved. An evaluation is necessary to help ensure there is a process for coaches to measure their work and receive feedback from others who are impacted by their practice. We used many different processes to evaluate coaches. For example, we used a professional skills checklist. We also would have coaches write individual goals and check their progress three times a year. We even used the state teacher evaluation for a few years. None of these totally captured the unique work of an instructional coach and gave them effective feedback.

I would encourage coaches to survey teachers for feedback on their coaching and make an informal meeting time with their principal to ask about what is going well, share celebrations of their progress, and ask for ideas on how to grow as a coach. As we shifted in our coaching model, we also found that the format of the evaluation needed to adjust to reflect the goals of our work. Often specific models have rubrics outlining the focus and goals of their work, and these can provide a way for coaches to see their strengths and areas for development. We would use the rubrics to self-reflect, but we never had a formal process for evaluation aligned to coaching work. I feel that really held us back from growing as a coaching team.

## Lesson 4

I learned how important it was to create a culture at the district and school levels for coaching—even prior to hiring coaches. Messaging, support structures, and leadership help create a culture where it is safe to share challenges, reflection is valued, and there are high levels of trust. This supportive culture opens doors of classrooms, making it safe to give and receive feedback, and allows teachers to feel comfortable and confident in sharing practices. Educators and administrators take a learning stance and feel encouraged to ask questions, express challenges, and celebrate growth. Thinking about a culture for coaching led us to consider the coaching models that we were supporting.

For years, coaching in our district was *teacher centered*. Coaches were often assigned to help roll out curriculum, provide professional learning for buildings around district initiatives, and work with new or struggling teachers. Meanwhile, the *fixing* coaching model, in which principals identified teachers needing support and then coaches were expected to work with them, was not effective. For coaching to work, the teachers partnering with the coach need to be open to support, feel comfortable and safe, and be willing to invest time and energy into improving their practices. We were sending a message that coaching was done *to* teachers, not *with* teachers. Other teachers were hesitant to work with a coach for fear that they would be perceived as ineffective.

We then shifted to an *opt-in model* where teachers had a choice if they wanted to work with a coach. Coaches would work to enroll teachers by starting with those who were eager for help, sharing a strategy and offering to model it in a classroom, and sending a survey and working with those who were interested in cycles. This had some impact, but it was limited to only those who engaged in cycles. This coaching helped individual teachers but was not always strategic, purposeful, and in connection with the larger focus of improvement at the school. It also did not provide evidence that our coaching work was impacting and increasing student achievement.

Our need for greater impact led us to an *all-in model* of coaching. This model establishes the understanding of how coaching impacts not just teachers but also students. Coaching was an added layer of support for specific classrooms, grade levels, or content areas based on data. The coach's work was prioritized to be with a teacher or teacher team for a specific time because of the needs of students. All teachers received coaching in some way. Coaches led professional learning based on building needs for all teachers. Coaching cycles were done in classrooms where students showed the most need. Coaches partnered with teachers to help impact student achievement. This shift to *all-in* coaching allowed coaching to be viewed as an integral part of schools rather than a support for specific teachers. Teachers are more open and willing to partner with the coach knowing that it is a support not only for them, but for students. Growing student achievement is the ultimate goal.

### Lesson 5

Finally, coaching—and large-scale change—takes time. Coaches must develop relationships and trust in a school to make an impact. The coach's role needs to be defined, understood, continually shared, marketed, and celebrated. Moreover, schools need to invest in coaching and allow the initiative time to grow before demanding results. Coaches need to have ongoing support and professional learning, and if we truly believe in the power of coaching, the coaches need a coach as well. When coaches are supported, and the work of a coach is understood and embraced, coaching can have a great impact. Coaching is complex and requires careful consideration of multiple factors—the content of coaching, the context for coaching, and the processes of coaching—for it to be a successful dimension of a school's professional learning program.

# Case 5: Changing the Community of Teaching, Learning, and Practice: A State Coaching Initiative

*Source: Ellen B. Eisenberg (Executive Director) and Bruce P. Eisenberg (Associate Director), The Professional Institute for Instructional Coaching*

In this case, Ellen and Bruce Eisenberg discuss the evolution of the Pennsylvania Institute for Instructional Coaching (PIIC), a statewide initiative to implement coaching in schools throughout the Commonwealth of Pennsylvania. This initiative started in 2005, and although it has evolved throughout the years, it is still a force in districts in the state.

---

### QUESTIONS TO PONDER

- What factors might account for the longevity and breadth of this coaching initiative?
- What are the primary beliefs and assumptions underlying coaching in this initiative?
- Of the lessons that are identified in this case, which resonate with you the most? How can they influence your coaching work?

---

The Professional Institute for Instructional Coaching (TPIIC) evolved from the Pennsylvania Institute for Instructional Coaching (PIIC) in 2009. The concept, however, of high-quality, effective teacher preparation started in 2005 with the private–public partnership between the Annenberg Foundation and the Pennsylvania Department of Education. Together, they crafted a multi-tiered statewide system of instructional coaching designed to prepare and support instructional coaches who provided job-embedded professional development for teachers and administrators in 26 schools within 16 different districts across Pennsylvania. These coaches were able to provide professional learning by offering ongoing, consistent "over the shoulder" support across all content areas and all grades. Below we describe key elements of PIIC, which are still important components of the current coaching framework.

## *Coaching Framework*

PIIC (and its successor, TPIIC) provides ongoing professional development for instructional coaches on four core elements: (1) working one-on-one and in small groups to support teachers and other school leaders; (2) focusing on data collection, analysis, and use; (3) using evidence-based literacy practices, applied across all content areas; and (4) supporting reflective and nonevaluative practice. PIIC instructional coaches provide teachers with tools to help them improve their practice and deliver quality instruction.

Instructional coaches team with teachers and provide one-on-one, side-by-side assistance, working together on specific needs in their classrooms. They provide professional development for teachers and school leaders with real-time support focused on changing practice, increasing student engagement, and improving student achievement.

The following BDA cycle of consultation describes how coaches work one-on-one and in small groups with teachers and other school leaders.

## *The BDA Cycle of Consultation*

Central to the coaching model is the BDA (before, during, and after) cycle of consultation and feedback. It is a cycle of communication, collaboration, confidentiality, and collective problem solving. In brief, the process works in the following way: In *before*-class visits, coaches co-plan with teachers to create goals, determine strategies, and identify materials and resources to use. The coach and teacher identify what data to collect during the class period. This list is limited and is constructed once the coach and teacher collaborate on the expectations of that class lesson. At this time, the teacher and coach also schedule the *after* visit, with the specific day and time devoted to debriefing and providing feedback for the class period visited. *During* class visits, coaches work with teachers to implement a specific literacy-based instructional approach, which emphasizes the consistency of language and practice across all content areas. Coaches concentrate on the mutually agreed-upon items from the co-designed visitation list and think about ways to help support the teacher's individual needs. This can be accomplished through co-teaching or modeling parts of the lesson. While a coach is modeling a specific strategy or concept, the teacher should have an identified focus as well. The purpose of this time is for the teacher to watch the coach share their expertise and then provide feedback at the scheduled meeting time. The coach is modeling the BDA process with the teacher and asking the teacher to follow the cycle of consultation, with roles modified for the occasion. *After* the visit, coaches and teachers discuss which goals were met and what worked effectively, focusing on their next steps to improve student performance. This is a nonevaluative process that encourages teachers to try innovative ways to engage students in a risk-free environment.

## *Mentoring*

Mentoring has always been an important aspect of this coaching framework, although given funding restrictions, the source of mentoring has changed. Generally, however, coaches in districts are mentored on a regular basis by experienced professionals who meet with school leaders to help administrators learn more about how to support their coaches. These mentors also meet with coaches to help them to gain a better understanding of the system in which they work and their place in it.

They also provide a sounding board for coaches, giving them opportunities to bring up challenges or issues that they may be facing.

## Content Framework

The underlying content framework advocates for evidence-based literacy strategies, techniques, and supports so that all students are exposed to literacy practices that teach them how to engage with their text. It's not about teaching students to read and write; it's all about teaching students and their teachers how to use literacy (reading, writing, and communication) to enhance learning. Research indicates that the effective development of literacy skills influences student learning and achievement. In the initial stages, the Penn Literacy Network, based at the Graduate School of Education at the University of Pennsylvania, served as a technical advisor for the initiative. They provided a graduate-level course for coaches and selected school teams, helping them identify effective teaching strategies appropriate for content areas. Participants completed in-class assignments, practiced with their coaches and mentors, and designed an end-of-year project to apply their learning. Coaches also facilitated turnaround training on the various concepts and instructional practices learned, enabling schools to provide consistency in language and practice.

## Updates about This Statewide Initiative

Because this statewide system was successful in improving student learning, increasing student engagement, and building teacher capacity, we were able to continue our partnership with 25 of the 29 Pennsylvania intermediate units from 2009 through 2018, and we currently work closely with one of the intermediate units that shares our vision and mission for sustaining schoolwide improvement. Coaches, administrators, and others interested in the transformation of teaching and learning in all 50 states and 30-plus countries use the TPIIC resources through our websites and blogs:

- Culture of Coaching (blog): *www.cultureofcoaching.blogspot.com*
- Institute for Instructional Coaching: *www.instituteforinstructionalcoaching.org*
- Professional Institute for Instructional Coaching: *www.tpiic.org*

Yet we still ask the same questions that are integral to an instructional coach's practice: "What am I doing as a coach to help teachers improve their practice?" and "What am I doing as a coach to help teachers improve student engagement and student outcomes?" These are the questions each instructional coach needs to answer when thinking about practice. When the school community fosters growth in ways that can answer these questions, instructional coaching improves teaching and learning.

While we believe that our framework and model (Eisenberg et al., 2017), Educator-Centered Instructional Coaching (ECIC), focus on the critical and effective components of instructional coaching implementation, we have learned that the model or framework matters less than the implementation of elements fostering consistent, ongoing learning that results in growth for all. Instructional coaching is not for the faint of heart, nor is it a deficit or "fix-it" model designed to take on the evaluative role and "judge" teacher performance. Instructional coaching is all about a systems approach that helps learners take ownership of their own learning and understand how students and their teachers learn. Embracing a schoolwide professional learning community and processes that are not "drop in" or "spray and pray" provides individualized and personal guidance for teachers and administrators. It deepens everyone's knowledge base and gives opportunities for highly skilled teachers to take on leadership roles while maintaining a presence in their classroom environments.

For instructional coaching to make a difference in teaching and learning, the elements of successful implementation must include a system that connects, supports, and strengthens teaching and learning. There must be a sustainable network of practitioners who believe in the same things: (1) There is a need to identify common goals and purposes for learning; (2) All students and their teachers can learn in a variety of ways; (3) Instructional coaching is a nonevaluative process and must be provided in a nonthreatening environment; and (4) All involved care about teaching and learning in schools.

As Lauren Resnick states in the foreword to West and Staub's (2003) book *Content-Focused Coaching:*

> No one expects an athlete or a musician to become great without a coach—an over-the-shoulder mentor who pushes and supports, watches and intervenes at critical moments, analyzes learners' actions and challenges them to become self-critical analysts of their own performances. Just so with teaching. It is a demanding craft, requiring of its practitioners both careful planning and finely tuned adaptation to the flow of classroom activity and conversation. The craft can be learned, but not from a textbook. It must be learned through guided practice. (p. xiv)

In the business world, executives jump at the chance for an opportunity to improve their skills; the same is true with athletes, performers, and now, even those interested in weight loss. What do they know that educators are less inclined to recognize? All are targeting sustainability, identification of goals, and the achievement of those goals in ways that make sense to the "audience." News flash: School communities are no different. We want to improve teaching, learning, leadership, performance, and, of course, outcomes. We all want to build stronger relationships and teams, all pulling in the same direction. We want to reduce isolation, strengthen community, build successful teams, safeguard confidentiality, and ensure that collaboration and collective problem solving are the norms in our schools. We want to support each other in a nonthreatening environment, build trusting relationships, and learn from each other without the risk of failure where the evaluation process determines our success; rather, we need to think "outside the box."

In our practice, we have found three essential components to successfully implement instructional coaching: fidelity, ubiquity, and dosage (Eisenberg et al., 2017). Without these three components, a model or framework will have no direction or clear path to success.

ECIC has seen that *fidelity* to a model or framework provides consistency in practice and language. All members in the community of practice need to be on the same page. By doing so, all the members understand the expectations and intentionally discuss a variety of ways to make those expectations a reality. The effect is cumulative, and students begin to expect the same kind of instructional delivery as they move from classroom to classroom. In schools where there is consistency or fidelity, there is a greater likelihood of an increase in student achievement.

If schools want schoolwide improvement, everyone in the school must participate. Every school stakeholder must be part of the conversation and share a vision for that improvement. A few teachers or classrooms implementing instructional coaching is just that—a few implementers, with no real shared goal or expectation for improvement. Within the ECIC framework, however, coaching is everywhere—the fact that it is common or *ubiquitous* is part of the reason for successful implementation.

If schools want to transform student learning, classroom learning, and professional learning, the support must provide an opportunity for everyone to be part of the process (e.g., everyone gets a "dose" of instructional support). This *dosage* builds teacher capacity and needs to be ongoing, consistent, deliberate, and focused. All the learners take responsibility for teaching and learning and ultimately learn from each other because they are part of the process and continually provide opportunities for critical thinking. Coaching does not work if a few teachers get instructional coaching only a few times a year. That kind of "drop-in" service doesn't yield anything positive except a quick "fix," which is the antithesis of effective instructional coaching. If every member of the community receives the same opportunity for coaching, shares in the accountability for teaching and learning, and believes in the learning capacity of all, those coaching interactions will change outcomes.

## Final Thoughts about the PIIC

As we reflect on our past and project to the future of schoolwide improvement and the impact of instructional coaching, we are reminded that instructional coaching is situational, and there are issues and conditions that exist in every school. Our goal is not to focus on the negatives but rather to highlight the positives and continue to make the changes we can and understand those we can't. Here we identify some of the lessons we learned along the way:

1. *Always begin with the end in mind, and recognize the power of the learning community.* The staff is critical for the implementation of a systems approach, determining the issues around teaching and learning and creating the necessary interventions essential to achieving the shared vision and common goals.
2. *Build a partnership, and foster collective problem-solving and critical friends' groups to engage in ongoing conversations about teaching and learning.* Practice the craft together, and reflect individually and collectively. Be a feedback giver and receiver.
3. *Tame the data monster.* Data collection, both qualitative and quantitative, is important, but some data are "need to know" and some are "nice to know." Participate in data dialogues to inform decision making, and use self-assessment tools to drive practice forward. Don't collect data you are not planning to use.
4. *Create a culture of teaching and learning by hiring appropriately skilled instructional coaches and allowing them to work with their colleagues in a nonevaluative system of support.* Protect their roles, and give them time to support each other, nourish their own growth, and reflect on what works effectively in classrooms and with teachers.
5. *The most important criterion for student success is teacher quality.* Sustain instructional coaching and relevant professional learning because that's what makes a difference in classroom instruction, student engagement, and student learning.

## APPENDIX A

# Thinking and Working Like a Coach: Note-Taking Organizer

This template may be helpful to readers wishing to reflect on their own practice as they read this book. In what ways do instructional coaches think and act when working on specific tasks or with specific groups? In what ways are you already thinking and working like a change agent, facilitator, designer, and advocate in your current role? Where do you see room for growth? (A downloadable version of this appendix is available on the book's companion website. See the box at the end of the table of contents for details.)

*(continued)*

---

From *Cultivating Coaching Mindsets, Second Edition: An Action Guide for Instructional Leaders* by Rita M. Bean and Jacy Ippolito. Copyright © 2025 The Guilford Press. Permission to photocopy this material, or to download and print enlarged versions (*www.guilford.com/bean3-materials*), is granted to purchasers of this book for personal use or use with students; see copyright page for details.

Thinking and Working Like a Coach: Note-Taking Organizer *(page 2 of 5)*

| | Thinking and Working Like a . . . | | | |
|---|---|---|---|---|
| | Change Agent | Facilitator | Designer | Advocate | Possibilities for me as a coach |
| **Chapter 3** Understanding and Shaping School Culture through Systems Thinking | | | | | |

| | Thinking and Working Like a . . . | | | |
|---|---|---|---|---|
| | Change Agent | Facilitator | Designer | Advocate | Possibilities for me as a coach |
| **Chapter 4** Ways of Working with Teachers | | | | | |

*(continued)*

Thinking and Working Like a Coach: Note-Taking Organizer *(page 3 of 5)*

| | Thinking and Working Like a . . . | | | | |
|---|---|---|---|---|---|
| | Change Agent | Facilitator | Designer | Advocate | Possibilities for me as a coach |
| **Chapter 5** Working with Individual Teachers | | | | | |

| | Thinking and Working Like a . . . | | | | |
|---|---|---|---|---|---|
| | Change Agent | Facilitator | Designer | Advocate | Possibilities for me as a coach |
| **Chapter 6** Working with Groups | | | | | |

*(continued)*

Thinking and Working Like a Coach: Note-Taking Organizer *(page 4 of 5)*

| | Thinking and Working Like a . . . | | | |
|---|---|---|---|---|
| | Change Agent | Facilitator | Designer | Advocate | Possibilities for me as a coach |
| **Chapter 7** Using Assessment to Guide Student Learning and School Improvement | | | | | |

| | Thinking and Working Like a . . . | | | |
|---|---|---|---|---|
| | Change Agent | Facilitator | Designer | Advocate | Possibilities for me as a coach |
| **Chapter 8** Developing, Implementing, and Sustaining Schoolwide Instructional Programs | | | | | |

*(continued)*

Thinking and Working Like a Coach: Note-Taking Organizer *(page 5 of 5)*

| | Thinking and Working Like a . . . | | | |
|---|---|---|---|---|
| | Change Agent | Facilitator | Designer | Advocate | Possibilities for me as a coach |
| **Chapter 9** Working with Families and Communities | | | | | |

| | Thinking and Working Like a . . . | | | |
|---|---|---|---|---|
| | Change Agent | Facilitator | Designer | Advocate | Possibilities for me as a coach |
| **Chapter 10** Coaches as Lifelong Learners | | | | | |

**APPENDIX B**

# Note-Taking Organizer
# When Coach Is Modeling Instruction

**Teacher:** _____

**School/Grade/Department:** _____

**Coach:** _____

**Date/Time(s):** _____

**Goals of Lesson:** _____

**Look-fors:** _____

**Teacher Activities (e.g., monitoring, assisting):** _____

TEACHER: Use the following chart to take notes during the lesson. We can address questions and comments in the post-lesson conversation. (A downloadable version of this appendix is available on the book's companion website. See the box at the end of the table of contents for details.)

| What is the coach doing? | What are students doing? | Comments/Questions |
|---|---|---|
|  |  |  |

From *Cultivating Coaching Mindsets, Second Edition: An Action Guide for Instructional Leaders* by Rita M. Bean and Jacy Ippolito. Copyright © 2025 The Guilford Press. Permission to photocopy this material, or to download and print enlarged versions (*www.guilford.com/bean3-materials*), is granted to purchasers of this book for personal use or use with students; see copyright page for details.

**APPENDIX C**

# Observation Protocol for Discipline-Specific Instruction

**Teacher:** _____ **Date:** _____

**Content Area / Grade Level:** _____

**Time Begin:** _____ **Time End:** _____

**Number of Students Present:** _____

**Special Circumstances to Note:** _____

**Lesson Focus:** _____

**Materials Being Used (check all that apply):**
- ☐ Textbook(s) / Other texts
- ☐ Board / Chart(s)
- ☐ Computer(s) / SMART Board / Projector
- ☐ Worksheet(s)
- ☐ Student-generated work
- ☐ Manipulatives: _____
- ☐ Other: _____

**Grouping (check all that apply):**
- ☐ Whole class
- ☐ Small groups
- ☐ Pairs
- ☐ Individuals
- ☐ Other: _____

Protocol to be used as a guide. Scale to be completed after the observation has been completed.

|  | Great Extent (3) | Some Extent (2) | Minimal Extent (1) | Not Observed (0) |
|---|---|---|---|---|
| **Classroom Environment** | | | | |
| **Materials supporting disciplinary content and literacy learning**<br>*Books, visuals, print, and nonprint materials about topic are evident* | ☐ | ☐ | ☐ | ☐ |
| **Peer-to-peer interaction opportunities**<br>*Seating for small groups, partners, etc.* | ☐ | ☐ | ☐ | ☐ |
| **Learning strategies displayed**<br>*Strategies displayed in anchor charts (e.g., why and how of Claim, Evidence, Reasoning routine)* | ☐ | ☐ | ☐ | ☐ |

*(continued)*

---

Adapted with permission from Bean and Goatley (2021). Copyright © 2021 The Guilford Press. From *Cultivating Coaching Mindsets, Second Edition: An Action Guide for Instructional Leaders* by Rita M. Bean and Jacy Ippolito. Copyright © 2025 The Guilford Press. Permission to photocopy this material, or to download and print enlarged versions (*www.guilford.com/bean3-materials*), is granted to purchasers of this book for personal use or use with students; see copyright page for details.

# Observation Protocol for Discipline-Specific Instruction *(page 2 of 3)*

|  | Great Extent (3) | Some Extent (2) | Minimal Extent (1) | Not Observed (0) |
|---|---|---|---|---|
| **Instruction** | | | | |
| **Warm-Up / Lesson Introduction** | | | | |
| T. sets purpose/goals, thinks aloud while modeling procedures/strategies | ☐ | ☐ | ☐ | ☐ |
| Activates student background knowledge, makes connections to past content and students' lives | ☐ | ☐ | ☐ | ☐ |
| Develops discipline-specific and general academic vocabulary | ☐ | ☐ | ☐ | ☐ |
| **Teacher Coaching of Students during Independent Practice** | | | | |
| Students prompted to engage in peer-to-peer discussions | ☐ | ☐ | ☐ | ☐ |
| Students prompted to engage in authentic tasks, eliciting their thinking and questions | ☐ | ☐ | ☐ | ☐ |
| T. coaches students in small groups, pairs, individually | ☐ | ☐ | ☐ | ☐ |
| T. questioning requires high-level thinking by students | ☐ | ☐ | ☐ | ☐ |
| Small-group reading, discussion, and writing activities, requiring deep engagement with/ responses to text | ☐ | ☐ | ☐ | ☐ |
| All activities require high-level thinking | ☐ | ☐ | ☐ | ☐ |
| Opportunities for differentiation to meet student needs | ☐ | ☐ | ☐ | ☐ |
| Teacher monitors and supports student work across the lesson | ☐ | ☐ | ☐ | ☐ |
| **Cool-Down / Lesson Conclusion** | | | | |
| T. provides opportunities for students to reflect and consolidate knowledge | | | | |
| Small-group and whole-class discussion opportunities provided | | | | |
| Connections to homework and next lessons are made | | | | |

*(continued)*

# Observation Protocol for Discipline-Specific Instruction *(page 3 of 3)*

|  | Great Extent (3) | Some Extent (2) | Minimal Extent (1) | Not Observed (0) |
|---|---|---|---|---|
| **Classroom Climate / Engagement of Students** | | | | |
| **High levels of student participation** <br> *Students are actively engaged with content, T., each other* | | | | |
| **Positive learning environment** <br> *Interactions are respectful and supportive, encouraging risk taking* | | | | |
| **Students use strategies to learn** <br> *Evidence of students knowing when, how, and which strategies to use (e.g., note-taking, summarizing, questioning)* | | | | |
| **Students show evidence of being able to think about their own learning** <br> *Provide justification for thinking, evidence of being able to organize their own learning* | | | | |

**Notes:**

## APPENDIX D

# Lesson Analysis Guide for Post-Observation Coaching Conversations

Teacher: _____ Coach: _____ Date: _____

Focus of Lesson/Objectives: _____

In Column 1, the coach can write notes about the observed lesson. In Column 2, the coach can summarize the post-observation conversation, indicating follow-up steps. The guide then serves as a record of both what the coach observed and what the coach and teacher discussed post-observation. Together, the columns help the coach–teacher pair plan next steps as a result of the observation and follow-up discussion.

| Coach Note-Taking During and After Observation | Coach Post-Observation Conversation Planner and Note-Taking |
|---|---|
| **Summary of Lesson Analysis**<br><br>• Overall, what did you see?<br><br>• Think?<br><br>• Wonder?<br><br>• Draft comments and focus questions to include in your post-observation conversation | **Results of Discussion with Teacher (after Post-Observation Conversation)**<br><br>• What should be / was the conversational focus?<br><br>• What action steps were agreed upon?<br><br>• Who will do what, in terms of next steps? Teacher? Coach? |
| **Instructional Strategies / Approaches That the Teacher Used:**<br><br>• Active engagement of students?<br><br>• Appropriate for lesson?<br><br>• Need for differentiation? | |

*(continued)*

From *Cultivating Coaching Mindsets, Second Edition: An Action Guide for Instructional Leaders* by Rita M. Bean and Jacy Ippolito. Copyright © 2025 The Guilford Press. Permission to photocopy this material, or to download and print enlarged versions (*www.guilford.com/bean3-materials*), is granted to purchasers of this book for personal use or use with students; see copyright page for details.

## Lesson Analysis Guide *(page 2 of 2)*

| Coach Note-Taking<br>During and After Observation | Coach Post-Observation Conversation<br>Planner and Note-Taking |
|---|---|
| **Materials Teacher / Students Used:**<br><br>• List materials used<br><br>• Are they appropriate for this lesson?<br><br>• Used effectively? | |
| **Classroom Management:**<br><br>• Were students attentive and engaged?<br><br>• Grouped appropriately? | |
| **Classroom Environment:**<br><br>• Did the environment provide for maximum learning?<br><br>• Were all students involved in meaningful work? | |
| **Other Notes:** | **Other Notes:** |

## APPENDIX E

# Analysis of State and District Assessments

Use this chart to identify and describe the assessment tools currently used in your district, responding to the headings. Then use the completed chart as a means of discussing whether each assessment is required, necessary (of great use), or perhaps unneeded. Participation in this activity can guide coaches and teacher teams as they consider the ways in which they use assessment to identify student learning needs. **Overarching question: Do these assessments provide for a well-aligned, coherent assessment system?**

*In Column 3, tests are identified as summative (S) or Formative (F) (screening, diagnostic, benchmark/progress monitoring).
**In Column 5, indicate whether all students or selected students are assessed.

| Assessment (e.g., math benchmark assessments) | Required By (e.g., district, state, federal?) | *Type (e.g., S or F) | Grade Levels Included (e.g., grades 3–8) | **Students (e.g., K–2, all) | Purpose of Assessment (e.g., determining start-of-grade math knowledge) | Time for Administration (e.g., 1 hour) | Frequency Administered (e.g., 1 × year) | Comments |
|---|---|---|---|---|---|---|---|---|
| | | | | | | | | |
| | | | | | | | | |
| | | | | | | | | |
| | | | | | | | | |
| | | | | | | | | |
| | | | | | | | | |
| | | | | | | | | |

From *Cultivating Coaching Mindsets, Second Edition: An Action Guide for Instructional Leaders* by Rita M. Bean and Jacy Ippolito. Copyright © 2025 The Guilford Press. Permission to photocopy this material, or to download and print enlarged versions (*www.guilford.com/bean3-materials*), is granted to purchasers of this book for personal use or use with students; see copyright page for details.

**APPENDIX F**

# A Sample Process for Guiding Assessment-Focused Self-Study and Professional Learning

We see the development of assessment-related professional learning as a three-stage process: (1) design and development, (2) implementation (which includes professional learning for staff), and (3) evaluation of the process.

**1. Design and Development**

   a) The district can form a leadership team composed of representative stakeholders: administrators, coaches, specialists, teachers, a school board member, and parents/caregivers to begin thinking about the vision and mission of a comprehensive assessment and professional learning system across schools, grades, and content areas. Often districts will ask a director of assessment to lead this team.

   b) Establish a set of goals for the team (see suggested questions below). As the team is thinking about the questions, it would be beneficial for individual members to lead several meetings with small groups of teachers at various grade levels and content areas to solicit their views about the current assessment program, its strengths, and how it might be improved. Here are some suggested questions:
   - What is the purpose of the district's comprehensive assessment plan? Its function?
   - Is there a clearly stated mission and vision for the plan?
   - What does the district believe about assessment (what is the role of assessment in improving student learning)?
   - In what ways do current tools address diversity, equity, and belonging in student assessment?
   - In what ways can the district provide a balance of summative and formative assessments?

   c) Analyze the current assessment tools that are used in the district (see Appendix E for a template to support this task). What are some possible ways in which to improve the current system of assessment? What is missing? Redundant?
   - Continue to share this information with small groups of faculty to solicit their feedback about the work and decisions of the leadership team. A survey might also be conducted to solicit their perceptions.

   d) Based on analysis results, the team can develop a set of recommendations regarding specific assessment instruments to be used, a schedule for administration, and an assessment-focused professional learning plan to be shared with all district faculty and stakeholders. This set of recommendations should also be shared with the school board/committee for feedback and approval. (Committee members should also be kept in the loop during the entire process.)

*(continued)*

---

From *Cultivating Coaching Mindsets, Second Edition: An Action Guide for Instructional Leaders* by Rita M. Bean and Jacy Ippolito. Copyright © 2025 The Guilford Press. Permission to photocopy this material, or to download and print enlarged versions (*www.guilford.com/bean3-materials*), is granted to purchasers of this book for personal use or use with students; see copyright page for details.

# A Sample Process *(page 2 of 2)*

2. **Implementation**
   a) Begin by holding a large-group meeting to introduce teachers to the overall framework for the assessment plan and the importance of assessment data for informing instruction. Such large groups may be school-based or even districtwide, depending on the number and size of schools.
   b) Introduce the assessment plan to the participants and ask them to discuss the following: the tools that are most useful to them for making instructional decisions, the proposed schedule for administration, and most importantly, what they think they need to learn to be able to implement this new plan effectively.
   c) Follow-up meetings with smaller groups can address the specifics of how to collect data and interpret them (e.g., What does it mean? How can it be used?). In the first of these meetings, a sample data set might be used to help teachers practice their interpretation skills, perhaps using a specific data analysis protocol (see, e.g., *www.clee.org/resources/data-driven-dialogue*). Questions that teachers should address include the following:
      - What do these results indicate in terms of student strengths? Needs?
      - What do the data mean? Is there a need for additional instruction or a change in instruction? What questions do the data raise?
      - What specific recommendations for instruction might be useful?
   d) Coaches can support teachers in following the recommendations made in the data-analysis process. In follow-up meetings, coaches and teachers can share the results of their work. Coaches may also find that they need to work with specific individuals who may need modeling or additional support in their instructional efforts. They may also find that learning walks with groups of teachers can lead to a more consistent, aligned process of instruction and understanding of data results (see Ippolito & Bean, 2024).

3. **Monitoring and Evaluation of the Process**
   a) Coaches and other school/district leaders must continue to monitor the results of the assessment tools to determine whether they are providing the necessary information needed to meet the needs of students. This can be done on a regular basis by instructional leadership teams at the school and district level.

**Additional Resource:**

Nelson, N., Cook, S., Caudle, T., Orozco, K. & Graupman K. (2020). *Comprehensive assessment plan*. Coeur d'Alene Public Schools. *www.cdaschools.org/documents/departments/assessments/welcome/607050*

### APPENDIX G

# Assessing Teacher Perceptions of Professional Learning Experiences

**Dear Teacher:** To what extent do you agree with the statements below about the professional learning (PL) available to you?

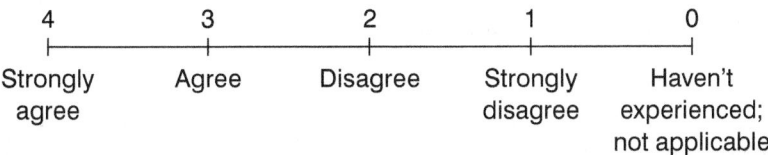

| 4 | 3 | 2 | 1 | 0 |
|---|---|---|---|---|
| Strongly agree | Agree | Disagree | Strongly disagree | Haven't experienced; not applicable |

### Content of Professional Learning

| Score | Description |
|---|---|
| | The district has established student learning goals and standards across grade levels and content areas that are used as a framework to guide PL. |
| | Standards for students' performance at each grade level have been identified (e.g., what should students know and be able to do?). |
| | Curriculum and instructional practices are evidence-based. |
| | Curriculum and instructional practices set high expectations for all students. |
| | Multiple sources of data are used to determine curriculum and instructional practices. |
| | PL resources (e.g., journals, webinars, professional books) are available and help me gain an in-depth understanding of the theory and research underlying practices (why a practice is important). |

### Collaboration and Sense of Community in the School

| Score | Description |
|---|---|
| | I play a decision-making role in deciding what/how I engage in professional learning to achieve the teaching and learning goals set by the school. |
| | I am given opportunities to work with my colleagues to learn from them (e.g., grade-level meetings, study groups). |
| | There is a focus on the value of families and their role as members of the community. |
| | I am recognized for the work that I do. |
| | I have opportunities to serve as a leader in planning and implementing PL activities. |

*(continued)*

---

Adapted with permission from Bean and Goatley (2021). Copyright © 2021 The Guilford Press. From *Cultivating Coaching Mindsets, Second Edition: An Action Guide for Instructional Leaders* by Rita M. Bean and Jacy Ippolito. Copyright © 2025 The Guilford Press. Permission to photocopy this material, or to download and print enlarged versions (*www.guilford.com/bean3-materials*), is granted to purchasers of this book for personal use or use with students; see copyright page for details.

# Assessing Teacher Perceptions *(page 2 of 2)*

## Duration and Amount of Time

| Score | Description |
|---|---|
| | PL activities are ongoing (over time) and give me opportunities to develop an in-depth understanding of what I am learning. |
| | I have sufficient contact hours related to the PL topic, enough to help me begin to feel a sense of competence and confidence. |

## Active Learning

| Score | Description |
|---|---|
| | PL activities make use of new technologies in helping me achieve my professional goals. |
| | I am encouraged to use information from my classroom and students in my PL experiences (e.g., student assessments, work samples). |
| | I am given PL choices based on the knowledge and skills I need to support my students. |
| | I have opportunities to participate in inquiry-based PL activities that help me reflect and think critically. |
| | I have opportunities to practice what I am learning with my peers. |
| | If coaching is available, it is useful in guiding and supporting my professional learning/growth. |
| | I find observation of teaching colleagues to be helpful to my learning. |
| | My participation in a book study group is helpful to my learning. |
| | I find outside technology resources (e.g., blogs, videos, podcasts, social media) to be useful for my own learning. |

## Applying What We Are Learning

| Score | Description |
|---|---|
| | I have opportunities to apply what I am learning in PL to my classroom. |
| | I have opportunities to try out what I am learning in a risk-free environment. |
| | Feedback is geared toward supporting and guiding my teaching practices; it is not evaluative. |
| | I am recognized for what I know and do in my classroom. |
| | I have opportunities to self-evaluate and reflect on my work. |

## Additional Comments:

**APPENDIX H**

# Template for a Professional Learning Action Plan

This template for a professional learning (PL) action plan guides coaches, along with groups of leaders and teachers, as they assess the current status of school- and/or district-based PL opportunities. The results of the process should be an "action plan" supporting next steps in designing and delivering PL.

### Part 1: Why?

- At the beginning of the process, establish your "why" (some coaches begin by asking the team to watch Simon Sinek's TED Talk on starting with "why," found here: *www.ted.com/talks/simon_sinek_how_great_leaders_inspire_action*).
- Write a brief, narrative rationale for developing this PL plan.
- What are you hoping to accomplish with this plan? Why?
- How does your plan build on existing data (e.g., about student demographics, student learning [tests, observational data, informal assessments, student work], perceptions, and processes [what we see in classrooms, instruction, materials])?
- How is your plan connected to demonstrated needs in your school/district?
- What other information may need to be collected to support the plan?

### Part 2: How?

- How will you achieve your purpose?
- What are the details of your plan so that you can move forward with clarity and coherence?
- Complete the table on the following page, detailing your specific plans in bulleted form.

*(continued)*

---

For an additional template to guide planning, see Ippolito and Bean's (2024, p. 42) "Theory of Action Template." From *Cultivating Coaching Mindsets, Second Edition: An Action Guide for Instructional Leaders* by Rita M. Bean and Jacy Ippolito. Copyright © 2025 The Guilford Press. Permission to photocopy this material, or to download and print enlarged versions (*www.guilford.com/bean3-materials*), is granted to purchasers of this book for personal use or use with students; see copyright page for details.

Template for a Professional Learning Action Plan *(page 2 of 3)*

| WHY: Professional Learning Focus | HOW: Action Steps | HOW: Lead Person | HOW: Time Line | HOW: Resources Needed | WHAT: Evidence of Implementation and Impact |
|---|---|---|---|---|---|
|  |  |  |  |  |  |
|  |  |  |  |  |  |

*(continued)*

## Template for a Professional Learning Action Plan *(page 3 of 3)*

### Part 3: What?

- What are the best-case-scenario intended outcomes of your plan? In six months? One year? Two years?
- How will you know if your plan is working? Which short-term and longer-term outcomes will you look for?

### Part 4: Wonderings?

- What are your team's lingering questions?
- What potential obstacles do you foresee, and how might you overcome them?
- What additional support is needed from your school, your district, the state?

## APPENDIX I

# Coach Skills, Knowledge, and Dispositions Self-Assessment Tool

| Domain | Emerging | Developing | Proficient |
|---|---|---|---|
| **Disciplinary Knowledge**<br>• Knowledge of the discipline (with extensive coursework based on standards of appropriate professional organization, such as ILA, NCTE, or NCTM[a])<br>• Knowledge of the research evidence regarding instruction<br>• Can translate knowledge into practice for teachers | | | |
| **Adult Learning**<br>• Understanding of how adults learn (need for meaningful, authentic experiences)<br>• Understanding of adult development (i.e., the notion that adults differ in how they make meaning and learn)<br>• Ability to apply knowledge of adult learning/development in developing professional learning experiences | | | |

*(continued)*

---

[a]ILA = International Literacy Association, NCTE = National Council of Teachers of English, NCTM = National Council of Teachers of Mathematics. From *Cultivating Coaching Mindsets, Second Edition: An Action Guide for Instructional Leaders* by Rita M. Bean and Jacy Ippolito. Copyright © 2025 The Guilford Press. Permission to photocopy this material, or to download and print enlarged versions (*www.guilford.com/bean3-materials*), is granted to purchasers of this book for personal use or use with students; see copyright page for details.

## Self-Assessment Tool *(page 2 of 4)*

| Domain | Emerging | Developing | Proficient |
|---|---|---|---|
| **Organizational Leadership and School Improvement**<br>• Understanding of school reform models that indicate need for both top-down and bottom-up efforts<br>• Understanding of the importance of collaborative efforts to remodel schools<br>• Understanding of how to assist in developing conditions that create schools as places of learning for students and teachers<br>• Ability to establish relationships with internal and external audiences about school change | | | |
| **Professional Learning (PL)**<br>• Understanding of research findings about effective PL (e.g., authentic, job-embedded, long-term)<br>• Ability to use knowledge to lead, facilitate, and evaluate effective PL experiences in schools | | | |

*(continued)*

## Self-Assessment Tool *(page 3 of 4)*

| Domain | Emerging | Developing | Proficient |
|---|---|---|---|
| **Facilitative Leadership**<br>• Understanding of research findings about importance of shared, distributed leadership in schools<br>• Ability to facilitate in ways that develop capacity of others to lead and participate collaboratively in individual and school change efforts<br>• Ability to choose and use discussion-based protocols and other adult learning routines<br>• Understanding of how to craft agendas and lead effective meetings | | | |
| **Assessment**<br>• Understanding of assessment and its use for accountability and for instructional decision making<br>• Understanding of how technology can be used for assessment purposes and for analyzing data | | | |

*(continued)*

## Self-Assessment Tool *(page 4 of 4)*

| Domain | Emerging | Developing | Proficient |
|---|---|---|---|
| **Coaching Processes/ Approaches**<br>• Understanding of how to work effectively with individual teachers<br>• Understanding of how to work effectively with groups of teachers (small and large)<br>• Ability to work with educators both in person and virtually<br>• Ability to analyze instructional practice and provide meaningful feedback to teachers<br>• Understanding of barriers to effective coaching and ability to work with others to address these barriers<br>• Understanding of how to advocate for teachers, programs, and students | | | |
| **Overall Assessment of Myself as a Coach:**<br><br>Based on this self-assessment, what are my current strengths?<br><br>Current needs?<br><br>What are my short-term improvement goals? How can I best achieve these?<br><br>What are my long-term improvement goals? How can I best achieve these? | | | |

# APPENDIX J

# Sample Disciplinary Literacy Protocols Shared by Michael P. Henry

### 1. Physics Key Terms Protocol

Name: _____

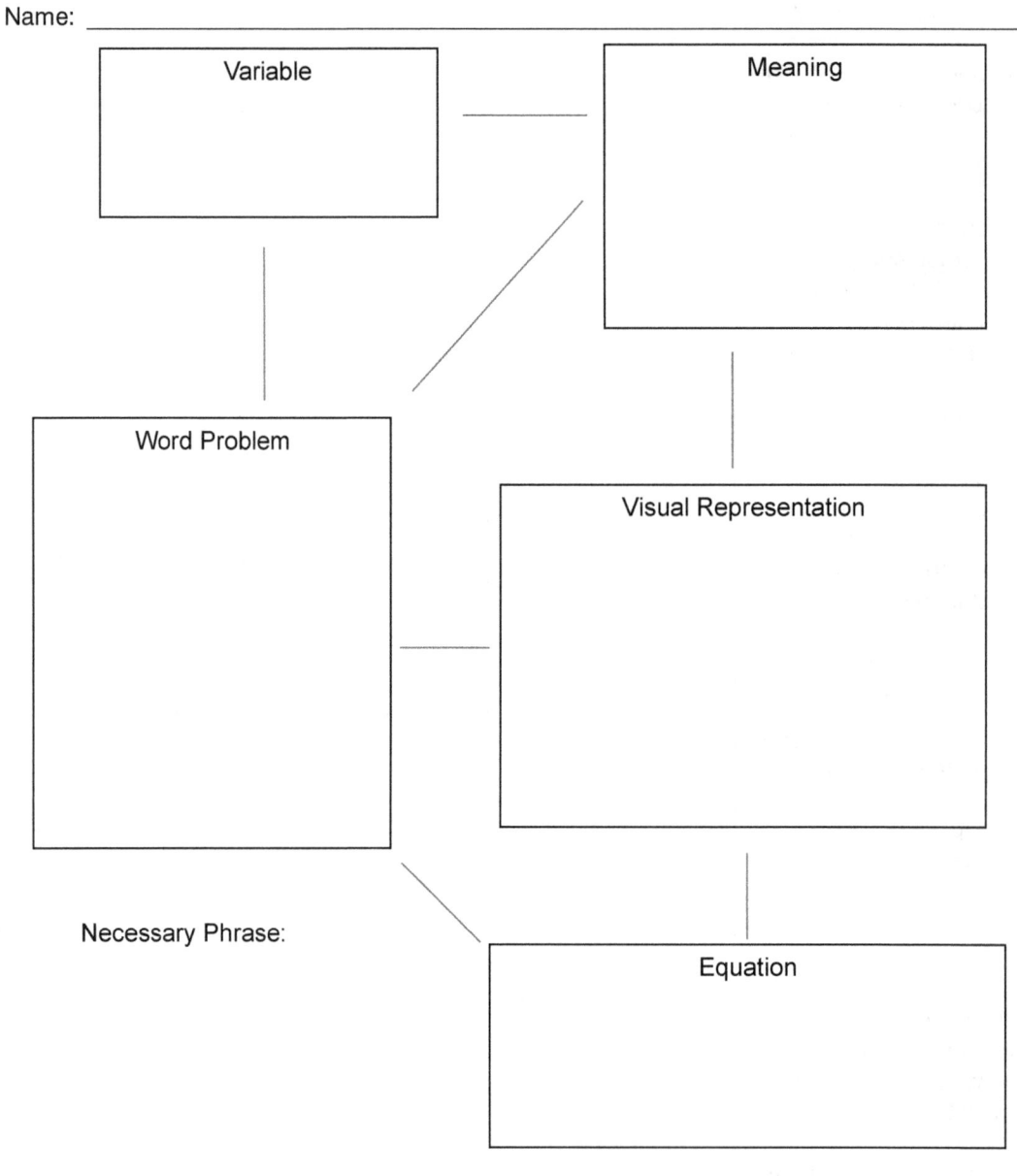

*(continued)*

From *Cultivating Coaching Mindsets, Second Edition: An Action Guide for Instructional Leaders* by Rita M. Bean and Jacy Ippolito. Copyright © 2025 The Guilford Press. Permission to photocopy this material, or to download and print enlarged versions (*www.guilford.com/bean3-materials*), is granted to purchasers of this book for personal use or use with students; see copyright page for details.

# Sample Disciplinary Literacy Protocols *(page 2 of 2)*

| **2. Physics Problem-Solving Process Protocol** <br> (Students complete right column) | |
|---|---|
| **Step 1:** List Assumptions | What pertinent background information might help you solve the problem; e.g., gravity is 9.8 m/s$^2$; Inertia makes acceleration = 0 |
| **Step 2:** Identify Necessary Variables | Write out a list of variables and their values that are relevant to solving the problem; e.g., $v_i$ = 10 m/s; $v_f$ = 0 m/s |
| **Step 3:** Create the Visual | Draw a picture or a diagram illustrating the event in the problem—a person should be able to look at the diagram and understand what event is occurring |
| **Step 4:** Label the Visual with Variables | The diagram should have the variables and their numbers on the drawing from step 3 |
| **Step 5:** Select the Appropriate Equation | Write out which equations are needed; after the equation is written, replace the variables with numbers from step 2 |
| **Step 6:** Complete Calculations | Solve the equation—get an answer |
| **Step 7:** Reinterpret and solve | Reread the problem and choose a word or phrase or assumption—change it in such a way that will result in using a different set of equations and or get a different answer |

# References

Adams, S. R., & Breidenstein, A. (Eds.). (2023). *Exploring meaningful and sustainable intentional learning communities for P-20 educators*. IGI Global.
Adisa, A. (2020, June 16). *What is the flywheel effect*. LinkedIn. *www.linkedin.com/pulse/what-flywheel-effect-wale-adisa*
Afflerbach, P. (2014, May). *What's new in literacy teaching?: Assessment* [Paper presentation]. International Reading Association Annual Meeting, New Orleans.
Afflerbach, P. (2018). *Understanding and using reading assessment, K–12*. ASCD.
Afflerbach, P. (2022). *Teaching readers (not reading): Moving beyond skills and strategies to reader-focused instruction*. Guilford Press.
Afflerbach, P. P., & Cho, B. (2011). The classroom assessment of reading. In M. Kamil, P. D. Pearson, E. B. Moje, & P. P. Afflerach (Eds.), *The handbook of reading research* (Vol. IV, pp. 487–514). Routledge.
Afflerbach, P., Kim, J., Crassas, M. E., & Cho, B. (2011). Best practices in literacy assessment. In L. M. Morrow & L. B. Gambrell (Eds.), *Best practices in literacy instruction* (4th ed., pp. 319–340). Guilford Press.
Aguilar, E. (2016). *The art of coaching teams: Building resilient communities that transform schools*. Jossey-Bass.
Aguilar, E. (2024). *Arise: The art of transformational coaching*. Jossey-Bass.
Alexander, K. L., Entwisle, D. R., & Olson, L. S. (2007). Summer learning and its implications: Insights from the Beginning School Study. *New Directions for Youth Development, 2007*(114), 11–32.
Allen, D., & Blythe, T. (2004). *The facilitator's book of questions: Resources for looking together at student and teacher work*. Teachers College Press.
Allen, D., & Blythe, T. (2015). *Facilitating for learning: Tools for teacher groups of all kinds*. Teachers College Press.
Allen, D., & Blythe, T. (2018). Aesthetics of facilitation: Cultivating teacher leadership. *International Journal of Teacher Leadership, 9*(2), 48–68.
Allen, D., Blythe, T., Dichter, A., & Lynch, T. (2018). *Protocols in the classroom: Tools to help students read, write, think, & collaborate*. Teachers College Press.

Argyris, C., & Schön, D. A. (1974). *Theory in practice: Increasing professional effectiveness*. Jossey-Bass.

Argyris, C., & Schön, D. A. (1996). *Organizational learning II: Theory, method and practice*. Addison-Wesley.

Association of Science and Technology Centers. (n.d.). *Professional competencies for the informal STEM learning field*. www.astc.org/isl-framework

Bean, R., & DeFord, D. (2012). Do's and don'ts for literacy coaches: Advice from the field. *Literacy Coaching Clearinghouse*. https://files.eric.ed.gov/fulltext/ED530365.pdf

Bean, R. M., Draper, J. A., Hall, V., Vandermolen, J., & Zigmond, N. (2010). Coaches and coaching in Reading First schools. *Elementary School Journal, 111*(1), 87–114.

Bean, R. M., & Goatley, V. J. (2021). *The literacy specialist: Leadership and coaching for the classroom, school, and community* (4th ed.). Guilford Press.

Bean, R. M., Goatley, V., Kern, D., Brieske-Ulenski, A., Ippolito, J., & Smith, K. (2024, April). *The multiple roles of specialized literacy professionals: An update from a national survey* [Paper presentation]. American Educational Research Association Annual Meeting, Philadelphia, PA, United States.

Bean, R. M., & Ippolito, J. (2016). *Cultivating coaching mindsets: An action guide for literacy leaders*. Learning Sciences International.

Bean, R. M., Kern, D., Goatley, V., Ortlieb, E., Shettel, J., Calo, K., et al. (2015). Specialized literacy professionals as literacy leaders: Results of a national survey. *Literacy Research and Instruction, 54*(2), 83–114.

Bean, R. M., & Lillenstein, J. (2012). Response to intervention and the changing roles of schoolwide personnel. *The Reading Teacher, 65*(7), 491–501.

Bean, R. M., Swan Dagen, A., Ippolito, J., & Kern, D. (2018). Principals' perspectives on the roles of specialized literacy professionals. *Elementary School Journal, 119*(2), 327–350.

Bean, R. M., Turner, G. H., & Belski, K. (2002). Implementing a successful America Reads Challenge tutoring program: Lessons learned. In P. E. Linder, M. B. Sampson, J. Dugan, & B. Brancato (Eds.), *24th yearbook of the College Reading Association* (pp. 169–187). College Reading Association.

Beck, I. L., McKeown, M. G., & Kucan, L. (2013). *Bringing words to life: Robust vocabulary instruction* (2nd ed.). Guilford Press.

Benson, T. A., & Fiarman, S. E. (2020). *Unconscious bias in schools: A developmental approach to exploring race and racism*. Harvard Education Press.

Berebitsky, D., Goddard, R. D., & Carlisle, J. F. (2014). An examination of teachers' perceptions of principal support for change and teachers' collaboration and communication around literacy instruction in reading first schools. *Teachers College Record, 116*(4), 1–28.

Berger, J. G. (2019). *Unlocking leadership mindtraps: How to thrive in complexity*. Stanford University Press.

Bernhardt, V. (2013). *Data analysis for continuous school improvement* (3rd ed.). Routledge.

Bernhardt, V. L. (2017). *Data analysis for continuous school improvement* (4th ed.). Routledge.

Biancarosa, G., Bryk, A. B., & Dexter, E. (2010). Assessing the value-added effects of Literacy Collaborative professional development on student learning. *Elementary School Journal, 111*(1), 7–34.

Bishop, R. S. (1990). Mirrors, windows, and sliding glass doors. *Perspectives: Choosing and Using Books for the Classroom, 6*(3), ix–xi.

Blythe, T., Allen, D., & Powell, B. S. (2015). *Looking together at student work* (3rd ed.). Teachers College Press.

Bocala, C., & Holman, R. R. (2021). Coaching for equity demands deeper dialogue. *Educational Leadership, 78*(6), 66–71. *www.ascd.org/el/articles/coaching-for-equity-demands-deeper-dialogue*

Bolden, F. (2023). *How instructional coaches can support the mental health of educators*. The Learning Counsel. *https://thelearningcounsel.com/articles/how-instructional-coaches-can-support-the-mental-health-of-educators*

Booker, L., & Russell, J. L. (2022). *Design principles for improving practice with instructional coaching*. EdResearch for Action. *https://edresearchforaction.com/research-briefs/design-principles-for-improving-practice-with-instructional-coaching*

Botel, M., & Paparo, L. (2016). *The plainer truths of teaching, learning and literacy: A comprehensive guide to reading, writing, speaking and listening pre-K–12 across the curriculum*. Owl Publishing.

Boudett, K. P., & City, E. A. (2014). *Meeting wise: Making the most of collaborative time for educators*. Harvard Education Press.

Boudett, K. P., City, E. A., & Murnane, R. J. (Eds.). (2020). *Data wise, revised and expanded edition: A step-by-step guide to using assessment results to improve teaching and learning*. Harvard Education Press.

Boutte, G. S., & Johnson, G. L. (2014). Community and family involvement in urban schools. In H. R. Milner & K. Lomotey (Eds.), *Handbook of urban education* (pp. 167–187). Routledge.

Bradford, D. L., & Cohen, A. R. (1998). *Power up: Transforming organizations through shared leadership*. John Wiley & Sons.

Breidenstein, A., Fahey, K., Glickman, C., & Hensley, F. (2012). *Leading for powerful learning: A guide for instructional leaders*. Teachers College Press.

Briars, D. J. (2014, November). *Curriculum materials matter: Evaluating the evaluation process*. National Council of Teachers of Mathematics. *www.nctm.org/News-and-Calendar/Messages-from-the-President/Archive/Diane-Briars/Curriculum-Materials-Matter-Evaluating-the-Evaluation-Process*

Brieske-Ulenski, A., & Kelley, M. J. (2023). Development and validation of the Literacy Coach Self-Efficacy Scale. *Literacy Research and Instruction*, 1–22.

Brookhart, S. (2023). *Classroom assessment essentials*. ASCD.

Bryk, A. S. (2015). 2014 AERA distinguished lecture: Accelerating how we learn to improve. *Educational Researcher, 44*(9), 467–477.

Bryk, A. S., Gomez, L. M., Grunow, A., & LeMahieu, P. G. (2015). *Learning to improve: How America's schools can get better at getting better*. Harvard Education Press.

Bryk, A. S. (2021). *Improvement in action: Advancing quality in America's schools*. Harvard Education Press.

Bryk, A. S., Gomez, L. M., Grunow, A., & LeMahieu, P. G. (2015). *Learning to improve: How America's schools can get better at getting better*. Harvard Education Press.

Bryk, A. S., Sebring, P. B., Allensworth, F. E., Luppescu, S., & Easton, J. A. (2010). *Organizing schools for improvement: Lessons from Chicago*. University of Chicago Press.

Buly, M., & Valencia, S. (2002). Below the bar: Profiles of students who fail state reading assessments. *Educational Evaluation and Policy Analysis, 24*(3), 219–239.

Burke, P., & Kennedy, E. (2024). "Why do you think that?" Exploring disciplinary literacy in elementary science, history and visual arts. *The Reading Teacher*. *https://ila.onlinelibrary.wiley.com/doi/10.1002/trtr.2283*

Burton, E. (2013, January 8). *Parent involvement in early literacy*. Edutopia. *www.edutopia.org/blog/parent-involvement-in-early-literacy-erika-burton*

CAST. (2018). *Universal design for learning guidelines* (Version 2.2). *http://udlguidelines.cast.org*

Chappuis, J., & Stiggins, R. J. (2019). *Classroom assessment for student learning: Doing it right—Using it well* (3rd ed.). Pearson.

Chappuis, J., Stiggins, R. J., Chappuis, S., & Arter, J. (2012). *Classroom assessment for student learning: Doing it right—Using it well.* Pearson.

City, E. A., Elmore, R. F., Fiarman, S. E., & Teitel, L. (2009). *Instructional rounds in education: A networked approach to improving teaching and learning.* Harvard Education Press.

Coburn, C. E., & Woulfin, S. L. (2012). Reading coaches and the relationship between policy and practice. *Reading Research Quarterly, 47*(1), 5–30.

Cochran-Smith, M., & Lytle, S. L. (2009). *Inquiry as stance: Practitioner research for the next generation.* Teachers College Press.

Coiro, J. (2005). Every teacher a Miss Rumphius: Empowering teachers with effective professional development. In R. A. Karchmer, M. Mallette, J. Kara-Soteriou, & D. J. Leu, Jr. (Eds.), *New literacies for new times: Innovative models of literacy education using the Internet* (pp. 199–219). International Reading Association.

Coiro, J. (2021). Toward a multifaceted heuristic of digital reading to inform assessment, research, practice, and policy. *Reading Research Quarterly, 56*(1), 9–31.

Coleman, A. L., Negrón, F. M., Jr., & Lipper, K. E. (2011). *Achieving educational excellence for all: A guide to diversity-related policy strategies for school districts.* National School Board Association. *https://highered.collegeboard.org/media/pdf/achieving-educational-excellence-for-all.pdf*

Collet, V. S. (2019). *Collaborative lesson study: ReVisioning teacher professional development.* Teachers College Press.

Collins, J. (n.d.). *The flywheel effect. www.jimcollins.com/article_topics/articles/the-flywheel-effect.html*

Collins, J. (2001). *Good to great: Why some companies make the leap . . . and others don't.* HarperCollins.

Collins, J. (2005). *Good to great and the social sectors: Why business thinking is not the answer.* HarperCollins.

Collins, J. (2019). *Turning the flywheel: A monograph to accompany good to great.* Random House.

Constantino, S. M. (2008). *101 ways to create real family engagement.* ENGAGE! Press.

Conyers, T. (2023). *Engagement matters: Tips for facilitating large groups.* Medium. *https://medium.com/@tricia.conyers/engagement-matters-d0250aa9bf02*

Cooper, J. (2023). 7 tips for improving parent engagement in schools. *SchoolNow. www.schoolnow.com/blog/parent-involvement-school-another*

Corbett, J., & Redding, S. (2017). *Using needs assessments for school and district improvement: A tactical guide.* Center on School Turnaround at WestEd and Council of Chief State School Officers. *www.adi.org/downloads/NeedsAssessment-Final.pdf*

Costa, A., & Garmston, R. (2002). *Cognitive coaching: A foundation for renaissance schools* (2nd ed.). Christopher-Gordon.

Costa, A., & Garmston, R. (2015). *Cognitive coaching: Developing self-directed leaders and learners* (3rd ed.). Rowman & Littlefield.

Cuiccio, C., & Husby-Slater, M. (2018). *Needs assessment guidebook: Supporting the development of district and school needs assessments.* American Institutes for Research. *http://oese.ed.gov/files/2020/10/needsassessmentguidebook-508_003.pdf*

Daly, A., & Little, J. W. (Eds.). (2010). *Social network theory and educational change.* Harvard Education Press.

Dana, N. F., & Yendol-Hoppey, D. (2008). *The reflective educator's guide to professional development: Coaching inquiry-oriented learning communities.* Corwin Press.

Darling-Hammond, L. (2010). *The flat world and education: How America's commitment to equity will determine our future.* Teachers College Press.

Darling-Hammond, L., Hyler, M. E., & Gardner, M. (2017). *Effective teacher professional development.* Learning Policy Institute.

Datnow, A., & Park, V. (2018). Opening or closing doors for students? Equity and data use in schools. *Journal of Educational Change, 19,* 131–152.

Deussen, T., Coskie, T., Robinson, L., & Autio, E. (2007). *"Coach" can mean many things: Five categories of literacy coaches in Reading First* (Issues & Answers Report, REL 2007-No. 005). U.S. Department of Education, Institute of Education Sciences, National Center for Education Evaluation and Regional Assistance. https://nces.ed.gov/pubsearch/pubsinfo.asp?pubid=REL2007005

Dimitriadis, M. (2024). *What is design thinking? A handy guide for teachers.* Makers Empire. www.makersempire.com/what-is-design-thinking-a-handy-guide-for-classroom-teachers

Donaldson, M. L., Johnson, S. M., Kirkpatrick, C. L., Marinell, W. H., Steele, J. L., & Szczesiul, S. A. (2008). Angling for access, bartering for change: How second-stage teachers experience differentiated roles in schools. *Teachers College Record, 110*(5), 1088–1114.

Donohoo, J., Hattie, J., & Eells, M. (2018). The power of collective efficacy. *Educational Leadership, 75*(6), 41–44.

Donohoo, J., & Katz, S. (2017). When teachers believe, students achieve. Collaborative inquiry builds teacher efficacy for better student outcomes. *The Learning Professional, 38*(6), 20–27.

Drago-Severson, E. (2009). *Leading adult learning: Supporting adult development in our schools.* Corwin Press.

Drago-Severson, E., & Blum-DeStefano, J. (2017). *Tell me so I can hear you: A developmental approach to feedback for educators.* Harvard Education Press.

DuFour, R. (2004). What is a "professional learning community"? *Educational Leadership, 61*(8), 6–11.

DuFour, R., DuFour, R., Eaker, R., Many, T., & Mattos, M. (2016). *Learning by doing: A handbook for professional learning communities at work* (3rd ed.). Solution Tree Press.

Dumay, X. (2009). Origins and consequences of schools' organizational culture for student achievement. *Educational Administration Quarterly, 45*(4), 523–555.

Duncan, M. (2006). *Literacy coaching: Developing effective teachers through instructional dialogue.* Richard C. Owen Publishers.

Edwards, P. (2016). *New ways to engage parents: Strategies and tools for teachers and leaders, K–12.* Teachers College Press.

Edwards, P. A., Paratore, J. R., & Sweeney, J. S. (2014). Working with parents and the community. In S. B. Wepner, D. S. Strickland, & D. J. Quatroche (Eds.), *The administration and supervision of reading programs* (5th ed., pp. 214–222). Teachers College Press.

Eisenberg, E. B., Eisenberg, B. P., Medrich, E. A., & Charner, I. (2017). *Instructional coaching in action: An integrated approach that transforms thinking, practice, and schools.* ASCD.

Eisold, K. (1997). The task of leadership: Leadership as an attribute of group life. *ADE Bulletin, 116,* 33–37.

Elish-Piper, L., & L'Allier, S. (2011). Examining the relationship between literacy coaching and student reading gains in grades K–3. *Elementary School Journal, 112*(1), 83–106.

Elish-Piper, L., L'Allier, S. K., Manderino, M., & Di Domenico, P. (2016). *Collaborative coaching for disciplinary literacy: Strategies to support teachers in grades 6–12.* Guilford Press.

Elish-Piper, L., Matthews, M. W., & Risko, V. J. (2022). *Reading assessment to promote equitable learning: An empowering approach for grades K–5.* Guilford Press.

Elmore, R. F. (2004). *School reform from the inside out: Policy, practice, and performance.* Harvard Education Press.

Epstein, J., Sanders, M. G., Sheldon, S., Simon, B. S., Salinas, K. C., Jansorn, N. R., et al. (2009). *School, family, and community partnerships: Your handbook for action* (3rd ed.). Corwin Press.

Epstein, J. L., Sanders, M. G., Sheldon, S. B., Simon, B. S., Salinas, K. C., Jansorn, N. R., et al. (2018). *School, family, and community partnerships: Your handbook for action* (4th ed.). Corwin Press.

Evans, R. (2007). The authentic leader. In J. L. Perry (Ed.), *The Jossey-Bass reader on educational leadership* (2nd ed., pp. 135–156). Jossey-Bass.

Fahey, K., Breidenstein, A., Ippolito, J., & Hensley, F. (2019). *An uncommon theory of school change: Leadership for reinventing schools.* Teachers College Press.

Fahey, K., & Ippolito, J. (2015). *Towards a general theory of SRI's intentional learning communities.* School Reform Initiative. https://works.bepress.com/jacy-ippolito/28/download

Ferman, B. (Ed.). (2017). *The fight for America's schools: Grassroots organizing in education.* Harvard Education Press.

Fisher, D., & Frey, N. (2023). The technology-enhanced school. *Educational Leadership, 80*(6), 76–77. www.ascd.org/el/articles/the-technology-enhanced-school

Fixsen, D. L., Naoom, S. F., Blasé, K. A., Friedman, R. M., & Wallace, F. (2006). *Implementation research: A synthesis of the literature* (FMHI Publication No. 231). National Implementation Research Network. https://nirn.fpg.unc.edu/resources/implementation-research-synthesis-literature

Foorman, B., Beyler, N., Borradaile, K., Coyne, M., Denton, C. A., Dimino, J., et al. (2016, July). *Foundational skills to support reading for understanding in kindergarten through 3rd grade: Educator's practice guide* (NCEE 2016-4008). What Works Clearinghouse. https://ies.ed.gov/ncee/wwc/PracticeGuide/21

Fullan, M. (1993). Why teachers must become change agents. *Educational Leadership, 50*(6), 12–17.

Fullan, M. (2015). *The new meaning of educational change* (5th ed.). Teachers College Press.

Fullan, M. (2020). *Leading in a culture of change* (2nd ed.). Jossey-Bass.

Fullan, M., & Langworthy, M. (2014, January). *A rich seam: How new pedagogies find deep learning.* Pearson. www.michaelfullan.ca/wp-content/uploads/2014/01/3897.Rich_Seam_web.pdf

Gabriel, R. (2023). *Doing disciplinary literacy: Teaching reading and writing across the content areas.* Teachers College Press.

Galey-Horn, S. (2020). Capacity-building for district reform: The role of instructional-coach teams. *Teachers College Record, 122*(10), 1–40.

Galey-Horn, S., & Woulfin, S. L. (2021). Muddy waters: The micropolitics of instructional coaches' work in evaluation. *American Journal of Education, 127*(3), 441–470.

Ganimian, A. J., Vegas, E., & Hess, F. M. (2020). *Realizing the promise: How can education technology improve learning for all?* The Brookings Institution. www.brookings.edu/articles/realizing-the-promise-how-can-education-technology-improve-learning-for-all/

Garmston, R. (2005). *The presenter's handbook: A practical guide* (2nd ed.). Christopher-Gordon.

Gawande, A. (2011, October 3). Personal best. *The New Yorker.* www.newyorker.com/magazine/2011/10/03/personal-best

Gawande, A. (2017). *Want to get great at something? Get a coach* [Video]. TED. www.ted.com/talks/atul_gawande_want_to_get_great_at_something_get_a_coach

Genest, M. T. (2014). Reading is a BLAST! Inside an innovative literacy collaboration between public schools and the public library. *Reading Horizons, 53*(1), 4.

Genest, M. T., & Bean, R. M. (2007). *Bringing libraries and schools together (BLAST): A collaborative program between Carnegie Library of Pittsburgh and the Pittsburgh Public School District (year 5)* [Unpublished technical report].

Gibbons, L. K., & Cobb, P. (2016). Content-focused coaching: Five key practices. *The Elementary School Journal, 117*(2), 237–260.

Gibbons, L. K., & Cobb, P. (2017). Focusing on teacher learning opportunities to identify potentially productive coaching activities. *Journal of Teacher Education, 68*(4), 411–425.

Gillespie, R., & Amador, J. M. (2024). Video annotations contribute to coach and teacher conversations during coaching cycles. *The Elementary School Journal, 125*(1), 106–131.

Gladwell, M. (2000). *The tipping point: How little things can make a big difference*. Little, Brown.

Goldstein, J. (2009). Designing transparent teacher evaluation: The role of oversight panels for professional accountability. *The Teachers College Record, 111*(4), 893–933.

Gorski, P. C., & Swalwell, K. (2015). Equity literacy for all. *Educational Leadership, 72*(6), 34–40.

Gorski, P., & Swalwell, K. (2023a). *Fix injustice, not kids and other principles for transformative equity leadership*. ASCD.

Gorski, P., & Swalwell, K. (2023b). Moving from equity awareness to action. *Educational Leadership, 80*(8), 20–27.

Gray, L., & Lewis, L. (2021). *Use of educational technology for instruction in public schools: 2019–20* (NCES 2021-017). U.S. Department of Education, Institute of Education Sciences, National Center for Education Statistics. https://nces.ed.gov/pubsearch/pubsinfo.asp?pubid=2021017

Gray-Lobe, G., Pathak, P. A., & Walters, C. R. (2023). The long-term effects of universal preschool in Boston. *The Quarterly Journal of Economics, 138*(1), 363–411.

Grierson, A. (2011, April). *Walking the talk: Supporting teachers' growth with differentiated professional learning* [Paper presentation]. American Educational Research Association Annual Conference, New Orleans, LA, United States.

Grose, J. (2024, January 17). Don't ditch standardized tests. Fix them. *The New York Times.* www.nytimes.com/2024/01/17/opinion/standardized-tests.html

Grossman, P. (2020). Making the complex work of teaching visible. *Phi Delta Kappan, 101*(6), 8–13.

Guskey, T. R., & Yoon, K. S. (2009). What works in professional development? *Phi Delta Kappan, 90*(7), 495–500.

Hall, April. (2014, July 2). *IRA takes positions on high-stakes assessments, leisure reading*. International Literacy Association. www.literacyworldwide.org/blog/literacy-now/2014/07/02/ira-takes-positions-on-high-stakes-assessments-leisure-reading

Hamilton, L., Halverson, R., Jackson, S., Mandinach, E., Supovitz, J., & Wayman, J. (2009). *Using student achievement data to support instructional decision making* (NCEE 2009–4067). U.S. Department of Education, Institute of Education Sciences, National Center for Education Evaluation and Regional Assistance. https://ies.ed.gov/ncee/wwc/Docs/PracticeGuide/dddm_pg_092909.pdf

Haneda, M., Teemant, A., & Sherman, B. (2017). Instructional coaching through dialogic interaction: Helping a teacher to become agentive in her practice. *Language and Education, 31*(1), 46–64.

Hannan, M. Q., & Russell, J. L. (2020). Coaching in context: Exploring conditions that shape instructional coaching practice. *Teachers College Record, 122*(10), 1–40.

Hanover Research. (2023, January 25). *2023 trends in K–12 education*. www.hanoverresearch.com/reports-and-briefs/2023-trends-in-k-12-education/

Hattie, J. (2012). *Visible learning for teachers: Maximizing impact on learning*. Routledge.

Hattie, J. (2016, July). *Mindframes and maximizers* [Keynote speech]. Visible Learning 3rd Annual Conference, Washington, DC, United States.

Hattie, J. (2023). *Visible learning: The sequel*. Routledge.

Heifetz, R., Grashow, A., & Linsky, M. (2009). *The practice of adaptive leadership: Tools and tactics for changing your organization and the world*. Harvard Business Press.

Henderson, A., & Mapp, K. (2002). *A new wave of evidence: The impact of school, family, and community connections on student achievement (annual synthesis)*. National Center for Family and Community Connections with Schools, Southwest Educational Development Laboratory.

Hersey, P., & Blanchard, K. (1977). *Management of organizational behavior: Utilizing human resources* (3rd ed.). Prentice-Hall.

Hess, K. (2023). *Rigor by design, not chance: Deeper thinking through actionable instruction and assessment*. ASCD.

Hill, H. C., & Papay, J. P. (2022, October 25). *Building better PL: How to strengthen teacher learning*. Research Partnership for Professional Learning. https://wrap2fasd.org/wp-content/uploads/2022/11/rppl-building-better-pl.pdf

Hill, H., Papay, J., Schwartz, N., Johnson, S., Freitag, E., Donohue, K., et al. (2021). *A learning agenda for improving teacher professional learning at scale*. Research Partnership for Professional Learning. www.annenberginstitute.org/sites/default/files/rppl-agenda.pdf

Hong, S. (2020). *Natural allies: Hope and possibility in teacher–family partnerships*. Harvard Education Press.

Hu, Y., & Tuten, J. (2017). Literacy teachers' learning through a recursive coaching cycle. *The Reading Professor, 40*(2), Article 18.

IDEO. (n.d.). *Design thinking for educators* [with toolkit]. http://page.ideo.com/design-thinking-edu-toolkit

International Literacy Association. (n.d.-a). *Standards 2010: Role 5: Reading specialist/literacy coach*. www.literacyworldwide.org/get-resources/standards/standards-for-reading-professionals/standards-2010-role-5

International Literacy Association. (2015). *The multiple roles of school-based specialized literacy professionals* [Research brief]. https://www.literacyworldwide.org/docs/default-source/where-we-stand/literacy-professionals-research-brief.pdf

International Literacy Association. (2018a). *Literacy coaching for change: Choices matter* [Literacy leadership brief]. Author. www.literacyworldwide.org/docs/default-source/where-we-stand/ila-literacy-coaching-for-change-choices-matter.pdf

International Literacy Association. (2018b). *Standards 2017: Standards for the preparation of literacy professionals*. www.literacyworldwide.org/get-resources/standards/standards-2017

Ippolito, J. (2010). Three ways that literacy coaches balance responsive and directive relationships with teachers. *Elementary School Journal, 111*(1), 164–190.

Ippolito, J., & Bean, R. M. (2018). *Unpacking coaching mindsets: Collaboration between principals and coaches*. Learning Sciences International.

Ippolito, J., & Bean, R. M. (2019). A principal's guide to supporting instructional coaching. *Educational Leadership, 77*(3), 68–73.

Ippolito, J., & Bean, R. M. (2024). *The power of instructional coaching in context: A systems view for aligning content and coaching.* Guilford Press.

Ippolito, J., Bean, R. M., & Sacha, K. (2023). Innovations in elementary literacy coaching: Sustaining coaching practices in virtual spaces. In D. Robertson, L. A. Hall, & C. Brock (Eds.), *Innovations in literacy professional learning: Strengthening equity, access, and sustainability* (pp. 213–239). Guilford Press.

Ippolito, J., Dobbs, C. L., & Charner-Laird, M. (2019). *Disciplinary literacy inquiry and instruction.* Learning Sciences International.

Ippolito, J., Dobbs, C. L., & Charner-Laird, M. (2024). *Disciplinary literacy inquiry and instruction* (2nd ed.). Harvard Education Press.

Ippolito, J., & Lieberman, J. (2012). Reading specialists and literacy coaches in secondary schools. In R. M. Bean & A. Swan Dagen (Eds.), *Best practices of literacy leaders: Keys to school improvement* (pp. 63–85). Guilford Press.

Ippolito, J., & Lieberman, J. (2020). Literacy coaches as literacy leaders. In A. Swan Dagen & R. M. Bean (Eds.), *Best practices of literacy leaders: Keys to school improvement* (2nd ed., pp. 69–88). Guilford Press.

Jacobs, J., Boardman, A., Potvin, A., & Wang, C. (2018). Understanding teacher resistance to instructional coaching. *Professional Development in Education, 44*(5), 690–703.

Jakob, E., Porter, A., Podos, J., Braun, B., Johnson, N., & Vessey, S. (2010, December 5). How to fail in grant writing. *The Chronicle of Higher Education. www.chronicle.com/article/how-to-fail-in-grant-writing*

Jerald, C. (2005, August). *The implementation trap: Helping schools overcome barriers to change* [Policy brief]. The Center for Comprehensive School Reform and Improvement. *https://files.eric.ed.gov/fulltext/ED494092.pdf*

Jewett, L. (2022, September 12). Teachers as advocates and leaders of the profession. *Homeroom: The Official Blog of the U.S. Department of Education. https://blog.ed.gov/2022/09/teachers-as-advocates-and-leaders-of-the-profession*

Johnson, D. T., Boyce, L. N., & VanTassel-Baska, J. (1995). Science curriculum review: Evaluating materials for high-ability learners. *Gifted Child Quarterly, 39*(1), 36–42.

Johnson, D. W., & Johnson, F. P. (2003). *Joining together: Group theory and group skills* (8th ed.). Allyn-Bacon.

Jung, E., & Zhang, Y. (2016). Parental involvement, children's aspirations, and achievement in new immigrant families. *The Journal of Educational Research, 109*(4), 333–350.

Kaner, S. (Ed.). (2014). *Facilitator's guide to participatory decision-making* (3rd ed.). Jossey-Bass.

Kegan, R. (1998). *In over our heads: The mental demands of modern life.* Harvard University Press.

Kennedy, J. F. (1963). *Address in the Assembly Hall at the Paulskirche in Frankfurt.* Available at *www.presidency.ucsb.edu/documents/address-the-assembly-hall-the-paulskirche-frankfurt*

Kiili, C., Lakkala, M., Ilomäki, L., Toom, A., Coiro, J., Hämäläinen, E., & Sormunen, E. (2021). Designing classroom practices for teaching online inquiry: Experiences from the field. *Journal of Adolescent & Adult Literacy, 65*(4), 297–308.

Killion, J. (2008). Are you coaching heavy or light? *Teachers Teaching Teachers, 3*(8), 1–4.

Killion, J. (2010). Reprising coaching heavy and coaching light. *Learning Forward, 6*(4), 8–9.

Killion, J., & Harrison, C. (2017). *Taking the lead: New roles for teachers and school-based coaches* (2nd ed.). Learning Forward.

Kim, J. S., Burkhauser, M. A., Quinn, D. M., Guryan, J., Kingston, H. C., & Aleman, K. (2017). Effectiveness of structured teacher adaptations to an evidence-based summer literacy program. *Reading Research Quarterly, 52*(4), 443–467.

Kinnucan-Welsch, K., Rosemary, C. A., & Grogan, P. R. (2006). Accountability by design in literacy professional development. *The Reading Teacher, 59*(5), 426–435.

Knight, J. (2016). *Better conversations: Coaching ourselves and each other to be more credible, caring, and connected.* Corwin Press.

Knight, J. (2017). *The impact cycle: What instructional coaches should do to foster powerful improvements in teaching.* Corwin Press.

Knight, J. (2019). Instructional coaching for implementing visible learning: A model for translating research into practice. *Education Sciences, 9*(2), 1–16. http://files.eric.ed.gov/fulltext/EJ1220410.pdf

Knight, J. (Host). (2024). Art Costa & Bob Garmston. *Coaching conversations with Jim Knight* [Audio podcast]. Apple Podcasts. http://podcasts.apple.com/au/podcast/art-costa-bob-garmston/id1649791348?i=1000638305772

Knowles, M. S., Holton, E. F., III, Swanson, R. A., & Robinson, P. A. (2020). *The adult learner: The definitive classic in adult education and human resource development* (9th ed.). Routledge.

Kraft, M. A., & Blazar, D. (2017). Individualized coaching to improve teacher practice across grades and subjects: New experimental evidence. *Educational Policy, 31*(7), 1033–1068.

Kraft, M. A., Blazar, D., & Hogan, D. (2018). The effect of teacher coaching on instruction and achievement: A meta-analysis of the causal evidence. *Review of Educational Research, 88*(4), 547–588.

Lazar, A. M., Edwards, P. A., & McMillon, G. T. (2012). *Bridging literacy and equity: The essential guide to social equity teaching.* Teachers College Press.

Leana, C. R. (2011). The missing link in school reform. *Stanford Social Innovation Review, 9*(4), 30–35.

Leana, C. R., & Pil, F. K. (2006). Social capital and organizational performance: Evidence from urban public schools. *Organization Science, 17*(3), 353–366.

Learning Forward. (n.d.). *Action guide for the coach: Standards for professional learning.* https://standards.learningforward.org/wp-content/uploads/sites/29/2022/04/coach-action-guide-1.pdf

Learning Forward. (2015, February). 3 steps to great coaching: A simple but powerful instructional coaching cycle nets results. *The Learning Professional.* https://learningforward.org/journal/february-2015-issue/3-steps-to-great-coaching

Leithwood, K., & Jantzi, D. (2008). Linking leadership to student learning: The contributions of leader efficacy. *Educational Administration Quarterly, 44*(4), 496–528.

Lencioni, P. (2002). *The five dysfunctions of a team: A leadership fable.* Jossey-Bass.

Leonhardt, D. (2024, January 7). The misguided war on the SAT. *The New York Times.* www.nytimes.com/2024/01/07/briefing/the-misguided-war-on-the-sat.html

Long, C. (2023, March 30). Standardized testing is still failing students. *NEA Today.* www.nea.org/nea-today/all-news-articles/standardized-testing-still-failing-students

Lortie, D. C. (1975). *Schoolteacher: A sociological study* (2nd ed.). University of Chicago Press.

Louis, K. S., Leithwood, K., Wahlstrom, K. L., & Anderson, S. E. (2010). *Investigating the links to improved student learning: Final report of research findings.* The University of Minnesota, University of Toronto, and The Wallace Foundation. https://conservancy.umn.edu/server/api/core/bitstreams/a72a3b69-ce13-4a9e-9e3e-210055524eaf/content

Mangin, M. M., & Dunsmore, K. (2015). How the framing of instructional coaching as a lever for systemic or individual reform influences the enactment of coaching. *Educational Administration Quarterly, 51*(2), 179–213.

Mapp, K. L., & Bergman, E. (2019). *The dual capacity-building framework for family–school partnerships* (Version 2). www.dualcapacity.org

Matsumura, L. C., Garnier, H. E., & Spybrook, J. (2013). Literacy coaching to improve student reading achievement: A multi-level mediation model. *Learning and Instruction, 25,* 35–48.

Matsumura, L. C., Sartoris, M., Bickel, D. D., & Garnier, H. (2009). Leadership for literacy coaching: The principal's role in launching a new coaching program. *Educational Administration Quarterly, 45*(5), 655–693.

McDonald, J. P., & Cities and Schools Research Group. (2024). *American school reform: What works, what fails, and why.* University of Chicago Press.

McDonald, J. P., Mohr, N., Dichter, A., & McDonald, E. C. (2013). *The power of protocols: An educator's guide to better practice* (3rd ed.). Teachers College Press.

McDonald, J. P., Zydney, J. M., Dichter, A., & McDonald, E. C. (2012). *Going online with protocols: New tools for teaching and learning.* Teachers College Press.

McKenna, M. C., & Walpole, S. (2008). *The literacy coaching challenge: Models and methods for grades K–8.* Guilford Press.

McLaughlin, M. W. (1990). The RAND change agent study revisited: Macro perspectives and micro realities. *Educational Researcher, 19*(9), 11–16.

McTighe, J. (2019). *Designing authentic performance tasks and projects: Tools for meaningful learning and assessment.* ASCD.

Meader, D. (2019, March 7). *9 tips for textbook adoption.* ThoughtCo. www.thoughtco.com/suggestions-to-guide-textbook-adoption-3194692

Messina, L. (2013). Disciplinary literacy in practice: The disciplinary literacy network as vehicle for strengthening instruction across content areas. In J. Ippolito, J. F. Lawrence, & C. Zaller (Eds.), *Adolescent literacy in the era of the Common Core: From research into practice* (pp. 37–60). Harvard Education Press.

Mezirow, J. (2000). *Learning as transformation: Critical perspectives on a theory in progress.* Jossey-Bass.

Miller, A. (2020, January 3). *Creating effective professional learning communities.* Edutopia. www.edutopia.org/article/creating-effective-professional-learning-communities

Mindlin, C. (2024, March 8). Digital literacy can close or widen economic and academic inequality. *Pittsburgh Post-Gazette.* www.post-gazette.com/opinion/guest-columns/2024/03/08/digital-internet-access-economic-inequality-casey-mindlin/stories/202402140004

Moje, E. B. (2015). Doing and teaching disciplinary literacy with adolescent learners: A social and cultural enterprise. *Harvard Educational Review, 85*(2), 254–278.

Moll, L. (2000). The diversity of schooling: A cultural-historical approach. In M. Reyes & J. Halcon (Eds.), *The best for our children: Critical perspectives on literacy for Latino students* (pp. 29–47). Teachers College Press.

Morrow, L. M., Morrell, E., & Casey, H. K. (Eds.). (2023). *Best practices in literacy instruction* (7th ed.). Guilford Press.

Munson, J., & Saclarides, E. S. (2022). Getting a foot in the door: Examining content-focused coaches' strategies for gaining access to classrooms. *The Elementary School Journal, 123*(1), 128–154.

Munson, J., & Saclarides, E. S. (2023, September 25). How coaches get in. *Kappan, 105*(2), 32–36.

Nalkur, P. (2024a). The JEDI coach: Embracing inclusivity. *Coaching Today, 50,* 8–13.

Nalkur, P. (2024b). *Stumbling towards inclusion: Finding grace in imperfect leadership.* Amplify Publishing.

Nash, J. B. (2019). *Design thinking in schools: A leader's guide to collaborating for improvement.* Harvard Education Press.

National Center for Literacy Education. (2014). *Remodeling literacy learning together: Paths to standards implementation.* National Council of Teachers of English. https://cdn.ncte.org/nctefiles/ncle/2014-ncle-report.pdf

National Council for the Social Studies. (n.d.). *NCSS social studies standards.* www.socialstudies.org/standards

National Council of Teachers of Mathematics. (n.d.). *NCTM standards.* www.nctm.org/Standards-and-Positions/NCTM-Standards

National Education Association. (n.d.). *Wraparound services: An NEA policy brief.*

National Science Teaching Association. (n.d.). *Science standards.* www.nsta.org/science-standards

National Youth Rights Association. (n.d.). *Student bill of rights.* www.youthrights.org/issues/student-rights/student-bill-of-rights

Nelson, N., Cook, S., Caudle, T., Orozco, K., & Graupman, K. (2020). *Comprehensive assessment plan.* Coeur d'Alene Public Schools. www.cdaschools.org/documents/departments/assessments/welcome/607050

New Teacher Center. (2018). *Continuum of instructional coaching practice.* https://newteachercenter.org/wp-content/uploads/2021/07/Cont-of-IC-Practice_RB21.pdf

Nielson, D. C., Barry, A. L., & Staab, P. T. (2008). Teachers' reflections on professional change during a literacy-reform initiative. *Teaching and Teacher Education, 24*(5), 1288–1303.

OECD. (2023, December 5). *PISA 2022 results (Volume II): Learning during—and from—disruption.* OECD Publishing. www.oecd-ilibrary.org/education/pisa-2022-results-volume-ii_a97db61c-en

Opper, I. M. (2019, December 4). *Teachers matter: Understanding teachers' impact on student achievement.* RAND. www.rand.org/pubs/research_reports/RR4312.html

Paratore, J., Steiner, L. M., & Dougherty, S. M. (2020). Developing effective home–school literacy partnerships. In A. Swan Dagen & R. M. Bean (Eds.), *Best practices of literacy leaders: Keys to school improvement* (2nd ed., pp. 346–363). Guilford Press.

Pendhankar, E. (2023, April 18). Equity audits in school districts: An explainer. *Education Week.* www.edweek.org/leadership/equity-audits-in-school-districts-an-explainer/2023/04

Pennsylvania Department of Education. (2016, December). *The framework for instructional coach endorsement guidelines.* www.education.pa.gov/Documents/Teachers-Administrators/Certification%20Preparation%20Programs/Specific%20Program%20Guidelines/Instructional%20Coach%20Endorsement%20Guidelines.pdf

Pennsylvania Department of Education. (2019). *Pennsylvania state literacy plan.* www.education.pa.gov/Documents/Teachers-Administrators/Curriculum/ELA/PaSLP/PaSLP%20Final.pdf

Peterson, D. S., Taylor, B. M., Burnham, B., & Schock, R. (2009). Reflective coaching conversations: A missing piece. *The Reading Teacher, 62*(6), 500–509.

Pierce, J. D. (2019, November 1). How good coaches build alliance with teachers. *Educational Leadership, 77*(3), 78–82. www.ascd.org/el/articles/how-good-coaches-build-alliance-with-teachers

Piper, B., & Zuilkowski, S. S. (2015). Teacher coaching in Kenya: Examining instructional support in public and nonformal schools. *Teaching and Teacher Education, 47,* 173–183.

PowerSchool. (2023, November 16). *The PLC handbook for educators: Unlocking professional learning communities.* www.powerschool.com/blog/plc-handbook

Preston, B. C., & Donohoo, J. (2021). It's not collective efficacy if it's easy. *Educational Leadership, 79*(3), 27–31.

Printy, S. (2008). Leadership for teacher learning: A community of practice perspective. *Educational Administration Quarterly, 44*(2), 187–226.

Rainville, K. N., & Jones, S. (2008). Situated identities: Power and positioning in the work of a literacy coach. *The Reading Teacher, 61*(6), 440–448.

Reed, M. (2015). To find solutions, look inward. *Educational Leadership, 72*(9), 80–85.

Reeves, D. (2023). *Fearless coaching: Resilience and results from the classroom to the boardroom.* Archway Publishing.

Risko, V. J., & Vogt, M. E. (2016). *Professional learning in action: An inquiry approach for teachers of literacy.* Teachers College Press.

Robbins, P. (1991). *How to implement a peer coaching program.* ASCD.

Robertson, D. A., Ford-Connors, E., Frahm, T., Bock, K., & Paratore, J. R. (2020a). Unpacking productive coaching interactions: Identifying coaching approaches that support instructional uptake. *Professional Development in Education, 46*(3), 405–423.

Robertson, D. A., Padesky, L. B., Ford-Connors, E., & Paratore, J. R. (2020b). What does it mean to say coaching is relational? *Journal of Literacy Research, 52*(1), 55–78.

Rothstein, A. L. (2019). *Creating winning grant proposals: A step-by-step guide.* Guilford Press.

Russell, J. L., Correnti, R., Stein, M. K., Thomas, A., Bill, V., & Speranzo, L. (2020). Mathematics coaching for conceptual understanding: Promising evidence regarding the Tennessee math coaching model. *Educational Evaluation and Policy Analysis, 42*(3), 439–466.

Saclarides, E. S. (2022). Reflecting on the past and looking ahead: An exploration of coach–teacher talk during reflection meetings. *School Science and Mathematics, 122*(4), 195–208.

Saclarides, E. S., & Munson, J. (2021). Exploring the foci and depth of coach–teacher interactions during modeled lessons. *Teaching and Teacher Education, 105*, 103418. https://doi.org/10.1016/j.tate.2021.103418

Saclardies, E. S., & Munson, J. (2024). Forces that shape coaches' classroom access. *The Learning Professional, 45*(4), 68–71.

Safir, S. (2017). *The listening leader: Creating the conditions for equitable school transformation.* Jossey-Bass.

Safir, S., & Dugan, J. (2021). *Street data: A next-generation model for equity, pedagogy, and school transformation.* Corwin Press.

Scharmer, C. O. (2009). *Theory U: Learning from the future as it emerges.* Berrett-Koehler.

Schein, E. H. (2010). *Organizational culture and leadership* (4th ed.). Jossey-Bass.

Schildkamp, K. (2019). Data-based decision-making for school improvement: Research insights and gaps. *Educational Research, 61*(3), 257–273. www.tandfonline.com/doi/full/10.1080/00131881.2019.1625716

Schmoker, M. (2011). *Elevating the essentials to radically improve student learning.* ASCD.

Schön, D. A., & Rein, M. (1994). *Frame reflection: Toward the resolution of intractable policy controversies.* Basic Books.

Schwanke, J. (2024). The principal as mentor and coach. *Educational Leadership, 82*(1), 28–33.

Schwartz, H. L., McCombs, J. S., Augustine, C. H., & Leschitz, J. T. (2018). *Getting to work on summer learning.* RAND Corporation.

Shanahan, C., & Shanahan, T. (2014). Does disciplinary literacy have a place in elementary school? *The Reading Teacher, 67*(8), 636–639.

Shanahan, T., & Shanahan, C. (2008). Teaching disciplinary literacy to adolescents: Rethinking content-area literacy. *Harvard Educational Review, 78*(1), 40–59.

Shanahan, T., & Shanahan, C. (2012). What is disciplinary literacy and why does it matter? *Topics in Language Disorders, 32*(1), 7–18.

Shand, R., & Batts, J. (2023). Toward more inclusive professional learning communities. *Journal of Education Human Resources, 41*(1), 110–141.

Singleton, G. E. (2014). *Courageous conversations about race: A field guide for achieving equity in schools*. Corwin Press.

Spangler, D. (2023a, June 14). *7 ways to measure instructional coaching for impact, not activity*. SmartBrief. www.smartbrief.com/original/7-ways-to-measure-instructional-coaching-for-impact-not-activity

Spangler, D. (2023b, October 10). *PLC coaching: 12 ways to achieve effective results*. SmartBrief. www.smartbrief.com/original/plc-coaching-impact-cycle

Stanford d.school. (2024). Getting started with design thinking for K12. https://dschool.stanford.edu/resources-collections/getting-started-with-design-thinking

Steiner, D., Magee, J., & Jensen, B. (2019, January). *High-quality curriculum and system improvement*. Learning First and Johns Hopkins Institute for Education Policy. https://jscholarship.library.jhu.edu/bitstream/handle/1774.2/62966/Quality-curriculum-and-system-improvement.pdf

Steinbacher-Reed, C., & Rotella, S. A. (2017). Windows into instructional practice. *Educational Leadership, 74*(8), 68–72. https://ascd.org/el/articles/windows-into-instructional-practice

Stiggins, R. J. (2014). Improve assessment literacy outside of schools too. *Phi Delta Kappan, 96*(2), 67–72.

Stiggins, R. (2017). *The perfect assessment system*. ASCD.

Supovitz, J., Sirinides, P., & May, H. (2010). How principals and peers influence teaching and learning. *Educational Administration Quarterly, 46*(1), 31–56.

Swan Dagen, A., & Bean, R. M. (2014). High-quality, research-based professional development: An essential for enhancing high-quality teaching. In L. E. Martin, S. Kragler, D. J. Quatroche, & K. L. Bauserman (Eds.). *Handbook of professional development in education: Successful models and practices, preK–12* (pp. 42–63). Guilford Press.

Swan Dagen, A., & Bean, R. M. (Eds.). (2020). *Best practices of literacy leaders: Keys to school improvement* (2nd ed.). Guilford Press.

Sweeney, D., & Harris, L. S. (2016). *Student-centered coaching: The moves*. Corwin Press.

Taylor, B. M. (2011). *Catching schools: An action guide to schoolwide reading improvement*. Heinemann.

Thiers, N. (2017, September 1). Unlocking families' potential: A conversation with Karen L. Mapp. *Educational Leadership, 75*(1), 40–44. www.ascd.org/el/articles/unlocking-families-potential-a-conversation-with-karen-l.-mapp

Thomas, S., S., Knight, J., Harris, M., & Hoffman, A. (2022). *Evaluating instructional coaching: People, programs, and partnerships*. ASCD.

Timperley, H. (2008). *Teacher professional learning and development*. International Academy of Education. www.iaoed.org/downloads/EdPractices_18.pdf

Timperley, H. (2010). *Using evidence in the classroom for professional learning* [Paper presentation]. Ontario Education Research Symposium, Toronto, Canada. https://cdn.auckland.ac.nz/assets/education/about/schools/tchldv/docs/Using%20Evidence%20in%20the%20Classroom%20for%20Professional%20Learning.pdf

Toll, C. A. (2006). Separating coaching from supervising. *Teachers Teaching Teachers, 2*(4), 1–4.

Tomasic, M. (2024, January 6). "Terribly broken": Pittsburgh-area superintendents frustrated over standardized tests. *Pittsburgh Post-Gazette*. www.post-gazette.com/news/education/2024/01/06/pittsburgh-superintendents-standardized-testing/stories/202401040105

Torgeson, J. K., & Miller, D. H. (2009). *Assessments to guide adolescent literacy instruction*. RMC Research Corporation, Center on Instruction.

Ulenski, A., Gill, M., & Kelley, M. (2019). Developing and validating the Elementary Literacy Coach Self-Efficacy Survey. *The Teacher Educator, 54*(3), 225–243.

Vanderburg, M., & Stephens, D. (2009). What teachers say they changed because of their coach and how they think their coach helped them. *Literacy Coaching Clearinghouse.* http://files.eric.ed.gov/fulltext/ED530297.pdf

Vanderburg, M., & Stephens, D. (2010). The impact of literacy coaches: What teachers value and how teachers change. *The Elementary School Journal, 111*(1), 141–163.

Vangrieken, K., Grosemans, I., Dochy, F., & Kyndt, E. (2017). Teacher autonomy and collaboration: A paradox? Conceptualising and measuring teachers' autonomy and collaborative attitude. *Teaching and Teacher Education, 67,* 302–315. https://doi.org/10.1016/j.tate.2017.06.021

Van Soelen, T. M. (2021). *Meeting goals: Protocols for leading effective, purpose-driven discussion in schools.* Solution Tree Press.

Venables, D. R. (2017). *Facilitating teacher teams and authentic PLCs: The human side of leading people, protocols, and practices.* ASCD.

Vescio, V., Ross, D., & Adams, A. (2008). A review of research on the impact of professional learning communities on teaching practice and student learning. *Teaching and Teacher Education, 24*(1), 80–91.

Visscher, A. J. (2021). On the value of data-based decision making in education: The evidence from six intervention studies. *Studies in Educational Evaluation, 69,* Article 100899. https://doi.org/10.1016/j.stueduc.2020.100899

Wagner, T., Kegan, R., Lahey, L. L., Lemons, R. W., Garnier, J., Helsing, D., et al. (2012). *Change leadership: A practical guide to transforming our schools.* John Wiley & Sons.

Walker-Dalhouse, D., & Risko, V. J. (2020). Culturally responsive literacy instruction. In A. Swan Dagen & R. M. Bean (Eds.), *Best practices of literacy leaders: Keys to school improvement* (2nd ed., pp. 304–322). Guilford Press.

Walker-Dalhouse, D., & Risko, V. J. (2024). *Equitable literacy instruction for students in poverty.* Teachers College Press.

Walpole, S., & Beauchat, K. A. (2008). Facilitating teacher study groups. *Literacy Coaching Clearinghouse.* http://files.eric.ed.gov/fulltext/ED530302.pdf

Warren, M. (2005). Communities and schools: A new view of urban education reform. *Harvard Educational Review, 75*(2), 133–173.

Wasley, P. A., Hampel, R. L., & Clark, R. W. (1997). *Kids and school reform.* Jossey-Bass.

Welch, S. (2010). *10-10-10: A fast and powerful way to get unstuck in love, at work, and with your family.* Scribner.

West, L., & Staub, F. C. (2003). *Content-focused coaching: Transforming mathematics lessons.* Heinemann.

Wiener, R., & Pimentel, S. (2017). *Practice what you teach: Connecting curriculum and professional learning in schools.* The Aspen Institute. www.aspeninstitute.org/wp-content/uploads/2017/04/Practice-What-You-Teach.pdf

Wilder, P. (2013). *"I can only cognitively coach so much": Heavy coaching efforts amidst disciplinary complexities in secondary school classrooms* [Dissertation]. University of Illinois at Urbana–Champaign.

Woulfin, S. L. (2020). Crystallizing coaching: An examination of the institutionalization of instructional coaching in three educational systems. *Teachers College Record, 122*(10), 1–32.

Woulfin, S. L., & Rigby, J. G. (2017). Coaching for coherence: How instructional coaches lead change in the evaluation era. *Educational Researcher, 46*(6), 323–328.

Woulfin, S. L., Stevenson, I., & Lord, K. (2023). *Making coaching matter: Leading continuous improvement in schools.* Teachers College Press.

Zigmond, N., Bean, R. M., Kloo, A., & Brydon, M. (2011). Policy, research, and reading first. In A. McGill-Franzen & R. L. Allington (Eds.), *Handbook of reading disability research* (pp. 464–476). Routledge.

Zoch, M. (2015). Growing the good stuff: One literacy coach's approach to support teachers with high-stakes testing. *Journal of Literacy Research, 47*(3), 328–369.

# Index

Accountability, 142, 145, 151–152, 154, 162
Action plans, 164f, 168–172, 170f, 251–253
Adaptive change agents, 14–15. *See also* Change agent mindset
Administrative leaders, 50–51, 161, 177–178. *See also* Leadership; Principals
Adult learning and development, 27–29, 65–67, 128. *See also* Professional learning for coaches; Professional learning for teachers; Teacher learning
Advocate mindset. *See also* Coaching mindsets
   advocating for community partnerships, 37–38
   advocating for particular practices, models, and programs, 38–39
   advocating for students, 36
   advocating for teachers, 36–37
   assessment and, 145
   community resources and, 189–190
   curriculum and materials and, 177–178
   one-on-one coaching with teachers and, 110
   overview, 12–14, 13f, 21, 35–39, 198
   schoolwide learning and changes and, 160
   self-reflection and, 206
Agenda use
   benefits of, 82
   group coaching and, 120, 124, 129
   high-leverage coaching moves and, 79–80
   overview, 58
Analysis of observations, 97f, 102–104. *See also* Observation
Apps on smart devices. *See* Technology tools
Artificial intelligence, 3, 173–174. *See also* Technology tools
Assessment of students. *See also* Data-based decision making; Needs assessment
   Analysis of State and District Assessments form, 246
   designer mindset and, 33
   example illustrating with an elementary math coach, 216–219
   facilitating conversations regarding, 81–82
   formative assessments, 145–146
   high-stakes assessments and, 142–145
   intensity in coaching and, 30t
   overview, 138–139, 140–146, 141f, 154–155
   problem solving and, 81
   purposes of, 142
   school and district improvement and, 151–154
   self-study and professional learning and, 247–248
   using data to improve classroom instruction and, 128, 146–154, 147f, 148f
Assistant principals, 59–60. *See also* Leadership
Audio-recorded lessons, 100–101. *See also* Recording lessons

## B

Balanced stance, 107, 109, 209–216
BDA (<u>b</u>efore, <u>d</u>uring, and <u>a</u>fter) cycle of consultation, 230
Beliefs regarding coaching, 3–12, 17
Belonging, 51–54
Benefits of coaching, 5, 6–7, 115–117
Bias, 52–53, 184
Bill of Assessment Rights, 150–151
Book clubs, 132, 184

## C

Calendars, coaching, 55–56, 77
Capacity, educator. *See also* Professional learning for teachers; Teachers
   benefits of coaching and, 6–7
   collaboration and, 50–51
   content of coaching work and, 8
   designer mindset and, 32
   example of a school change initiative and, 60
   facilitator mindset and, 31
   small-group coaching and, 125

277

Case examples. *See* Examples illustrating coaching
Cell phones. *See* Technology tools
Change agent mindset. *See also* Coaching mindsets
  building a collaborative culture and, 44–45
  group coaching and, 116–117
  one-on-one coaching with teachers and, 110
  overview, 12–15, 13*f*, 21–25, 198
  post-observation/debriefing conversation, 106–107
  self-reflection and, 206
Checklists, 99, 124, 146, 173
Classroom learning walks, 30*t*, 114, 133–134, 134*f*
Classrooms, visiting informally, 82–83. *See also* Conversations; Observation; One-on-one coaching
Coaching cycles, 89, 97. *See also* Group coaching; Observation cycle of coaching; One-on-one coaching
Coaching mindsets. *See also* Advocate mindset; Change agent mindset; Designer mindset; Examples illustrating coaching; Facilitator mindset
  importance of, 14–15
  note-taking organizers and, 235–240
  overview, 11–17, 12*f*, 13*f*, 20–21, 39
  self-reflection and, 206
Collaboration
  avoiding the expertise trap and, 66
  change agent mindset and, 23
  culture of, 44–45, 59–60, 61
  designer mindset and, 33
  example of a school change initiative, 60
  grant writing and, 193
  high-stakes assessments and, 144–145
  intensity in coaching and, 30*t*
  large-group coaching and, 128–129
  organizational change to improve instruction and, 50–51
  principals' support of coaching and, 55–57
  problem solving and, 32, 149–150
  supporting the development of PLCs and, 131–135
Collaborative inquiry, 11, 134–135. *See also* Inquiry
Communication. *See also* Conversations; Discussion-based approaches; Listening
  co-planning conversations and, 81
  developing relationships with teachers and, 77, 78*f*, 84
  group coaching and, 119–120
  home–school communication, 182, 185–189
  instructional leadership teams (ILTs) and, 162, 163*f*
  between principals and coaches, 56, 58
  questioning techniques and, 68–70
  with teachers, 67–71, 70*f*
Community agreements, 117–119, 117*f*
Community engagement. *See also* School–community partnership
  community resources and, 189–192
  importance of, 182–183
  overview, 181, 194
  school culture and, 183–185, 184*f*
  volunteer opportunities in the school and, 182, 187–188

Computers. *See* Technology tools
Content and Coaching in Context (CCIC) Framework, 11–12, 12*f*. *See also* Coaching mindsets
Content of coaching work, 8–9, 231
Content-area teams, 24, 28, 29, 32–33, 121. *See also* Subject-area teams; Teams
Context of coaching work, 9–10, 216. *See also* Systems
Conversations. *See also* Communication; Discussion-based approaches; Feedback
  analysis of the observation and, 102–103
  family and community engagement and, 183, 184*f*
  instructional leadership teams (ILTs) and, 162, 163*f*
  large-group coaching and, 128
  learning walks and, 134*f*
  modeling and, 91
  observation and, 96–97, 105
  post-observation/debriefing conversation, 97*f*, 104–110, 244–245
  pre-observation/planning conversation, 97*f*, 98
Co-planning, 3–11, 30*t*, 81, 89, 92, 95. *See also* Communication; Discussion-based approaches; Planning
Co-teaching, 30*t*, 89, 92–95, 110
COVID-19, 3, 22, 173–174
Credibility, 66, 77, 79, 93
Culture, 43–44, 52–53, 116. *See also* School culture
Curriculum
  advocating for, 38–39, 177–178
  content of coaching work and, 8–9
  designer mindset and, 32–33
  developing or selecting, 172–178
  diversity, equity, and belonging and, 53
  elementary compared to secondary coaching and, 8
  family and community engagement and, 184–185
  group coaching and, 117
  high-stakes assessments and, 144
  large-group coaching and, 128
  needs assessment and, 163–164
  problem solving and, 80
  stance and positionality of coaches and, 26
Curriculum directors/coordinators. *See* Leadership
Cycles of coaching, 89, 97. *See also* Coaching cycles; Group coaching; Observation cycle of coaching; One-on-one coaching

# D

Data analysis, 164*f*, 167–168
Data collection, 164*f*, 166–167, 234
Data sources, 164*f*, 165–166
Data teams, 133, 147–148, 148*f*, 149–150, 152–153
Data walks. *See* Learning walks
Data-based decision making. *See also* Assessment of students; Decision making; Needs assessment
  example of a school change initiative, 60
  needs assessment and, 164*f*
  overview, 51

school culture and, 147f, 154
using data to improve classroom instruction and, 146–154, 147f, 148f
Data-focused coaching work, 81–82, 99–101, 100f, 216–219. *See also* Assessment of students
Debriefing conversation, 97f, 102, 104–110, 134f, 244–245. *See also* Conversations; Observation
Decision making. *See also* Instructional decision making
  group coaching and, 121, 124–125
  involving families in, 182, 188
  using data for, 51, 60
Descriptive approaches, 96, 99, 100f
Designer mindset. *See also* Coaching mindsets
  assessment and, 145
  group coaching and, 119
  one-on-one coaching with teachers and, 87–88, 110
  organizational change to improve instruction and, 50–51
  overview, 12–14, 13f, 21, 32–35
  self-reflection and, 206
Development, adult, 27–29, 128
Differentiation, 27–29, 175
Digital devices. *See* Technology tools
Directive stance
  example illustrating the evolution of a coach, 209–216
  facilitator mindset and, 26, 31
  observation and, 103
  post-observation/debriefing conversation and, 106–107, 109
Discussion-based approaches. *See also* Communication; Conversations
  agenda use and, 80
  co-planning conversations and, 81
  data-team meetings and, 149
  group coaching and, 119–120
  intensity in coaching and, 30t
  overview, 71, 72–74, 84
District improvement, 151–154. *See also* Systemwide instructional change
District-based leaders. *See* Leadership
Diversity, 3, 51–54, 183–185, 184f

# E

Early childhood education, 190
Elementary school instruction, 8, 26, 82, 94
Engagement, 120, 129, 175. *See also* Community engagement; Family engagement
Equity
  at the core of a school's mission/vision, 51–54
  facilitator mindset and, 31
  group coaching and, 118–119
  needs assessment and, 164
  technology as a tool and, 174
Examples illustrating coaching
  evolution of a coach, 209–216
  instructional coach liaison, 224–228
  part-time instructional coach who also teaches, 219–224
  Pennsylvania Institute for Instructional Coaching and, 229–234
  school-based elementary math coach, 216–219
Expertise, 65–67, 84, 106–107, 197–202. *See also* Directive stance

# F

Facilitator mindset. *See also* Coaching mindsets
  assessment and, 145
  avoiding the expertise trap and, 65–67
  communication with teachers and, 67–71, 70f
  discussion-based protocols and, 72–74
  high-leverage coaching moves and, 79–83
  instructional leadership teams (ILTs) and, 161
  one-on-one coaching with teachers and, 87–88, 110
  overview, 12–14, 13f, 21, 25–32, 30t, 84
  self-reflection and, 206
  stance and positionality of coaches and, 25–27
Family engagement. *See also* School–community partnership
  community resources and, 189–192
  home–school communication and, 53–54, 182, 185–189
  importance of, 182–183
  overview, 181, 194
  school culture and, 183–185, 184f
Feedback. *See also* Conversations
  for coaches, 56, 202, 205–206
  communication with teachers and, 70–71
  following large-group coaching, 130–131
  formative assessments and, 146
  observation and, 96, 104, 105–110
  supporting a culture of collaboration and, 59–60
  for teachers, 57
Focus, 49, 60, 98, 99, 102
Formative assessments, 145–146, 152. *See also* Assessment of students

# G

Goals. *See also* Mission/vision; Vision
  developing relationships with teachers and, 78f
  instructional leadership teams (ILTs) and, 162
  large-group coaching and, 129
  modeling and, 90–91
  needs assessment and, 164–165, 164f
  observation and, 98, 99, 102, 104
  organizational change to improve instruction and, 48–49
  set by students, 150–151
  small-group coaching and, 122, 125
Grade-level teams
  change agent mindset and, 24
  designer mindset and, 32–33

Grade-level teams *(cont.)*
   differentiating coaching and, 28
   group coaching and, 121
   intensity in coaching and, 29
   supporting the development of PLCs and, 133
Grant writing, 192–193
Group coaching. *See also* Large-group coaching; Professional learning communities (PLC); Small-group coaching; Teams
   benefits of, 115–117
   differentiating coaching and, 28
   discussion-based protocols and, 72–74
   facilitator mindset and, 31
   guidelines for, 117–121, 119*f*
   high-leverage coaching moves and, 79–80, 83
   instructional leadership teams (ILTs) and, 161–162
   intensity in coaching and, 29, 30*t*
   overview, 113–114, 135–136
   professional learning communities and, 131–135, 134*f*
   strategies for working with large groups, 128–131, 129*f*, 136
   strategies for working with small groups, 121–127, 123*f*

## H

High-stakes assessments, 142–145. *See also* Assessment of students
Home–school communication, 182, 185–189. *See also* Communication; Family engagement; Technology tools
Human capital, 45–47, 47*f*, 52
Hybrid learning. *See* Technology tools

## I

Implementation, 169–171, 170*f*
Individual coaching. *See* One-on-one coaching
Inequity, 51, 174. *See also* Equity
Informal classroom visits, 82–83. *See also* Conversations; Observation; One-on-one coaching; Relationships
Inquiry
   assessment and, 145
   avoiding the expertise trap and, 66
   change agent mindset and, 22, 23
   collaborative cycles of, 134–135
   collaborative inquiry, 11, 134–135
   facilitator mindset and, 31
   intensity in coaching and, 30*t*
   post-observation/debriefing conversation, 107
Instruction. *See also* Curriculum; Instructional decision making; Schoolwide learning; Systemwide instructional change; Teachers
   advocating for, 38–39
   assessment cycle and, 146–150, 147*f*, 148*f*
   content of coaching work and, 8–9
   designer mindset and, 32–33
   elementary compared to secondary coaching and, 8
   observation and, 96
   organizational change to improve, 47–51
   problem solving and, 80
   technology as a tool and, 173–177
   using data to improve, 146–154, 147*f*, 148*f*
Instructional decision making. *See also* Decision making; Instruction
   assessment and, 142, 143–144, 145–146, 151–152
   benefits of coaching and, 7
   intensity in coaching and, 30*t*
   using data to improve classroom instruction and, 146–154, 147*f*, 148*f*
Instructional improvement cycle, 146–150, 147*f*, 148*f*
Instructional leadership team (ILT). *See also* Schoolwide learning; Systemwide instructional change; Teams
   assessment and, 152–153
   coach's support of, 160–162, 163*f*
   differentiating coaching and, 28
   high-leverage coaching moves and, 83
   intensity in coaching and, 29
   overview, 178–179
   supporting the establishment of, 48
Instructional rounds. *See* Learning walks; Visiting classrooms
Instrumental learning, 28, 29, 108, 109
Intensity in coaching, 29–32, 30*t*, 74

## L

Language, 67–71, 70*f*
Large-group coaching, 128–131, 129*f*, 136. *See also* Group coaching
Large-scale assessment measures, 142–145. *See also* Assessment of students
Leadership. *See also* Principals
   advocating for programs or materials and, 177–178
   building a collaborative culture and, 44–45
   coaching mindsets and, 13
   data-team meetings and, 147–148
   distributing leadership across roles, 49–50
   expertise of coaches and, 197–198
   group leadership, 120
   high-stakes assessments and, 144–145
   importance of, 15–16
   leadership teams, 56–57, 152–153, 161
   organizational change to improve instruction and, 48–50
   school culture and, 61
   supporting a culture of collaboration, 59–60
Learning, adult, 14, 31. *See also* Professional learning for coaches; Professional learning for teachers; Teacher learning
Learning, student
   advocating for programs or materials and, 177–178
   assessment and, 142–143, 153, 154

developing or selecting curriculum and materials, 172–173
technology as a tool and, 173–177
Learning walks, 30*t*, 114, 133–134, 134*f*
Lesson Analysis Guide, 102, 244–245
Lesson planning. *See* Co-planning
Lesson study format, 133
Levels of Intensity model, 29–32, 30*t*, 74, 100–101
Libraries, local, 191
Listening. *See also* Communication
avoiding the expertise trap and, 66
communication with teachers and, 67–68
facilitator mindset and, 31
group coaching and, 119–120
post-observation/debriefing conversation, 107–108
tips for, 70*f*
Literacy assessment, 152–153, 154–155. *See also* Assessment of students

## M

Materials, 172–178, 184–185. *See also* Curriculum
Mentoring, 200, 230–231
Mindsets, coaching. *See* Coaching mindsets
Mirror, coach as, 107–108. *See also* Responsive stance
Mission/vision. *See also* Vision
coaching mindsets and, 13
diversity, equity, and belonging at the core of, 51–54
importance of, 15, 16
organizational change to improve instruction and, 48–49
school culture and, 61
Modeling, 89, 90–93, 110, 240
Multi-tiered systems of support (MTSS), 59–60, 147–148, 147*f*

## N

Needs assessment, 163–172, 164*f*, 170*f*. *See also* Assessment of students; Data-based decision making; Systemwide instructional change
Needs of adult learners, 27–29. *See also* Teachers
Needs of students, 3, 36. *See also* Diversity; Students
Nonverbal communication, 68. *See also* Communication
Note-taking, 68, 96, 108, 235–240

## O

Observation. *See also* Observation cycle of coaching
as assessment, 141*f*
facilitator mindset and, 31
learning walks and, 30*t*, 114, 133–134, 134*f*
modeling and, 91–92
Observation Protocol for Discipline-Specific Instruction form, 241–243
one-on-one coaching with teachers and, 89, 95–97

overview, 97*f*, 99–102, 100*f*, 110–111
small-group coaching and, 122
Observation cycle of coaching. *See also* Coaching cycles; Observation
analysis, 97*f*, 102–104
observation, 97*f*, 99–102, 100*f*
overview, 87, 97–98, 97*f*, 110
post-observation/debriefing conversation, 97*f*, 104–110
pre-observation/planning conversation, 97*f*, 98
One-on-one coaching. *See also* Individual needs; Teachers
co-teaching, 92–95
group coaching and, 116
modeling and, 90–92
observation and, 95–110, 97*f*, 100*f*
overview, 7–8, 87–90, 110–111
Online learning. *See* Technology tools
On-the-fly coaching, 82
Organizational culture. *See* Culture

## P

Parallel teaching, 93–94
Parents. *See* Family engagement
Partnerships, 66, 189–192. *See also* Collaboration; Community engagement; School–community partnership
Peer support and coaching, 107, 114, 119–120, 131–135, 200. *See also* Balanced stance
Pennsylvania Institute for Instructional Coaching (PIIC), 229–234
Planning, 79–80, 104–105. *See also* Co-planning; Pre-observation/planning conversation
Policy, 202
Positionality of coaches, 25–27, 36, 209–216
Post-COVID-19 era of education, 3, 22, 173–174
Post-observation/debriefing conversation, 97*f*, 102, 104–110, 134*f*, 244–245. *See also* Conversations; Observation
Pre-observation/planning conversation, 97*f*, 98. *See also* Conversations; Observation
Preschool education, 190
Presentations, 128–131, 129*f*. *See also* Large-group coaching
Principals. *See also* Leadership; Relationships
Coach's support of, 57–59
data-team meetings and, 147–148
instructional leadership teams (ILTs) and, 161
role of in supporting coaching, 55–57, 77, 226–227
school culture and, 54–59
supporting a culture of collaboration, 59–60
Problem-solution focus
avoiding the expertise trap and, 66
data-team meetings and, 149
designer mindset and, 32
distributing leadership across roles and, 49–50
high-leverage coaching moves and, 80–81
overview, 14

Problem-solving team meetings, 149–150
Professional learning communities (PLC). *See also* Group coaching
  collaborative cycles of inquiry and, 134–135
  high-leverage coaching moves and, 83
  intensity in coaching and, 30*t*
  overview, 114
  supporting the development of, 131–135, 134*f*
Professional learning for coaches
  focus of, 204–205
  knowledge that supports coaching and, 199–202
  lifelong learning focus and, 67
  overview, 4, 196–197, 206–207
  Pennsylvania Institute for Instructional Coaching and, 229–234
  principals and, 54
  reflective tools for coaches, 202–206, 204*f*
Professional learning for staff, 184
Professional learning for teachers. *See also* Teacher learning; Teachers
  Assessing Teacher Perceptions of Professional Learning Experiences form, 249–250
  assessment and, 154
  avoiding the expertise trap and, 65–67
  benefits of coaching and, 6–7
  coaching mindsets and, 14
  content of coaching work and, 9
  differentiating coaching and, 27–29
  discussion-based protocols and, 72–74
  example of a school change initiative and, 60
  family and community engagement and, 184
  importance of coaching and, 3
  large-group coaching and, 128–131, 129*f*
  lifelong learning focus and, 67
  problem solving and, 81
  schoolwide learning and changes and, 158–159
Progress monitoring, 145–146, 148*f*, 149

## Q

Questioning techniques. *See also* Communication
  analysis of the observation and, 102–103
  communication with teachers and, 68–70
  developing relationships with teachers and, 78*f*
  discussion-based protocols and, 72
  informal classroom visits and, 82–83
  instructional leadership teams (ILTs) and, 162, 163*f*

## R

Reading current research, 201–202
Recording lessons, 30*t*, 100–101, 121
Reflection
  assessment cycle and, 148*f*
  coaching mindsets and, 206
  keeping a journal and, 201
  modeling and, 91
  observation and, 97, 102–104
  post-observation/debriefing conversation, 107
  reflective tools for coaches, 202–206, 204*f*
Reflective log, 201, 204, 204*f*
Reflective practice, 14, 32, 48, 70. *See also* Reflection
Relationships. *See also* Administrative leaders; Community engagement; Examples illustrating coaching; Family engagement; Principals; Teachers
  advocating for teachers and, 37
  building a collaborative culture and, 44–45
  coaching mindsets and, 13
  developing with individual and groups of teachers, 74–79, 78*f*, 84
  diversity, equity, and belonging and, 53–54
  high-leverage coaching moves and, 79
  importance of, 15, 16, 226–227
  intensity in coaching and, 30*t*
  organizational change to improve instruction and, 50–51
  positionality of coaches and, 25–27
  school culture and, 45–46
Reluctant or resistant teachers, 75–77, 126. *See also* Teachers
Response to Intervention (RtI), 54, 59–60
Responsibilities of coaches, 4, 7–8, 44–45, 51–54
Responsive stance
  example illustrating the evolution of a coach, 209–216
  facilitator mindset and, 25–26, 31
  observation and, 103
  post-observation/debriefing conversation, 107–108, 109
Role of coaches. *See also* Advocate mindset; Assessment of students; Change agent mindset; Designer mindset; Facilitator mindset; Group coaching; One-on-one coaching
  building a collaborative culture and, 44–45
  compared to activity of coaching, 4
  data-team meetings and, 147–148
  developing relationships with teachers and, 77
  focusing on both individuals and systems and, 7–8
  grant writing and, 192–193
  instructional leadership teams (ILTs) and, 160–162, 163*f*
  organizational change to improve instruction and, 47–51
  overview, 226
  schoolwide learning and, 158–160
  using data to improve classroom instruction and, 146–154, 147*f*, 148*f*
Roles of group members, 122–123, 123*f*

## S

Schedules, coaching, 55–56, 77
School culture. *See also* School improvement; Schoolwide learning
  change agent mindset and, 24
  collaboration and, 59–60

data-based decision making and, 147, 147f, 154
diversity, equity, and belonging and, 53–54
diversity, equity, and belonging at the core of, 51–54
example of a school change initiative, 60–61
family and community engagement and, 183–185, 184f
group coaching and, 116, 124–125
importance of, 45–47, 47f
organizational change to improve instruction and, 47–51
overview, 42–45, 61
Pennsylvania Institute for Instructional Coaching and, 234
principals and, 54–59
shared leadership and, 44–45
School improvement. *See also* Needs assessment; School culture; Schoolwide learning; Systemwide instructional change
assessment data and, 151–154
coaching mindsets and, 11–17, 12f, 13f, 21–25
community partnerships and, 37
diversity, equity, and belonging and, 51–54
example of a school change initiative, 60–61
improving instruction and, 47–51
intensity in coaching and, 30t
partnering with principals and, 54–59
role of coaching in, 2–3
School–community partnership, 30t, 37–38, 45–46, 53–54, 189–192. *See also* Community engagement; Family engagement
School–university partnerships, 191–192
Schoolwide learning. *See also* Culture; Instruction; Instructional leadership team (ILT); School improvement; Systemwide instructional change
action planning and, 168–172, 170f
advocating for programs or materials and, 177–178
assessment data and, 147f, 152–153
coaching mindsets and, 26
developing or selecting curriculum and materials, 172–178
expertise of coaches and, 198
family and community engagement and, 183–185, 184f
group coaching and, 116–117
needs-assessment process and, 163–168, 164f
one-on-one coaching with teachers and, 89
overview, 157–160, 178–179
role of coaching in, 158–160
technology as a tool and, 173–177
Secondary grade instruction, 5, 8, 82, 94–95
Self-assessment, 147f, 150–151, 202–206, 204f, 254–257. *See also* Assessment of students
Self-authoring learning, 28, 29, 107, 109
Self-reflection, 107, 201, 206. *See also* Reflection
Slide presentations, 129–130, 129f. *See also* Large-group coaching; Presentations
Small-group coaching. *See also* Group coaching
benefits of, 117
collaborative cycles of inquiry and, 134–135
following large-group coaching, 130

during large-group coaching and, 128–129
overview, 136
strategies for, 121–127, 123f
Smart devices. *See* Technology tools
Social justice, 51, 118–119. *See also* Equity
Social-emotional learning (SEL), 3
Socializing learning, 28, 29, 107, 109
Specialists, 147–148
Staff, 45, 183–184, 184f. *See also* Assistant principals; Leadership; Principals; Teachers
Standardized assessments, 142–145. *See also* Assessment of students
Standards
coaching mindsets and, 24, 33, 34
knowledge that supports coaching and, 200
needs assessment and, 164–165, 164f
schoolwide learning and changes and, 159
using data to improve classroom instruction and, 150
Standards for Professional Learning, 158
Students, 3, 36, 147f, 150–151. *See also* Assessment of students; Diversity; Learning, student
Subject-area teams, 24, 28, 29, 32–33, 121
Summative assessments, 142–145, 151–152. *See also* Assessment of students
Systems, 7–8, 13, 15, 17, 216. *See also* Systemwide instructional change
Systemwide instructional change. *See also* Instruction; Instructional leadership team (ILT); School improvement; Schoolwide learning
action planning and, 168–172, 170f
advocating for programs or materials and, 177–178
diversity, equity, and belonging and, 51–54
example of a school change initiative, 60–61
expertise of coaches and, 198
family and community engagement and, 183–185, 184f
focusing on both individuals and systems and, 7–8
group coaching and, 116–117, 128
needs-assessment process and, 163–168, 164f
organizational change to improve instruction and, 47–51
overview, 178–179
role of coaching in, 158–160
supporting a culture of collaboration and, 59–60

# T

Targeted coaching. *See* One-on-one coaching
Teacher leaders, 147–148. *See also* Leadership
Teacher learning. *See* Professional learning for teachers
Teachers. *See also* Capacity, educator; One-on-one coaching; Professional learning for teachers
advocating for, 36–37
advocating for programs or materials and, 177–178
asking for feedback from, 204–205
benefits of coaching and, 5, 6–7
coaching mindsets and, 14, 25–27, 31
communication with, 67–71, 70f

Teachers *(cont.)*
  content of coaching work and, 8–9
  co-teaching and, 93
  developing relationships with, 74–79, 78*f*
  differentiating coaching for, 27–29
  discussion-based protocols and, 72–74
  distributing leadership across roles, 49–50
  diversity, equity, and belonging and, 52–54
  expertise of coaches and, 197–198
  family and community engagement and, 183–184, 184*f*, 185
  focusing on both individuals and systems and, 7–8
  high-leverage coaching moves and, 79–83
  home–school communication and, 182, 185–189
  impact of coaching on, 10
  intensity in coaching and, 29–32, 30*t*
  involving during modeling, 91
  organizational change to improve instruction and, 48–49
  Pennsylvania Institute for Instructional Coaching and, 234
  Principals' support of coaching and, 55
  school culture and, 45–46
  schoolwide learning and changes and, 170
  support of principals and, 57
  supporting a culture of collaboration, 59–60
  systems thinking and, 17
  technology as a tool and, 176–177
Team teaching, 94
Teams, 29, 30*t*, 48, 59–60. *See also* Content-area teams; Grade-level teams; Group coaching; Instructional leadership team (ILT)
Technical change agents, 14–15, 106–107. *See also* Change agent mindset
Technology tools
  developing or selecting curriculum and materials, 173–177
  group coaching and, 129, 129*f*
  home–school communication and, 182, 185–189
  importance of coaching and, 3
Training of coaches. *See* Professional learning for coaches
Trust, 31, 79, 80, 84, 162. *See also* Relationships

**U**

Universities, 191–192
Upper grade instruction. *See* Secondary grade instruction

**V**

Video-recorded lessons, 30*t*, 100–101. *See also* Recording lessons
Virtual presentations, 130. *See also* Large-group coaching; Presentations; Technology tools
Vision, 48–49, 51–54, 151–154. *See also* Mission/vision
Visiting classrooms, 82–83. *See also* Conversations; Observation; One-on-one coaching; Relationships
Volunteer opportunities in the school, 182, 187–188. *See also* Community engagement; Family engagement

**W**

Walk-throughs. *See* Learning walks; Visiting classrooms